Economy, Emotion, and Ethics in Chinese Cinema

The First and Second Comings of Capitalism are conceptual shorthand used to capture the radical changes in global geopolitics from the Opium Wars to the end of the Cold War and beyond. Centering the role of capitalism in the Chinese everyday, the framework can be employed to comprehend contemporary Chinese culture in general and, as in this study, Chinese cinema in particular.

This book investigates major Chinese-language films from mainland China, Taiwan, and Hong Kong in order to unpack a hypercompressed capitalist modernity with distinctive Chinese characteristics. As a dialogue between the film genre as a mediation of microscopic social life and the narrative of economic development as a macroscopic political abstraction, it engages two otherwise remotely related worlds, illustrating how the State and the Subject are reconstituted cinematically in late capitalism. A deeply cultural, determinedly historical, and deliberately interdisciplinary study, it approaches "culture" anthropologically, as a way of life emanating from the everyday, and aesthetically, as imaginative forms and creative expressions.

Economy, Emotion, and Ethics in Chinese Cinema will appeal to students and scholars of Chinese cinema, cultural studies, Asian studies, and interdisciplinary studies of politics and culture.

David Leiwei Li is Professor of English and Collins Professor of the Humanities at the University of Oregon, USA.

Routledge Contemporary China Series

Economy, Emotion, and Ethics in Chinese Cinema

Globalization on speed

David Leiwei Li

Routledge
Taylor & Francis Group

LONDON AND NEW YORK

First published 2016
by Routledge
2 Park Square, Milton Park, Abingdon, Oxon OX14 4RN

and by Routledge
711 Third Avenue, New York, NY 10017

First issued in paperback 2017

Routledge is an imprint of the Taylor & Francis Group, an informa business

© 2016 David Leiwei Li

British Library Cataloguing in Publication Data
A catalogue record for this book is available from the British Library

Library of Congress Cataloging-in-Publication Data
Name: Li, David Leiwei, 1959–
Title: Economy, emotion, and ethics in Chinese cinema : globalization on
    speed / David Leiwei Li.
Description: Milton Park, Abingdon, Oxon : New York, NY : Routledge,
    2016. | Series: Routledge contemporary China series ; 142 | Includes
    bibliographical references and index.
Identifiers: LCCN 2015035188 | ISBN 9781138120969 (hardback) |
    ISBN 9781315651385 (ebook)
Subjects: LCSH: Motion pictures—China—History and criticism. | Motion
    pictures—Taiwan—History and criticism. | Motion pictures—China—
    Hong Kong—History and criticsm. | Motion pictures and globalization.
Classification: LCC PN1993.5.C4 L4656 2016 | DDC 791.430951—dc23
LC record available at http://lccn.loc.gov/2015035188

ISBN 13: 978-1-138-01931-7 (pbk)
ISBN 13: 978-1-138-12096-9 (hbk)

Typeset in Times New Roman
by Apex CoVantage, LLC

Contents

Acknowledgments

Parts of the book in their earlier versions have appeared in the following venues: *Cahiers du Cinéma* (December 2008), *Texas Studies in Literature and Language* 49.3 (Fall 2007), *Globalization and the Humanities* (Hong Kong UP, 2004), *Chinese Films in Focus: 25 New Takes* (British Film Institute, 2003), and *Comparative Literature* 53.4 (2001).

Gratitude is also due to my selection as the Fulbright Distinguished Chair at the University of the Arts, London (January–June 2013): the award has made possible the successful completion of this book.

Introduction

Culture and contemporary Chinese cinema in the Second Coming of Capitalism

Shortly after the Manchu Dynasty of China lost the world's first recorded war against drugs to the British Armada in 1842, with partial surrender of its sovereignty and the introduction of "free trade" in China under the gun, the authors of *The Communist Manifesto* (1848)[1] had this observation:

> The bourgeoisie, by the rapid improvement of all instruments of production, by the immensely facilitated means of communication, draws all, even the most barbarian nations into civilization. The cheap prices of its commodities are the heavy artillery with which it batters down all Chinese walls, with which it forces the barbarians' intense obstinate hatred of foreigners to capitulate. *It compels all nations, on pain of extinction, to adopt the bourgeois mode of production*; it compels them to introduce what it calls civilization into their midst, *i.e.* to become bourgeois themselves. In one word, it creates a world after its own image.
>
> (Tucker 477, italics mine)

Aside from its well-critiqued Orientalist tone, the profundity of Marx and Engels's prophecy is as pertinent as, if not more so today than when these sentences were originally in print. They were the original observers of "the First Coming of Capital" in China, that this courtesy call and worldly arrival should entail a reversal of the civilization and barbarity antinomy in history.[2] If the Europeans from whose stock the bourgeoisie arise used to be "barbarians" in the ancient assurance of a Chinese "celestial" centrality, the Chinese became barbarians in the confident conquest by the bourgeoisie of the ancient world and its redefinition of "what it calls civilization." While Marx and Engels seem to engage in this instance in an act of stylistic equivocation – for it is not Western commodities but Western cannonballs that shattered the landlocked empire's territorial defense and with it a Chinese cultural superiority long taken for granted and until then historically undercontested – their metaphorical extension of meaning to the bourgeois power to bend the world to its will remains indisputably prescient.

Note here the swift shift of reference from the Chinese confrontation with and submission to the invading bourgeoisie as a particular encounter to a universalization of this colonial conquest in the combined figure of a global geopolitical and historical inevitability. For Marx and Engels, not only are China's "feudal, patri-archal, idyllic relations" subject to the logic of radical industrial enclosure, but agrarian societies the world over are also compelled to yield to the ruthless exploi-tation of the environment for surplus value, or they will together risk collective "extinction" (Ibid. 475, 477). In their estimate, the bourgeoisie as an emergent class hailed from Western Europe shall eventually force with its unique mode of production the transformation of immense aggregate communities in lands distant or near, of languages and cultural practices distinct or not, into a singular race of people of near-identical rationalities, similar sentiments, and kindred habits. Since "the bourgeoisie cannot exist without constantly revolutionizing the instrument of production, and thereby the relations of production, and with them, the whole relations of society," they conclude, it is able to both transform vitriolic hatred against itself into idolatrous love and remake the planet and its people "after its own image" – an approximate image of what can be accurately designated in our time as "globalization" (Ibid. 476–77).

Let us set aside for now Marx's analytic imaging of capitalism and his teleol-ogy of communist triumph, and turn instead to a historical juncture more than a century later, amid the heat of the Cold War and the tumult of China's Great Proletarian Cultural Revolution. It is then, when the ideological conflicts of the two hegemonic camps were still raging, that Guy Debord, the French Situationist and an intellectual heir of Marx, provided the following trajectory of capitalism in relation to China's future political economy. For Debord, the march of Western industrial capitalism since the late eighteenth century has developed "two antago-nistic tendencies": "progression towards the highest form of commodity produc-tion and the project of its total negation [i.e. pollution] . . . grow ever stronger in parallel with each other" (1971/2008, 77). In eschewing the entropic lot of West-ern bourgeois development, however, the march of the Chinese communist revo-lution has stagnated in its horrendous paucity of commodities and abject poverty of the populace. While "the degradation of the totality of the natural and human environment" by industrial capitalism "has now become the more fundamental one of whether a world that pursues such a course can preserve its *material exis-tence*," "a country such as China, if it is to retain respect as a power among impov-erished nations," Debord speaks as a matter of fact, "has no choice but to sacrifice a disproportionate part of its slim budget to the generation of a decent quantity of pollution" (Ibid. 79, 87). For "such a high quotient of poverty," he continues as if echoing Marx and Engels's hypothesis of geopolitical survival after the bourgeois arrival, "amounts to a death warrant for the bureaucracies presently in power" (Ibid. 87). As Debord frames this matter of political economy in stark dialectical terms, a healthy capitalist economy is tantamount to "a sick planet," while lack-luster economic growth spells the doom of political regimes everywhere.

Mind-boggling as it sounds, we find Debord in *The Society of the Spectacle* both historically resonant and eccentrically at odds with Marx and Engels in an earlier stage of industrial capitalism. As theorists of contemporary globalization avant la lettre, the authors of *The Communist Manifesto* prophesied the politi-cal death of nations had they dared to refuse the bourgeois mode of production.

As their true spiritual offspring, Debord forewarned the physical death of the earth had all nation-states of the world joined the bandwagon of capitalist growth. Marx, Engels, and Debord's shared reference to China as a geopolitical alterity upon which world historical destiny appears to pivot only illuminates the supreme historical irony not only of China's pendulum swings between the actually existing communist and capitalist alternatives but also of contemporary political and planetary fates which have, since the First Coming of Capitalism, become incontrovertibly integrated and indivisible. Despite their alleged "obstinate hatred of foreigners," as history has it, the Chinese have in effect listened to the advice of the "barbarians" twice on record, Mao for Marx as one and Deng Xiaoping for Guy Debord as the other (Tucker 477).

As though responding to *The Communist Manifesto* some eighty years ago, we have Mao's Marxist ventriloquism of 1939:

> Foreign capitalism played an important part in the disintegration of China's social economy; on the one hand, it undermined the foundations of her self-sufficient natural economy and wrecked the handicraft industries . . . and on the other hand, it hastened the growth of commodity economy . . . The history of China's transformation into semi-colony and colony by imperialism in collusion with Chinese feudalism is at the same time a history of struggle by the Chinese people against imperialism and its lackeys.
>
> (Editorial collective, *The Opium War* 1–2)

Mao's restoration of Chinese sovereignty entails both a rejection of the "commodity economy" of the free market and a refusal of the traditional "handicraft industries" of dynastic China (Ibid. 111). He is convinced that Chinese communist revolution shall hasten the productive power of the bourgeoisie to the point of its destruction. At his projected demise of capitalism and colonialism and with his recalibration of politics and economics, a Chinese socialist modernity is supposed to emerge toward a global communist utopia. Mao's nationalist independence has indeed succeeded ten years after this pronouncement, ending decisively the era of Capitalism's First Coming in China since the Opium Wars. However, Mao has conjured up neither the material abundance of his wish fulfillment nor the egalitarian governance of communism. By the time of the Cultural Revolution, the constant ideological purge of the party and the people has resulted in such "poverty, both material and mental" that makes Debord's proposal of generating pollution in "the highest form of commodity production" sound almost reasonable (1971/2008, 77, 87).

Although his own days of French sojourn predated the birth of the Situationist, Deng Xiaoping possesses such a utilitarian instinct of bureaucratic survival – "be it white or black, the cat that catches the mouse is the good cat" – that he will disavow his own proletarian revolutionary past and alter the tortured communist course of "the Great Helmsman." Following Mao's meeting with Nixon in 1972 and his passing in 1976, the return of Deng as China's new paramount leader has a twofold significance. It means, first, a total reassessment of China's "revolutionary mode of socialist production," *and* second, the nation-state's resolute (re)turn to the "bourgeois mode of production," just as Marx and Engels originally defined it in Capitalism's First Coming. The difference is that the same "bourgeois mode of production" has in its Second Coming acquired the status of euphemistic neologism as China's "socialist market economy."

From the Tiananmen crackdown of 1989, Deng's southern China tour of 1992, and Hong Kong's repatriation in 1997 under "one country, two systems" to China's entry into the World Trade Organization (WTO) in 2001 and its subsequent constitutional amendment to recognize "private property" in 2004, Deng has had the People's Republic renege its historic "delinking" from the world system (Amin) and "connect the tracks" with the global market (与世界接轨).[3] The great walls of communism have indeed been "battered down," and China has "on pain of extinction" both "adopt[ed] the bourgeois mode of production" and "capitulate[d]" to the capitalist way of life (Tucker 477). In a feverish embrace of the "oceanic civilizations" that occasioned the historical downfall of its own landlocked dynasty, China has by now completed the planetary picture of what should be properly called the post–Cold War "Reagan-Thatcher-Deng Xiaoping Revolution."[4] This is the picture of neoliberal globalization and "Capitalism's Second Coming," in which "the bourgeois mode of production" dominates without the apparent need for imperialist incursion and through which whole relations of precapitalist societies and cultures the world over are being refashioned, compulsively and reflexively, in the image of the bourgeoisie.[5]

Globalization on Speed scrutinizes the convoluted and compressed processes of capitalist transformation in the Sinophone region through the lens of contemporary Chinese cinema, examining the film discourse's conscientious imaging of bourgeois society and its critical mediation of bourgeois subjectivity in global modernity. The study is therefore deeply cultural, determinedly historical, and deliberately interdisciplinary. I approach "culture" anthropologically, as a way of life emanating from the everyday, *and* aesthetically, as imaginative forms and creative expressions. It is through interpretations of the latter, of film texts in particular, that I make my general arguments about the former, about how the practice of daily life embodies values and how culture as symbolic acts is materially manifest. For this emphasis on material culture, I consider "capitalism" not only as a historically specific economic system originated from Western Europe, but also an encompassing system of culture that has since turned hegemonic and gone viral, increasingly constitutive of both contemporary social practices writ large and individual aspirations in matters of the heart. "No matter how hard we perceive ourselves as being embedded in a particular culture," as Slavoj Zizek states so succinctly, "the moment we participate in global capitalism, this culture is always already de-naturalized" (144). It is at the moment of global capital contact with greater China that contemporary Chinese cinema has zoomed in both on the changing material conditions of its societies and mental structures of its subjects, and it is at these cinematic mediations that I now cast my critical eye.

We are ready now to approach the temporal and spatial parameter of contemporary Chinese cinema. To start, "contemporary" specifically frames the film production within the mise-en-scène of Capitalism's Second Coming. If the First Coming expresses itself as European colonial and capitalist conquest, both in the worldwide accumulation of wealth and the consolidation of its nation-states, leading to the scattered sovereignty of the Sinophone region, the Second Coming – following the apparent dissolution of the internecine Cold War and buttressed by the US military superpower with its promised peace and prosperity regime hinged on the free market – evidences a global expansion of the capitalist regime and an anxious Chinese convergence with it. Despite the repatriation of Hong Kong as a sign of Chinese sovereign recovery, this post–Opium War and post–Cold War partial healing of Hong Kong, Taiwan, and China's geopolitical splinter, however, is realized not in the full integration of Chinese territories but in the consolidation of its developmental patterns. Because the People's Republic of China models after the precedents of its Sinophone peripheries (i.e., the earlier "economic miracles" of Taiwan and Hong Kong), its reunion with the lost siblings is simultaneously a remarriage with global capital.[6] As such, the Chinese reintegration after its geopolitical disintegration in the First Coming of Capitalism is nothing but a regional economic integration of capitalist production, circulation, and consumption of goods, services, and sights and sounds. It is part and parcel of capital's globalization that makes natural a mapping of a "greater China" and makes possible a new conceptualization of "cultural China" (Shambaugh; Tu 1991a).

The naming of "greater China" or "cultural China" has rendered untenable a taken-for-granted, transhistorical understanding of what is "Chinese." The neologism attempts to provide a more accurate description of a postcolonial and transnational condition in which an isomorphism of land, language, and cultural lineage can no longer be automatically assumed. Yet, because of the diasporic locations of this new discursive formation and the fact that the desire to reposition Chinese culture in the new world order originates from a Chinese geopolitical periphery in advanced capitalist countries and intellectual metropolis, say, the elite institutions of Western learning in North America, such "cosmopolitan" redefinitions of cultural China, though ambitious undertakings, could be oblivious to the role of class and power in the reconstruction of knowledge and become inattentive to the materiality of cultural practice. For the most part, they are inclined to evoke and encrypt a lost ancient Chinese civilizational centrality as well as continuity. The neo-Confucian confrontation with Max Weber's "Protestant ethic" is an earlier example of this scholarly address (1930/1993), while the poststructural preoccupation with "Chinese-ness," although admittedly "anti-essentialist" in spirit, appears not entirely devoid of similar culturalist overtones. Both have importantly enabled the episteme of a cosmopolitan China that critically challenges the Euro-American tradition but neither seems sufficient in articulating the historical specificity of Chinese-ness in Capital's Second Coming and its significance in inquiring after a better world community.[7]

To fully interrogate the postcolonial construction and transnational circulation of China, and to adequately account for the interpretation of film texts in this study, I propose for the moment a working usage of Chinese both in transcendence of its semantic origin as a racial and national signifier *and* in retention of it as morphological and material signs. What this means in terms of film classification is to move beyond a geopolitically discrete grouping while refusing to presume an identity based on common cultural content. Here, I find critical kinship with leading scholars who abandon an exclusive focus on the cinema of either Hong Kong, Taiwan, or (mainland) China and share with their interpretive outlook in assembling my selective films on a categorical unity of language and image. The Chinese in contemporary Chinese cinema, in this instance, becomes transnational, first to suggest the dispersal of the people from its ancestral mainland since the First Coming of Capitalism; second, to delineate the border-transcending production, distribution, and reception of its cinemas in Capitalism's Second Coming; and third, to denote the Sinophonic medium as the linguistic common denominator that gives the filmic corpus a classificatory coherence. Following the course of its debates, my use of the "Chinese" in Chinese cinema concurs with the emerging critical consensus that reconfigures Chinese cinema as semantic shorthand for "Chinese-language cinema," downplaying geopolitical divisions while heightening a shared Sinophonic-phenotypical visual identity.[8] In this conception, contemporary Chinese cinema has begun to embody film texts that feature distinctive Chinese subjects in variegated Chinese communities and star Chinese actors who speak Chinese in its conceivable dialects, whether in Taiwan, Hong Kong, China, or the Chinese diaspora. It has come to stand for a transnational representational regime of Sinophonic-phenotypical screen culture in sight, sound, and motion, constituting as it were an alternative site of cultural production in a world dominated by US media conglomerates, late capitalist ideologies, and Euro-American images.

Globalization on Speed approaches contemporary Sinophonic-phenotypical screen culture as aesthetic artifacts to apprehend the anthropological alterations wrought by the progressive spread of global capitalism. In this analytical attempt, the sight and sound of the Chinese are arrested not as scientific mirrors of permanent traditions but sensorial mediations of historical motions and transformations. I assume no equivalence between looking, sounding, and acting Chinese and I reject hermeneutic exercises redolent of what Edward Said famously characterizes as Orientalism and what Johannes Fabian succinctly calls "the denial of coevalness," the kind of hegemonic epistemology of culture that partitions peoples spatially and distances their practices temporally. Instead of relying on a "geographic distribution of culture traits" and a "taxonomy of space" organized by the antinomy of the East and the West with its implicit racialized meanings, nationalized comprehensions, and overall transcendent essence, I treat Chineseness in this study as a practice particular to time and place, which is defined in relation both to its historical past and to its historical encounters with the post-Enlightenment capitalist West (Fabian 54–55).

Indeed, the emergence of industrial capitalism at the heel of the European Enlightenment is for me the most crucial divide in world historical destiny that not only marks a radical reconstitution of subjectivity and society but also a nationalization and racialization of cultures. Karl Polanyi has identified this capitalist market reorientation of culture as "the great transformation," a pivotal moment that may also be regarded as "the great differentiation" of humanity. By the latter, I refer to a presumptive universal narrative of material progress through industrial capitalism and free market economy, within which geographical and racial others are deemed as either culturally incompatible or incompetent, condemned to a position of being either impossible to convert or in dire need of catching up. It is in this teleology of human progress with its associated discursive arsenal of tradition and modernity, civilization and barbarity (to which the authors of *The Communist Manifesto* were not at all immune) that we presently locate the historical origins of "commonsense" Chinese-ness, or for that matter, American-ness.

What is glaringly absent from this ahistorical common sense, however, is a much-needed recognition that precapitalist Chinese practice has in fact a lot in common with precapitalist European cultural practice. Confucian Chinese-ness and Aristotelian Greek-ness, for example, have more overlaps between them than we would normally recognize and register because of the shared features of their agrarian cultures. What is also inexcusably overlooked in this ahistorical common sense is the uneven conditions of European capitalist development. Areas and peoples of Europe other than those at the heart of the British Empire were compelled to assimilate a capitalist way of life with its distinctive conceptions of subjectivity and society just as peoples in Asia, Africa, and Latin America do. The difference is the relative completion of its transformation for Europeans and North Americans in Capitalism's First Coming, and the continuing accommodation and resistance of peoples elsewhere in the Second Coming of Capitalism.[9]

A historical examination of Chinese-ness, in this context, is a simultaneous historical engagement with the expansion of capitalism from its native grounds into societies beyond its geopolitical origins as well as an examination of the reorganization by capital of preexisting social orders, whether it is in the East, West, North, or South. As Marx describes its double nature in *Grundrisse*, capital must on the one hand "strive to tear down every spatial barrier to intercourse, i.e. to exchange, and conquer the whole earth for its market," while on the other hand "to annihilate this space with time, i.e. to reduce to a minimum the time spent in motion from one place to another" (Marx 539). The Second Coming of Capitalism in China seems to evidence not only capital's overcoming of geophysical distance and psychocultural resistance in time but also the temporal compression with which it sweeps over spaces formerly impermeable to its colonization. David Harvey succinctly captures this annihilation of space through capitalized time, and this acceleration of production and consumption in specific and of social life in general, as the "time-space compression" of globalization (1990, 147, 240, 284–87). In its extremely condensed experience of capitalism, the Chinese instance crystallizes a unique form of global modernity perhaps like no other.[10]

This form of hyperaccelerated and compressed modernity is best delineated as *Globalization on Speed*. I use the titular "speed" to convey the sense of unprecedented velocity with which capitalist development in Taiwan, Hong Kong, and

China is compressed into a miraculous mirage, materializing in a short span of three decades what has taken the West three centuries to accomplish. "Speed" thus signifies the substratal reconstitution of both the physical and psychic universe in the Sinophonic region through rapid industrialization and individualization, urbanization and embourgeoisment, marketization and commodification. It suggests the condensed processes of "deterritorialization," evident in the neo-enclosure acts and the proletarianization of peasants, in the migration from ascribed conditions of living and the making-over of historically grounded ways of human affiliation, and above all in the systemic phasing out of all territorially rooted modes of attachments and belongings (Appadurai; Deleuze and Guattari 1972, 1980; Virilio). Similarly, speed represents the hastened processes of "disembedding," the separation of a prior time-place integrity that amounts to the "'lifting out' of social relations from local contexts of interaction and their restructuring across indefinite spans of time-space" (Giddens 21). Speed reveals a previously unimaginable but presently pervasive form of spatial and temporal aporia in greater China, the simultaneous yet disjunctive existence in approximate social space of the different modes of production, the agrarian and the artisanal, the industrial and the informational, as well as the contradictions of a mixed modernity they inhere and entail. In this sense, speed is an indicator more of social division than economic integration, complicating our comprehension of "contemporaneity" as that in which "things from different historical periods can exist at the same time but belong to different worlds" (Chakrabarty, 1997, 49). Indeed, speed is "the new opium" in the Second Coming of Capitalism, the methamphetamine to which the brave neoliberal world is addicted, for it portends a freedom from social encumbrances, an exhilaration of flight, and "an unbearable lightness of being" that could readily morph into "euphoria in unhappiness" (Kundera; Marcuse, 1964, 5).

Born of the precipitation of developmental history and induced by entrancing speed, contemporary Chinese cinema necessarily refracts global capital's abrupt integration of local cultures, revealing their drastic convergence and contradiction in the revision of everyday life. Screening the subject of China thus enables us to grasp how macroscopic transformations in economy and polity impact East–West and North–South relationships, *and* how microscopic diurnal thinking and feeling both make sense of and cope with such sea changes. Such a scholarly quest joins the plethora of inquiries already taking place on modernity and capitalism – one thinks of the discourses of modernity, be it "post," "late," "singular," "multiple," "second," "reflexive," "alternative," "provincializing," or more recently, "postsocialist" and "uneven" (Beck, Giddens, and Lash; Calhoun; Chakrabarty, 2000; Dirlik and Zhang; Eisenstadt; Gaonkar; Gong; Jameson, 1991, 2002; Jameson and Miyoshi; McGrath). Or, one notes the pluralization of capitalism: what I characterize as "the Second Coming of Capitalism" is more commonly referred to as "global capitalism," "transnational capitalism," and their variants, "disorganized capital" (Lash and Urry), "post-Fordist capitalism"/"flexible capitalism" (Harvey, 1990), "late capital" (Mandel; Jameson, 1991), "casino capitalism" (Strange), "neoliberal capitalism" (Brown), "millennial capitalism" (Comaroff and

Comaroff), "disaster capitalism" (Klein), and so forth. Although the People's Republic of China and the Soviet Union had their forms of modernity that were distinctly socialist, modernity is predominantly taken to be Western and capitalist. I shall use the aforementioned host of capitalisms often interchangeably in the text because they seem more capacious categorical umbrellas not only to include a contemporary modernity through and beyond the geopolitical West but also specifically include it in the age of the Reagan-Thatcher-Deng Xiaoping Revolution.

As such, this study interrupts the conventional boundaries of humanistic and social scientific disciplines and area studies in a spirit of interdisciplinary inquiry that is yet to gain its genuine institutional footing.[11] This is not to say that I dismiss older ways of knowing the world, through such convenient categories of "race," "nation," and "culture/civilization." The fact remains that they have neither lost their hold on popular imagination nor been rendered obsolete with the easy prefixes of "inter-," "trans-," or "multi-." What I want to accomplish with this scholarly undertaking is to highlight the urgent need to confront capitalism in its Second Coming as the most formidable contemporary disciplinary power. To recognize this power is to register capital's "creative destruction" of the world's natural and social orders and imagine possibilities of cultural resistance (Schumpeter). If the contribution of postcolonial and multicultural studies since the 1970s has illuminated the imbricated social evolution of the West and the rest, and the coproduction of a global modernity since the European Enlightenment, have we reached, with the progressive planetary expansion of capitalism, "the end of history" (Fukuyama), which could mean the end of the earth as we know it? Are we ready to reconcile ourselves with the secession of "grand narratives" (Lyotard) and the demise of President Johnson's Great Society by disregarding the flawed legacy of liberalism, dismissing the subject of justice while acquiescing to the neoliberal myth of an asocial individual liberty and the fate of a cosmopolitan commercial nirvana (Brown; Li 2012)?

In posing and probing these overarching questions, *Globalization on Speed* conceives itself as an interdisciplinary cultural studies project, which, while recognizing transnational economic and cultural flows, remains hopeful for the revitalization of democratic societies against both "the tyranny of the market" and the planetary plutocracy of the new millennium (Bourdieu). Because "ours are cinematic societies," opines Virilio, "not only societies of movement, but of the acceleration of that very movement" (Armitage 27), and because "capital is not a thing," intones Harvey, "but rather a process that only exists in motion" (2010, 12), cinema, as the celluloid or digital circulation of images, appears the most appropriate medium to picture and capture globalization in motion. Cinema is an exemplary medium of "disappearance," according to Virilio, because "things [on the screen] owe their existence to the fact they vanish afterwards."[12] But it is also a medium of appearance, a slice of space-time on-screen as "change mummified," to echo Andre Bazin's classic definition of filmic art, that preserves life "by representation of life" (15, 9). Above all, cinema is a visual as well as a vital medium of "the imaginary"; let me borrow Cornelius Castoriadis's original formulation for our purposes, "the unceasing and essentially *undetermined* (social-historical and psychical) creation of figures/forms/images, on the basis of which [. . .] what we call 'reality' and 'rationality' are its works" (3).

What makes *Globalization on Speed* distinctive, then, is its particular deployment of the film medium in deliberate dialogue with social and political theory on the persistent imaginary of capitalist modernity. By calling attention to the hypercompressed cycle of Sinophonic capitalist development while focusing on the cinematic expressions to which such compression has specifically given rise, this project is able to articulate the historical uniqueness of a Chinese modernity on speed while making visible and visceral the always abstract theories of a global imaginary. Unlike the developed West, whose evolution of capitalism is stretched over a longer historical span, the characteristic speed with which Chinese capitalist compression is accomplished and is still being accomplished cannot possibly smooth over the fissures of seismic social change that globalization has occasioned. When time is compressed, its harried "annihilation of space" cannot but leave rough edges and gaping holes, remnants and residuals of history in the embodied present that the Marx of *Grundrisse* has captured in an enigmatic trope – "human anatomy contains the key to the anatomy of the ape" (Tucker 241).

This aphorism finds its perfect analogy in the representative potentials of contemporary Chinese cinema, for the film form "allows insights," as I would argue along with Marx's description of a then emerging bourgeois society, "into the structure and relations of production of all the vanished social formations out of the ruins and elements it [the bourgeois society] built itself up" (Ibid.). Chinese cinematic texts are microscopic manifestations of otherwise unfathomable macroscopic forces of global capitalist transformation, for not only do they retain those "partly still unconquered remnants that are carried along" within the brief trajectory of Sinophonic bourgeois development, but they also render into salient relief in ways the advanced cultural industry of the West seems incapable of the contradictions of capitalist sea change in the everyday (Ibid.). In this light, *Globalization on Speed* is as much a scholarly tracking shot of Chinese cinema's creation of figures/forms/images about Capitalism's Second Coming as it is a "symptomatic interpretation" of Chinese cinema's mediation and contestation of a neobourgeois reality, rationality, and affectivity (Bordwell 71–104).

Suggested by the title, the book is structured as a threefold analysis, each part keyed in with the apparently independent yet actually interrelated concepts of *economy, emotion,* and *ethics* to round out a world picture of Chinese capitalist encounter in its various compressed forms. The successive figures of *Homo economicus, Homo sentimentalis,* and *Homo ethicus* imply neither the chronological order of their thematic development nor their distinctive conceptual boundaries in the book's nominal triptych. By identifying capitalism as both the foundational source and the fundamental force field in the cross-constitution of contemporary economic, emotional, and ethical beings, I wish to throw light on Chinese film texts' particular revelation of global processes that are reordering, in unprecedented speed and scale, local societies and indigenous subjectivities. Apparent arenas of "affects" are thus addressed along with obvious concerns of "interests," for example, so that emotions and ethics, ostensibly siphoned off for later parts of the book, make their advanced appearance in Part I, as does economics and its associated rationalities in Parts II and III. This is to eschew a stereotypical repetition of Marx's base- and superstructure determinism in favor of a dialectic engagement of contrarian ideas over the linearity of their progression.

We need to be reminded that one approaches an understanding of culture the best when s/he historicizes. As we recall, the etymological origin in the Greek language for the English word economy (*Oikos*) also gives birth to its linguistic twin, ecology. *Oikos* means household. When coupled with *nomia* (management) and *nomos* (law), economy has the foundational sense of a management of a household. When coupled with *logos* (systematic study), ecology has developed the sense of *habitat* and the study of the relations of plants and animals and the species environment. As late as 1931, H.G. Wells still regarded economics as a "branch of ecology, the ecology of the human species" in its myriad social and natural relationships (Williams, 110–11). But the repression of ecological sense and the exile of ethical reason in the redefinition of economy in fact occurred much earlier in history. It happened along the rise of the capitalist mode of production and reached a significant turning point in nineteenth-century Europe and America when the original "motive of subsistence," the ultimate economic purpose of administering and sustaining life as though in a household, locally, morally, and on the ground was "substituted for that of gain" (Polanyi).

As the capitalist motive of surplus began to drive the economy, disembedding it from locality and alienating it from nature, the raison d'être of *Oikos*, "the principle of householding" in the preservation of life and "maintenance of social ties," gave way to one's "self-interest in the possession of material goods" (Polanyi 53, 41, 46). As though a Pandora's box, an instrumental economic irrationality was let loose in the world, at once energized and exacerbated by a fossil-fueled industrialization. "God forbid that India should ever take to industrialization after the manner of the west," Gandhi forewarned at the eve of his motherland's independence. "If an entire nation of 300 million took to similar economic exploitation, it would strip the world like locusts" (Gandhi quoted in Arrighi 386). While Gandhi is as successful as is Mao in his tactical achievement of national sovereignty against European colonialism in the First Coming of Capitalism, a capitalism not of territorial conquest but deterritorial consent seems to be winning strategic global victory. As Karl Marx is thrown out of the Forbidden Palace and Adam Smith is now welcome in Beijing, Capitalism of the Second Coming has certainly come home to roost, "creating a world after its own image": it not only "profane[s] all that is holy" but also "melt[s] all that is solid into air," including the ozone layer (Tucker 476–77). The *Oikos* of the Earth, our planetary household, is in doubtless peril.

The triptych of the book tells the story of *Oikos*, its rise and fall as well as its compulsory restoration. Part I, *Homo economicus*, posits that the hyperaccelerated capitalist development in the economic realm entails the hypercompressed process of psychosocial individualization, the manic and makeshift construction of both the liberal and neoliberal Chinese subjects of globalization. Chapter 1 approaches two works by what is known as China's "Fifth Generation" of film directors, Zhang Yimou's *Red Sorghum* (1987) and Zhou Xiaowen's *Ermo* (1994). I read the tales of wine brewing and noodle selling as cinematic allegories of "primitive accumulation" and "self-possession," liberal appeals to the transformation of the socialist subject into the ideal of "the economic (wo)man." Taking on the Sixth Generation director Zhang Yuan's *Crazy English* (1999), Chapter 2 approaches the documentary feature's protagonist Li Yang as an exemplary figure of an emergent neoliberalism, his motivational biography, English pedagogy, and marketing strategy expressive of the flexible forging of a Chinese entrepreneurial subject that loosens the liberal "state/citizen bind."

To what extent the market-driven rewiring of subjectivity and community enables individual liberty and social equality is a crucial matter of feeling for Part II, *Homo sentimentalis*. Chapter 3 reads the genres of melodrama and romantic comedy in an investigation of the family form in diverse Chinese contexts. Locating the transition from extended family to nuclear family in tropes of "(re)production" and "(re)creation," I tease out the ambivalence as well as the humor of Ang Lee's "Father Trilogy" and Zhang Yimou's *Happy Times* in their penetrating representations of gender and generation in Capital's Second Coming. That economic deregulation is coupled with emotional deregulation is the special insight of the two Taiwanese New Wave directors in Chapter 4. By encapsulating his oeuvre in a triptych, Hou Hsiao-hsien's *Three Times* compares the affective modalities in 1911, 1966, and 2005 to highlight sentimental cultures of the different times. With his eyes on the island state's sudden rise in wealth, Edward Yang's *A Confucian Confusion* (1994), *Majiang* (1996; *Mahjong* and *Majiang* are variant forms of the same film, 麻将; it shall be referred to exclusively as *Majiang* hereafter in the text), and *Yi Yi: A One and a Two* (2000) probe the "normal chaos of love" when societies become open-ended and risky. The "transformation of intimacy" so perspicuously portrayed in Hou's and Yang's cinema illuminates the enervation of society amid the exponential growth of the market.

While *Homo ethicus* is its key figure, Part III privileges *Homo sacer* over *Homo economicus* (Agamben) to favor a vision of an equitable ecological world. Here, economy, emotion, and ethics are brought together in a full chorus when Marx's "industrial reserve army" meets Heidegger's "standing reserve" of nature, and the figure of *Oikos* and its integrity that inaugurated the book's analysis is given an encore. In this effort, Chapter 5 provides an in-depth exegesis of Jia Zhangke's Golden Lion winner at the Venice Film Festival, *Still Life* (2006), set at the actual construction site of the Three Gorges Dam. I consider Jia's neorealist aesthetics and surrealistic strategies a conservational practice against neoliberal capital's devastating exploitation of world resources. This inquiry assumes new significance in Hong Kong director Fruit Chan's *Dumplings* (2004), where forbidden food is devoured with abandon. Confronting the challenge of cultural intelligibility the film poses for the kind of boundary disturbance central to both the horror genre and the histories of cannibalism and colonialism, I examine the director's deliberate departure from particular aesthetic conventions in the context of specific historical mutations of capitalism. Unless and until we halt the speed of Capital's Second Coming, our delirium of autopoiesis and endless growth may well be our last breath on earth.

Notes

1 The citations of *The Communist Manifesto* refer to Tucker's edition.

2 I coin the term "the First Coming of Capital" to indicate the historical process of its evolution from its origin of industrial capitalism in the UK to its transformation into monopoly capitalism, imperialism, and colonialism till the third-world decolonization of the mid-twentieth century. Between the end of World War II and the beginning of the 1970s it materializes as Western welfare capitalism, also known as Fordism or Keynesian economics.

3 Although China is still governed by the communist state, the Amendment to the Constitution of the People's Republic of China on March 14, 2004, effectively empties the meaning of the communist signifier. Article 13 of the Constitution, "Citizens Lawful Private Property Shall Not Be Violated," reads: "The State protects the right of citizens to own lawfully earned income, savings, houses and other lawful property. The State protects according to law the right of citizens to inherit private property." (http://news.bbc.co.uk/2/hi/asia-pacific/3509850.stm)

4 With "oceanic" I am alluding to the critique by *River Elegy* 河殇 (1988) of mainland China's historical land-bound insularity. Extrapolating from Harvey's *A Brief History of Neoliberalism*, I coin the "Reagan-Thatcher-Deng Xiaoping Revolution" to illuminate the actual evolution of global capitalism in view of the Tiananmen Incident (June 4, 1989) prior to the fall of the Berlin Wall on November 9, 1989 (Li, 2009). The fall of the Berlin Wall or the wall of communism has meant not the disappearance of social, economic, or political barriers, but the erection, in Mike Davis's words, of "the great wall of capital."

5 The Capitalism of the Second Coming, as I've been referring to it, is a transnational form of capitalism that has assumed world hegemony since the Reagan-Thatcher-Deng Xiaoping Revolution. In the West, it means the dismantling of post–World War II welfare capitalism and the deregulation of the market. For the rest of the world, it signals the infiltration of a largely Anglo-American form of free market capitalism into local economies and everyday lives. No longer through colonial occupation of foreign lands, though the planetary presence of US military force is palpable, this is a global capitalism of apparent indigenous consent, a neocolonial and neoliberal biopolitics through the International Monetary Fund (IMF) and the WTO that bears not, despite its neocolonial influence, the ugly name of domination. I am partially indebted to Comaroff and Comaroff's "Millennial Capitalism" for my formulation of "Capital's Second Coming."

6 The islands of Taiwan and Hong Kong, as well as the diasporic city-state of Singapore, remain peripheral in the paternalist conception of "the central kingdom," or "Zhong Guo" (中国), as China is literally translated, although those Sinophonic margins initiated the center's contemporary capitalist development.

7 For an illuminating debate on the concept of Chinese-ness, see Tu Weiming, *Daedalus* 120.2 (1991b), Rey Chow (2000), Tong and Chan, and the monographs by Wang Gungwu, Ien Ang, and Shu-mei Shih.

8 For a sampling of the field's redefinitions, see Chris Berry, Sheldon Lu and Emily Yeh, Chris Berry and Mary Farquhar, Rey Chow (2007), and Yingjin Zhang.

9 We recall the belated rise of German industrial capitalism and the pioneering effort of the Japanese in the Asia Pacific, both of which led to the catastrophe of imperialism in World War II. We need to keep in mind not only the Cold War opposition between communism and capitalism but also the divergence between Anglo-American capitalism and European social democratic capitalism.

Approaching capital in terms of culture, this interpretive project on Chinese cinema is not another exercise of "historicism." While the Second Coming of Capitalism means the domination of a neoliberal free market fundamentalism and its hijacking of the deeply flawed liberal teleology of universal progress, I suggest neither as our world historical destiny. What Chakrabarty argues for in *Provincializing Europe* is the recognition of indigenous cultures as the living "diversity of human life-worlds" within a "capital or bourgeois [that still] read 'Europe' or 'European'" (2000, 18, 30). What *Globalization on Speed* addresses is the Chinese recuperation of capitalism after its earlier rejection, when capital itself is losing its racial and national distinction. Although in agreement with Chakrabarty's rejection of capital's presumptive fait accompli, the retention or restoration of "the diversity of human life-worlds" for me entails not only a deconstruction of capital's totalizing logic but also a demolition of capital's globalizing institutions.

10 I have described "the historically mixed and compressed modernity in East Asia" in *Globalization and the Humanities* (2003, 1–16, 249–72). Extending Harvey and Beck, Chang Kyung-Sup offers a sociological account of "compressed modernity," drawing from South Korean and other East Asian examples. Of interest as well are Xudong Zhang's Chinese "postsocialism" (see my 2010 review in *Comparative Literature*) and Haomin Gong's "uneven modernity" in China (2012). Though intellectually intriguing, these analyses seem to take for granted the fait accompli of a world capitalist modernity, an implicit ideological position against which this book stakes its argument.

11 Although "department of literature(s)" has been instituted in a few American universities to transcend "methodological nationalism" (Beck 2011), and the work of the scholar/teacher in the tertiary institutions has become more consciously comparative, the annual MLA job list as a cartography of the profession remains by and large discrete by nation, period, and genre. For discussion on disciplines and area studies, see Chow (2000, 1–25), Readings, and Li (2003).

12 For Virilio, "an aesthetic of appearance means that there was a material support to the image. Wood or canvas in the case of paintings; marble in the case of sculptures." However, "from the moment of cinematography," one encounters "aesthetics of disappearance," because cinema is a "sequential phenomenon where "an enduring material support to the image" is no longer (Armitage 41). This insistence on the material support of the image is the specific focus of Chapter 5, where Jia Zhangke's neorealist aesthetics and ecological consciousness are analyzed through Bazin and Heidegger.

Works cited

Agamben, Giorgio. *Homo Sacer: Sovereign Power and Bare Life*. Trans. Daniel Heller-Roazen. Stanford: Stanford UP, 1998.

Amin, Samir. *Delinking: Towards a Polycentric World*. Trans. Michael Wolfers. London: Zed Books, 1990.

Ang, Ien. *On Not Speaking Chinese: Living Between Asia and the West*. London and New York: Routledge, 2001.

Appadurai, Arjun. *Modernity at Large: Cultural Dimensions of Globalization*. Minneapolis: U of Minnesota P, 1996.

Armitage, John. "From Modernism to Hypermodernism and Beyond: An Interview with Paul Virilio." *Theory, Culture, & Society* 11.5–6 (1999): 25–55.

Arrighi, Giovanni. *Adam Smith in Beijing: Lineages of the Twentieth-First Century*. Cambridge: London/New York: Verso, 2007.

Bazin, André. *What Is Cinema?* Trans. Hugh Gray. Berkeley: U of California P, 1967.

Beck, Ulrich. "We Do Not Live in an Age of Cosmopolitanism But in an Age of Cosmopolitanization: The Global Other Is in Our Midst." *Irish Journal of Sociology* 19.1 (2011): 16–34.

Beck, Ulrich, Anthony Giddens, and Scott Lash. *Reflexive Modernization: Politics, Tradition, and Aesthetics in the Modern Social Order*. Stanford: Stanford UP, 1994.

Berry, Chris, ed. *Perspectives on Chinese Cinema*. London: The British Film Institute, 1991.

Berry, Chris, and Mary Farquhar. *China on Screen: Cinema and Nation*. New York: Columbia UP, 2006.

Bordwell, David. *Making Meaning: Inference and Rhetoric in the Interpretation of Cinema*. Cambridge: Harvard UP, 2000.

Bourdieu, Pierre. *Acts of Resistance: Against the Tyranny of the Market*. Trans. Richard Rice. New York: The New Press, 1998.

Brown, Wendy. "Neo-liberalism and the End of Liberal Democracy." *Theory and Event* 7.1 (2003): 1–43.

Calhoun, Craig. "Beck, Asia, and Second Modernity." *The British Journal of Sociology* 61.3 (2010): 597–619.

Castoriadis, Cornelius. *The Imaginary Institution of Society*. Trans. Kathleen Blamey. Boston: MIT Press, 1987/1998.

Chakrabarty, Dipesh. *Provincializing Europe: Postcolonial Thought and Historical Difference*. Princeton: Princeton UP, 2000.

———. "The Time of History and the Times of Gods." *The Politics of Culture in the Shadow of Capital*. Eds. Lisa Lowe and David Lloyd. Durham: Duke UP, 1997. 35–60.

Chang, Kyung-Sup. "The Second Modern Condition? Compressed Modernity as Internalized Reflexive Cosmopolitanization." *The British Journal of Sociology* 61.3 (2010): 444–64.

Chow, Rey, ed. *Modern Chinese Literary and Cultural Studies in the Age of Theory*. Durham: Duke UP, 2000. 1–25.

———. *Sentimental Fabulations, Contemporary Chinese Films*. New York: Columbia UP, 2007.

Comaroff, Jean, and John L. Comaroff. "Millennial Capitalism: First Thoughts on a Second Coming." *Public Culture* 12.2 (2000): 291–343.

Davis, Mike. "The Great Wall of Capital." *Socialist Review* (February, 2004). *http://www.socialistreview.org.uk/article.php?articlenumber=8770*.

Debord, Guy. *A Sick Planet*. Trans. Donald Nicholson-Smith. Oxford, England: Seagull Books, 1971/2008.

———. *The Society of the Spectacle*. Trans. Donald Nicholson-Smith. New York: Zone Books, 1967/1995.

Deleuze, Gilles, and Felix Guattari. *Anti-Oedipus: Capitalism and Schizophrenia*. Trans. Robert Hurley et al. Minneapolis: U of Minnesota P, 1972/1983.

Deleuze, Gilles, and Felix Guattari. *A Thousand Plateaus: Capitalism and Schizophrenia*. Trans. Brian Massumi. Minneapolis: U of Minnesota P, 1980/1987.

Dirlik, Arif, and Xudong Zhang, eds. "Postmodernism and China." A Special Issue of *boundary 2: An International Journal of Literature and Culture* 24.3 (Fall, 1997): 1–275.

Editorial Collective. *The Opium War*. The History Departments of Fudan University and Shanghai Teachers' University, Peking: Foreign Languages Press, 1976. 111 and 1–2.

Eisenstadt, Shmuel Noah, ed. *Daedalus: "Multiple Modernities, A Special Issue"* 129.1 (Winter, 2000): 1–260.

Fabian, Johannes. *Time and the Other: How Anthropology Makes Its Object*. New York: Columbia UP, 1983.

Fukuyama, Francis. "The End of History?" *Globalization and the Challenges of a New Century*. Eds. Patrick O'Meara, Howard D. Mehlinger, and Matthew Krain. Bloomington: Indiana UP, 2000. 161–80.

Gaonkar, Dilip Parameshwar, ed. *Alternative Modernities*. Durham: Duke UP, 2001.

Giddens, Anthony. *The Consequences of Modernity*. Stanford: Stanford UP, 1990.

Gong, Haomin. *Uneven Modernity: Literature, Film, and Intellectual Discourse in Postso-cialist China*. Honolulu: U of Hawaii P, 2012.

Harvey, David. *A Brief History of Neoliberalism*. New York: Oxford UP, 2005.

———. *A Companion to Marx's Capital*. London and New York: Verso, 2010.

———. *The Condition of Postmodernity: An Enquiry into the Origins of Social Change*. Cambridge: Blackwell Publishers, 1990.

Jameson, Fredric. *Postmodernism: Or the Cultural Logic of Late Capitalism*. Durham: Duke UP, 1991.

———. *A Singular Modernity: Essay on the Ontology of the Present*. London: Verso, 2002.

Jameson, Fredric, and Masao Miyoshi. *The Cultures of Globalization*. Durham: Duke UP, 1998.

Klein, Naomi. *The Shock Doctrine: The Rise of Disaster Capitalism*. New York: Picador, 2008.

Kundera, Milan. *The Unbearable Lightness of Being: A Novel*. New York: Harper Peren-nial, 2009.

Lash, Scott, and John Urry. *The End of Organized Capitalism*. Madison WI: U of Wiscon-sin P, 1987.

Li, David Leiwei, ed. *Globalization and the Humanities*. Hong Kong: Hong Kong UP, 2003.

———. "(In Lieu of an) Introduction: The Asian American Subject between Liberalism and Neoliberalism." *Asian American Literature: Volume I. Literary History: Criticism and Theory*. Ed. David Leiwei Li. Abingdon, UK/New York, NY: Routledge, 2012. 1–29.

———. "Remembrance against Manufactured Amnesia: On the 20th Anniversary of the Tiananmen Incident." *Jumpcut: A Review of Contemporary Media* 51 (Spring, 2009). *http://www.ejumpcut.org/currentissue/Tiananmen/index.html*.

———. "Review of *Postsocialism and Cultural Politics: China in the Last Decade of the Twentieth Century* by Xudong Zhang." *Comparative Literature* 62.3 (2010): 311–14.

Lu, Sheldon, and Emily Yueh-yu Yeh, eds. *Chinese-Language Film: Historiography, Poet-ics, Politics*. Honolulu: U of Hawaii P, 2005.

Lyotard, Jean-François. *The Postmodern Condition: A Report on Knowledge*. Trans. Geoff Bennington and Brian Massumi. Minneapolis: U of Minnesota P, 1984/1997.

Mandel, Ernest. *Late Capitalism*. Trans. Joris de Bres. London: NLB, 1975.

Marcuse, Herbert. *One-Dimensional Man: Studies in the Ideology of Advanced Industrial Society*. Boston: Beacon Press, 1964/1991.

Marx, Karl. *Grundrisse: Foundations of the Critique of Political Economy*. New York: Penguin Classics, 1993.

McGrath, Jason. *Postsocialist Modernity: Chinese Cinema, Literature, and Criticism in the Market Age*. Stanford: Stanford UP, 2010.

Polanyi, Karl. *The Great Transformation: The Political and Economic Origins of Our Time*. Boston: Beacon, 1944/1957.

Readings, Bill. *The University in Ruins*. Cambridge: Harvard UP, 1997.

Schumpeter, Joseph A. *Capitalism, Socialism, and Democracy*. New York: Harper, 1950.

Shambaugh, David, ed. *Greater China: The Next Superpower?* New York: Oxford UP, 1995.

Shih, Shu-mei. *Visuality and Identity: Sinophone Articulations across the Pacific*. Durham: Duke UP, 2007.

Strange, Susan. *Casino Capitalism*. Manchester, Manchester UP, 1997.

Tong, Chee-kiong, and Chan Kwok-bun. "One Face, Many Masks: The Singularity and Plurality of Chinese Identity." *Diaspora: A Journal of Transnational Studies* 10.3 (2001): 361–89.

Tu, Weiming. "Cultural China: The Periphery as the Center." *Daedalus* 120.2 (1991a): 1–32.
———, ed. "The Living Tree: The Changing Meaning of Being Chinese Today, A Special Issue." *Daedalus* 120.2 (1991b): 1–226.
Tucker, Robert C. *The Marx-Engels Reader* (2nd ed.). New York: W. W. Norton, 1978.
Virilio, Paul. *Speed and Politics: An Essay on Dromology*. Trans. M. Polizzotti. New York: Semiotext(e), 1977/1986.
Wang, Gungwu. *The Chinese Overseas: From Earthbound China to the Quest of Autonomy*. Cambridge: Harvard UP, 2000.
Weber, Max. *The Protestant Ethic and the Spirit of Capitalism*. Trans. Talcott Parsons. Intro. by Anthony Giddens. London and New York: Routledge, 1930/1993.
Williams, Raymond. *Keywords: A Vocabulary of Culture and Society* (Revised Edition). New York: Oxford UP, 1983.
Zhang, Yingjin. "Comparative Film Studies, Transnational Film Studies: Interdisciplinarity, Crossmediality, and Transcultural Visuality in Chinese Cinema." *Journal of Chinese Cinemas* 1.1 (2007): 27–40.
Zizek, Slavoj. *First as Tragedy, Then as Farce*. London/New York: Verso, 2009.

Part I

Homo economicus

Individual liberty and market dependency

1 Primitive accumulation and the emergence of the liberal subject in the People's Republic

Zhang Yimou's *Red Sorghum* and Zhou Xiaowen's *Ermo*

Indubitably China's best-known film director both domestically and abroad, Zhang Yimou 张艺谋 comes onto the stage of world cinema just when the People's Republic (PRC) ends its self-willing socialist economic and cultural isolation. If the international success of *Red Sorghum* 红高粱 in 1987 marks China's opening after its "delinking" from the world system, Zhang's phantasmagoric opening of the 2008 Beijing Olympic Games signals China's success of "relinking" after becoming the belated 143rd member and a significant player in the World Trade Organization.[1] This convergence with Capital's Second Coming involves not only the radical pendulum swing in political ideology and state governance but also a fundamental reconstitution of the Chinese subject as an individual, social, economic, and emotional being. Chinese cinema in the reform era – of which the works of Zhang and his lesser known cohort Zhou Xiaowen 周晓文 are a constitutive part – plays the crucial role of mediating the shock of the new and unintelligible, anticipating the arrival of liberal subjects while adjudicating the adjustment of historical subjects of socialism.

With its extravagant display of exotic colors and peasant customs and its exuberant celebration of the repressed spirit yearning its rightful release, Zhang's *Red Sorghum* enacts an aesthetic rupture from the drab social landscape of Mao's China and expresses itself as a renewed desire for an enlightened modernity in the 1980s. Instead of treating it as "autoethnography" wherein the third world subject represents itself to a projected first world audience, I reread this classic of the Chinese Fifth Generation of film directors primarily as an allegory of primitive accumulation.[2] The film's figuration of the rural society enacts "the invention of tradition" in Hobsbawm and Ranger's sense of the term. It serves to secure a spotlight in the international arena of spectacle production as well as to meet the challenge posed by the Second Coming of Capitalism. The Yellow River plateau and its peasantry, long held as the cradle of Chinese civilization, appear a persistent problem of agrarianism that begs filmic representation in the globalization of industrial capitalism. If Zhang tackles this historical problem by conjuring up an apparently ahistorical agrarian community with an apparent anachronistic spirit of acquisition, naturalizing economic interests in tropes of erotic conflicts, his contemporary Zhou Xiaowen attends the transformation of a precapitalist habitat by focusing on a hinterland village with all the verisimilitude of a Chinese present under political and economic reform. What appears as the myth of romantic rivalry in *Red Sorghum* is realized as actual market competition in *Ermo* 二嫫 (1994), indicated early on in a heckling match when the title character tries to win customers for her handmade noodles. But Zhou's seemingly more realistic cinematic narration is as allegorical as Zhang's apparently more legendary mode of storytelling: both *Red Sorghum* and *Ermo* exemplify the kind of "cognitive mapping" and "allegorical thinking" that allow "the most random, minute, or isolated landscapes to function as a figurative machinery in which questions about the system and its control over the ceaseless local rise and fall," and through which "a host of partial subjects . . . can often now stand in allegorically for trends and forces in the world system" (Jameson, 1995, 3, 5).

In this first chapter I want to demonstrate how such "partial subjects" are produced in China's transition from socialism to capitalism, from the agrarian structures of feeling insufficiently revolutionized by and intransigently persisted through Mao's reign to their uneasy makeover in the Deng Xiaoping era into something resembling "the habits of the heart" (Bellah et al.). I begin with *Red Sorghum*'s allegorical figuration of "passions and interests" in association and advocacy of PRC's reversal of political and economic direction (Hirschman). Turning briefly to *River Elegy* 河殤, the television documentary that gripped China in 1988, chronologically between Zhang's and Zhou's films, I identify the reformist urge in its embrace of an oceanic culture and view the series as an attempt to modernize the historical peasantry, the core of Chinese citizenry at the time. Following this is a reading of *Ermo* as a telling tale of "dis-embedding" the Chinese rural society through the rise of market economy (Giddens). I show Zhou's filmic illumination of both Karl Polanyi's classic argument against a market's hegemony over society and C. P. Macpherson's original theory of possessive individualism. The exegesis of the ascending spirit of acquisition and instrumental rationality in these Chinese media texts also addresses the resurgence of Max Weber in the neo-Confucian justification of East Asian economic miracles and culture particular capitalisms.[3] Not at all implying that China is reproducing the kind of Western liberalism of yesteryear, I want to demonstrate its manifestation, mutation, as well as its rupture of historical Chinese-ness.[4]

1

Typical of the Fifth Generation of film directors, Zhang's work shares the intellectual tension of the time as China opens up to the Second Coming of Capital. On the one hand, *Red Sorghum* revives the legacy of May 4th in Capital's First Coming and renews its iconoclastic assault on precapitalist Chinese tradition. On the other hand, its passion for capitalist modernity is wedded to a national soul-searching. This double movement of cultural reflection and national articulation against the landlocked past and toward an oceanic future is achieved in cinema through a salient stylization.[5] The spectacular capture of quaint color and landscape functions as much as the Fifth Generation's inoffensive disavowal of communist rule and socialist realism as its deliberate pitch of aesthetic distinction to the international film market (X. Zhang, 205–06). For Dai Jinhua, "the novel film language" betrays "a biography of a generation's spiritual exile" (2002, 16). For Rey Chow, it is an instance of "primitive passion" at the moment of a "cultural crisis." The primitive as a figure for this "irretrievable *common/place*" becomes necessarily the "fabrication of a *pre* that occurs in the time of the *post*" (Chow, 22). Zhang Yimou's mythical agrarian appears an ethnographic self-invention that figures an Eastern tradition against a Western modernity.

But Zhang's 1980s is not an era of nineteenth-century colonialism, and China's encounter with Capital's First Coming has left indelible traces of its semicolonial and semicapitalist past. In this light, the founding of the People's Republic of China at once rejects a dominant capitalist modernity and carves a divergent path of socialist modernity: the establishment of the PRC constitutes both a monumental delinking from the world system and a critical alternative to Soviet communism during the Cold War. For Zhang to evoke the primitive at the moment of Western reorganization of world capitalism from a welfare state form of "Fordism" to "Flexible Accumulation" is to negotiate a cultural crisis not of classical colonialism or capitalism in its imperial phase (Harvey; Jameson 1988). Rather, Zhang has to negotiate the Second Coming of Capital with his technology of the moving image, which does not involve territorial occupations but entails a transnational geo-economic submission by indigenous societies and the body and soul of their subjects.

By emptying the immediate past of macabre socialism and harking back to a precapitalist China, Zhang's use of the 'primitive' reimagines a blank slate so that PRC's present embrace of capitalism could be reconfigured as teleological progress rather than regression. A story of "primitive passion," *Red Sorghum* is best appreciated as a prototypical narration of "primitive accumulation." The film ingeniously subsumes the pursuit of material interests in the tropes of sexual passion, at once mystifying the naked operation of power and mythologizing the origin of property and possession. Along with *Ju Dou* 菊豆 (1990) and *Raise the Red Lantern* 大红灯笼高高挂 (1991), *Red Sorghum* has inaugurated an allegorical trilogy of forbidden love and its transgression. The opposition to the totalitarian socialist state finds its metaphor in the revolt against tyrannical landlords while the appropriation of their women comes to justify the natural rise of capitalist enterprise. In so transfiguring the historical difference between socialist and capitalist political economies into a timeless romantic rivalry, *Red Sorghum* has become a successful article of imagistic and ideological persuasion that eventually valorizes a type of hero and favors a type of subjectivity supportive of Capital's Second Coming.

Framed by the voice-over of the grandson, the film opens with rowdy festivity. Concealed in a wedding sedan, "Grandma," the young bride, is being married off to an old, leprous winery owner in exchange for a mule. The sedan is waylaid on its way to the groom, but under the heroic leadership of "Grandpa," the head sedan carrier, the team finishes off the gun-toting bandit. Three days later, as the bride is visiting her widowed father, she is again kidnapped by no other man than Grandpa himself. Are we to interpret it as rape, or view it as the mutual consummation of Grandpa and Grandma, a spontaneous merging of body and soul against the prison house of feudalism?

Zhang sets up the sequence with an establishing shot of Grandma on a donkey, riding leisurely into the sorghum fields. Out jumps a hooded man, who grabs her sideways against her struggle, runs into the depth of the field, and throws her down on the ground. Grandma escapes; the kidnapper chases in a quick crosscutting of the two amid the dense underbrush over Grandma's loud panting, until she stops in exhaustion, only to find her way blocked. Tearing apart his hood, Grandpa reveals himself, his face tense, and his gaze piercing. A reverse shot of Grandma shows her shock of recognition, mouth agape, motionless. Grandpa tramples down the windswept sorghum in frenzy. A close-up of Grandma follows, backlit by the dazzling sun, her eyes closed and her face sweaty. As she falls and fades out of frame in the blinding sunlight, the camera angles up with a bird's-eye view of the circular clearing made by Grandpa amid the jungle of wild sorghum. He kneels, with her prostrate on the ground, as the rhythmic beat of the drums gains intensity, ringing in the full blast of Shouna, the Chinese horn. This is "a moment of returning the human to its natural elements, and the moment of triumph of the primitive 'body,' in all its violence and life force, over the repressive tradition of the Chinese patriarchal society" (Y. Zhang 210).

Leaving aside for now the sequence's transformation of the intent of rape into an effect of rapture, I would argue that the apparent release of the libidinal here is neither natural nor antipatriarchal. Grandpa's gesture of clearing the unruly sorghum and claiming the woman is reminiscent of "the lay of the land": man's colonization of nature and conquest of women have become in this instance one and the same (Kolodny). The triumph of the body is not about its immersion in divine nature but about the domination and alienation of nature; for the trampling of the sorghum bush merely anticipates the all-too-real transformations of the Chinese landscape into local sites of industrial production for global consumption, not to mention turning it into the dumping ground for capitalism's inherent productive waste. The genius of Zhang, however, rests on the way he cinematically encodes such direct acts of cultural violence in expressions of irrepressible sexual passion. Grandma's apparent acquiescence to Grandpa, for example, could reasonably be taken as her desire for virility and vitality while her physical paralysis in front of him could be taken for her powerless submission to his irresistible charm. After all, Grandpa is both muscular and masculine, with such reckless energy and irreverent charisma that his succession of the leper has to be natural and his conquest of Grandma consensual.

It is not incidental that the naturalization of the couple's romantic passion is followed by their interesting and interested symbolic patricide. In a fit of rage against her father, who insists that Grandma return to the leper so she may inherit his property, the daughter literally disowns him: you're not my Dad, she screams. Meanwhile, the Grandson's voice-over discloses that the leprous owner of the distillery and the lawful husband of Grandma roughly three decades her senior are mysteriously murdered. This "imaginary killing of the father" is for Dai Jinhua the "myth making" of the Fifth Generation that must by historical necessity bypass both the horror of the Cultural Revolution and "the shock of the onslaught of Western/Other culture" (2002, 32–33). *Red Sorghum* thus heralds "the coming of age of the Fifth Generation" by "push[ing it] back into a 'prehistoric era' in a wilderness outside Ur-society itself" (Ibid. 34).

Instead of regarding Zhang's fabrication of the prehistoric as an escape into a wilderness outside Ur-society, I consider the symbolic patricide in *Red Sorghum* a deliberate mediation of China's historical present of the 1980s. If the biological father of Grandma stands for the arbitrary authority of ancient feudalism, then Big Head Li, the Big Boss of the winery, who exists in the name of the Father but never appears on the screen, serves as an invisible trope of historical communism/ socialism. It is important that the Big Boss of the winery is unseen, not because the phallus is always more powerful when concealed, as a Lacanian reading may suggest, but because the only visible figuration of authority in China during the Cultural Revolution (1966–76) is the ubiquitous image of Mao. Zhang's analogy and allusion would be too blatant and too politically risky if the equation of the two patriarchs was directly and visibly drawn, for both Chinese feudalism and state socialism are patriarchal hierarchies steeped in hereditary succession, whether through actual blood lineage or revolutionary heritage. Like the removal of wild sorghum that stands in the way of Grandpa and Grandma's libidinal fulfillment, the inhumanity and unreason of patrilineal political economies must also be eradicated on their road to heaven. This, I believe, is Zhang Yimou's active participation in the 1980s Chinese cultural reflection and political and economic reform: in wading through the historical sediments of China's feudalism and socialism while conveniently skipping its semicolonial and semicapitalist history, the director seems encouraged by the nation-state's very capitalist (re)turn. In an ingenuous cinematic figuration of history, both the capitalist system and its ideal subject are represented anew. The recreation of the Oedipal hero in the Chinese context is a radical disavowal of a system of thick filial exchange rooted in land and lineage. It is simultaneously an enthusiastic introduction if not an endorsement of a system of transparent commodity exchange based on the voluntary alienation as well as vigorous competition of labor via the boundless market.

In this light, the death of the leper is an insufficient representational demise of the agrarian aristocratic system, because for the violent replacement of the old political economy to succeed, the new one has to prove its superiority not only rationally but also emotionally. As an emblem of the new spirit of capitalism, in other words, Grandpa has to shine against other real or imagined rivals. Zhang achieves this aesthetic effect with two scenes. In the first, Grandpa appears as an intoxicated lunatic, bragging of his sexual conquest of Grandma in front of everyone, thus dashing the hope of Luohan, the ex-foreman who is a secret admirer of Grandma and who stays on after the Big Boss's homicide to revive her distillery. In the second, Grandpa confronts the real gangster, Crackpot Sanbao, by accusing him of "defiling" his woman and then eluding his gunfire, miraculously unharmed. Not only do these two sequences establish Grandma's virginity until the primal scene in the sorghum fields, but they also further secure Grandpa's exclusive right of sexual access. In the first instance, the potential threat by Brother Luohan is dissolved precisely because of his brotherly affection for Grandma. In his deference to her, Luohan exudes conformity and femininity; he represents a mode of emotional economy wherein labor is integrated into loving care, or rather the pain of asexual devotion more often than not substitutes and sublimates sexual abandon. In the second instance, Sanbao the bandit, who has an equally impressive physique as Grandpa, however, is so plagued by the paranoia of leprous contamination that he is afraid to touch her. Neither the spontaneous care of Luohan nor the superstitious fear of Sanbao seems right; as particular expressions of frustrated longing, they appear anachronistic if not antiquated.

This line of cinematic persuasion reaches its apex in a final scene that fully justifies Grandpa's claim of Grandma, and by extension naturalizes his logical possession of the winery. At the party celebrating the new wine, Grandpa publicly takes off his pants, pees right into the gigantic amphora, and then grabs Grandma and takes her to the bedroom.[6] If the trampling of wild sorghum introduces a new cultural order of nature's submission, mutual sexual attraction, resulting ultimately in fecund reproduction, then the discharge of urine, as the grandson's voice-over now tells us, leads to a phenomenal production of the spirits. This batch of sorghum wine turns out to be the best brew of the distillery ever. Primitive and penile passions of the procreative kind have been transformed into a miraculous force of industrial production, serving both the ends of personal pleasure and the interests of a burgeoning economy. Beyond an impromptu gesture of defiance, the public urination is at once an act of liberating the hitherto suppressed productive energy and an act of clearing the leprous production system of its legitimacy. Acquiring the catalytic power of deregulation, Grandpa's pee has become a paean to the superior capitalist spirit(s). Not coincidentally, the discovery of the wine's urine-induced superiority should lead to its naming as "Eighteen Mile Red." It is not the red in socialist symbolism, the passionate flame of Mao's revolutionary utopia and attendant fanaticism. Rather, the red is metaphorically the intoxicating fever of capitalist accumulation, which shall literally turn into "red obsession," the Chinese craze for French Bordeaux decades later.[7] The product branding of Eighteen Mile Red thereby anticipates the "libidinalization of the market" as a new form of psychosocial discipline in place of previous puritanical prohibition, just when *Red Sorghum* itself signals a beginning transformation of commodities into images and images into commodities (Jameson 1998, 69).

In thus turning the story of primitive accumulation into a story of timeless romantic passion for imagistic consumption and subject interpellation, Zhang Yimou appears to have conjoined Thomas Jefferson and Adam Smith, as the individual pursuit of happiness and lust for material gain converge in a self-regulating market which will supposedly maximize collective social benefit (Stone 236). Zhang's apparently unique form of cinematic allegory, intriguingly, has its precise parallel in 1980s discourse of "the New Enlightenment," which, according to Wang Hui, couches its critique of socialism as "a critique of tradition and feudalism" (157). Rallying "symbols of individual autonomy" in opposition to "a powerful state" allows Chinese intellectuals of the time to identify with the old "antichurch and anti-aristocratic bourgeois[ie]" of eighteenth-century European Enlightenment while simultaneously promoting a postsocialist Chinese integration into the fin de siècle system of neoliberal capitalism (Ibid. 157, 160).

Grandpa's rebellion against the leper in *Red Sorghum* not only invites a similar identification against the feudal socialist state but also accentuates this opposition with the technology of the cinematic image, even though the leper is diegetically evoked only and never really shown on the screen. By making the state the natural enemy and overlooking its viable role in ensuring democracy and equality, however, such cinematic allegories of antinomianism as *Red Sorghum*, *Ju Dou*, and *Raise the Red Lantern* have initiated in China a classic liberal understanding of the self-possessive individual as the sovereign agent and the market as the sole outlet of individual liberty. While I shall elaborate later on how a capital-generated liberalism finds and reforms its Chinese peasant subject in *Ermo*, and how the documentary *Crazy English* reveals the remaking of a Chinese urban subject into a neoliberal, it is fair to say that in *Red Sorghum* we already witness the strange discursive convergence between the 1980s antistate rhetoric in Deng Xiaoping's China and the anti–big government slogan of the Reagan-Thatcher West. This antinomian discourse turns out to be variegated local responses to the same pressure of ascending global capitalism, as it both obscures the essential function of the reforming state in guiding China's marketization and anticipates the neoliberal conception of "the market as self-sustaining, correcting, and foundational" on a planetary scale (Bové 172; H. Wang 43).[8]

2

This treatment of *Red Sorghum* seems against the grain. First, by reading cinematic signs of "passion" in terms of economic "interests," I interpret the film's representation of nature, the bloody sorghum fields and the muddy plateaus, as a cinematic prelude to capitalist culture. In this, I share with Rey Chow's perceptive remark that for the Fifth Generation nature "signifies a deliberate *emptying*" of "communist state discourse," but for me "returning to nature" far exceeds "aestheticizing old China as 'ancient' and 'backward'" while insisting on "the first-ness and uniqueness of what is Chinese" (40, 37). The Fifth Generation's gaze at nature reveals not "the quest for the 'Chineseness' of their origins" as it does the puzzling out of Chinese-ness dramatically destabilized by Capitalism's Second Coming. The remark by Chen Kaige, the director of *Yellow Earth* 黄土地 (1984; cinematography by Zhang Yimou), that his choice of the Yellow River plateau merely follows the Chinese revolutionary movement from the west to the east must be apprehended beyond its face value (quoted in Chow 39). The Fifth Generation has pioneered a "cultural revolution after the Cultural Revolution," both rejecting the old communist teleology and reversing its inward-looking direction (Berry). Chen and Zhang's rendition of the yellow earth, though a cinematic act of national soul-searching, is clearly oriented toward the capitalist Pacific Rim rather than a recuperation of Mao's patriotism. Granted, Mao has succeeded in founding the People's Republic via the strategy of having the country surrounding and strangling the city, but he has since mired China in the country despite his "great-leap" fantasy of Soviet-style industrialization. Chen and Zhang's turn to the yellow earth is to awaken the country, after Deng Xiaoping's invisible handshake with Reagan-Thatcher, to the new prospects of the city from China's millennia of agrarianism. The country, in short, must forsake its tenacious historical attachment to the yellow earth and confront the challenge brought on by industrial capitalism in its second global incarnation.

Second, this reading is at odds with what I call "the bifurcation thesis" on the Fifth Generation. Unlike most critics who see their collective corpus through an exclusive lens of the rural, Fredric Jameson recognizes early on the Fifth Generation's preoccupation with both the rural and the urban. For him, the representation of the rural is epitomized by an "epic narrativity," unfolding like a "cinematic scroll" on two principal levels. Politically "it claims to constitute some new way of appropriating tradition which is neither iconoclastic nor given over to Western individualism." Aesthetically, its inclusion of the countryside "reaffirms the immense agricultural hinterland of the peasant masses." "Urban PRC film," on the other hand, "take[s] a very different stylistic turn, as though its relations were not those that led into the Chinese land mass, but rather the discontinuous vertical openings onto the media and the Pacific Rim." Citing Zhou Xiaowen's *Desperation* 最后的疯狂, which came out in 1987 as with *Red Sorghum*, Jameson argues that the film's yearning toward the capitalist West expresses itself by a representational removal of "the reminders of a socialist economy of the PRC," precluding the audience from realizing their existential distance from the "world of contemporary industrial production and consumption" and from raising questions of any "ideological struggle" (Jameson 1995, 118–19 passim). If the epic shot of the rural is a nostalgic evocation of the Chinese "collective imaginary" and the "de-identification procedures" of the urban a "representational laundering of ideologically marked contents," the Fifth Generation seems in this bifurcated reading unable to bring China's landlocked socialist modernity and an oceanic capitalist modernity into one single horizon of cinematic vision.

What I have contended with *Red Sorghum* and what I shall argue with Zhou Xiaowen's subsequent film, *Ermo*, is the contrary: the Fifth Generation's obsession with the rural in fact addresses the problems of a historically bounded agrarian culture now made urgent by Capital's Second Coming and the "economic miracles" of China's Confucian cousins, such as Hong Kong, Taiwan, and Singapore, if not also South Korea and Japan. Even in the pastoral of Grandpa and Grandma frolicking in the sorghum fields, pristine nature in the raw form of the peasant body and the fecund land has already taken on an acquisitive spirit every bit infused by the dawning directorial awareness of the world beyond the People's Republic in which China is no longer the beacon of international socialism. The landmass with its yellow earth and the peasantry of seeming eternity are neither reaffirmed as "tradition," as Jameson seems to suggest, nor privileged as distinctive "Chinese-ness," as Chow appears to have it. Rather, they are presented as a weighty historical condition not to be ideologically neutralized (Jameson 1995, 119), but aesthetically negotiated with, and above all, culturally reformed. Indeed, *Red Sorghum* has in my opinion participated in the larger intellectual discourse of reform of 1980s China as well as anticipated, with its unique cinematic drama and stylistic innovation, the themes and thrusts of *River Elegy*, the television documentary that gripped the nation in 1988, a year after the appearance of Zhang's film.[9]

The film *Red Sorghum* and the documentary *River Elegy* represent the emerging media market in the 1980s transcendent of state control in their ubiquitous articulation of "high culture fever" (Jing Wang). They show that postsocialist reform is neither exclusively dictated by the state nor passively accepted by the populace but brokered by an emergent mass media and its entrepreneurs, who are supplanting the elite Chinese intellectuals historically affiliated with state institutions or imperial bureaucracies. Crucial to this development is the televisual media's inestimable role in the reform of the Chinese peasantry, the salt of the yellow earth or origin of historical Chinese-ness, the fountainhead of agrarian insurgency that once ensured Mao's successful communist revolution and China's socialist identity. By the Deng Xiaoping era, the Chinese peasantry is both the subject and object of the revolution after the Cultural Revolution: it has to be made ready and made over for the nation's precipitous passage to Capitalism's Second Coming. If *Red Sorghum* mediates more cryptically and *Ermo* more realistically China's national reorientation toward industrial capitalism from its socialist commitment to a nonaligned third world to its close engagement with the newly industrialized countries of the Pacific Rim, these movements are the explicit subjects of *River Elegy*'s melancholic advocacy.

A six-part miniseries broadcast on China's Central Television in 1988, *River Elegy* is both a popular cultural reflection on China's traumatic "Yellow River culture" and a national incitation in favor of "the oceanic blue culture." Su Xiaokang and Wang Luxiang's lament on China's international weakness resonates with the Chinese enlightenment movement of the 1920s. Unlike the May 4th intellectuals who attribute China's defeat by Western powers as the consequence of both dynastic corruption and colonial aggression, Su and Wang consider China's failure as exclusively indigenous and inherently cultural in origin. The Chinese preference for stability through the defense mechanism of self-enclosure is at the root of its inevitable ruin. Su and Wang's new assignment of historical causality leads to their condemnation of such national symbols as the Yellow River and the Great Wall so that an anxious embrace of the image of the blue ocean can be absolutely affirmed. Similarly, the arguments of Adam Smith and Max Weber have found their way into Su and Wang's fundamental question: "Why had Industrial Civilization with its promise of vast wealth never appeared in Chinese history?" (Bodman and Wan 162). In the very manner it is phrased, the raison d'être of the nation-state and its subject are proclaimed to be economic. Wealth through capitalist accumulation is advocated as the sole path of China's salvation.

In place of a socialist nationalism that once consolidated the Chinese peasantry in a struggle against imperialist invasions is Su and Wang's new nationalism, the core of which contains the wholesale conversion of Chinese peasantry and the radical modernization of a Chinese-ness historically rooted in the agrarian way of life. Theirs is a unique brand of "assimilationist nationalism" as opposed to the near-concomitant phenomenon of an "antagonist nationalism" of the neo-Confucian kind. Antagonistic nationalism is generated from the periphery of the

Sinophonic Asia Pacific – not paradoxically the central developmental space in the Second Coming of a truly global capitalism – where the system has already produced "economic miracles." It is thus characterized by a reverse Orientalist impulse to revise the Weberian thesis and to claim the superiority of Confucian capitalism over the capitalism of Occidental origin. It is not without irony that antagonist nationalism is not antagonist to capitalism as an economic system; it merely insists on its own apparent cultural specificity. If neo-Confucian antagonist nationalism is motivated by the spirit of civilizational superiority, the assimilationist nationalism of Su and Wang is driven by a self-deprecating Chinese cultural inferiority measured by the yardstick of a Western turned global capitalist material culture.[10] Assimilationist nationalism is a concessional and motivational nationalism, conceding to the universal trajectory of capitalist development and motivating the Chinese populace to catch up with the world system in speed.

In view of their ideological orientation, Su and Wang's analyses of and answers to China's historical failure are straightforward:

> China, a large country made up of peasants with small landholdings, had never had a true concept of commodities, even though commerce had always been highly developed . . . In the vast, backwards rural areas, there are common problems in the peasant makeup such as a weak spirit of enterprise, a very low ability to accept risk, a deep psychology of dependency and a strong sense of passive acceptance of fate . . . This is truly an agricultural civilization caught in a vicious cycle.
>
> (Bodman and Wan 163–64, 169–70)

The voice-over's condemnation of the "deep psychology of dependency and a strong sense of passive acceptance of fate" is interspersed with visuals – footage liberally lifted from dramatic films as well as documentaries, such as Chen Kaige's *Yellow Earth* and Wu Tianming's *Old Well* 老井 (1986, starring none other than Zhang Yimou before his directorial debut) along with actual interviews – that foreground the figures of the praying peasants as evidential symbols of China's primitive condition and historical mishap. The medium and the message are consistent for Su and Wang: China, which has lost "its once-in-a-millennium chance to develop capitalism," will have to "acquire the mechanism of revitalization"; to do so, it must transform the historical makeup of the Chinese peasantry, the mainstay of the Chinese population (Ibid. 165, 162).

3

Ermo, Zhou Xiaowen's film about the title protagonist's quest for the biggest television set in her county, dramatizes with extraordinary cinematic power and precision the global processes of market transformation on local social relations and individual psyches.[11] In Zhou's skillful hands, a peasant woman's yearning to transcend her agrarian limitations, to marshal her fate on the market, to fulfill her desire, and to develop herself becomes simultaneously a masterful allegory of Su and Wang's impassioned plea of reform as well as China's rush to embrace the Second Coming of Capitalism. The spatial bifurcation of the rural and the urban visible in the Fifth Generation's corpus is unified in *Ermo* with one single cinematic scope of vision. The industrial capitalism of *River Elegy*'s assimilationist dream is for Zhou not only the conceptual parameter but also the material context through which to cinematically reconfigure China's ancient agrarianism. Unlike Chen Kaige and Zhang Yimou, who tend to mediate the maddening pace of China's capitalist revolution through specious evocations of the agrarian and the archaic, Zhou Xiaowen zeroes in on the countryside of a postsocialist China in its fervent embrace of the capitalist market. It is true that the village in *Ermo* initially figures an "earthbound" China, an ethnocentric continental mind-set and a landlocked way of life that have come to stand for the particularity of historical Chinese-ness, a makeup or essential quality of the people that is increasingly suspect (G. Wang). But the project of a peasant woman purchasing her TV already heralds a centrifugal outlook, inextricably infused with the work of globalization both as the planetary dissemination of capitalist logics and practices and as the evolution of a spectacle economy in which "ends are nothing and development is all" (Debord 15–16). Ermo's departure from the village and eventual return to her unsettled origin enact an archetypal allegory of economic and emotional development, requisite for the development of capitalism, but the partial fulfillment and painful frustration of her desires raise serious doubts not only about the logic of a growth-driven and image-oriented consumption but also its fundamental desirability.

The movie begins with a scrupulously framed medium shot of the peasant woman Ermo, wrapped in her dull yellow babushka, hawking twisted noodles at the outskirts of an unnamed northern Chinese village. Her visage is intermittently blocked in the long take by the traffic in the foreground – passing pedestrians, bicyclists, donkey carts, and finally a rusty rundown truck, different modes of transportation as mixed modes of modernity in simultaneity. Xiazi, the proud owner-driver of the only motorized vehicle in the village and an independent contactor, offers his neighbor a ride to town for better sales, but Ermo declines. The camera follows her heading home on a dirt road, exchanging greetings with an old man squatting on a haystack, and passing old women sunning at the village boundary stones. As the audio shifts from chirping birds to crowing ravens, one senses an ominous change in the hamlet. On arrival home, her moping husband, the former village chief and communist party boss now permanently disabled, greets Ermo with the news that the commune has refused to buy the baskets it commissioned her to weave because unexpected hail has destroyed all the fruit. While husband and wife eat dinner, still shocked that a caprice of nature could impact the centralized planning of the co-op, their son Huzi is summoned by the daughter of Xiazi because "the show is on." As Huzi rushes next door, the camera pans to a courtyard of children all wishing to catch a glimpse of Xiazi's TV. Behind the children, in the distance, the old women are still basking in the setting sun, abiding by the celestial clock and traditional codes of living, set in stone, as it were, by the boundaries of the village. The young, however, are irresistibly drawn to the programmable time of the tube and the virtual space beyond their physical confines.[12]

It is perhaps incidental yet particularly illuminating if we consider the opening sequence of *Ermo* as director Zhou Xiaowen's purposeful imaging of Adam Smith's key idea in *The Wealth of Nations* that a presupposed propensity in human nature to "barter, to truck and exchange" leads to the division of labor and consequently the creation of the capitalist market. After all, Ermo's peddling and Xiazi's trucking provide the movie's mise-en-scène of the emergent capitalist market, but it is in Zhou's representation of their metamorphoses in postsocialist China that the film achieves a sociological significance comparable to Karl Polanyi's classic study of European society in tumultuous transition in the previous century. Like *The Great Transformation, Ermo* delineates the tipping of a historical equilibrium between economy and society as it sharpens our apprehension of the rise of "the idea of a self-adjusting market" (Polanyi 3). As shown in Polanyi's penetrating analyses, all societies possess an economy and a market of sorts, but not until the nineteenth century do we witness the coming into hegemony the kind of cultural logic that "the motive of subsistence" is "substituted for that of gain," and "the maintenance of social ties" gives way to safeguarding one's "self-interest in the possession of material goods" (41, 46). However, as Polanyi notes about Smith's own lifetime, "individual economic interest" is "submerged in his social relationships," for it is the principle of reciprocal obligation that ensures collective as well as individual survival (46). Indeed, Ermo's initial reluctance to jump on Xiazi's truck to exchange her noodles for a better price in the city suggests a similar social sentiment to what is prevalent in Euro-American societies prior to the saturation of "a market economy" (Ibid.).

Although Chinese socialist economy is a modern state economy fundamentally different from the residually feudal and increasingly capitalist economy of eighteenth-century Europe, it shares with the latter a quintessential social embeddedness common to what Wang Shaoguang terms, via his reading of Polanyi, the "moral economy," wherein economic activities are "subordinated to political, religious, and social relations" (16). Citing the influential work of Liang Shuming, a Chinese philosopher and reformer of the 1930s, that the traditional Chinese society through millennia is one that has subjected all economic relations to "kinship relations and ethical norms," Wang argues that this historical subjection remains basically untouched after the founding of the PRC in 1949: while "collective and national interests replaced familial relations as the most important of social values," he writes, "the subordination of economic relations to social ethics remained the same . . . under the planned economy" (16–17). If the state machinery and its bureaucratic management of national economy betray the sign of modernity in its rational ordering of people and production, pace Max Weber, this socialist modernity of the People's Republic, however, exhibits a remarkable continuity with the tradition of Chinese agrarianism in its ethical and earthbound outlook as well as its corresponding social arrangements.[13] For all the draconian state measures and political movements, the communist revolution before the Reagan-Thatcher-Deng Xiaoping Revolution seems unable to produce a fundamental rupture in a

Chinese way of life that has been rooted in *Oikos*, a principle of householding that is both land and lineage bound.

With striking stylistic economy, Zhou shows us precisely how a cultural continuity accomplished by the absorption of economic production within the primacy of social reproduction is being challenged. By pairing the two neighboring families he contrasts the fading state-regulated economy with the burgeoning market practices of the Deng reform era. Physically handicapped and sexually impotent, Ermo's husband stands for the defunct socialist economy and the relative decline of the state in centralized economic control. The ex-chief and party boss can no longer guarantee the sale of baskets that his wife has woven and he seems powerless in the social stagnancy of the village. In his black leather jacket and fume-pumping truck, his neighbor Xiazi, however, exudes masculine energy and exemplifies the entrepreneurial possibilities of a postsocialist order. He is offering to truck the baskets for sale in the provincial city. Between the old state and the new capital, equal opportunity impoverishment and "getting rich is glorious": Ermo has decided on the latter.[14] Ermo's choice is metaphorically a decisive Chinese choice after its historical rejection of market economy, for Deng Xiaoping's punch line urging the mass pursuit of wealth appears none other than an explicit endorsement of Adam Smith and a willful contemporary gesture of relinking. From this point on Ermo's personal journey assumes the shape of a globalizing history with all its potential allegorical significance: it is in substituting the motive of personal gain for that of social subsistence and survival and in subscribing to "the self-regulating market system uniquely derived from this principle [of gain]" that Zhou Xiaowen unpacks the planetary domination of capitalism and marks *the* historical moment when the steadfast continuity of Chinese agrarian civilization is broken (Polanyi 30, 41).

The next morning Ermo stacks her baskets and ropes them onto Xiazi's jalopy truck before hurling herself on top with nothing to secure her but gravity. As the bandwagon of capitalist mobility rolls out of the village gate, nearly throwing her overboard, Ermo screams "Mama!" and begs it to stop. But the vehicle of marketization and material prosperity has a momentum of its own: once she is on, Ermo is compelled to stay straddled, as the truck snakes through the winding and muddy highways of the yellow earth that once inspired Mao's utopian peasant revolution. The revolution Ermo experiences is of an entirely different kind, however, for its engine of self-interest and perpetual growth and development will ultimately uproot the peasantry from the soil that has anchored the Chinese filial ethos and a culture steeped in the imperatives of social reproduction. In this sense, the bumpy motion of the truck and Ermo's motion sickness betray the rough rupture that has presently seized upon Chinese socialist modernity and started to sweep away its historically rooted collective ethos. They symbolize the transformation of the mainland Chinese modernity into the archetypal modernity of Euro-American capitalism, which Anthony Giddens holds as radically "discontinuous" and whose contemporary manifestation Arjun Appadurai characterizes as "cultural flows" of "disjunction" (Appadurai 33; Giddens 12). What for Giddens are the mechanisms of "disembedding," "the 'lifting out' of social relations from local contexts of interaction and their restructuring across infinite spans of time-space" are for Zhou simply the act of leaving the household, and he visualizes the motorized movement away from the hamlet as abandoning the principle of householding (21).

As Polanyi reminds us, catering to the needs of one's household being the essential feature of production, the pattern of economy before the domination of the capitalist market is enclosed both within a social group and a circumscribed geography (53). Aristotle's denunciation of production for profit and Confucius's contempt for tradesmen clearly share the same ethical impulse of agrarian social solidarity as does the twentieth-century Chinese communist concern for national sovereignty and economic self-sufficiency, all of which are "aiming at a crucial point, namely the divorcedness of a separate economic motive from the social relations in which these limitations inhered" (Ibid. 54). But the motive to truck and barter has undermined the foundation of householding and reversed economy's subordination to its ethical authorities and emotional imperatives. "Instead of economy being embedded in social relations," notes Polanyi, "social relations are embedded in the economic system" (57). This act of economic "'lifting out' of social relations from local contexts" constitutes for the director of *Ermo* the historical mise-en-scène of capital's global Second Coming as well as a new challenge to historical Chinese-ness (Giddens 21).[15]

When Xiazi's truck honks its way into the crowd-packed county seat, Ermo seems to have not only survived her departure from the household proper but also become ready for the adventure of bartering as well as sightseeing. After selling her baskets and noodles for a previously unimagined price, she steps into the general store where a merry crowd is gathered around a shelf of TV sets. Ermo cranes her neck from behind the audience of various ages and attires to catch a dubbed episode of *Dynasty*: "What will become of us if we don't stop? What will happen if we just go on like this?" a Caucasian woman mouths in perfectly dubbed Mandarin as a man kisses her, the sticker of the 29″ TV prominently pasted above their foreplay on the screen. Although an abrupt power shortage literally curtails the answer to this overwhelming question – the blackout being a reminder as it were of the material limitations of a Chinese underdevelopment – Ermo is practically transfixed. "The TV is so big," the awestruck Ermo comments to Xiazi as the disappointed crowd disperses. "Yeah, the only one in the county seat. Even the head of the county cannot afford it," Xiazi adds. "How come the foreigners speak Chinese?" Ermo quizzes further, to which Xiazi replies without apparent irony, "The TV speaks whatever language it pleases."

In this loaded scene of bewildered spectatorship and open-ended televisual interpellation, disembedding acquires added significance beyond leaving the household or lifting the economy from the local community. Granted that Polanyi is indisputably correct that "market economy can only function in a market society" (57), Zhou Xiaowen wants to show how a subject appropriate for the smooth function of both will have to be carved out of the old socialist economy if not compelled into being. In this context, the 29″ TV is not so much an inanimate object of Ermo's desire but an assimilating subject positioned to lift her out of agrarian encumbrance and convert her into a free agent of disembedded desires. Zhou's camera reveals with characteristic brilliance that the introduction of rational interests governing the market alone is not going to facilitate its operation, for the ideology of the market materializes itself less as an abstract set of ideas than a rich system of signs, perceptions, and images. It is sight specific, involving audiovisual representations of a particular social order as natural and real while at the same time working on the spectator's imaginary conception of the self within that social order. The shot of Ermo staring at the television set and the reverse shot of the TV looking at Ermo and the peasants gawking constitute Zhou's succinct sequence of "interpellation," in the Althusserian meanings of "summoning" and "hailing," in which the seeing TV, with its steamy scene from *Dynasty*, invites the audience's identification, while the latter, though irrepressibly drawn, are yet unable to see themselves mirrored.[16]

It is worthy of noting that Zhou's innovative use of TV's interpellating "eye/I" is appropriated with freshness in Peter Chan's *Comrades, Almost a Love Story* 甜蜜蜜 (1996), a similar story of migration about two mainland provincial city dwellers finding their fortune in the global metropolis of the yet to be repatriated Hong Kong. The seeing "I" that does the work of interpellating the pair of "comrades," however, is the omniscient "eye" of the automatic teller machine (ATM), which in the course of the film reveals the joy and sorrow of the protagonists through the rise and fall of the stock market along with their savings accounts. In Zhou and Chan's creative rendition, the television screen and the ATM screen have become telling machines of subjective incorporation and social transformation, the constitutive media of a global market and its mediation of the new consuming subject and society, a point to which I shall return.

For the moment at the county store, however, the 29″ TV's representation of a palpitating market society appears yet to familiarize itself with its target audience in another country so that Ermo and company can eventually imagine themselves and feel at home in it. But the pedagogy for the production of prospective market subjects has already been under way, as has the civilizing mission of Capitalism's Second Coming. The solicitation of the tube or the seduction of capital does not go unheeded, for the symbolic order embodied by the television set is already dissolving the hierarchy of the socialist state, with its embedded, territorialized, and hereditary authority. In its place arises the authority of price as an instrument of democratization that brings the county head down to the level of an average peasant woman. Intuiting the new possibilities opened up by the emerging market and mediated *infinitus* by the television, Ermo is now able to imagine herself on par with the county head and see herself as central in the apparent autonomous arena of accumulation and consumption.

If Xiazi's truck has helped physically remove Ermo from the village proper, the TV set in the general store is a supplementary instrument of capitalist disembedding that has widened her virtual horizon of market expectations. While sight specific, the TV seems also site universal, causing the kind of cognitive disjuncture and geopolitical deterritorialization that Appadurai theorizes (27–47 passim). No wonder Ermo is flummoxed by the incongruity of white Americans speaking pitch-perfect Chinese on the screen. As she was initially unsettled on top of Xiazi's rolling truck when the speed of motion upsets her inbred relationship with the land, Ermo is now dumbfounded by the loss of a "natural" integrity between race and language. Such shock and confusion, Zhou Xiaowen wants to impress upon his audience, are mere effects of a global capitalism that separates time from space, the practice of culture from the specificity of locality. The TV practically shatters the bounded social order of face-to-face interactions and inserts itself as an extraterrestrial dimensionality, reconstituting the human sensorium through a face-to-screen relation in the new order of a boundless media state.

This does not mean that Ermo has ceased to live her life in actual physical localities; it simply means that her place, the physical settings of her social activity, to use Giddens, is being "penetrated by and shaped in terms of social influences quite distant from it," that is, the space and the stories televised through the screen or transmitted in all sorts of electronic devices of virtuality (19). The 29″ TV not only disrupts the space and time continuum of her hamlet and by extension "the imagined community" of the Chinese nation (Anderson), but it also empties both Ermo's existential space and the assurance of local communal experience of their original meaning. Thus disembedded from the ontological security and stagnancy of an enclosed socialist modernity, Ermo is made answerable to the sirens and summons of unknown origins, and she will have to reembed her subjectivity by taking possession of the means with which to restructure her life "across indefinite spans of time-space" (Giddens 21).

Zhou Xiaowen's perspective on China's economic reform and Ermo's refashioning of herself – the parallel projects of political and personal development, if you will – is ambivalent at best. While registering the liberating possibilities of capitalist lifting, he seems equally concerned with the potential disintegration of self and society, as market and media take on a life of their own, subjecting human welfare to corporate interests. Xiazi's answer to Ermo's puzzle over the language, "the TV speaks whatever language it pleases," seems in this case a ventriloquism of the director's uncanny understanding. It is not that the foreigners are speaking Chinese but that capitalist commerce is turning global, capable of assuming local accents while absorbing indigenous languages into its cultural grammar of insatiable appetites. The televisual presence of *Dynasty* in the Chinese countryside, however, does not diminish for Zhou the remarkable absence of mutual traffic between the hyperreality of American TV and the everyday reality of rural China. In fact, the gap between border-crossing and locality-transcending media and the insurmountable materiality of national boundaries generates the film's most productive artistic tension, as we shall see later. The quotation from *Dynasty* in that same scene, "What will become of us if we don't stop?" thus fast-forwards an insight to which, and, allegorically, both the majority of Chinese in a fever of capital accumulation and the fully fledged American consumers seem equally blind: it is a question of the end, that is, the objective and outcome of a global market society that late capitalism is spreading planetwide.

Counting her earnings in bed, Ermo seems to have the answer for now. Inviting her husband to smell the new bills, she rhapsodizes about the 29″ screen, the beautiful color and the high resolution that "make visible" in her words "the foreigners' blond hair one by one." If the innocent reference to blond hair is an indirect expression of Ermo's thwarted sexuality, the direct achievement of desire, ironically, has to be mediated through vicarious image consumption. The media and the market thus converge in the sexy symbol of the 29″ TV with scenes of seduction from an American *Dynasty*, propagating a "new transnational culture-ideology of consumption," as Jameson puts it, that is "changing traditional psychic habits and practices and sweeping all before it into something resembling the American Way of Life" (1998, 69). This money-counting scene, which recurs throughout the movie, strategically ties Ermo's developmental project of self-interested social mobility with the complementarily disembedding media of the television and the market as well as money. As "a means of bracketing time and so of lifting transactions out of particular milieu of exchange," argues Giddens, money is in its developed form essential to the "disembedding mechanisms associated with [capitalist] modernity" (24–25). Although China is credited for the invention of paper money, and rural China under socialism has been an integral part of the nation's monetary system, Zhou's cinematic reiteration of Ermo's money counting emphasizes the increasing individual command of financial resources after the recent opening of the Chinese market and the liberation of money from the strictures of a once-dominant collective social ethos and method of standardized distribution. The scene also suggests the power of private accumulation as a means of loosening the agrarian and authoritarian bounds of land, family, and community, and foreshadows money's power both to erode patriarchy and enable new gender identities.

It is only natural that the contradiction between the state-centralized and market-oriented economies should come to a headlong collision in Ermo's spousal dispute with her husband over the proper use of what are apparently their newly acquired riches. Disregarding Ermo's plan to own the 29″ TV that even the county head cannot afford, the former chief of the village and still titular head of the household has called in a contractor for house addition and renovation. After Ermo dismisses his building scheme and scares away the contractor, her husband flies into a futile fit of rage: "The TV is an egg while the house is a hen. Why would one want an egg instead of a hen? Why don't you act like a woman?" With her head still buried in the pile of money, Ermo retorts, "Why don't you do it like a man?" insinuating both his sexual malfunction and economic dependency on her for his livelihood. Ermo's command of her own productive labor and its monetary rewards has made a mockery of ancient patriarchy and socialist authority as well as her husband's impotence to enforce it. "I've found a job with better pay," she announces flatly. "I'm leaving for the city tomorrow morning. And I am going to buy the biggest TV in the county."

4

In declaring her determined departure from home for better economic opportunities in the city and the liberty of consummating her desire for commodities, Ermo has intuitively subscribed to the cultural assumptions of a liberal society and enunciated her becoming of what C. B. Macpherson has called the "possessive individual." Just as Polanyi identifies nineteenth-century Euro-America as the time-space of great transformation through which traditional society's principle of reciprocity and redistribution is overtaken by market principles, Macpherson traces this transformation to its philosophical origin in Hobbes, Harrington, and Locke, its realization in the social order of industrial capitalism, and finally its embodiment in and embrace by the self-sovereign subject. First among those precepts and practices is a conception of the subject as one who is the sole proprietor of his/her own person, owing nothing to society but capable of alienating his/her capacity for labor. Second, such a self-possessive subject is essentially independent from the will of others and free from any relations with people except those willingly entered into according to self-interest. Third, human society is seen as consisting of no more than a series of market relations (Macpherson 263–64). As Joseph Carens highlights for us, the distinctive contribution of Macpherson lies in his theoretical elaboration of "how a conception of property relationship had shaped liberal thinking about individualism" (2). The contribution of Zhou Xiaowen, on the other hand, rests on his scintillating illustration of Macpherson's chain of equivalences – "to be an individual is to be an owner . . . of one's own person and capacities . . . of what one acquires through one's capacities . . . to be free is to be an owner" (Carens 2) – as it impinges on a national and individual psyche historically yet unaccustomed to the liberal ways of thinking and feeling. Calling attention to the economic and emotional processes of self-ownership as it changes the Chinese peasantry, the mainstay of Chinese citizenry in the 1980s, Zhou makes immediately visible the transformative effects of possessive individualism on the female protagonist's project of liberal self-development in and through her body.

The body appears to be, first and foremost, the only article Ermo can claim potential ownership of and is capable of alienating to achieve market freedom. Aware now of the possibility to truck and barter the productive power of her labor, Ermo quickly mines her body's property value through her disciplining mind. The camera focuses on her direct channeling of her repressed sexuality into noodle making: her feet are the manual blender of dough, her arms the practical muscle energy that presses the noodles into shape, and she even works at night while others sleep, thus siphoning off the portion of "biological time" essential for life's somnolent sustenance and increasing the duration of "industrial time" for more profit (Hareven). Possessive individualism seems to have infused Ermo with the kind of agency and self-assertion atypical of the traditional Chinese peasantry, who were cast as the oppressed lot in a state of torpor before the communist revolution, recast in the socialist era as the collective strength of the nation, and in the postsocialist age of Deng turned into an ambiguous subject figuring "anew a long standing concern over China's 'failure' to attain the modernity that has proved so elusive" (Anagnost 86). As a figure of this failure, Ann Anagnost writes persuasively, the body of the Chinese peasantry is in need of reform: the peasantry has thus become once more the target of the state's "civilization work," "its incitements to labor, its disciplinization and enhancement of [the people's] 'quality'" (Ibid. 75, 86–87). Anagnost echoes the argumentative tenor in Su and Wang's *River Elegy*. Sharp in their observation, they all overlook China's history of zigzagging modernity and the specificity of its agents. As a response to Capital's First Coming, the PRC's socialist industrialization assumes a centralized national modernization development delinked from the world system. Under the leadership of the communist party, the peasantry along with workers and soldiers represents China's model citizenry. Capital's Second Coming, however, witnesses the unprecedented convergence of the authoritarian Chinese state and the authoritative market. It is this marriage of capital and state that encumbers itself on the civilizing mission: to enhance the Chinese people's overall "quality" is but to convert them into bourgeois subjects of capitalist propriety. New codes of civility, however, are divorced from both the traditional allegiance to historical filial piety and its socialist transfiguration into a love of the state and its leaders. Like the decollectivization of the socialist body politic through economic devolution, the body of the Chinese subject has to be individualized and privatized, unmoored from its economic and ethical encumbrances so that the liberty of the market, almost always evoked in the name of individual freedom, can march on unhindered. Once disembedded, deterritorialized, and civilized into disciplined and docile labor, the Chinese peasantry turned the new international proletariat is then fully incorporated.

Although Zhou's film does not explicitly link its protagonist's labor to the mushrooming of Chinese factories that begin to feed the Walmarts of the world, *Ermo* nevertheless illuminates the macroscopic processes of capitalist modernization as the microscopic processes of individual subjective rebuilding and bodily makeover. It is the process of capitalizing on the body in a conscious effort at self-willing alienation and self-possession. Unlike the prostrate and passive Grandma in *Red Sorghum*, as feminine nature open for capitalist colonization, and unlike her gaunt and impotent husband, emblematic of the sterile socialist economy, Ermo seems in full possession of her laboring body, awakened from the stagnancy of feudal history and the stupor under socialist regulation, and active in her market participation. The kind of backward psychology of dependency and high tolerance of fate *River Elegy* accuses of the Chinese peasantry is being made over, epitomized in the very physical and psychic metamorphosis of Ermo.

While quite affirmative of the productive energy released by possessive individualism on the emerging Chinese market, Zhou retains his suspicion about the alienation of labor as the precondition of individual freedom and social integration. The figuration of Ermo's body as alienable labor power is thus coupled with two other seemingly unrelated scenes, the death of a donkey and the amputation of a worker's arm. In the first, Xiazi's truck accidentally knocks down a roadside donkey, killing it. That the truck should sweep the donkey off the highway signifies more than just modernity's unstoppable march and the incompatibility of mule power in the age of fossil-fueled mechanization. The fallen ass is not just a figure of disposability, either, but also the usher of the new ideology of money: the bitter barter between Xiazi and the older peasant and mule owner that follows shows that nothing now escapes the law of price under which "all transactions are turned into money transactions" (Polanyi 41). In the second scene, Zhou evokes off camera the mangling of a noodle maker's arm in an electric blender at the shop where Ermo has been hired as the supervisor. Of mule and man, a parallel between animal and human maiming reminiscent of fin-de-siècle European and American literary naturalism at the height of Western capitalist industrialization is drawn in the context of China toward the end of the twentieth century. Although this scene serves to highlight the peril and dehumanization of industrialization, casting doubt on the spell of technology (as does the failure of Xiazi's truck to start at the time of this emergency), Zhou's primary purpose is not to show incidental damage caused by machines but other volitionally inflicted wounds inherent in the proprietary regime of liberty and individual autonomy.

To save their coworker, Ermo and her group volunteer to donate blood at the county hospital. In a prolonged facial close-up evocative of the one during her first visit to the city, we witness Ermo's helpless terror as her blood slowly fills the syringe. "Enough now. I am scared. Stop, please stop," a tearful Ermo entreats the nurse, who, like Xiazi the driver in the earlier scene, does not heed her plea. After she gets her pint, the nurse hands Ermo a receipt instructing her to "collect her pay." Ermo is initially bewildered, for despite her hunger for money, she has not connected her act of helping a fellow human being survive with the idea of remuneration. In Ermo's bewilderment, Zhou has captured the residual of a peasant consciousness, an illiberal civility that I am tempted to call "traditional Chinese-ness." It is "peasant" because it springs from an agrarian rootedness and localized sympathy, from a sort of *Gemeinschaft* "community," which Ferdinand Tönnies has made famous as that which is replaced by *Gesellschaft*, "association" or "[civil] society" (1887/2001).[17] It is "illiberal" not because of its presumed narrow-mindedness or stinginess but because it is not fully contained or contaminated by liberalism, which is "a doctrine of certain necessary kinds of freedom but also, and essentially, a doctrine of possessive individualism" (Williams 181). It is traditionally Chinese not because it represents a code of behavior and mode of affect exclusively Chinese in the racial or ethnic sense of the word but because it is inclusively agrarian, locally embedded, and definitely precapitalist. Instead of Su and Wang's construction of the peasant as a figure of backwardness in need of radical reform, Zhou Xiaowen offers an alternative view of the peasant that casts its retention of tradition in a positive light. Ermo's gifting of blood to a practical stranger, albeit a member of the community within sight and on-site, is represented as an act of preliberal civility both before the individual is remade as a proprietor of himself/herself owing nothing to society and before society is reconstituted as nothing other than the total sum of individual interests. Zhou figures in the donation of blood an expression of historical Chinese-ness, in the slightly variable semantic chain of the Confucian, communal, and collectivist construction of society and subjectivity, that the modernity of state socialism has retained.

But the *Gesellschaft* of rational calculation in Capital's Second Coming is sounding the death knell to Ermo's intuitive gifting of blood, a gesture of reciprocal and obligatory exchange that has kept the *Gemeinschaft* of face-to-face, homogenous, and regulated local community alive. As is well known through Marcel Mauss,

The Gift is an expression of donor and recipient relationship in archaic societies wherein economic exchange is inseparable from other social fields. Like Polanyi before him, Mauss considers it misguided to separate the rational and the nonrational, interest and affect. Unlike Polanyi, however, Mauss seems to believe economic relations are always infused with value judgments and moral relations in every society. What Zhou Xiaowen has seized cinematically is a Polanyian "great transformation" in China: one shot of Ermo's altruistic blood donation is succeeded by a sequence of her procuring profit, revealing the astonishing speed with which exchange economy takes over gift economy in Ermo's sudden rebirth as the rational subject of *Homo economicus*. The scent of money and the no-fuss naturalness with which the nurse presents Ermo the payment slip convinces her in no time that "a woman's blood will run away anyway" (as in menstruation) and "it would be a terrible waste" not to profit from it. What was nature's endowment is now a mere commodity on the market. The work of a liberal capitalist civilization on Ermo the backward peasant appears instantaneously evident. Zhou's camera cuts incisively to Ermo drinking bowls after bowls of salt water to dilute the content of her blood and to her repeated visits to the medical office, deliberately timing her "donation" with different nurses' shifts. Our protagonist of the new economy seems to have finally come to her senses that the last frontier of her materialist conquest does not lie outside herself but within: the body as the reservoir of her entrepreneurial vitality is also an indispensable natural resource to be rationally extracted.

From the extraction of the body's labor power to the extraction of the body's vital fluid, a compressed completion of the commodification process and a disjuncture of capitalist development seem to have occurred with the bat of an eye. Zhou has highlighted two conditions of China's process of fast-track liberalization. First, for the rural poor who have no means of production or other marketable skills, selling menial labor and becoming the industrial reserve army for hire is not so much a choice but a compulsion. Second, for those whose access to the liberal promise of possessive individualism is at once abrupt and absolute, life itself may be endangered. On Ermo's body is thus writ not only the development of the economic (wo)man and ecological insanity but also China's contradictory return to capitalism and relinking with the world system. But there are additional problems of developmental trajectories and foreclosed possibilities. Zhou makes explicit that Ermo has no shortage of the asceticism or abstinence necessary for the evolution of primitive capitalism. Besides her capacity for toil, she refuses to eat in restaurants because of her inarticulate conception that to do so would be a squandering of resources. As Xiazi literally drags her feet into the door of the restaurant, Ermo stubbornly backs off, insisting "it's a waste of money," for a penny saved from the rudimentary maintenance of the body will be a penny applied toward the purchase of the TV, her fundamental if not fundamentalist developmental project. Although Ermo's work ethic and desire for wealth exemplify the kind of habits of heart to which Max Weber attributes the rise of early Protestant capitalism, her project does not lead to investments in advanced machinery and hiring of cheap labor in the typical trajectory of a renewable capitalist enterprise.

Zhou Xiaowen recasts Ermo's deviation from the established norm of capital-ist development as a row over Chinese home economics – the chicken-and-egg problem of either expanding the house or acquiring the TV. Here, the ex-chief's renovation project still falls within the model of what Polanyi identifies in the etymological origin of Greek household production: it is an economy of subsis-tence and immediate use. Ermo's purchasing project, on the other hand, represents a double departure, at once from the satiation of necessities of survival and from the pure pursuit of surplus. Instead, the accumulation of Ermo's capital is directed toward the immediate consumption of the very medium of consumption, the 29" TV set. If the ex-chief's remodeling idea still falls under the rubric of fulfilling basic "needs" (food, clothing, and shelter), Ermo's acquisitive project belongs more appropriately to the satisfaction of "wants."[18] The conflict between needs and wants, which Daniel Bell pinpoints as one of the major "cultural contradic-tions of capitalism" in the US when America moved from an industrial to a postin-dustrial or consumer society, seems to have already prematurely and convulsively seized China, a society that is yet fully to industrialize. If the dynamo of American late capitalism seeks to resolve this contradiction by ceaselessly converting wants into needs, Ermo's submission to this logic of capital and her husband's rejec-tion come to embody not merely individual or familial conflict in the modes of consumption, but the impossibility, generally speaking, for developing nations to follow the West's unilinear model of industrial capitalism.

As Zhou Xiaowen shrewdly shows, when Ermo finally acquires her long-sought-after object of desire, the 29" TV, it cannot even be carried through the narrow doorframe of her house. The scene betrays the contradiction between normative consuming ideals from afar and material limitations at home. It also reveals that global capital inevitably infringes on, if not determines, the overall terms and local conditions of development, occasioning rapid social change and radical psychological confusion. Deeply rooted in the mentality of a precredit village economy, while helplessly seduced by the power and pleasure of a distant yet now dominant consumption ethic, Ermo cannot but embody the disparities of capitalist globalization at the local level. For the moment, however, Ermo has emerged as the unambiguous victor of mass cultural consumption, though, unlike the perfect consumers of metropolitan centers, she is constitutionally unable to "take the waiting out of the wanting" (Bauman 7). While Zhou encourages a read-ing of the husband's defeat as a triumph of the postmodern logic of fantasy and pleasure over the (pre)modern logic of utility and subsistence, he also demon-strates that instant commodity satiation is not within Ermo's reach. The paucity of her resources and the time she needs to improve and develop herself entail an essential element of postponement. Such temporal delay is endemic to the geo-economic particularity of Ermo's place. By highlighting this time-space contra-diction, Zhou complicates the applicability of a universal consumer culture and embeds concerns as to whether Ermo will be able to catch up or whether indeed she has a choice of an alternative course.

Meanwhile, the husband's failure to control the household finance also becomes at this juncture Zhou's tribute to the triumph of acquisitive spirit in postsocialist

China over the historical hold of ascriptive status, either secured by decades of communist party governance or older Confucian customs and gender roles. Despite the director's strong reservation about its inescapable effect of alienation, the incorporation of possessive individualism also evidences liberating possibilities. The liberalization of political economy through the logic of possessive individualism not only upsets rural patriarchies of former communes but also triggers more fundamental changes in the traditional Chinese regimes of body, sexuality, and family. The turning point of this transformation is Ermo's second departure from the village, not to sell her homemade noodles as in the film's opening, but to seek gainful employment at the noodle factory in the city. Zhou signals to the audience that Ermo's autonomy is largely mobilized by the liberal promises of capital in the "rational" exchange and "organization of (formally) free labor" (Weber 21). Her newfound freedom from the sterility of the country and the shackles of its gender stratification, in short, depends on freeing herself and her economic activity from the Greek *Oikos*, the household – in this context both the encumbrances of her original family and the time-space of the vanishing commune.

By extricating herself from home for employment in the city, Ermo has fulfilled a crucial condition of capitalist enterprise that distinguishes capitalism, according to Weber, from earlier forms of mercantile exchange prevalent in ancient China and India, that is, "the separation of business from the household" (21–22). This separation of economic activity from an edict and an everyday practice embedded in the ecological welfare of the household, if we recall Karl Polanyi and Wang Shaoguang's reading of him in the Chinese context, has a deleterious impact on social solidarity, be it the family or the immediate community, especially when economic ends overtake ethical ends. Although it is not uncommon during the period of Chinese socialism for the state to relocate labor from its original location, such lifting is never free, either formally or volitionally speaking. It is almost always forcibly and quickly reintegrated into the local community while the autonomy of the individual subject remains suppressed in the raison d'être of the socialist state. What Zhou's film wants to illustrate, however, is different: the separation of economy from the household in Ermo's literal and allegorical act of moving out constitutes the precondition for the birth of a new emotional economy under capitalism. It subordinates the motive of collective subsistence to judgments of self-interests, thus shifting the locus of ethics from its primary concern with social order to its preoccupation with personal fulfillment.

Zhou renders this rapid process of capitalist economic and emotional development in China in a cinematic montage: as "possessive individualism" is instrumental in Ermo's economic development, so "affective individualism" of the kind that prizes romantic love becomes pivotal in her emotional satisfaction (Stone). Capital as an impersonal engine for remaking the world and the personal engine for remaking the self culminates in Ermo's and Xiazi's lovemaking. Not surprisingly, the fulfillment of individual desire and the satiation of the body should take place in the jalopy truck on the winding highways of the barren hills, the stereotypical country setting for the Fifth Generation Chinese film directors and a central symbol of *River Elegy*'s indictment. This mise-en-scène of the yellow earth is thus rich in cross-cultural suggestion. Given his expert employment of the *Dynasty* footage and his evident knowledge of US popular culture, Zhou is clearly alluding to the American association of automobiles and adolescent sexuality. Although the director's portrayal of the middle-aged Ermo and Xiazi's passion in the manner of American teenagers romping in the car could look a bit jarring, aesthetic defamiliarization is precisely his strategy. Here, Zhou deliberately rewrites the Fifth Generation's visual trope of the land and in doing so suggests macroscopic cultural change in the minutia of individual feelings. The arid topography of the yellow earth plateau, which Zhang Yimou and Chen Kaige have elevated to unprecedented aesthetic heights to stand for the indefatigable Chinese instinct for social survival, is dissolving in Zhou Xiaowen's close-up of the protagonists' lovemaking. No longer the determining element in human endurance and no longer the symbol of reproductive necessity, the yellow earth is rejuvenated through pure sexuality.

As the night falls, Xiazi stops his truck on the pretense of a fatal mechanical failure and pounces on Ermo without any preliminary gestures of intimacy. A violent struggle ensues as Ermo disentangles herself from Xiazi's passionate grip and plunges her hand right below his belt, instantly stopping him in his tracks. Still panting, Ermo slowly removes her babushka and the many layers of her winter clothing, as a perplexed Xiazi looks on passively. The camera cuts to a long shot of the truck in a no-man's-land with a swirl of silvery dirt gently lifted against the dark blue of the night. The rhythmic ecstasy of Ermo follows as a haunting flute in the familiar tune of her hawking slowly takes over, recalling the now unspoken words that once accompanied that tune: "buy my twisty noodles."

For Zhou, this consummation represents the pinnacle of Ermo's self-actualization and her exercise of agency free from male intimidation. Ermo has become the willing and willfully self-possessive subject not only of economy as such but of her own sexuality. The subtle and poetic affirmation of the adulterous affair significantly transcends the traditional morality rooted in reproductive imperatives, powerful in the dynasties and still residual in socialist China, where the value of women depends on the perception of their virtue if not their virginity (Larson 74–75). It is not that Zhou approaches his characters in an amoral frame of reference. Rather, he is presenting an ethical alternative that emerges with the recent Chinese assimilation of capitalism when economy is being alienated from family and community and the individual subject from the society that used to contain as well as sustain it. To risk simplicity for now, we may say that Ermo's past worldview favors goods conceived in concrete social networks and the immutable teleology of life, while her present worldview clearly favors goods of individual consumption and personal fulfillment. At least in that Edenic moment, neither Ermo nor Xiazi seems concerned with the consequences of their coupling. Their wild abandon and their obliviousness to the consequences of libidinal coupling are, as the narrative buildup adequately illustrates, the consequence of the capitalist decoupling of economy and family, sexuality and society. Changes in economic modes of production are accompanied by similar changes in popular ethos and ethical practice. If the feudal codes of agrarian China bind women to the whipping post of chastity, it is the notions of chastity and monogamy themselves and not the gender exclusivity with which they are historically conceived that have become suspiciously outdated. Perhaps the Chinese modernist proposal of gender equality based on reciprocal ethical restraint at the turn of the last century has become inescapably anachronistic at the turn of the new millennium, for China, however belatedly, has reached the end of history "after virtue" where the absolute self-possessive individual and the new ethic of personal fulfillment begin to rule (MacIntyre).[19]

The lovemaking is in many respects the climax of Ermo's romance with globalization, a Chinese infatuation with the Second Coming of Capital after puritanical communist repression, and the liberation of an unregistered civilizational pubescence from the burdens of its history. However, having captured this rapture of capital mobility, Zhou ruthlessly returns his audience to the rueful existence his heroine has to face. In the seedy hotel room that Xiazi has reserved, Ermo looks at her face in the broken looking glass, the cubist image mirroring either a tormented realization of a hitherto suppressed individual or the schizophrenia of capitalism itself. It is an image of the split, revealing the contradictory effects of a freedom from local constraints and a frustrating and fragmented interpellation of a countrywoman into consumerist ideal of global metropolis. Zhou has created an uncanny intertextual resonance between this secret rendezvous and the previous clip from *Dynasty* to hint at a temporary convergence of media narrative and life stories. Ermo has indeed gone from a bewildered fascination with television romance to an enactment of her own version of that romance. Similarly, she seems to have become accustomed to seeing herself through the eyes of televisual media and the products it promotes. With great pride, she shows Xiazi her newly purchased bra, muttering with glistening eyes, "Don't I look like a city girl?" In response, Xiazi unpacks his gift of antiwrinkle cream and smears it in generous blobs onto her seminaked body, chanting all along its youth-enhancing magic like a salesman for Revlon.

Zhou's deadpan delivery of the scene conjures up the shrill image of "a truncated and warped modernization," or "the modernism of underdevelopment," as Marshall Berman writes, that is "forced to build on fantasies and dreams of [capitalist] modernity, to nourish itself on an intimacy and a struggle with mirages and ghosts" (232). In their anxious assimilation of the culture of "the global city" (Sassen, 1991), both Ermo and Xiazi have submitted themselves to the imperializing eye/I of a transnational consumerism, whose regime of spectacle, surface, and sexuality constitutes their simultaneous "subjection and subjectivation" (Balibar). For some, Ermo's emergence as a sexualized subject of desire may be progress from gender erasure under "state feminism" (M. Yang 63–64), but one has to question if desire's commodification in the postsocialist return of prostitution and trafficking of women in China are true liberations. Engaging it in gender-neutral terms, Zhou couches commodification in the language of anti-alienation humanism that responded to the initial rise of industrial capitalism in Europe. Stunned by Ermo's bruised veins, apparently caused by her repetitive blood drawing, Xiazi shouts, "You sell blood again? Don't you want to live anymore?" The seducer of Ermo's self-possessive and affective individualist yearnings has emerged unexpectedly as the voice of sobriety against the frenzy of her pursuit and her resultant dehumanization. Shocked and stuttering, he calls her blood sale an act of "barbarism," once again reversing the terms of civility and barbarity at the core of the recent Chinese embrace of capitalism, and questioning the postsocialist "civilization work" that attempts to reform the obstinate residual of agrarian ethics.

As means to end Ermo's blood sale and to redeem her humanity, Xiazi volunteers his "loads" to buy her the 29″ TV so that she may reach her goal of acquisition and consummate her consumer dreams. What he could not have imagined is Ermo's resolute rejection of his offer of money. What Ermo desires is self-possession in the liberal individualistic sense of self-interest and personal fulfillment, and what she dreads is to be possessed by another man, whether it is the communist party boss or the capitalist sugar daddy. Although she is willing to alienate her labor and blood, Ermo is not ready to violate the integrity of her sexuality, the validity of her libidinal fulfillment, and the romantic projection of her marriage with Xiazi in order ultimately to sanctify her affections and aspirations. With one foot still mired in the traditional structures of feeling that value and valorize reciprocity and stability the institution of marriage seems to embody, Ermo refuses the final leap toward a total split of sexuality and family.

Her defiance of Xiazi appears almost flamboyant, especially if viewed in relation to another *Dynasty* clip near the movie's end in which a woman in a compromising position is begging her boss for a raise. Perhaps her resistance to the system of absolute exchange is exceptional, reflecting an incomplete Chinese capitalist modernization in matters of rationality and affectivity. Perhaps her gesture is merely Zhou's nostalgic idealization of the local "non-exchangist practices" (Lowe 173). The implicit contrast between women in fledgling and advanced capitalist societies seems to illuminate the different degrees to which the market has saturated their individual consciousness. There is beauty to Ermo's defiance, a beauty consistent with her recalcitrant will and dignity, a beauty derived from the material and ethical solidity of a disappearing China. However, such a gendered beauty of transcendent virtue and blind dedication, as the film later makes obvious, is neither individually desirable nor socially sustainable in Capital's Second Coming.

5

Just as Ermo breaks up with Xiazi where the dusty highway and the narrow mountain path part, so Zhou shifts his film from an exuberant departure from the village to a determined return of the native, thus shunning the Hollywood narrative of romantic sunsets and the developmental narrative of a global village where the sun never sets. Such a narrative resolution helps tease out the complex issues of Capital's Second Coming, for the protagonist's leave-taking from her precapitalist agrarian origin and her eventual fall back to the postsocialist Chinese village is yet a miniature story of the zigzag course of grand Chinese history. Film narrative intimates, it seems, political and economic alternatives. Ermo's repatriation to the village resonates with such contemporaneous populist outcries as *China Can Say No* to oceanic capital (Qiang Song et al.). But Zhou is not reviving a nationalist fantasy of *Gemeinschaft* after China's historical relinking with neoliberal capitalism, but exploring if social alternatives are available for a "No" to be materially viable.

In suspending Ermo and Xiazi from further migration to the coastal cities, Zhou could be expressing awareness that struggles for rights to the city have become seminal in developing nations and democracies in globalization (Holston and Appadurai 196–97). Ermo's return could then suggest the foreclosed struggle of rural migrants to attain benefits reserved for urbanites. The coming of the markets to China cannot readily convert country denizens into citizens by making them dwellers of new urban centers and helping them achieve national membership through access to the state's allocation of socioeconomic resources. Known as the problem of "floating population" (Cheng Li), this exploitation of the rural migrant workforce for rapid urban development through a deregulated labor market, as Dorothy Solinger makes cogent, stands parallel to the sharp decline of the welfare state in the West. Where "the [American] welfare state" or "[Chinese] state socialism" fails to "allay the influence of the market . . . capitalism, rather than promoting citizenship, may be antagonistic and detrimental to it" (Solinger 278). Ermo's agrarian retreat thus challenges the assumption that capitalism and democracy are twin engines of development and that capitalism necessarily fosters laissez-faire economic competition, egalitarian governance, and the guarantee of human rights. As a failed exemplar of "flexible citizenship" (Ong), Ermo's very "inflexibility" heightens the contradiction between the instantaneous mobility of finance capital, on the one hand, and the overall immobility of the human body, on the other, that the speed of globalization has only intensified. The regulation of and capitalization on rural influx to the cities within China, it is worth noting, bears striking similarity to the control and profiting of illegal immigrants within the US borders.

Aside from viewing it as symptomatic of an institutional failure, we may parallel Ermo's return with the resurgence of neo-Confucianist discourse in its reaffirmation of Chinese-ness. When Ermo unloads her bundle of thick quilts on the family bed, the camera appears to suggest that she has literally reembedded herself in the grounding order of the Chinese local after her disembedding foray into a global capitalist modernity. Perhaps she has now reconciled with human finitude and the limits of capital. Perhaps she has recognized that ascriptive circumstances can only be transcended to a certain degree, nature can only be exploited to a certain degree, and her rapacious acquisition in the context of the market, instead of being a vehicle of her personal freedom, has turned her into a vassal of possession.[20] She has perhaps grasped ever so intuitively Amartya Sen's argument that economic freedom alone may not necessarily prolong life spans or proffer more fruitful existences.[21] Consequently, she has decided to say "No" to the unfettered market rationality and "No" to the unencumbered individual affectivity by embracing once more the ideal of a Confucian mean in the spatial and temporal scheme of the village, with its routinized domestic chores and demands of making a living, not to mention its mandatory codes of ethics. Indeed, to simulate the narrative authenticity of Ermo's return, Zhou has to subject his characters to a Chinese agrarian system of discipline of which their earlier affective abandon makes a mockery. After Xiazi deliberately has himself caught patronizing prostitutes in the city, thus exonerating Ermo of the potential stigma of the scarlet letter, the two neighboring families apparently reclaim their tranquility. They enjoy the Spring Festival fanfare together, bring the 29″ TV back home together, and the ex-chief invites the whole village over for the biggest TV show ever.

Harmony and happiness seem to smile again on the descendants of the yellow earth, but this picture of Ermo's China is a far cry from the Singaporean model of East Asian modernity that energizes much argument in favor of "Asian Values" (Han). It is true that the application of the TV set betrays a Chinese difference; it is brought into a private home but turned on for the entire village to see, transforming the normative practice of nuclear familial or individual viewing into a communal and public experience. This seeming closeness of the village may even resemble such a neo-Confucian construct as the "concentric circles" of "self, family, society, nation, world, and cosmos," but its cloistral closure defies at every level the promise of Tu Weiming's circular ideal and the sense of village cohesion appears at best a momentary solidarity (1998, 302). Zhou's picture is a community punctuated with contradictions and marred with splits. The self looks unfulfilled: Ermo passes out before the show and sleeps through most of the program. The family seems dysfunctional: the bedding has to be removed to make room for the TV. The society becomes more competitive: Xiazi's wife now inquires after an even bigger TV. Although the occasion to have the villagers over to his house restores the ex-chief's patriarchal authority on the back of Ermo's sweat, the Singaporean model of the strong and caring state that secures for its citizenry a high material standard of living and mandates in return its moral discipline is nowhere in sight in this Chinese context of the film. In Ermo's case at least, the varied modes of Chinese communalism – themselves products of historical rootedness in land, lineage, and loyalty, be it premodern Confucianism or modern state communism – appear to be irreversibly undermined by the ascending logic of the global market and its companion gospel of individual mobility. The desirability and applicability of the Singaporean model aside, Ermo's China seems to have made dubious the claim for the endurance of a transnational and transhistorical Chinese-ness and its materialization in distinctive capitalisms and alternative modernities.[22] Zhou Xiaowen's film has thus embedded a central question as to whether the kinds of cultural capital we inherit from a prior historical mode of production are capable of retaining the habitus and regenerating forms of individual agency appropriate to Capital's Second Coming (Bourdieu 1977).

The recovery of familial integrity with Ermo's return aside, we have to note the film's resonance with the well-known Victorian narrative recuperation of wayward women into patriarchy. Ermo's self-possessive developmental project is in short qualified by the historical limitations of liberal individualist capitalism on gender. As Virginia Held remarks in her feminist reevaluation of Macpherson, while freedom requires women's access to the means of life and labor, the gendered division within the household may place unfair demands on women, both psychologically and economically (138–44 passim). Liberal capitalism's systemic gender bias devalues women's necessary labor as private and nonproductive. The freedom purportedly guaranteed by one's capacity to alienate her labor puts women in a double bind, for either their labor is not properly priced or it cannot be fully exchanged because of traditional social requirements and reproductive restrictions. On the other hand, however, in emphasizing the feminist valuation of relations of trust, care, and shared welfare, Held seems to echo C. B. Macpherson's original critique of the deeply individualist and narrowly possessive nature of liberalism as it is manifest in the capitalist economy (149–52).

By bringing his protagonist home, Zhou Xiaowen neither suggests that women's proper place is in the home nor is he sanctioning patriarchal control over women. Rather, in subjecting Ermo to the burdens that both precede and succeed her encounter with and exercise of possessive individualism, Zhou complicates the gender problems inherent in liberalism and authoritarian socialism while anticipating our reading of Ang Lee's treatment of family and reproductive care in Chapter 3. With his knowledge of her affair, however, Ermo's husband, the ex-party chief, is blackmailing her emotionally. The camera cuts to Ermo cooking and later massaging him as a gesture of acquiescing servitude, exposing the reassertion of male domination, though with a twist. If this shot evidences the impossibility of women to become absolute self-possessive individuals free of patriarchal strictures or vestiges of agrarian tradition, the shot of Ermo collapsing, after her extreme alienation of her labor and her blood, seems to indicate the inescapable exhaustion of liberal reason and the potential negative outcome when self-possessive individuals achieve their sovereignty. Zhou Xiaowen thus partakes in film language the theoretical preoccupations of Macpherson and Held as well as the larger debate of liberalism and communitarianism both in the US and in the Chinese diaspora. This discursive convergence is not coincidental but conditioned by the compelling thrust of global political and economic forces. Because of China's subscription to the Second Coming of Capitalism concurs with the Reagan-Thatcher-Deng Xiaoping Revolution, its primary social concerns now dovetail with those of the West. Thus, the discourse of neo-Confucianism, despite its ethnocultural overtones, in fact shares with Western communitarianism the anxiety of societal dissolution when capital transcends national boundaries and the new captain of industry is reaping instant profits. The tension between rooted communitarianism and liberal cosmopolitanism thus betrays the fundamental tension of globalization when capitalism intensifies the split between economy and society as well as individual desires for both security and mobility.

In the deepest cultural sense, globalization is nothing but the planetary domination of the values of market divinity and individual mobility based on an uneven capacity of subject nations and peoples to consume natural resources, material goods, and human services. Ermo may have reasons to value the ontological security the village once provided, but Zhou makes palpable that such psychosocial stability is not at all viable in a world of constant change. Now that her noodle-making strainer is turned into a makeshift TV antenna, even the basic means of her production seems to have been emptied of its meaning. Despite her preference, Ermo cannot truly return to the site of an original producer society to observe its material limits and social regulation of desire (Bauman, 1995, 153–54). Global capital, as the process of "creative destruction" and the "reproduction of social life through commodity production," has forced her strainer's obsolescence (Harvey 343), signifying not only the near impossibility of small-scale local economy but also a way of life dependent on it. As the Ford-ferrying land surveyors and joint venturers loom upon Ermo's yellow earth, Zhou seems to say that Nabisco and Monsanto are not far behind.

As an arrested producer without prospects to sustain a valid mode of economic life, a frustrated citizen unable to fully access urban resources, Ermo is also an abortive consumer without the command of its essential cultural grammar, for arrival and gratification are death in another name. No wonder she looks lethargic and lost, her image now imperceptibly blended with that of the old peasant women squatting at the village boundary slabs. Having gone global with all the sound and fury she could muster, Ermo is eventually condemned to the role of the local in a world where, as Zygmunt Bauman has it, "the 'globals' set the tone and compose the rules of the life-game," while the locals are fixed in their place, "losing their meaning-generating and meaning-negotiating capacity" (1998, 2–3). Such infiltration of cosmopolitan consciousness often in the shape of a commodity awareness at the individual level and such incongruities of its materialization on the international scale are for Zhou Xiaowen the crux of a global contradiction whether in the inner cities or reservations of the US or in the Chinese hinterlands. Has Ermo turned out to be inherently and insufficiently self-possessive, therefore an impossible subject of liberalism, or is she proof of the failed civilization work of capitalism to remake the Chinese peasantry as it used to reform Max Weber's Catholics? Rather than seeking a neat narrative resolution to such political and philosophical questions, Zhou deploys a series of intercutting visual frames and audio tracks in the film's closing to enhance his picture of a seriously divided "one world, ready or not" (Greider).

Recall Ermo's question the first time she sees the 29″ TV. She asks why the foreigners speak Chinese, to which Xiazi responds, "The TV speaks whatever language it pleases." By the time she has saved enough to buy the set at the store, Ermo is again puzzled, this time asking "why they [the Chinese TV hosts] speak the foreign language [English]." When Xiazi explains that "they'll have to speak a bit of foreign language every day," Ermo wonders if "they are going back to speaking Chinese afterwards." The question Zhou is pursuing by the film's conclusion is no longer "what will become of us if we do not stop?" Rather, it is whether we can speak the lingua franca of global capitalism just "a bit every day," whether we can realistically "go back to speaking [a native precapitalist] Chinese," and whether stopping is indeed a desirable option or a reluctant sign of imposed deprivation. With these details in mind, the grand finale of *Ermo* the film turns out particularly striking.

An aerial shot of the snow-covered village in sleepy darkness fades to the chill of Ermo's uninsulated house, where the entire family is huddled together in heavily padded cotton jackets, snoring. A steamy shower scene from *Dynasty* fills up the 29″ TV as the lovers finish their bargain of money and sex and embark on the journey of "having more fun." Like the bubbly fluidity of the shower that seems to smirk at Ermo's muddy flat without running water, the misty heat of sexual excitement on the screen and the laughter of the TV lovers appear to jeer at Ermo's somnolent family. Zhou's juxtaposition of the real and virtual worlds is deliberate and his representation of their split is dazzling, condensing in the final mise-en-scène the many meaningful questions the film text has previously posed. It is no longer the economy and society split or the split between a rooted existence and an uprooted one that Zhou Xiaowen wants to make emphatic, but more fundamentally the split of two simultaneous modes of production that are tearing Ermo asunder. On the one hand, it is the mode of industrial production and capital accumulation that extracts the yield of Ermo's physical labor. On the other hand, it is the new mode of spectacle production that regulates her psychic labor. Ermo's state of exhaustion is symptomatic of the double demands that "the society of spectacle" exacts on subjects of late capitalism, more painfully so especially for subjects of developing societies.

While in the context of the film China was far from being such a society as Debord first characterizes it, its subscription to the capitalist logic of perpetual growth has already set in motion the "ruling economic order, [where] ends are nothing and development is all – although the only thing into which the spectacle plans to develop is itself" (15–16). As Jonathan Beller's elaboration of Marx, Debord, and Deleuze convinces us, cinema in specific and by extension virtual-visual media in general constitute the capital of the twentieth and twenty-first centuries. As such, virtual media "work to organize previous forms of discipline and control, which remain extant" (para. 6). If primitive accumulation and early capitalist industrialization require that labor be lifted from its indigenous origin, corralled in the factory, and fixed at the assembly lines for maximum value extraction, the late capital of spectacle economy entails "the technological positioning of bodies for the purpose of [additional] value extraction, [when] to look is to labor" (Ibid., paras. 10–11).

The sight of Ermo's exhaustion evidences the cumulative effects of capitalist extraction of human value, from the overcoming of "geographical limitations" and national boundaries to the "positing the human body as the next frontier." "Capital expands not only outwards, geographically," Beller writes quite incisively, "but burrows into the flesh" (Ibid., para. 12). The image of the tired Ermo at the end of her possessed pursuit of the spectacle – from being initially seduced to watch, thus performing the labor of giving attention, to her toiling at the noodle press and selling blood in order to acquire the instrument of watching, thus furthering the cycle of watching and working for more consumption – is the film director's cinematic vehicle to leave open the conceptual challenge to endless capitalist development. Perhaps Zhou Xiaowen has Guy Debord's insights in mind:

> Economic growth liberates societies from the natural pressures of survival, but they still need to be liberated from their liberators . . . The economy transforms the world, but it transforms it into a world of economy . . . In these

circumstances an abundance of commodities, which is to say and abundance of commodity relations, can be no more than an *augmented survival*.

(28)

As Ermo and family sleep, the central Chinese TV station winds up its programming with "weather forecasts of world cities." Not ironically and consistent with China's determined opening up, the state-owned media is no longer forecasting national weather, simulating and substantiating Walter Benjamin's notion of "homogenous, empty time" that Benedict Anderson later elaborates into the time-space of the nation-state as that of the "imagined community." Instead, on the TV screen with the map of the world in the background, Beijing, Tokyo, Bangkok, Sydney, Karachi, Cairo, Moscow, Frankfurt, Paris, London, and New York all zoom out of their respective locations, performing a cartography of mobile capital connections, or an "interurban geography" that calls our attention to their distinctive landmarks and disparate locations while conveniently telescoping by the vast rural terrains.[23] After the metropolitan cities exit their planetary televisual stage, and the huge Chinese characters, "Zai Jian 再见" ("See you again") fill the 29" screen, we see what Ermo has not quite seen: the world is speeding by her while she remains trapped in her enervated body and stranded in her rural locality. Ermo's predicament of impossible venture and impossible return turns out to be Zhou's apt allegory not only for China but also for all the locals of the world, East and West, North and South, who are thrown into the giddy whirlpool of global capitalism over which they have little control. Only the cacophonous buzz of the sign-off rouses Ermo from her Rip Van Winkle–like slumber and alerts us to the gaping economic, social, and spatial polarization in a paradoxically interlinked world. Face expressionless and eyes wide open, Ermo stares at the TV, which has nothing on but static snow, an image of flickering uncertainty and chaotic velocity that bespeaks the human condition in globalization.

Notes

1 "Delinking" is Samir Amin's concept. It suggests a partial disengagement from the international capitalist world system in which the "core" countries subordinate developing countries on the "periphery" to their political and economic interests. It also proposes the transformation of countries by initiating a transition to socialism, which both abolishes the exploitive relations of capitalism and enhances democratic participation of citizens. The first three decades of the People's Republic of China since 1949 could be conceived as a social experiment of such delinking. However, China's entry into the WTO in 2001 officially concludes its socialist history of delinking.

   Zhang's film is adapted from the novel of the same name by the now Nobel laureate in literature, Mo Yan.

2 Autoethnography as a strategy for "colonized subjects to represent themselves in ways that engage with the colonized own terms" is from Mary Louis Pratt, who Rey Chow appropriates for her analyses of the Fifth Generation (Chow 38). The Fifth Generation of film directors refers to the graduates of the Beijing Film Academy in the early 1980s, such as Chen Kaige, Zhang Yimou, and Tian Zhuangzhuang, who were the products of Chinese reform in higher education after the Cultural Revolution. Like any term of periodization, the use of "generation" is inexact and without consensus; it is

more for critical convenience than for precise analysis of individual directors or their works because the generation does not encompass a uniformity of styles and subjects. The beginning use of generation to designate mainland Chinese film production in the 1980s is very much part of a "retrogressive naming syndrome" (Dai 2002, 237, 73). For a clear discussion of the term Fifth Generation in English, see Dai, "A Scene in the Fog: Reading the Sixth Generation Films" (2002, 71–98), and Xudong Zhang, "Generational Politics: What is the Fifth Generation?" (215–32). For original Chinese literature on the generational subject, see Dai (1989) and Ni. See note 11 of Chapter 5 on related discussions.

3 See Berger and Hsiao for an earlier probe into the neo-Confucian legitimization of East Asian development, Tu (1998), Dirlik, and Pye's later revision of the thesis.

4 Liberalism is a loaded term in economic and political theory. It is primarily defined in opposition to two historical regimes, first against feudalism and second against authoritarianism. Liberalism denotes the individual's rational deployment of labor or resources in the marketplace in systemic pursuit of his or her own self-interest. In its classic form, liberalism is a theory of rights based on private property and a theory of governance based on a social contract between the minimum intervention of the state and the free-choosing citizenry. My use of the term in the Chinese context leans toward an emphasis on the liberal accents of self-interest, self-possession, and self-choice through the capitalist market, as the PRC is not a liberal state by any definition. The freeing of liberalism from the frame of social contract theory and its evolution into neoliberalism with Chinese characteristics is the subject of my analysis in Chapter 2. (See Raymond Williams, Gordon Marshall, Colin Gordon, and Wendy Brown.)

5 The Chinese expression for reaching out to the capitalist West and the adoption of the global market is "Xiahai下海" or "plunging into the ocean."

6 Grandpa's urination, instead of being read in the mode of the Bakhtinian carnivalesque and its Dionysian community making (Y. Zhang 211–12), is to me more an act of animal scent-marking symbolic of aggressive individual possession.

7 See the documentary *Red Obsession* (2013 Tribeca Film Festival).

8 Treating *Red Sorghum* as an allegorical film sympathetic to the capitalistic structure of feeling is not to say that it is a propaganda piece for neoliberal capitalism. In fact, the distillery emblematizes an artisanal form of earlier capitalism that retains elements of socialist collectivism. Such idealized artisanal capital, however, suffers a brutal death in the hands of monopoly capital, symbolized by the Japanese invasion of China in the second half of the film.

9 *River Elegy* has been translated into English as *Deathsong of the River* by Richard Bodman and Pin Wan. Citations in the text refer to this edition.

10 Their strategy could be traced to a national "superiority-inferiority complex" after China's encounter with Western imperialism since the mid-nineteenth century (J. Wang 124).

11 Rayns's critical biography provides helpful English sources on Zhou, while the special section devoted to him in the Chinese *Dangdai dianying* 当代电影 (*Contemporary Film* 5 [1994]) is highly informative. The video of the film is available in the US through Arrow Releasing/Evergreen Entertainment. Citations in the text are based on this edition with my translation.

12 For contemporary Chinese TV culture in general, see Barmé and Zhao.

13 Given the PRC's residential registry system in its socialist era known as "Hukouzi," the urban population is as attached to its assigned place as is the rural population, securing a sort of demographic stability only to be interrupted by the postsocialist economic development in the surge of "floating population," the multitude of migrant labor.

14 The punch line encouraging the pursuit of wealth comes from Deng Xiaoping. See Greider (146–70), and Goldman and MacFarquhar (3–29). Notably, the film's figurative opposition of the state and capital downplays the Chinese government's top-down economic policy as well as the crucial role of the state not only in East Asia but also in Euro-America in Capital's Second Coming.

15 According to Giddens, modernity involves two distinct organizational complexes of "the *nation-state* and *systematic capitalist production*." While modernity as such is "distinctively a Western project," its "globalization" – the diffusion of its dual institutional agencies across the world, the ensuing "process of [its] uneven development that fragments as it coordinates" and that leaves out no "others" – has meant that modernity cannot be Western as a consequence (Giddens 174–75; see also Appadurai and Jameson 2002). What I argue in the text is that modernity could have taken the form of a socialist nation-state and a planned economy as in the case of the People's Republic, yet the PRC's relinking with world capital as much confirms Giddens's thesis as it throws additional light on Capital's Second Coming, which is impossible to comprehend without the Chinese experience.

16 Althusser (100–40); also helpful is the Zizek edition that contains Althusser's essay.

17 While earlier English translations use "society" to stand for *Gesellschaft*, the Harris and Hollis edition I am referring to chooses "civil society" instead.

18 Zhou considers the choice of the 29″ TV crucial in contrasting the consumption gap in the earlier 1990s between Chinese urban dwellers, for whom it was no longer an item of unattainable luxury, and rural folk, for whom it remained a symbol of coveted wealth and status (W. Zhang 32).

19 In an earlier era of China's modernizing endeavor, both Lu Xun (1881–1936) and Hu Shi (1891–1962) advocated the applicability of virtue to both men and women (Larson 79), thus revising a gender-exclusive personal morality in traditional China. However, they did not anticipate MacIntyre's critique of modernity with ethical "emotivism" at its core.

20 The market "rarely has anything to do with choice or freedom," as Fredric Jameson reasons, "since those are all determined for us in advance." We select among new model cars or television programs, but "we can scarcely be said to have a say in actually choosing any of them" (1991, 266).

21 For Sen, the exercise of development should transcend its exclusively economic, technological, and industrial objectives. It should be geared toward overcoming deprivations and enhancing "substantive freedoms in judging individual advantage and in evaluating social achievements and failures" (285). Deeply committed to the complementarily of individual agency and social arrangements, Sen is concerned "with our capability to lead the kind of lives we have reasons to value" and with widening "the range of human choice" beyond the market (290, 295–96).

22 Since the success of Singapore hinges on its unique formation as a small city-state, this model is hardly "reproducible" in larger nation-states such as China (Ong 208).

23 As part of an emerging global grid, "interurban geography" joins major international financial and business centers but omits zones of the rural and the inner city (Sassen, 2000, 225).

Works cited

Althusser, Louis. "Ideology and Ideological State Apparatuses (Notes Towards an Investigation)." *Mapping Ideology*. Ed. Slavoj Zizek. New York: Verso, 1994. 100–140.

Amin, Samir. *Delinking: Towards a Polycentric World*. Trans. Michael Wolfers. London: Zed Books, 1990.

Anagnost, Ann. *National Past-Times: Narrative, Representation, and Power in Modern China*. Durham: Duke UP, 1997.

Anderson, Benedict. *Imagined Communities: Reflection on the Origin and Spread of Nationalism*. New York: Verso, 1991.

Appadurai, Arjun. *Modernity at Large: Cultural Dimensions of Globalization*. Minneapolis: U of Minnesota P, 1996.

Balibar, Etienne. "Subjection and Subjectivation." *Supposing the Subject*. Ed. Joan Copjec. New York: Verso, 1994. 1–15.

Barmé, Geremie R. *In the Red: On Contemporary Chinese Culture*. New York: Columbia UP, 1999.

Bauman, Zygmunt. *Globalization: The Human Consequences*. New York: Columbia UP, 1998.

———. *Life in Fragments: Essays in Postmodern Morality*. Oxford: Polity P, 1995.

———. *Liquid Love: On the Frailty of Human Bonds*. Cambridge: Polity P, 2003.

Bell, Daniel. *The Cultural Contradictions of Capitalism*. New York: Basic Books, 1976/1996.

Bellah, Robert N. et al. *Habits of the Heart: Individualism and Commitment in American Life*. Berkeley and Los Angeles: U of California P, 1985.

Beller, Jonathan. "Cinema, Capital of the Twentieth Century." *Postmodern Culture* 4.3 (May, 1994). *http://infomotions.com/serials/pmc/pmc-v4n3-beller-cinema.txt*.

Berger, Peter, and Hsin-huang Michael Hsiao, eds. *In Search of an East Asian Development Model*. New Brunswick: Transaction Books, 1988.

Berman, Marshall. *All That Is Solid Melts into Air: The Experience of Modernity*. New York: Penguin, 1988.

Berry, Chris. *Postsocialist Cinema in Post-Mao China: The Cultural Revolution after the Cultural Revolution*. New York: Routledge, 2004.

Bodman, W. Richard, and Pin P. Wan, eds. *Deathsong of the River: A Reader's Guide to the Chinese TV Series Heshang*. Ithaca, NY: East Asia Program, Cornell U, 1991.

Bourdieu, Pierre. *Outline of a Theory of Practice*. Trans. Richard Rice. Cambridge: Cambridge UP, 1977.

Bové, Paul A. "Rights Discourse in the Age of US-China Trade." *New Literary History* 33.1 (2002): 171–87.

Brown, Wendy. "Neo-liberalism and the End of Liberal Democracy." *Theory and Event* 7.1 (2003): 1–43.

Carens, Joseph, ed. *Democracy and Possessive Individualism: The Intellectual Legacy of C. B. Macpherson*. Albany: SUNY Press, 1993.

Chow, Rey. *Primitive Passions: Visuality, Sexuality, Ethnography, and Contemporary Chinese Cinema*. New York: Columbia UP, 1995.

Dai, Jinhua. *Cinema and Desire: Feminist Marxism and Cultural Politics in the Work of Dai Jinhua*. Eds. Jing Wang and Tani Barlow. London: Verso, 2002.

———. "Xiata: Chongdu dishidai/Leaning Tower: Re-reading the Fourth Generation." 《电影艺术》 *Film Arts* 4 (1989): 3–8.

Debord, Guy. *The Society of the Spectacle*. Trans. Donald Nicholson-Smith. New York: Zone Books, 1967/1995.

Dirlik, Arif. "Confucius in the Borderlands: Global Capitalism and the Reinvention of Confucianism." *boundary 2* 22.3 (Fall, 1995): 229–73.

Giddens, Anthony. *The Consequences of Modernity*. Stanford: Stanford UP, 1990.

Goldman, Merle, and Roderick MacFarquhar, eds. *The Paradox of China's Post-Mao Reforms*. Cambridge: Harvard UP, 1999.

Gordon, Colin. "Governmental Rationality: An Introduction." *The Foucault Effect: Studies in Governmentality*. Eds. Burchell, Graham, Colin Gordon, and Peter Miller. Chicago: U of Chicago P, 1991. 1–52.

Greider, William. *One World, Ready or Not: The Manic Logic of Global Capitalism*. New York: Touchstone, 1998.

Han, Sung-Joo, ed. *Changing Values in Asia: Their Impact on Governance and Development*. New York: Japan Center for International Exchange, 1999.

Hareven, Tamara. *Family Time and Industrial Time: The Relationship between the Family and Work in a New England Industrial Community*. Cambridge: Cambridge UP, 1982.

Harvey, David. *The Condition of Postmodernity: An Enquiry into the Origins of Social Change*. Cambridge: Blackwell Publishers, 1990.

Held, Virginia. "Freedom and Feminism." *Democracy and Possessive Individualism: The Intellectual Legacy of C. B. Macpherson*. Ed. Joseph Carens. Albany: SUNY Press, 1993. 138–52.

Hirschman, Albert O. *The Passions and the Interests: Political Arguments for Capitalism before its Triumph*. Princeton: Princeton UP, 1977/1997.

Hobsbawm, Eric, and Terence Ranger. *The Invention of Tradition*. Cambridge: Cambridge UP, 2012.

Holston, James, and Arjun Appadurai, eds. "Cities and Citizenship." *Public Culture* 8.2 (Winter, 1996): 187–204.

Jameson, Fredric. "Cognitive Mapping." *Marxism and the Interpretation of Culture*. Eds. Cary Nelson and Lawrence Grossberg. Urbana and Chicago: U of Illinois P, 1988. 347–57.

———. *The Geopolitical Aesthetic: Cinema and Space in the World System*. Bloomington: Indiana UP, 1995.

———. "Notes on Globalization as a Philosophical Issue." *The Cultures of Globalization*. Eds. Fredric Jameson and Masao Miyoshi. Durham: Duke UP, 1998. 54–77.

———. *Postmodernism: Or the Cultural Logic of Late Capitalism*. Durham: Duke UP, 1991.

———. *A Singular Modernity: Essay on the Ontology of the Present*. London: Verso, 2002.

Kolodny, Annette. *The Lay of the Land: Metaphor as Experience and History in American Life and Letters*. Chapel Hill: University of North Carolina P, 1975.

Larson, Wendy. *Women and Writing in Modern China*. Stanford: Stanford UP, 1998.

Li, Cheng. "200 Million Mouths Too Many: China's Surplus Rural Labor." *The China Reader: The Reform Era*. Eds. Orville Schell and David Shambaugh. New York: Vintage, 1999. 362–73.

Lowe, Donald. *The Body in Late-Capitalist USA*. Durham: Duke UP, 1995.

MacIntyre, Alasdair. *After Virtue: A Study in Moral Theory*. Notre Dame: U of Notre Dame P, 1984.

Macpherson, Crawford Brough. *The Political Theory of Possessive Individualism: Hobbes to Locke*. Oxford: Oxford UP, 1962.

Marshall, Gordon. "Liberalism." *A Dictionary of Sociology* (2nd Edition). New York: Oxford UP, 1998. 366–67.

Mauss, Marcel. *The Gift: Forms and Functions of Exchange in Archaic Societies*. Trans. Ian Cunnison. Glencoe, IL: Free Press, 1954.

Ni, Zhen. "Dianying yu dangdai shenghuo"/"Cinema and Contemporary Life." 《当代 电影》 *Contemporary Cinema* 2 (1985): 20–27.

Ong, Aihwa. *Flexible Citizenship: The Cultural Logics of Transnationality*. Durham: Duke UP, 1999.

Polanyi, Karl. *The Great Transformation: The Political and Economic Origins of Our Time*. Boston: Beacon, 1944/1957.

Pye, Lucian W. "'Asian Values': From Dynamos to Dominos?" *Culture Matters: How Values Shape Human Progress*. Eds. Lawrence E. Harrison and Samuel P. Huntington. New York: Basic Books, 2000. 244–55.

Rayns, Tony. "The Ups and Downs of Zhou Xiaowen." *Sight and Sound* 5.7 (July, 1995): 22–24.

Sassen, Saskia. *The Global City: New York, London, Tokyo*. Princeton: Princeton UP, 1991.

————. "Spatialities and Temporalities of the Global: Elements for a Theorization." *Public Culture* 8.2 (Winter, 2000): 215–32.

Sen, Amartya. *Development as Freedom*. New York: Anchor Books, 1999.

Solinger, Dorothy J. *Contesting Citizenship in Urban China: Peasant Migrants, the State, and the Logic of the Market*. Berkeley: U of California P, 1999.

Song, Qiang et al. 《中国可以说不》 (*China Can Say No*). Beijing: Zhonghua Gongshang Lianhe Books, 1996.

Stone, Lawrence. *The Family, Sex, and Marriage in England 1500–1800*. New York: Harper and Row, 1977.

Tönnies, Ferdinand. *Community and Civil Society/Gemeinschaft und Gesellschaft*. Trans. Jose Harris and Margaret Hollis. New York: Cambridge UP, 2001.

Tu, Weiming. "Human Rights as a Confucian Moral Discourse." *Confucianism and Human Rights*. Eds. Wm. Theodore de Barry and Tu Weiming. New York: Columbia UP, 1998. 297–307.

————, ed. "The Living Tree: The Changing Meaning of Being Chinese Today, a Special Issue." *Daedalus* 120.2 (1991).

Wang, Gungwu. *The Chinese Overseas: From Earthbound China to the Quest for Autonomy*. Cambridge: Harvard UP, 2002.

Wang, Hui. *China's New Order: Society, Politics, and Economy in Transition*. Ed. Theodore Huters. Cambridge: Harvard UP, 2003.

Wang, Jing. *High Culture Fever: Politics, Aesthetics, and Ideology in Deng's China*. Berkeley: U of California P, 1996.

Wang, Shaoguang. "The Great Transformation: The Double Movement in China." *Boundary 2* 35.2 (2008): 15–47.

Weber, Max. *The Protestant Ethic and the Spirit of Capitalism*. Trans. Talcott Parsons. Intro. by Anthony Giddens. London and New York: Routledge, 1930/1993.

Williams, Raymond. *Keywords: A Vocabulary of Culture and Society* (Revised Edition). New York: Oxford UP, 1983.

Yang, Mei-hui Mayfair. "From Gender Erasure to Gender Difference: State Feminism. Consumer Sexuality, and the Women's Public Sphere in China." *Spaces of Their Own: Women's Public Sphere in Transnational China*. Ed. Mayfair Yang. Minneapolis: U of Minnesota P, 1999. 35–67.

Zhang, Wei. "Xiao Wen Zi Bian,"/"The Transformation of Xiaowen: An Interview with Zhou Xiaowen." 《当代电影》 *Contemporary Cinema* 5 (1994): 28–36.

Zhang, Xudong. *Chinese Modernism in the Era of Reforms*. Durham: Duke UP, 1997.

Zhang, Yingjin. *Screening China: Critical Interventions, Cinematic Reconfigurations, and the Transnational Imaginary in Contemporary Chinese Cinema*. Ann Arbor: U of Michigan Center for Chinese Studies, 2002.

Zhao, Yuezhi, *Media, Market, and Democracy in China: Between the Party Line and the Bottom Line*. Urbana: U of Illinois P, 1998.

2 *Crazy English* with a Chinese face

Zhang Yuan's documentary on the neoliberal pedagogy of the self

Significant mutations in sovereignty and subjectivity have occurred on a global scale since the 1970s, becoming particularly and palpably salient after the Reagan-Thatcher-Deng Xiaoping Revolution. "Today, the problem is not so much the governability of society," writes Nikolas Rose, "as the governability of the passions of self-identified individuals and collectivities." Instead of "citizen-forming devices" of school and public broadcasting, "the commercial consumption regimes" increasingly "shape individuals and pluralities" (46). Rose attributes such drastic shifts in political and personal governance to a neoliberalism that takes "as its target not just an economy but society itself" (Ibid. 146). Wendy Brown agrees that neoliberalism is an emerging "mode of governance encompassing but not limited to the state, and one which produces subjects, forms of citizenship and behavior, and a new organization of the social" (1). For Aihwa Ong, finally, " 'American neoliberalism' has become [such] a global phenomenon" that it has both infiltrated Western liberal democracies and intervened in "postcolonial, authoritarian, and postsocialist situations in East and Southeast Asia" (2006, 3). The nightmare of an economy-driven society Polanyi dreaded is looming large on the world stage.

In their Michel Foucault–inflected analyses, Rose, Ong, and Brown transcend the common sense of neoliberal governmental rationality as mere free market–based policies that are "favorable to business and indifferent toward poverty, social deracination, cultural decimation, long term resource depletion and environmental destruction" (Brown; Ibid.). The art and science of neoliberal governmentality first signals a shift of state reason from its principal concern with the people of a national sovereignty to its primary concern with the economy. Second, it involves a strategic reorganization of the social by the market as well as a systemic refashioning of subjects on the liberal foundation of possessive individualism.[1] The ideal subject of neoliberalism – originally conceived by the Austrian philosopher Friedrich von Hayek, nursed in the Chicago School of economics, and fully grown in the heyday of the Reagan-Thatcher-Deng Xiaoping Revolution – is nothing short of the extension and a revision of *Homo sapiens* as "*homo economicus*, an instrumentalist figure forged in the effervescent conditions of market competition" (Ong, 2006, 10; Peters; Phillips 187–89).

In Chapter 1, we read *Red Sorghum* and *Ermo* in the old grain of Euro-American liberalism and approached Grandpa and Ermo as Chinese figurations of *Homo economicus* from the embrace of Capital's Second Coming by the People's Republic of China (PRC). In this Chinese liberal cast, *Homo economicus* is essentially a self-possessive individual in Macpherson's original sense: we have discovered how a particular conception of capitalist property relationship encouraged by the Chinese state reshapes the thinking, feeling, and doing of a postsocialist Chinese subject. Ermo's truncated metamorphosis into the liberal subject of self-ownership enacts at the individual level a new dialectic of freedom and serfdom just as it mirrors "the great transformation" of state governmentality when the raison d'être of society yields to the imperatives of economy. In Zhou Xiaowen's dramatization of China's capitalist development, however, Ermo remains an incomplete and incongruous subject of liberalism. Although s/he gains a dawning awareness of the self as an economic agent, Ermo is neither constitutionally fit for the competitive satiation of appetites nor entitled to the rights implicit in the ideal of a liberal democracy.

Though unique to China's express transition from its condition of socialist modernity, this incomplete and incongruous liberalization (i.e., the opening of market avenues for individual accumulation of wealth and the persistent closure of popular political participation) parallels the change in contemporary democratic nation-states of the West. There, radical economic liberalization and political conservatism are manifest in maximizing private profit and minimizing public welfare. *"The liberalism in what has come to be called neo-liberalism refers to liberalism's economic variant,"* clarifies Wendy Brown, "recuperating selected pre-Keynesian assumptions about the generation of wealth and its distribution" while "establish[ing] these principles on a significantly different analytic basis from those set forth by Adam Smith" (2). The neoliberal *Homo economicus* is both "a reactivation and a radical inversion" of the economic man "conceived by the liberalism of Smith, Hume, or Ferguson," comments Colin Gordon, as this reactivation "consists in positing a fundamental human faculty of *choice*, a principle which empowers economic calculation effectively to sweep aside the anthropological categories and frameworks of the human and social sciences" (43).

While Brown and Gordon provide a spirited scholarly synthesis of the neoliberal political agenda, its psychosocial reconstitution of the *Homo economicus* as the subject par excellence can be found in *Crazy English* 疯狂英语 (1999), a Chinese documentary biography that stars Li Yang, a self-taught student of English whose mission it is to convert a billion Chinese into an English-speaking folk. Once a shy and introverted youngster, Li Yang claims no special aptitude for foreign languages and admits flunking English examinations in college. To pull himself out of the heap of failures, he tried reading aloud with his materials, took TEM 4 (a standardized college English test in China), and succeeded in obtaining the second-highest score at Lanzhou University. Given his success as an English broadcaster and simultaneous translator in Guangzhou, he decides to popularize his method by establishing Li Yang Cliz English Promotion Studio in 1994, building his pedagogy on the personal example of English shout-out on rooftops. Besides his trademark English teaching shows that regularly draw stadium-sized audiences of 20,000, Li has made "Crazy English" a multimillion yuan and dollar brand name with a renewable product line that includes textbooks, tapes, training camps, and needless to say, the ubiquitous website of borderless dissemination (http://www.crazyenglish.org/). In the estimate of *Asiaweek*, Li is "China's most successful English teacher and a pop-cult figure" (R. Zhang).

At the height of his career, Li Yang approached Zhang Yuan 张元 – a prominent Sixth Generation independent filmmaker of such reputed works as *Beijing Bastards* 北京杂种 (1992), *East Place, West Palace* 东宫西宫 (1996), *Seventeen Years* 过年回家 (1999), *I Love You* 我爱你 (2002), and the winner of the Berlin Film Festival, *Red Flowers* 看上去很美 (2005) – with the proposal to be his documentary subject. Fascinated by Li's biography and his expanding commercial empire, Zhang decided to take up his "camera to understand this man" (M. Berry 152). The result is a vivid portrayal of one individual who crafts himself in the flesh from the abstract game of neoliberal enterprise. *Crazy English* brings to light the confluence between the political and philosophical discourse of neoliberalism and its personal and psychological actualization in its "crazy" Chinese protagonist.

1

Technically speaking, the film does not open with an image; it is led in with nondiegetic sound. An offscreen and off-story mechanical drone, which soon becomes distinguishable for the audience as that of a jumbo jet taking off, accompanies the rolling of credits before the bilingual title, 疯狂英语 *Crazy English* pops on the screen. The launching of the documentary subject simultaneously signifies the liftoff of the Chinese economy, now inextricably tied to exports and cargo planes. Against this audio backdrop of the globalizing industrial production comes the upper-body shot of a bespectacled yet vigorous looking Li Yang, striding, shouting, and gesticulating in a snow-covered street, uncontainable by the handheld camera: "Crazy English! Crazy life! Crazy work! Crazy study! Be crazy everyday, every minute, everywhere! I love this crazy game. I want to be crazy! Let's join this crazy game, crazy world!" As the lens withdraws to include more of the city and the protagonist's followers, presently chanting in chorus with a frenzy that puzzles the pedestrians in the distance, we have entered a China that is no longer the self-enclosed place of legendary "standstill" but the space on the move, opened up to transnational commerce. In this mise-en-scène, Li Yang's body language begins to personify the restless spirit of Capital's Second Coming while his vociferous slogans decry the moldy conventions of China's historical past. In his iconoclasm, being crazy is not being insane but being enthused about individual exertion in the brave new world of capitalist enterprise.

Fully cognizant of documentary genre's complex "factual-fictional typology," its impulse of informing the audience of the immediate historical milieu and its narrative urge of entertaining it by storytelling (Izod and Kilborn 426), Zhang Yuan effectively situates his protagonist in the post-Tiananmen and post–Cold

War context of China's deliberate movement to join the World Trade Organization. Unlike some of his colleagues who deploy cinema verité as ethnographic exploration of social outcasts left behind by progress and prosperity, Zhang's focus in *Crazy English* is on the socially ambitious.[2] Although Zhang's camera positions Li as a historical person, functioning throughout as a member of a radically changing social collectivity, the protagonist frequently obtains dimensions larger than real life. Right after its inaugurating rally in the street, for example, the film displays a gallery of *Crazy English* converts and a brief radio interview of its creator, Li. While the close-ups of anxious Chinese learners struggling with the foreign tongue in front the camera presents the new faces of English in its astounding non-Caucasian diversity, this sequence of individual shots also enables an ensemble effect that promotes Li's idiosyncratic tutelage. Similarly, the radio interview that follows uses the voice-over to further establish the truth-telling effect of the documentary mise-en-scène (the insertion of the radio soundtrack leading to shots in the studio coincides with sights of the cityscape unfolding from a moving vehicle, with a quick succession of billboards and high-rise buildings revealing the exponential growth of an urban China). As the radio announcer has it, the story of a tongue-tied youth turned motivational speaker with exceptional missionary zeal is not "an Arabian fantasy," but an actual exemplar for people to "master English and pull up China." Such journalistic framing in the nationalistic vein, which director Zhang borrows to frame his subject cinematically, has endowed Li Yang with an indisputable iconic status. Li has become the sign of the times just as the image of his energizing body opens up multiple possibilities of mass psychological identification if not virtual transubstantiation. One may logically ask at this point, "Is *Crazy English* a national allegory?"

Doubtless to evoke this question is to revisit the well-known controversy between Fredric Jameson and Aijaz Ahmad in the late 1980s, when China's course of development was increasingly aligned with the Second Coming of Capital. It is also to reconsider the vexed relationship between biography and history, the genre of the novel and its narration of the nation, recently animated by Joseph Slaughter's examination of the *Bildungsroman* in relation to the discourse of human rights. For me, these debates on rhetorical tropes and generic conventions manifest larger tensions in the geopolitical reorganization of national societies and individual subjectivities since Jameson/Ahmad's particular moment, tensions that are specific to the rocky global transition from the regime of liberalism to that of neoliberalism. Two quick points of contention are in order before we proceed with our discussion in that direction. I want to show first of all how the state and citizen bind at the heart of political liberalism is simultaneously the adhesive enabling the analogous fiction of individual liberty and national sovereignty. Second, I want to reveal how the loosening of the state and citizen bind in neoliberalism, and the dovetail of the active consumer to the free market, have confounded the constitutive terms of understanding the subject while giving credence to the rise of some "newer new humanity."[3] This shall pave the way for our grasp of *Crazy English* as a contradictory cinematic biography and a different form of *Bildungsroman* that documents as it mediates the pedagogy and technology of a neoliberal subject "with Chinese characteristics."

As we recall, the national allegory controversy is provoked by Jameson's essay, "Third World Literature in the Era of Multinational Capitalism," in which he declares, "Third-world texts necessarily project a political dimension in the form of national allegory: *the story of the private individual destiny is always an allegory of the embattled situation of the public third-world culture and society*" (69).[4] A conviction in the explanatory power of the "Marxian concept of modes of production" and a yearning for the "the principles of community interdependence" very much motivate this sweeping claim (68, 86). The residual "tribal" and "bureaucratic imperial systems" of the third world provide for Jameson both "infrastructural realities" of potential resistance and a unique literary form that integrates the lived experience of the individual with the abstraction of economic and political power in ways inconceivable in the industrialized first world where the split between the private and the public is almost absolute (68, 78). "[T]he radical difference of other national situations" and their incomplete privatization of the political are clearly where Jameson invests his desire for social alternatives to capitalism (77, 109).

This progressive desire, however, becomes precisely the object of critique for Ahmad, who reads such "national allegory" as nothing but "rhetoric of Otherness" (95). Ahmad disputes Jameson's division "between a capitalist First World and a presumably pre- or non-capitalist Third World," challenging his assumption that the third world is constituted by "the singular experience of colonialism and imperialism" to narrate it "nationalist[ically]" (101, 102). Crucial for Ahmad is the "proposition that we live not in three worlds but one," unified "by the global operation of a single mode of production, namely the capitalist one" (103). As soon as we recognize that "capitalism is not an externality but a shaping force within [the colonized/imperialized] formations," Ahmad states, "the separation between the public and private, so characteristic of capitalism, has occurred there as well, at least among the urban intelligentsia," the primary producers of literature (107).

Part of the confusion of "national allegory" can be attributed to a word that neither Jameson nor Ahmad directly uses but nonetheless holds a key to their dispute. The semantic fields of "ethnicity," an English word of mixed etymologies, in fact overlap Jameson's "nation" and Ahmad's "other." When derived from the Greek *ethnos*, ethnicity signifies "nation" or "people." Following its origin in Latin, *ethnicus*, however, ethnicity means "'heathen,' referring to people of non-Christian and non-Jewish" descent (Murji 112). Central to Ahmad's charge is Jameson's ethnicization not in the sense of religious exclusion but the marginalization of third-world people as the Other to capitalistic modernity. In a by now familiar postcolonial and multicultural maneuver, Ahmad contends that colonized peoples both contribute to and are constitutive of capitalist modernity. But Jameson is preoccupied specifically with China, whose post–World War II participation in global history until the late 1970s is marked by its unique passage of socialist modernity.[5] China was for Jameson an affirmative alterity, a system of social and economic organization that constituted an "outside" to expanding capitalism.

While insisting that the third-world subject is as divided and individualized by the category of class as the liberal subject of the first world, Ahmad is expressing his reservation as much about the homogenous conception of the nation and its elision of internal differences as about the presumed bind between the bourgeois state and its subject, secured by the rhetoric of "national allegory." Arguing for an allegorical integrity of "the private individual destiny" and "the public third-world culture and society," Jameson is drawing on an interpretive tradition in existence since the European Enlightenment, which regards the novelization of the emergent bourgeois subject as both a story of his secular individuation as his socialization into the emergent proto-nation-state. Benedict Anderson has written about the nation as the imaginative projection of the individual subject mediated by print capitalism. Etienne Balibar has contended that "citizenship *is* subjectivity," an equation which identifies "the task of self-emancipation from every domination and subjection by means of a collective and universal access in politics" (12). The interpretive coupling of the state and the citizen-subject informs much reading of metropolitan fiction as it does postcolonial and multiethnic writings of "nation and narration" (Bhabha). Thus, in an apt assessment of one critic, "Jameson's national allegory is a prescription for reading *Bildungsromane* according to the synecdochial, ethno-nationalist logic of *Bildung* itself" (Slaughter 114).

Crucial to the *Bildungsroman*, as Joseph Slaughter argues, is the genre's dual social role of "incorporating the problematic individual into the rights and responsibilities of citizenship" and "legitimating the democratic institutions of the emergent rights-based nation-state":

> The affirmative *Bildungsroman* normalizes the idealist vision of what Dipesh Chakrabarty calls the dominant transition narrative of development and modernization, which not only patterns the novel, biography, historiography, and human rights law, but also "underwrote, and was in turn underpinned by," the institutions of the modern European nation-state. This enlightenment-progress narrative centers the individual within a "state/citizen bind as the ultimate construction of sociality" . . . Through *Bildung*, German idealism assigns to culture the "political vocation" of centralizing the nation-state and centering its citizen-subjects . . . [I]t is here . . . the classical society/individual dyad becomes the modern Chakrabartian state/citizen bind, and the story of the emergent proto-nation-state becomes fully congruent with the stories of the national-historical emergence of its proto-citizens.
>
> (94, 113)

In highlighting the interdependency between *Bildungsroman*'s "narrative individualism" and "narrative nationalism," Slaughter offers valuable insight into Jameson's allegorical impulse, for without the inalienable bind between the state and the citizen the trope of national allegory cannot possibly hold (92). After nation-states became ubiquitous entities of international geopolitical organization, the modern subject has always until quite recently been inextricably embedded in sovereignty and territoriality, in state-inflected discourses, in ethnic and cultural evocations redolent of national sentiments. However, in his preoccupation with the Enlightenment origin of the *Bildungsroman*, Slaughter neither attempts an account of Ahmad's objection to "national allegory" nor does he fully engage Chakrabarty's critique of "the state/citizen bind" central to post-Enlightenment historiography and biography. As a result, his take on "contemporary postcolonial *Bildungsromane*" remains reliant on the structural bind of liberalism in its seemingly continuous and unproblematic "globalizing designs" (25).

Like the liberal tradition of Chakrabarty's celebration and critique from which he draws inspiration, Slaughter, like Jameson before him, instinctively and indefatigably holds on to the state/citizen bind "in its projection of an 'egalitarian imaginary'" (5). In doing so, he extends the classic *Bildungsroman* (and *Bildung*)'s requisite "harmonization of the individual and society" to the contemporary world, where society may behold a different reason of the state and the socialization of the individual may not be subjected to disciplines of citizenship. The Reagan-Thatcher-Deng Xiaoping Revolution may have already measurably loosened the state/citizen bind crucial to liberalism's conception and practice of sociality that its proclaimed egalitarian imaginary is under severe duress.

Ahmad's suspicion of "national allegory" is a genuine suspension of belief in the state's capacity to govern and to secure the welfare of its people. This suspicion is intimately tied to the death of grand narratives in the postmodern topos and linked with the birth of capitalism as "a [de facto] single mode of [world] production" (Ahmad 103; Lyotard). National allegory is indeed lost in translation, because, just when Ahmad and Jameson were debating, the very liberal foundation of its rhetorical and political translatability – the relative temporal homogeneity and spatial boundaries of the people that makes possible for the individual subject to stand for the identity of the nation – was fractured by the "disjunctive" flows of capital and followed by the "detotalization of [national] society" (Appadurai; Rose 135).

Although the socialist modernity of China was noncapitalist and illiberal, its proper subject was locked in the extreme form of the bureaucratic "state/citizen bind," with neither the property-generated rights of Western liberal democracies nor the privacy of bourgeois interiority. In its postsocialist embrace of capitalism, "the transnationalization of production [has turned] China into 'the industrial workshop of the world,' and transformed [its] traditional form of sovereignty [so much]," writes Wang Hui, that "domestic and international special interest relations have now seeped into state mechanisms and even the process of legislation to an unprecedented degree" (xxvi, xxviii). Consequently, "neoliberalism was able to take the place of state ideology to become a new ruling ideology, thus providing basic direction and rationality to state policy, international relations, and the emerging values of the media" (Ibid. 37). As the reason of the socialist state to "represent the 'universal interest'" of the Chinese masses has become so tenuous and the old state/citizen bind so "moribund," the PRC's "crisis of legitimacy" has to be "overcome through [promotion of] economic reform" under such "ubiquitously deployed tropes as 'transition' and 'development'" (Ibid. xxviii, 37, 20).

Wang Hui's seems a scintillating capture of the post-Tiananmen and post–Cold War Chinese transition and development. It complicates the Jameson/Ahmad controversy and contradicts Chakrabarty's critique of liberalism. Ironically, it is China's sudden subscription to capitalism that has made it susceptible to the foundational teleology of liberalism and "the problematics posed by this transition narrative," inherent in "most modern third-world histories," states Chakrabarty, "of which the overriding (if often implicit) themes are those of development, modernization, and capitalism" (27, 31). If China's earlier immunity to this set of problematics, say the Mao period of 1949–76, was the basis of its historical alterity and the projected alternative behind Jameson's "national allegory," its active participation of global capitalism has meant a significant loss of this immunity, not in terms of political sovereignty but rather a claim of cultural sovereignty.

Because in the universal history of capitalism, here I concur with Chakrabarty: "'Europe' remains the sovereign, theoretical subject of all histories, including the ones we call 'Indian,' 'Chinese,' [and] 'Kenyan'" (Ibid. 27). In its intransigent relinking with or voluntary self-inclusion in the course of capitalism, the PRC is consequently subject to the norms of both historicism and liberalism in Chakrabarty's senses. The Chinese nation-state is subject to the historicist developmental definitions of lack and inadequacy, just as its citizen is now subject to "the [liberal] public and private rituals of modern individualism" (Ibid. 35, 34). The post-Mao and pre-Tiananmen deregulation of the Chinese economy was particularly suggestive of this liberal trajectory of societal transformation and subject reformation, as our reading of *Ermo* in the previous chapter demonstrated.

But liberalism is not the word that Wang Hui uses to describe the post-Tiananmen Chinese turn; it is "neoliberalism," "a market radicalism" that simply realigns the state with corporate interests, thus dissolving the legendary liberal state/citizen bind central both to Chakrabarty's critique of bourgeois subjectivity and Slaughter's conceptualization of the *Bildungsroman* (31–32). In Wang's words, "neoliberals believe that it is possible to use the strength of multinational and domestic capital to reconfigure Chinese society [through state devolution and state violence]" (32). For him, the Tiananmen crackdown betrays the "mutual entanglement of neoliberalism and neo-authoritarianism" that effectively smothered liberal aspirations for "social justice and the democratization of economic life," catapulting – catastrophically as it were – the pre-Tiananmen liberalization and democratization into post-Tiananmen "radical privatization" (32–33). "In this sense," Wang concludes, "certain conflicts between neoliberalism and the state are different from the relationship between liberalism and the state in the nineteenth and early twentieth centuries; they are product of new relations of interests" (32).

Contrary to Chakrabarty, who considers the continual spread of capitalism as an uninterrupted historical expansion of the bourgeois state/citizen bind and its "universal and secular vision of the human" (4), Wang argues that this political ideal of the Enlightenment for social justice is being effectively eviscerated by "new relations of interests" in Capital's Second Coming (32). Though Wang does not state it explicitly, he clearly shows that this shift of relations of interests from liberalism to neoliberalism marks the waning of the state/citizen bind and the emergence of a state/capital bind. Such realignment of interests and their

immediate bearing on the new constitution of society and subjectivity are succinctly explicated by Nikolas Rose:

> No longer is there a conflict between the self-interest of the economic subject
> and the patriotic duty of the citizen: it now appears that one can best fulfill
> one's obligations to one's nation by most effectively pursuing the enhance-
> ment of the economic well-being of oneself . . . freedom is no longer freedom
> from want, which might be provided by a cosseted life on benefits: it is the
> capacity for self-realization which can be obtained through individual activ-
> ity. Hence an economic politics which enjoins work on all citizens is one
> which provides mutual benefit for the individual and the collective.
>
> (144–45)

While "market radicalism" of Wang's coinage spells out the organizational condition of China's denationalization of public ownership (31), the "economic
politics" of Rose's analysis articulates the subjective condition for "the will to
self-actualize" (144). Together, they provide us with a clear contour of the objective and subjective conditions of a neoliberal "governmentality," as the "conduct
of conduct" in Foucault's term, that actively reconceives the state and subject
relationship as "the relation between self and self" (Gordon 2). In place of the
apprenticeship of the liberal citizen-subject passively constrained by the rights
and duties within a territorial state of homogenous time is the training for the
new consumer-subject in the borderless marketplace, who is quintessentially "an
entrepreneur of him- or herself" actively "seeking to enhance and capitalize on
existence itself through calculated acts" (Rose 164). It is in the global mutation
of the meaning and practice of the (national/postnational) subject that we find the
meteoric rise of Li Yang, a new sort of *Homo economicus* in the guise of a populist
pedagogue of the English language.

2

Because of China's precipitous transition from socialist to capitalist modernity
short-circuits the consolidation of the liberal society and cultivation of the liberal subject, the documentary biography of Li Yang unveils both the making of a
new subjectivity and the mark of a new developmental narrative. For one, *Crazy
English* exemplifies the telling of "other narratives of the self and community
that do not look to the state/citizen bind as the ultimate construction of sociality"
(Chakrabarty 37). But its resemblance to the project of "provincializing Europe"
stops here, for Chakrabarty's is about a historical recuperation of subjectivities
that do not abide by the "universal and secular vision of the human" (4). Similarly,
Crazy English retains the function of the European *Bildungsroman* in socializ-
ing the national subject, but it replaces its "egalitarian imaginary" at the genre's
classic core with what I call "an entrepreneurial imaginary" of transnational
capitalism (Slaughter). Indeed, the documentary biography makes extraneous the
progressive attack on "the universalization of the nation-state," simply because

this "most desirable form of political community," coproduced through "modern European imperialism and third world nationalism," seems no longer psychologically desirable nor politically viable (Slaughter 42). When a liberal commitment to equality and justice through geopolitical sovereignty is yielding to neoliberal relations of interest and technologies of governmentality, whither "national allegory," whither *Bildungsroman*?

As a documentary of English pedagogy in contemporary China and the entrepreneurial education of Li Yang, *Crazy English* is the story of an inaugural Chinese subject forged out of the political triumph of an Anglo-American form of neoliberal capitalism and the domination of English as "the lingua franca of the TNC [transnational corporation] era."[6] The newness of this subject becomes truly fascinating if we recover a historical fact: the Anglophonic yet non-Anglo subject of capitalism is not a novel idea but the abortive dream of an earlier British imperialism in Capital's First Coming. On February 2, 1835, seven years prior to the British Armada's opening of Manchu China, Lord Thomas Babington Macaulay (1800–59), a member of the governing council of the East India Company (1834–38) and the Secretary of War (1839–41), delivered an infamous speech in the British Parliament. Known as the "Minute on Indian Education," it promoted English learning in the colony of India: "We must at present do our best to form . . . a class of persons, Indian in blood and colour, but English in taste, in opinions, in morals, and in intellect." Less well known, however, is the proselytization of English to the Chinese in the 1920s and '30s, decades after the Qing Dynasty's loss to Queen Victoria in Capital's First Coming to China. I.A. Richards, the English literary critic and linguist most renowned for the pioneering of "practical criticism," is the founder of the BASIC English education program. While there is no evidence that Li Yang is knowledgeable about Richards's evangelic efforts, his own brand of "Crazy English" has effectively amalgamated the acronymic elements of its predecessor, "*B*ritish, *A*merican, *S*cientific, *I*nternational, *C*ommercial" (Tong 338). The difference between the two is that Li has popularized English acquisition in China in scopes about which Richards could only fantasize. This comparison, however, is not about the Anglo-American debacle of the past and Chinese success at present. Rather, the excavation of Richards, Li's forerunner, serves a poignant reminder that linguistic and cultural conversions from outside China have been historically attempted, but these soft acts of imperialism – "cultural imperialism" in Tomlinson's coinage – are forestalled by ethnic recalcitrance either in the form of religious resistance or nationalist independence, or both. Such pedagogical projects as Macaulay's and Richards's are integral to the civilizing missions of earlier colonialism – liberalism's outer expression in Capital's First Coming, if you will. They are, in the wry felicity of Ngugi's phrasing, "the morning of the chalk and the blackboard" succeeding "the night of the sword and bullet" (quoted in Slaughter 121). Unlike liberalism's inner orientation in the classic *Bildungsroman*, which "consolidated a split between citizen and subject that, in Europe, the genre aimed to reconcile," "European civilizing colonialism [as liberalism's outer expression] persisted on the technical difference between citizens and subjects" (Slaughter 123–24). Subjecting the natives to the inculcation of English taste, opinion, and morals the Macaulay way is not to incorporate them as citizens of the empire, but to justify their subjugation in the teleology of capitalist progress within which the Anglophonic non-Anglo's subjectivation is always already deferred.

Richards's ill-fated endeavor to produce the Queen's colonial subject of BASIC English has to do with the incomplete domination of China by Euro-American powers. Contrary to colonial India, China has not been subject, except for the city of Hong Kong, to total territorial occupation, nor has it been subject to the linguistic hegemony of English integral to Anglo-American colonizing endeavors in the nineteenth and early twentieth centuries. Together, the history of China's semicolonialism, its communist-led nationalist independence, its ensuing political sovereignty hinged on a socialist economy, and a state-dictated collective subjectivity have come to account for the failure of liberal capitalism's first BASIC mission. However, it is precisely on account of this abortive annual that the heated ascent of "Crazy English" over and above the cold ashes of BASIC English betrays an unsurpassable aporia. It is in China's absolute political sovereignty and avid subordination to free market economy at Capital's Second Coming that we find the continuation of old colonialism in remarkable neoliberal clothing.

"The death of the West-for-itself" – here I borrow Serge Latouché's enigmatic sentence – "has not been the end of the West-in-itself" (3), for the passing of Richards is succeeded by Li Yang's rise, when the relay of the baton appears a global efficacy of the invisible hand. This is because "the West no longer means Europe, either geographically or historically"; it has become instead a "mad machine," "impersonal, soulless, and nowadays masterless, which has impressed mankind into its service" (Latouché 3). In this treatment of it as culturally abstracted and geopolitically deterritorialized from its historical moorings, the West begins to stand for an omnipresent world condition of capitalistic, industrial, urban, and rootless modernity (Ibid., xii). Indeed, the historical departure and renewal between Richards and Li confirms Latouché's insight that the successful spread of linguistic and economic systems from their European origins by non-European agents is a prevalent story of our time. Latouché enhances our understanding of the neoliberal specificity of Capital's Second Coming by noting the disintegration of the liberal state/citizen bind. When the materiality of the political and economic bind of a nation and its people is dissolving, the figurative analogy that holds its narration of subjectivity shall also fall apart. In this sense, *Crazy English* can no longer be "a national allegory" in the manner Jameson defines it and Ahmad disputes it. It does signal the arrival, though, of an allegory of "nationalitarianism," the conversion of nationalism as a feeling of territorial belonging into, as Latouché has it, "a process of constructing rootless mimetic states to manage [a global capitalist] economy" (xii).

Yet, Latouché's universalist framing of the neoliberal subject as "nowadays masterless" and faceless underestimates the history of Western capitalism and imperialism in relation to their colonial subjects and overlooks the "power geometry" in contemporary global capitalism (Latouché 3; Massey). He also seems insufficiently attentive to the age-old Euro-American proprietary claims to dominant linguistic and economic systems. It is incumbent upon us that we recognize that the worldwide dissemination of English and dispersal of capitalism do not necessarily dispel the historical dichotomy of center/margin and origin/copy that have buttressed liberalism's cultural distinction. Neoliberalism's global expansion and catholic claims have only intensified the contradiction of "the universal" and "the particular" in [old/historical] liberalism, when the non-European subjects of the English language and capitalist economy are now forced to regard themselves as being not quite "other" yet not quite "us" either. The new agents of phenotypical difference, in short, are subject to the teleology of identical progress while suffering from inadequate subjectivation. " 'Europe' remains the sovereign, theoretical subject of all histories, including the ones we call 'Indian,' 'Chinese,' 'Kenyan,' " as we recall Chakrabarty once more (27).

Crazy English tracks the problematics of the Chinese becoming an Anglophone subject of global capitalism, as it negotiates the contradictory struggle between the protagonist's identitarian and cultural claims. If *"Crazy English* with a Chinese face" suggests the process of reconstituting an indigenous subject through systems of language and economy alien to its origin, "a nationalitarian allegory" indicates the extent to which historical categories of culture and signs of value are redefined under the BASIC culture of neoliberal capitalism. Faithful to documentary biography's double charge of providing privileged access to empirically observable reality while dramatizing individual agency amid the demands of society, *Crazy English* informs the audience of a "China" as it confounds the very terms of its own representational intelligibility (Nichols 18–20).[7]

We shall clarify this confounding intelligibility by treating the aesthetic form of *Crazy English* as an abstract expression of postsocialist China's actual assimilation of both liberal and neoliberal capitalism. Yet, because it foregrounds at its beginning an interdependency between "narrative individualism and narrative nationalism," *Crazy English* appears at first glance a documentary biography in the guise of the original *Bildungsroman* (Slaughter 92). The story of Li Yang's rise seems simultaneously to be China's rise from the humiliation of its semicolonial history, economic underdevelopment, and abject poverty. While the text may invite this hermeneutic possibility, the narrative organization of the film as a whole, however, contradicts this reading at a deeper level and promises a richer and more exciting interpretive alternative. As we note, the film is made up of discrete scenes shot on location and sewn together in postproduction. Headlines are inserted on-screen both marking the geographical specificity of each episode and providing narrative causality for the protagonist's ceaseless ventures and tireless exhortations. If anything, *Crazy English* seems more a professional biography of Li than a personal one. Its coherence is achieved against the invisibility of familial and national histories of which the protagonist is a part, and it is realized in the hypervisibility of how Li independently fashions his professional life from being an enterprising student, to teacher, to a mogul of a commercial empire.

The film narrative does not emanate from a Bakhtinian dialogical imagination wherein the birth of the bourgeois subject is accomplished in and through the emergence of capitalist modernity (Slaughter 108). Instead, the documentary narrative is constituted monologically and episodically, determinedly against the spatiotemporal practices of Chinese socialism as well as the fable of the liberal subject and society. Li Yang's meteoric ascent is presented as immaculate conception without maternal gestation, be it by his biological mother or the PRC, his motherland. This simultaneous birth of the nation and the coming into maturity of the individual typical of *Bildungsroman*'s classic design in Capital's First Coming are not formative of *Crazy English*.

What is formative, however, are both the singularity of its documentary subject and the episodicity of its storytelling, formal features that promulgate the technologies of a neoliberal entrepreneurial subject against its historical others, be they Confucian, socialist, or Western liberal subjects. The singularity of Li as a nascent Chinese neoliberal subject is best evidenced in the episodic manner in which his life is plotted and his life story told. Granted, episodic narration is a historically significant feature of the *Bildungsroman*, whose secular and humanistic pattern allows for free and full character development without the strictures of predestined transcendental plots. "The generic sociological name for [the episodically chronological] plot is 'modernization,'" argues Slaughter, "the narrative pattern of European civilization's collective transition to modernity that repeat[s] itself in each life as the progressive manifestation of the human personality in time" (106–07). Since the *Bildungsroman* is a unique aesthetic mediation of political and economic liberalism, as we have learned, its plots to modernize the world and the individual are interrelated. "The individual narrative of self-formation is subsumed" by the *Bildungsroman*, in David Lloyd's incisive comment, "in the larger narrative of the civilizing process, the passage from savagery to civility, which is the master narrative of modernity" (134).

But this unalienable relationship between the individual narrative and the larger narrative of capitalist modernity is nowhere seen in *Crazy English*. All is not lost: the film biography unveils the articulation of a subjectivity that is resolutely independent of modernity's ideological claims while steadfastly adhering to modernity's instrumental reason. While a subjective interpellation with the nation-state, the enfolding of oneself through the unfolding of homogenous empty time is shown to be outdated, the incorporation of self-interest by the capitalist market becomes imperative. It is in this omission of the nation and selective retention of the principle of calculation, commodification, and competition that we find a global neoliberalization of both the Western liberal and the Chinese preliberal or socialist subjects. The divorce of liberalism's state/citizen binary is succeeded by the neoliberal arranged marriage of the consumer and the market.

Not surprisingly, the Mao-era political rallies and struggle sessions are replaced by Li's pedagogical rallies and self-motivational lessons. Here, the documentary subject's peripatetic and energetic performances already evidence an emergence of value as socially necessary labor time in China. Documentary episodicity thus reflects the ways in which time has been industrialized and instrumentalized, broken down into separate units and maximized for surplus value. It also reflects the spatiotemporal discipline of capitalism to which individuals are at present indentured in order to realize their desires as proper subjects. One could say that episodic production decollectivizes the Chinese socialist subject in its march toward the fulfillment of a glorious national destiny, just as it crucially enables an individualization of a neo-Chinese subject by tethering it to the mode of capitalist production. For Li the businessman, episodic production represents a continuous income stream. Giving lessons in small doses at regular intervals is the admitted "secret of his success": "we make them pay again and again and again" (quoted in Osnos 47). Watching Li from one teaching rally to another, the audience not only witness his dynamic reiterations of accumulation, but they also sense the internalization of a temporal discipline requisite for profitable subjectivation.

As each of Li's "Crazy English" shows pinpoints a particular location, be it the provincial city of Shaoyang or the global metropolis of Shanghai, documentary episodicity works also as a spatial approximation of the nation's geographic totality. Contrary to an identical socialist projection of Chinese spaces or the epic shot of the Fifth Generation signifying the collective ethos if not the spirit of the ethnos awakening from its historical trauma, the tiered rice paddy of Hunan Province and the glistening skyline on the Bund in *Crazy English* display a China in all its drastic developmental difference. This cinematic capture of social discrepancy is seized as a space for market mobilization. Unlike Mao's strategy of encirclement, wherein the wretched of the country shall surround and vanquish the metropolis in the process of bringing it forward to an egalitarian sameness and collective bliss, what Li Yang exemplifies is a reverse course of revolution in which the city shall incorporate the country in its civilizing and reforming mission. His successive ventures to the provinces emblemize a double movement of China's opening to global capital on the one hand, and of a Chinese coastal cosmopolitan conversion of the hinterland on the other. Very much like the theme of *River Elegy, Crazy English* idealizes the reiterative mobile Chinese subject of neoliberal capital as it denigrates the local Chinese subject as traditional, backward, parochial, and feudal. Departing from Mao's sanctioned hero, Lei Feng, a self-proclaimed cog in the socialist machine and a servant of the people, Li Yang brazenly fashions himself as an entrepreneurial paragon and an emissary of Capital's Second Coming.

Nowhere is this role more revealing than on his visit to Urumqi, the provincial seat of Xinjiang autonomous region of the Uighur, preaching the same gospel of English acquisition and wealth accumulation to the Chinese Muslims. In one of the film's most telling shots, we see Li Yang assembling a group of young and uniformed Uighur women in a public square covered with snow. Against the vehement protest of the ethnic women that he would catch cold, he threw off his overcoat, rolled up the sleeves of his turtleneck, and advised them to learn English with "passion." "No pain, no gain!" Dissolving to the next scene, the camera spotlights Li among a crowd of adoring Uighur children, chanting, "How are you?" under his gesticulating direction. The montage conveys, however unconsciously, a paternalistic Han tutelage of Uighur development very much reminiscent of the civilizing mission in Capital's First Coming. Li Yang's image performs an uncanny double displacement of identity in the double movement of global and coastal capital infusion. Since the Caucasian-looking Uighur are cast as willing converts to the BASIC culture of global capitalism of which Li has become

exemplary, he has by now gained a missionary and masculine authority historically reserved only for Euro-American modernizers.

This imagistic and gestural assumption of the "White man's burden" in Capital's Second Coming helps exorcise a latent anxiety of Anglo-American superiority, both conditioned by humiliating memories of past colonial and capitalist
conquests and triggered by Li's own manifest Han Chinese phenotype.[8] It evidences the opening possibility of capitalistic embodiment beyond ethnicity, in
a manner Latouché suggests, even if this means that Chinese subjects of Han
and Uighur origins alike shall live by the self-possessive entrepreneurial clock,
moving in a direction of capitalist modernity and teleological progress to which,
as Chakrabarty maintains, the West shall remain "sovereign" and the rest stay
inauthentic. While *Crazy English* seems to have disrupted the semantic chain of
race, nation, and capitalist modernity, what is also crucially missing, however, is
the coupling of the emergent bourgeois subject of rights and the rights-bearing
nation-state, typical of the classic *Bildungsroman*. In its absence from public
view, individual access to the markets has appeared to be the only legitimate time-
space of self-realization and freedom. While the name of the nation remains vital
and vibrant to Zhang Yuan's documentary biography, the nature of its existence
is being radically revised and the tokens of its evocation progressively privatized.

3

We are now ready to examine the various moments in *Crazy English* when Li
Yang fashions his entrepreneurial self by strategically deploying and transforming
extant nationalist, familialist, and civilizationalist discourses so that the cultural
logic of global capitalism is made thinkable, calculable, and realizable. Take for
example his refrain, "I love losing face / I welcome failures / I enjoy suffering / I
seek success." In its first cinematic citation, when Li leads a group jogging and
chanting in the street, this idiosyncratic motto is used as an inspirational narrative of individual exertion. The motto takes on an added significance in a
TIME interview, however, when a journalist inquired after Li's alleged antagonism toward Japan. His photo collection of the Japanese occupation of China
is to remind young people both of Japanese brutality and Chinese weakness, Li
argued, explaining that the recollection of historical shame could be an inspiration for national striving. The diffident learner of English and the defeated nation
in history are interlocked and invoked as though mirror images of each other. As
tempting as this correlation of individual fate with national destiny is for us to
regard *Crazy English* as yet another *Bildungsroman* or "national allegory," the
"nation" in the film no longer stands for collective welfare and social solidarity; it
is not a locus of affective investment but a site of economic competition. Patriotic
passion is stirred only by primitive accumulation, as Li Yang exhorts his audience
to abandon the myopia of local markets, "to teach English in Taiwan, Hong Kong,
Singapore, and Malaysia," and "to make money in the US, Europe, and Japan."

Li's call is an instance of discursive transfiguration: nationalism as geopolitical allegiance and affection is turned into "nationalitarianism," "a process of

constructing rootless mimetic states to manage economy" (Latouché xii). But this economization of emotion cannot be effective without a simultaneous and more substantive monetarization of filial piety, the Confucian belief and practice of parent–child bond and duty. In a lecture to the students of Qinghua University – the Chinese MIT, if you will – Li Yang confronts the crucial conflict between filial relationship and exchange relationship that the sudden introduction of capital in China has sharpened, while immediately dismissing it with a rhetorical sleight of hand.[9] "Making money is the biggest motivation to learn English," he preaches, while hastening to add, "it is also the best way to repay the debts to your parents." Within a single breath, Li has turned the instrumental logic of the bottom line into a prerequisite of individual and familial aspiration. "If you love your country, if you love your parents," he advises, "you'll love to study English well, study computer well, study international business well, and you'll make more money." The consummate example of fulfilling one's familial obligations becomes simply this: "Buy your parents a pair of open-jaw air-tickets and let them see the world."

This new interpretation of filial exercise signals Li's purposeful indigenization of market values still foreign to and fresh in China. As we recall, one major obstacle in the way of Mao's communist utopia is China's long history of feudalism, embodied by the patriarchal family and its Confucian structures of feeling hinged on reproductive lineage. To modernize and revolutionize it has meant a requisite transformation of filial piety. By detaching the loyalty originally circulating between parents and children and displacing it through mechanisms of transference onto the socialist state, epitomized by none other than the father of the nation, Mao hopes to pave way both for the eventual abolition of the private biological family and the realization of communism. In this vision, Chinese socialism marks the progressive stage above and beyond the residual filial structures of binding as well as the emergent structures of social affiliation based on communal belonging. Where Mao's success in bringing about a psychosocial transition from "filiation" to "affiliation" through political movements to an anticipated communist solidarity seems partial at best, Li Yang appears more ambitious in his project of changing the Chinese habits of the heart.[10] Ostensibly, the love of country and the love of one's progenitors have nothing to do with the love of money. The love of money can indeed impede the spontaneous overflow of more altruistic affects, if not running directly counter to the natural affection for land and lineage, roots and rootedness. Yet, as we witness in his pitch, Li Yang is revising both the subject's ascribed filial attachment to the natural family and his/her acquired affiliation with the state, be it socialist or liberal capitalist. The primordial feelings for the family and the nation are to be transubstantiated through his neoliberal proselytization into an inordinate passion for absolute abstract value. The cult of Mao is to be vanquished by the cult of gold.

One hears in this an argumentative echo of Reaganomics and Thatcherism as well as Deng Xiaoping's social vision in the new Chinese grain: patriotic and parental dedication is best exercised through the subjective securing of entrepreneurial skills and the objective enhancement of individual economic well-being (Rose 145).[11] The productive tension within the state/citizen bind that has long sustained nationalism, be it the liberal or the socialist kind, that Nikolas Rose describes as "the conflict between the self-interest of the economic subject and the patriotic duty of the citizen," seems to have miraculously disappeared with Li Yang's repetitive incitement (144). Its disappearance in nationalitariansm is at best make-believe, of course, for the contradiction between the self and society is historically irresolvable. What Li's rhetoric shows, however, is a successful revision of sound liberal sense by precisely a displacement of this productive tension. In other words, neoliberalism is able to cultivate a seductive appearance "that one can best fulfill one's obligations to one's nation by most effectively pursuing the enhancement of the economic well-being of oneself" (Ibid.). Such is the magic of neoliberal "governmentality" in a nutshell: it actively reconceives the state and subject relationship as "the relation between self and self" (Gordon 2). In Li Yang's particular translation, to love your country, to love your parents, is to love making more money: being self-serving in the English language has surely gained a crazy significance.

Li's strategy looks especially cunning if we recognize the sediments of history upon which he builds his empire of surplus value. Although British guns opened the borders of the Qing Dynasty in the mid-nineteenth century, enforcing "free trade," the capitalist form of circulation was prevented from domination in China by indigenous social structures that obstinately prioritize the welfare of society over economy, very much like Polanyi's description of precapitalist UK. While often attributed to the victory of communist-led nationalist independence, the debacle of Capital's First Coming in China in fact owes to its own inability to surmount the intense barriers of traditional Chinese society and family. After all, "MCM," the famous cycle from money to commodity and back to money, encapsulates Marx's simple yet elegant definition of capital: "Money as the beginning and end point of a distinctive circulation process [is] called capital" (Harvey, 2010, 77). The great wall of China that withstood the batter of foreign guns and commodities was not the prominent earthwork that American astronauts on the moon first spotted; it was instead the invisible and perhaps inscrutable cycle of indigenous resistance, "FMF," the circulation of money from family to family, if you will, that subordinates the currency of material exchange to a mere means in service of the ultimate end of social cohesion. As draconian and devastating as the cult of Mao was, the cult of money in capital as a system freed from the value system shall have far more disastrous effects on social and natural relations. Li's entrepreneurial exhortations are incorporating the logic of MCM to enervate the historical sinew of FMF that communist brainwashing has not been able to debilitate. By juxtaposing such different emotions as patriotism, familial allegiance, and material greed as though they were equivalent and interchangeable, Li Yang is able to change age-old aversions into newfound attachments. The traditional inhospitality to the accumulation of wealth for individual gain is transubstantiated – in the modest proposal of purchasing international flights for your parents – into a laudable form of filial piety for sale. Money is consequently mobilized and turned into a universal currency of capital circulation, where payments made in kind will have to be made from now on in money.

Not that money is a novelty in China – among the sensational news Marco Polo brought back to thirteenth-century Europe was the Chinese use of paper money – but

Li Yang's air tickets for parents betray money's increasing instrumentality in everyday practice. As a universal medium of absolute exchange, money empties the personal content of love and labor by substituting for them an impersonal standard and abstract value. Not only are gestures of care and concern separated from a palpable sociality of complex encumbrance, tangible personal involvement in affairs of the kinship network are minimized and recalibrated within a convenient cash nexus. As a result, the immediacy and immutability of generational interdependency central to filial feelings is invalidated by the impersonal balance sheet of debt and credit. If we follow Georg Simmel, that "a money transaction implies no commitment," Li Yang's proposal of purchasing travel packages as payment of one's existential dues eventually extricates the offspring from the necessity to maintain and "mediate [filial] relationships that require and assume durability" (Poggi 140). Just when the ancient Chinese ideal of unquantifiable generational devotion gets a second life, it is being rearticulated into a new law of quantifiable transaction, compressed and complete, presumably in a single and terminal settlement.

This revised transactional logic of filial intercourse also informs the film's own economy of representation. In the manner that an open-jaw ticket displaces the progenitors by sending them off literally and figuratively on a plane, the documentary achieves the same effect through cinematic elision of the parental image. Although the name of the father is occasionally mentioned, the figure of the father is strikingly absent in *Crazy English*. As a matter of fact, Li Yang's own mother and father are nowhere seen on the screen. Here, the verbal acknowledgment of his parents has substituted for a visual validation of his ancestral origins, making possible the emptying of space – the ascribed, involuntary, and ineluctable social conditions of one's ontology – and the emptying of time, the genealogical, ecological, and sociological time of reproductive continuity. With this ancestral absence in the documentary biography, Li Yang is practically turned into a blank slate of self-invention, lifted out from the dense web of filial affects, wiped clean of generational encumbrance, and liberated finally as a sovereign individual for the open market of endless entrepreneurialism. As such, the ancestral failure to achieve visibility proves crucial to the documentary's deconstruction of "generation" as a generative structure of film narrative and mise-en-scène; it facilitates the episodic construction of the individualistic protagonist as though in a typical Western road movie, at once authorizing a new Chinese documentary biography and a neoliberal subject with Chinese characteristics.[12] Similar to Max Weber who rationalizes the rise of Western capitalism by locating its origin in the secularization of Calvinism, Li Yang's aphorism, "making money is the best way to repay the debts to your parents," is able to make the gospel of gold not only imaginable in the grammar of native culture but also totally justifiable in postsocialist China.

4

True to his claim, Li's proselytizing of English represents a project much more extensive than foreign language acquisition alone. "Crazy English" is a program of linguistic pedagogy, life philosophy, and even cognitive therapy, whose ultimate goal is, in Li's own phrase, to "reform Chinese personality." "Gaizhao," the phrase Li adopts in his Qinghua University interview, literally means to rebuild, which dovetails unmistakably with the state's agenda of "Gaige," or economic reform. This linguistic congruence in the political and personal call for reform does not, however, indicate a conscious alliance between the state and civil society, even though the Chinese government's accommodation of neoliberal capital would be unimaginable without endeavors like Li's that are bent on the psychosocial adjustments of ex-socialist subjects.[13] What astounds us is not the newness of this agenda to transform Chinese mind and body but its historical persistence. Li is remarkably oblivious that the Qinghua University in which he advocates his reform was where I. A. Richards founded "The Orthological (Basic English) Institute of China" in the mid-1930s (Tong 336). It is through that institute, under the direction of an American, R. D. Jameson, that Richards's *First Book of English for Chinese Learners* is published. Besides, it is through its lobby of the Chinese Ministry of Education that Richards's project finds its way into the ministry's "resolution," which mandates, along with the general objective of secondary English education in China, "[t]he modernization of *expressional habits* with regard to *thought, outlook, attitude, [and] feeling*" (Tong 336–37, italics mine). Besides the correction of faulty speech and undesirable behavior, this orthological operation launched from 1930s China is meant to institute, as Richards envisions it in *Nations and Peace*, a "geolinguistic unity" necessary for the constitution of a "World Government," whose burden "rests finally on the steel shoulders of the British and American fleets" (Ibid. 344–45, 346).

From the inculcation of language to the modification of outlook and feeling to conquest via military might for an Anglo-American hegemony, one witnesses a naked vision of global domination in Richards, which appears totally irreconcilable with his other image of an English gentleman, a benevolent pedagogue, and a harmless wordsmith. Such contradiction prompts Tong to justify in his otherwise critically perceptive essay on Richards's ideological innocence. In this context of interpretation, the insights of *Culture and Imperialism* have become especially timely and cogent: just as metropolitan culture can hardly elude the spell of empire building, Edward Said states, its intellectuals are always complicit in the exercise of imperial power. Notably, Richards's geolinguistic and geopolitical ambitions are both concealed and elaborated in the diplomatic cunning of Churchill who, upon receiving his honorary degree at Harvard in 1943, at once endorses the program of Basic English and speaks of the "common tongue" as a priceless "foundation of common citizenship," a "gain to us far more durable and fruitful than the annexation of great provinces" (Ibid. 346).

Although history does not follow the straight trajectory of Anglo-American triumph, as decolonization disrupts Richards's disciplinary design of an imperial world government, a neoliberal governmentality more seductive does emerge half a century later to annex the mind and body of wider populace in greater provinces. In this global hegemony without the appearance of external imposition, though the fleets, missiles, and drones are always available should voluntary allegiance to it fail, Richards's basic "modernization of expressional habits" eases seamlessly into Li's crazy methodology of "three superlatives: shouting the loudest, talking the fastest, enunciating the clearest."[14] Volume, speed, and clarity are the new gauges of linguistic competence as well as psychological confidence. Above all, they are indicators of an assertive and efficient style of exchange gone normative and sets of acquirable skills necessary as well for submissive subjects of the former socialist state to successfully metamorphose into competent subjects of borderless capital. "In order for the voice of China be heard all over," Li Yang advises his audience, they must "re-condition the Chinese style muscles." According to Li, American muscles are notoriously "stiff"; instead, the Chinese should tone theirs into "flexible" "international muscles."[15]

Such racialization of culture through the comparative merits of Chinese and American muscles is indicative of residual or resurgent nationalist sentiments in globalization. It is especially evocative of debates in the 1980s over the relative strengths of culture-particular capitalisms, when the disappearance of the Eastern communist bloc and the emergence of robust East Asian tiger economies made both the capitalistic mode of production palpably global and its local contestations inevitable. The revival of Confucianism from the peripheries of the historical Sinic center (mainland China), that is, the North American and (South)East Asian academic staging of what is later known as neo-Confucian discourses, is a case in point.

As Joel Kotkin observes, the neoliberalist makeover has led to a new "multiracial world order," "running along the British-American tracks of market capitalism," in which "the Calvinist tribe" acts rather indistinguishably from the "Confucian tribe" (256). Kotkin's emphasis on indistinguishability suggests a universalization of a neoliberal tribe that subsumes the particular ethnicity of its subjects. The Japanese, Chinese, and Indians are simply "new Calvinists" who, while "driven by unique histories and ethnicities of their own," "either choose or were forced to accept as their channel of expression the global ethnicity of Anglo-Americans – even to the point of adopting English, now the idiom of technological rationality" (A. Liu 66). For Alan Liu, Kotkin's contribution lies in his recognition that "corporate globalism *is* ethnic" (Ibid.). The historical meanings of ethnicity, of ethnos standing for a nation and a people and of *ethnicus* standing for an alterity or a unique mode of human existence, are collapsed in Kotkin, because for him global capitalism has in the totality of its "institutions, methods, ethics, and language" constituted its distinctive way of being and living – its own ethnicity, so to speak – that is now inclusive of people of different national origins (Ibid.). Neoliberal capitalism at the closing decades of the twentieth century was but an "ethnicity at large": it has transcended its locality in Anglo-America to become a true new world order, embraced and practiced as a way of life by Asian and Anglo subjects alike.[16]

While Kotkin is correct in highlighting the emergence of a universal identity in everyday practice, so much so that subjects from around the world are being denationalized in their economic behavior, he cannot possibly explain the concurrent "construction of social action around primary identities, either ascribed, rooted in history and geography or newly built in an anxious search for meaning and spirituality" (Castells 22). The ascent of neo-Confucian discourse demonstrates that the very dynamic of Capital's Second Coming does not follow Kotkin's friction-free developmental trajectory toward the eventual erasure of identity as such. Contrarily, it is only when global capitalism is leveling out actual alternatives of experiencing time and space that an irresistible urge of cultural distinction begins to proliferate. In the sense that the intensification of capital, informational, and imagistic flows makes universal this particular quest for "the increasingly fine-grained modes of identity presentation," neo-Confucianism enacts the two-fold process of globalization, that is, "the particularization of the universal and the universalization of the particular" (Robertson 177–78).

Not paradoxically, neo-Confucianism becomes a form of two-pronged neo-Orientalism. Like Ahmad's position that we covered earlier, neo-Orientalism rejects, in its determined universalizing move, old Orientalism's exclusion of the Asian in the construction of capitalist modernity. Yet, unlike Ahmad's position, it accepts with an equally determined will particularizing old Orientalism's geopoliticization of cultural differences. Hence, we find neo-Confucianism's vociferous charge against Max Weber's conclusion of Chinese incompatibility with the spirit of capitalism and its equally vehement retention of civilizational dichotomy, except that the East now proffers a better version of capitalism. In this neo-Orientalist self-identification and self-differentiation, neo-Confucianism serves as an evocative form of "cultural nationalism," which, in endowing East Asian capitalism with an apparent ethnic-specific contour, attempts to simultaneously assimilate "the dynamic force in the development of capitalism" and absorb "the disruptive effects of capitalist development" (Dirlik 115). In this particular manner, the cultural nationalist sentiment of neo-Confucianism is perhaps best apprehended in Latouché's concept of nationalitarianism that we encountered previously, which nominally retains the figure and feeling of the mimetic states to ensure the energetic local running of the global market. The crucial question of whether it is indeed materially feasible to counteract the negative impact of development and sustain substantive cultural difference in an identical practice of neoliberal capitalism, however, remains conveniently unanswered in neo-Confucian discourses. What the contradiction of neo-Confucianism betrays is therefore the reality that relations of antagonism between the universal and the particular, whether of regions or groups, "continue to articulate themselves on the model of 'national identities' (rather than in terms of social class)" despite actual transnational economic and cultural convergence (Jameson, 1998, xii).[17]

5

It is to director Zhang Yuan's credit that *Crazy English* takes up the central challenge of the universal and the particular within the discourse of neo-Confucianism as a fundamental problem of documentary figuration. If neo-Confucianism intends to valorize an East Asian participation in the Second Coming of Capital it is because the abstract representation of universal capitalism has always presumed a Euro-American contour and core, precluding its potential assumption of a specific Asian form. By zeroing in on Li Yang's "internationalization of Chinese muscles," Zhang makes visible a popular cultural version of academic and philosophical neo-Confucianism and probes its performative effects. His lens shows how Li's explicit evocation of the putative difference in American, Chinese, and international muscles has both made accessible a particular Chinese figuration of neoliberal capitalism and made its abstract law of cutthroat competition comprehensible for his mass audience.

In one of the film's most memorable scenes, Li Yang summons up Steve on the Qinghua stage. A balding Caucasian in his sixties, Li's American sidekick, Steve, is the Ed McMahon to Li's Johnny Carson, serving primarily to authenticate Li's brand of Crazy English on his traveling shows.[18] That day, however, rather than quieting the audience before Li's star entrance, Steve is asked to speak a few words of Chinese. Initially, none of the students comprehend Steve's Sinophonic hem and haw. Upon Li Yang's orthographical translation of Steve's intended pronunciation, however, the audience roars with laughter. Tellingly, the scene enacts at the level of visual economy the documentary's representational revision that the onset of a global capitalist economy has set in motion. It shows how "ways of seeing" within and without *Crazy English*'s documentary frame, to use the titular phrase of Berger's classic study, both correspond and contradict historical relations of power. In this specific encounter, Li Yang and his Chinese audience have become active agents of looking while the American Steve is being looked at. With his calculated comic performance, Li has flexed his reformed Chinese muscles and scored the significance of international muscles in more ways than one. Besides being the butt of a language joke, however benign and humorous, Steve has become an example of stiff American muscles in neoliberalism and an object lesson of someone whose adaptation in the new transnational economy appears embarrassingly arrested. A shift in spectatorial perspective betokens a shift in subject position, as the documentary eye/I reconstitutes the structures of gaze that have informed "the imperial eyes" (Pratt).

However, we cannot fully appreciate the significance of this spectatorial shift until calling forth two crucial historical encounters, a Chinese and an African American encounter with the same Japanese contestation of European imperialism. The principal subjects of these two transracial and transnational contacts are Lu Xun, father of modern Chinese literature, and W. E. B. Du Bois, cofounder of the NAACP and forerunner of the African American tradition; their shared context is the Japanese military triumph over Czarist Russia in 1904. Although there is a considerable temporal gap between the era of the Russo-Japanese War and that of the post–Cold War, I juxtapose the scenes in the First and Second Comings of Capital in order to give the local drama at the Qinghua auditorium a historical depth of vision. I shall review the scenes as divergent historical sites/sights of subject formation, with particular attention to mechanisms of visual spectacle, somatic scheme, and psychic identification.

Lu Xun's narrative about his abandoning the pursuit of medicine for the calling of the pen is legendary.[19] Equally illuminating is the juxtaposition he makes between his personal attainment of Western medicine and China's acquisition of

Western modernity. Because "Japanese Reformation owed its rise to the introduction of Western medical science to Japan," Lu Xun recalls, it fired his dream to "cure patients like [his] father[,] while . . . promoting [his] countrymen's faith in reform" upon his return to China (34). Like a proper bourgeois subject for the classic *Bildungsroman*, Lu Xun carves out the course of his individual development along with the trajectory of developing China's national strength. However, his ambitious pursuit of medicine experiences a radical shift at the sight of a summary execution. "[O]ne day," he writes,

> I saw a news-reel slide of a number of Chinese, one of them bound and the rest standing around him. They were all sturdy fellows but look completely apathetic. According to the commentary, the one with his hands bound was a spy working for the Russians who was to be beheaded by the Japanese military as a warning to others, while the Chinese beside him had come to enjoy the spectacle.
>
> (Ibid. 35)

Through the complex processes of sighting, Lu Xun is hit with an epiphany: "The people of a weak and backward country, however strong and healthy they might be could only serve to be made examples of or witnesses of such futile spectacles" (Ibid.). "The most important thing," he concludes, "was to change their spirit" (Ibid.).

This resolution for a revolution of the spirit appears anything but the shock effect of a spectacular cinematic mediation. It is in the presence of his fellow Japanese spectators, looking at the documentary representation of his Chinese compatriots looking at one of their own decapitated by Japanese soldiers that Lu Xun comes to privilege the reform of the Chinese mind over the healing of the Chinese body. The (in)voluntary and unanticipated change of vocation by Lu Xun reveals itself as a contradictory process of visual identification and disavowal, both reminiscent and transcendent of Du Bois's famous formulation of "double consciousness." The shock of virulent beheading, in other words, performs a double duty of dismembering and re-membering. The documentary spectacle unsettles Lu Xun's status as a private spectator among the Japanese audience so that his public identification as a Chinese citizen appears inevitable. While the dawning awareness of his Chinese exposure betrays a shared "two-ness" with which Du Bois delineates the African American subject – "this sense of always looking at one's self through the eyes of [dominant] others" (3) – Lu Xun's Chinese identification under Japanese eyes nevertheless complicates Du Bois's dichotomous and stable constitution of colonial subjectivity. As is evident in his autobiographical narration, Lu Xun's sense of estrangement is not a permanent condition of the visible but a contingent self-awareness of losing his ethnic anonymity. Unlike the black and white epidermal dichotomy that preoccupies Du Bois, the racial difference between the Chinese and the Japanese in the case of Lu Xun in specific and among East Asians in general is not an apparent matter of phenotypical distinction.[20] It is the becoming of a spectacular object of victimization from the original position of an innocent subject of gaze that triggers both Lu Xun's self-willed excommunication from the Japanese spectators in the theater and his imaginary identification with a Chinese collective helplessly persecuted on the screen. One can contend with reasonable conviction that there is no national (self)consciousness or Chinese-ness until it is crystallized in colonial contact at the moment of categorical crisis.

But Lu Xun's is a contradictory national identification that disavows an epidermal unity of the race. In fact, it entails a simultaneous rejection of the actual national body and projection of its ideal form. Both the pathological body of his father and the "sturdy" yet "apathetic" bodies that bear witness to the execution are for Lu Xun signs of Chinese physical decay and spiritual stupor. Chinese individual and national redemption can be achieved neither by acquiring Western medicine through Japanese mediation nor by imitating the Japanese reproduction of Western imperialism. It is only through the awakening of the power of Chinese letters that a materialization of a vigorous modern body politic and a vital spirit of the Chinese nation can become possible. Lu Xun's faith in reform expresses itself as a willing subscription to the Western and modern political constitution of the nation-state. His *Call to Arms* is a concomitant narration of the nation and transubstantiation of the individual within it. The spectacle of a Chinese death in the hands of the Japanese only heralds the psychic projection of a nation's birth in which the new Chinese subject finds somatic sublimation.[21]

"The Russo-Japanese War has marked [a rather different] epoch" for Du Bois, however. Instead of signifying the trauma of impending colonization of the Chinese, it is seen from the refracted and racialized perspective of Du Bois as a triumph of the colored people. "For the first time in a thousand years," he declares ecstatically in *Collier's Weekly*, "a great white nation has measured arms with a colored nation and been found wanting" (Mullen and Watson 34). Troubled by the "territorial, political, and economic expansion" of the West yet compelled by the prevalent racialist interpretation of culture in his time, Du Bois seizes the event as a symbolic redrawing of "the hegemony of civilization," celebrating at once the shattering of "the magic of the word 'white'" and "the cross[ing of] the Color Line" (Ibid. 33–34). In his willful desire for Afro-Asian unity, however, Du Bois falls knee-jerk fashion into the trap of imperial identification and colonial competition. Not only does he uncritically submit himself to an essentialist and hierarchical vision of civilization marked by a gradualist ascent through the color line – "The awakening of the yellow races is certain. That the awakening of the brown and black races will follow in time" – but he also seems unmindful of the dangerous realignment of the imperialist world order by monopoly capitalism of the time (Ibid. 34). This tinted look of civilizational struggle among the races on a unidirectional track of capitalistic development will lead to his conspicuous condoning of Japanese atrocity in China decades later. "It is to escape annihilation and subjection and the nameless slavery of Western Europe," Du Bois writes, "that Japan has gone into a horrible and bloody carnage with her own cousin," eventually blaming the predatory violence of the Japanese against its Asian neighbors on "the encroachment of racist and imperialist ideals onto Asia by the West" (Ibid. 90, xvii). Although not entirely insensitive to the brutality of Japanese imperialism and the capitalist colonial rivalry of his day, Du Bois is helplessly blinded by his romantic dream of a colored world coalition. It is this fantasy of the colored counterbalance to global white power and this sacrificial vision of the colored part for the colored whole that provide him with a critical alibi for the conquest by the consanguineous of the consanguineous, while leaving the rapacious and homicidal nature of colonialism and capitalism unscathed.[22]

6

Fast-forward to the contemporary scene of Li Yang and Steve at Qinghua University. Here, Lu Xun's nationalist sublimation and Du Bois's anticolonialist inversion of colored coalition help us revisit the persistent problem of colonial and postcolonial identification. Besides bringing to mind classic scenes of colonial pedagogy – be it Crusoe and Friday, or Mr. Higgins and Eliza – Li Yang's instruction on Steve's Chinese as well as Steve's role as his teaching assistant of English appear an inversion of the political and economic hierarchy built on centuries of Euro-American hegemony.[23] If "the epistemological foundation of colonial psychology was the political unconscious of the family romance, the relation between the child and its parents," it is hard not to detect *Crazy English*'s framing of Li Yang and Steve as a restaging of that romance (Kuan-Hsing Chen 8). The scene in Qinghua could even be potentially read as a Du Boisian reiteration in that the Chinese are apparently following the Japanese in the game of capitalist development and colonial domination. Here, the formerly "colonized [and colored] subjects" are no longer "poor in linguistic expression" or "lacking the capacity of clear conceptualization": they seem instead to have given up "their ancestors' superstition" and forsaken the belief in "supernatural powers and fatalism" (Ibid.). Nonetheless, the documentary's revision of colonial power relations is coupled concomitantly with the camera's crucial identification with the spirit of capital, which, in the unforgettable words of Marx, "has pitilessly torn asunder the motley feudal ties that bound man to his 'natural superiors,' and has left remaining no other nexus between man and man than naked self-interest" (Tucker 475). If Du Bois and Lu Xun seek to have their parochial subjects interpellated into the imagined community of race and nation, Zhang Yuan has situated his protagonist squarely in the terrain of the competitive marketplace. As a result, the documentary mise-en-scène of Steve and Li Yang becomes a family romance with a difference. As symptomatic of the geopolitical economy of neoliberal capital, it has significantly recast the Chinese romance of filial piety and national sovereignty into an ecumenical romance of Oedipal revolt suited for the proliferation of capital.

In this neoromance, what binds the generations ascriptively and vertically is expected to dissolve and make way for horizontal affiliations not so much in the image of an ethnic or national solidarity with roots and boundaries, but in the spirit of soaring self-interests. Having already dispatched his birth parents on a plane and offscreen, and thus achieved the kind of adult maturity so ordained in the *Bildungsroman* of liberal imagination, it is only natural for Li Yang to proceed with yet another symbolic patricide of his adoptive father, whose language he has mastered and whose flexibility he finds wanting. The shot of the Li Yang and Steve dyad is less a scene of anticolonialist pedagogy for the welfare of the people than a scene of cutthroat capitalist swashbuckling. But in observing *Crazy English*'s narrative orientation toward patricidal progress, one is also struck by its image of linguistic and visual incongruity. In fact, the camera manifests a mixed metaphor that profoundly frustrates an unambiguous identification of ethnic and cultural lineage. If Steve signifies the origin of the English language and the fountainhead of Anglo-American capitalism, Li Yang suffers from an ineluctable crisis of legitimacy, for given his ubiquitous Chinese face he cannot claim heir to either. For all the practical reasoning of kinship, Li simply does not resemble Steve physically to be his true "son," therefore given license in his Oedipal disavowal of the patriarch. On the other hand, by capturing the elder Steve and the younger Li side by side, the documentary camera has incorporated them in an emblematic frame of the father/son and its unmistakable trope of the generations. The youthful and robust Li and the aging and flabby Steve lend themselves suggestively to a neo-Orientalist vision of the East's rise and the West's decline, the denouement of an "American Century" and the dawn of "China's Century."[24]

Regardless of the particular embodiment of the progenitor and progeny, universal succession is justified in this discursive formation so that the capitalistic cycle of boom and bust continues in perpetuity, replacing in importance the cycle of natural reproduction and conservation, be it the species or the environment. Consequently, what matters in the transcendent life of the capital is no longer the specificity of its subject or agent: everyone is eminently disposable and nothing is truly personal. Although the cinematic dyad of Li and Steve appears to rekindle the story of civilizational clash, racial rivalry, and national striving to which Du Bois and Lu Xun have succumbed, Li's paternal displacement of Steve is ultimately unhinged from those older and grander narratives and their corresponding subjectivities. His story is not so motivated by the cultural fantasy of communal encumbrance and transcendence, which entails an attachment between the little self and the large social body, their allegorical mediation, disciplinary surveillance, and spiritual subsumption; it is instead determined by the logic of natural selection, of the naturalness of individual competition and social disaggregation, and of the desirability of getting ahead individually by elimination of all adversaries. When the laws of social Darwinism are held up by contemporary cultures of both Christian and Confucian historical origins, and practiced through the interdependent market of global production and consumption, the actual differences in the conception of civilizational, national, or personal "goods" disappear, except in appearance.

Crazy English both documents and demonstrates the extent to which Anglo-American neoliberal capitalism has turned China inside out: the nation has had a drastic turnabout from its socialist past and the people are becoming turncoats. Fluent in English, vigorous in image, cosmopolitan in outlook, competitive and commercial to the bone, Li Yang seems at once a specific embodiment and a spectral fulfillment of I.A. Richards's BASIC design. His bilingual agility and facile

handling of "cheap American labor" (as he jokingly referred to Steve) have qualified him to be what Aihwa Ong calls the "flexible citizen" in what Thomas Fried-
man has named, all too euphorically and quite erroneously in my view, "the flat
world."[25] Not that this construction of the elite and border-transcending subject
is either easily transferable to the masses or desirable for the world as a whole.
Zhang Yuan has nonetheless projected Li Yang as an image of such subjective possibility with which his Chinese documentary audience is encouraged to identify.

As early as the late nineteenth century, Marx pointed out in *Capital* that the
manipulation of production necessitates the modification of individual conduct. A
century later, Foucault picked up this insight and ran with it. The transition from
one form of production to another, he argues, entails not only "acquiring certain
skills" but also "certain attitudes" through which "an individual acts upon himself, in the technology of the self" (18–19). The Reagan-Thatcher-Deng Xiaoping
Revolution has remade the world with a new mode of governmental rationality as
well as a new technology of the self. On the one hand, neoliberal governmentality
rejects the incumbent duty of society or state to secure the conditions of the individual citizen/subject's thriving. On the other hand, it promulgates an economic
individualism that exhorts the will to self-actualize in a supposed self-regulating
free market. *Crazy English* seems a documentary biography that perfectly performs the process of this technological self-enactment, this willing reformation
of the Chinese mind, and this aggressive retoning of the Chinese muscle. Li Yang
seems but a shining specimen of the new subject of endless entrepreneurialism,
who no longer depends on the body politic for safety and security but seeks indi-
vidualistically to "maximize his quality of life through the artful assembly of a
life style" strung together with an ever-expanding variety of commodities and
services (Miller and Rose 329). From behind the Chinese face of *Crazy English*
a flattened psyche has finally loomed large in the neoliberal world order, at once
haunting and troubling our imagination.[26]

Notes

1 Without reference to Polanyi, who first locates the shift from society to economy in the
rise of industrial capitalism, Foucault offers the following:

> It was through the development of the science of government that the notion of
> economy came to be recentered on to that different plane of reality which we char-
> acterize today as the "economic," and it was also through this science that it became
> possible to identify problems specific to the population; but conversely we can say
> as well that it was thanks to the isolation of that area of reality that we call economy,
> that the problem of government finally came to be thought, reflected and calculated
> outside of the juridical framework of sovereignty.
>
> (Burchell, Gordon, and Miller 99)

Helpful as a seminal concept to apprehend the neoliberal governmental rationality,
Foucault's antisovereign conception of governmentality overlooks the changed nature
of the state in the era of global capitalism. It is not the disappearance of sovereignty but
its definitional departure from the liberal ideal of social contract and its constitutive bond
with "the people" or "citizenry" that bestows the governmental art of neoliberalism its

unique characteristics. Namely, the neoliberal state has become primarily the servant of capital whose logic of perpetual growth demands governmental deregulation and discipline as well as the self-regulation and self-discipline of the new *Homo economicus*.

2 See Chris Berry on the postsocialist Chinese documentary form. The documentary is a favorite form of the Urban Generation of Chinese filmmakers (Z. Zhang), whose aesthetic characteristics of handheld camera, antiglamour and antigloss rendition, and focus on the social margin tend to infuse such works as Zhang Yimou's feature *Not One Less* (1999), Li Yang's *Blind Shaft* (2003), and nearly the entirety of Jia Zhuangke that are dramatic features by definition. The stylistic roughness and philosophical determinism of these films seem redolent of European and American literary naturalism in the late nineteenth and early twentieth centuries. It is as though monopoly capital of the Gilded Age has been reincarnated a century later, when rapid industrialization and urbanization dominate Capital's Second Coming in scales unimaginable in the First. A naturalistic Chinese cinema has emerged as an aesthetic response in its wake.

3 "The Newer, New Humanity" was first coined in the mid-1990s in Taiwan, according to Liu Kang, but soon spread to the mainland. They "consist of middle-class Internet and e-commerce specialists, cartoon- and disco-loving generation, McDonalds, Coca Cola, tele-marketing, independent workers, avant-garde artists," "transforming the old values of life" to "fulfill the goal of more humane and self-pleasing existence" (205).

4 Although Jameson cites *Anti-Oedipus* in this essay, neither does he acknowledge nor do his critics point out his indebtedness to Deleuze and Guattari's other influential text, *Kafka: Toward a Minor Literature*. The tenor between Jameson's definition of "third-world literature" and the French theorists' characterization of "minor literature" is so similar that I quote the latter: "The three characteristics of minor literature are the deterritorialization of language, the connection of the individual to a political immediacy, and the collective assemblage of enunciation" (Deleuze and Guattari 18). For follow-up assessment of the Jameson/Ahmad controversy, see Szeman.

5 Although the socialist revolution in China is the context against which he makes his allegorical claims, Jameson draws exclusively and extensively from the father of Chinese literary modernism, Lu Xun. Besides generating debates in *Social Text*, Jameson's work on culture in multinational capitalism also spawns the special issue of *boundary 2* on "Postmodernism and China" (Dirlik and Zhang).

6 It is Lawrence Mitchell who identifies Anglo-American capitalism as the dominant mode of global capitalism over "Rhinish capitalism," while Masao Miyoshi specifically calls English the common language for the era of transnational corporations (90).

7 Despite the director's love–hate relationship toward his subject (M. Berry 152), *Crazy English* neither evidences such adversarial tension formally nor betrays signs of a "reflexive documentary," which questions its own truth-telling and typically contradicts "the truth" with an inclusion of multiple voices. *Crazy English* belongs more properly to the "observational mode [of documentary film]," as Zhang's lens appears mostly an unobtrusive recording of Li's action, reflecting Li's ideological inclinations. The reflexive and observational modes of documentary film are terms from Nichols (32–33).

8 The Urumqi sequence begins with Li posing for celebrity shots with local people at the bazaar and his correction of a Uighur man's "uncertain" and "soft" English pronunciation. My reading suggests that the neoliberal transformation of the subject always entails a reiteration of racial and gender hierarchies of old colonialism. Li's idolization by his Uighur audience betrays a Sinocentric slant of the documentary, which also conceals the deep local ambivalence toward the Second Coming of Capital. As Rob Gifford writes, although the Uighur Muslims consider the Han Chinese as "agents of this modernization," they realize as well that "it is not just Sinification that is going on, it is globalization" (263).

9 It is worth noting the Chinese phrase, "Qinghua," as in Qinghua University, literally means "purely or clearly Chinese." I highlight the ironic effect of this name and the

physical site to call attention not only to the impossibility of purity in contemporary global cultural flows but also to the university's historical significance as the seat of student revolution and national resistance.

10 The terms filiation and affiliation in this paragraph are from Edward Said: see in particular 18–20 and 174–77.

11 The successful production of the neoliberal subject is evident in the rise of China's "Me Generation" a dozen years after Li Yang's exhortations, as Simon Elegant quotes its middle-class spokesperson in a recent *TIME* article, "My parents lived for me. We live for ourselves, and that's good. We contribute to the economy. That's how our generation is going to help the country" (51).

12 For a trenchant critique of China's neoliberalism, see Wang Hui (19–66), and for an informative account of "neoliberalism with Chinese characteristics," see Harvey (2005, 210–51).

13 Rofel has pointed out the rise of a postsocialist "desiring subject" that replaces class subjectivity dominant in the Mao era (22), but she overlooks the important fact that such a consuming subject was nascent in the *Shanghai Modern* of Capital's First Coming (Leo Lee 1999).

14 The reality of the Iraqi War certainly shatters Hardt and Negri's conception of *Empire* without an imperial center, for the globalization of neoliberal capitalism is conducted with both carrots and sticks. For a critique of this centerless conception of global power, see Bové's "Afterword" to Li.

15 In the manner of Richards's "modernization of expressional habits," Li's *Crazy English* receives divergent responses from both local and foreign teachers of English. North American teachers in China are remarkably ambivalent about the Chinese missionary pedagogue. ("Crazy Place, Crazy English," Teaching English in China info: China-teachers.com, and "Doing the ESL Thing and Enjoying It: Monday, March 15, 2004," Ken & Judy's China Adventure: http://www.downwithup.com/china/). Chinese scholars of English education, on the other hand, tend to downplay Li's claim of his "revolutionary" methodology, pointing to the introduction of "audio-lingual immersion" and "total physical response" into China from the US since the late 1970s. However, their research validates *Crazy English*'s effectiveness and efficiency, especially the program's ability in enhancing self-assurance and in creating ideal affective conditions for optimal language learning (Shen and Gao 190, 200). For an intriguing examination of identity politics in the politicization of English learning in contemporary China, see Qu.

16 In inverted fashion, I allude here to Appadurai's book, *Modernity at Large*. While his emphases are on the rupture of media and migration and their "joint effect on the *work of imagination* as a constitutive feature of modern subjectivity," universally but unevenly experienced, I try to name this capitalist modernity as a historical ethnicity that has evolved beyond its parochial origins. In this naming, I concur with the views of both Latouché and Giddens (1, 174–78).

17 A similar point is made by Alain Touraine:

> In a post-industrial society, in which cultural services have replaced material goods at the core of production, *it is the defense of the subject, in its personality and in its culture, against the logic of apparatuses and markets, that replaces the idea of class struggle.*

(quoted in Castells 22)

18 The use of an American sidekick on his traveling shows to authenticate *Crazy English* is reproduced in the publication of Li's series of textbooks. Take "Crack Function" from his "Spoken English Crash Course," for example. While the text is framed cover to cover with Li's photos and endorsed with a news article on him from *Journal of Chinese Education*, its Chinese foreword is followed by "Kim's Words" in English, along

with the picture of a Caucasian woman lecturing a huge Chinese student audience. While the assertion of Chinese masculinity as the boss over his Caucasian employee is unmistakable, the brand of *Crazy English* still seems inadequate in the eyes of the Chinese without the authentication of a native speaker – in this case Kim, who turns out to be Li's American wife.

19 See Lu Xun's autobiographical account in "Preface to *Call to Arms*" (34–38) and its interpretation as a foundational story of modern Chinese literature by Lee (17–19) and Chow (4–10). Of interest to *Crazy English*'s revision of the East–West spectatorial relation is Ching's piece on Japanese colonial discourse and Shih's "Antagonism against the Western Gaze" (79–84).

20 This is not to say that matters of black and white are all that clearly visible, or we shall not have had such a historical strategy of color subversion as "passing." See Lott and Rogin respectively on blackface minstrelsy and Jewish immigrants in the Hollywood melting pot.

21 It is worth noting that the event of Lu Xun's recollection took place during the Russo-Japanese War while his *Call to Arms* was published in 1922. In between, the Manchu Empire was overthrown and the Republic of China established. Rey Chow offers an intriguing reading of the eyewitness account, interpreting Lu Xun's turn to literature as an act of anachronism (10–11). While her analogy of modernity and visuality is doubtless valid, it overlooks Lu Xun's significant suspicion of spectacle. It is only in the era of intensified transnational capital, of informational and imagistic flows, and the relative decline of the nation-state in instituting cultural meaning that the individual and the image have become the primary locus of subjectivity. The eclipsing of verbal culture by visual culture is symptomatic of Capital's Second Coming and the rise of media states. One major consequence of this evolution is the tragic diminution of national languages and dialects and the status of English as de facto lingua franca of the world.

22 See Mullen and Watson's useful editorial introduction, which outlines Du Bois's complex yet often contradictory exercise of "racial romanticism" and "Afro-Orientalism" as an effort to "undo the form of white supremacy" (xiv–xv).

23 A recent NPR story about a potential Indian purchase of Ford's Jaguar division betrays the kind of post/neocolonial anxiety that an inversion of power brings. Since the global game of capitalism dictates that developed countries provide "technology, entrepreneurship, and management" while developing countries supply "cheap resources and cheap labor," the prospect of "English workers working for an Indian management" will take time to "get used to." As the commentator in the story remarks, if it takes two decades for European and North American employees to accept their Japanese employers, at least this much time is needed for China and India (Davidson).

24 For me, neo-Orientalism can mean either neo-Confucianism from the borderlands or a revised version of old Orientalism from Euro-America. Interestingly, the narrative of Euro-American decline was first heralded by the rise of a "Pacific Century" in the 1980s context of East Asian "tiger economies" (South Korea, Taiwan, Singapore, and Hong Kong). Popular journalism has narrowed it of late to such particular coinage as "China's Century" (*Newsweek*, May 9, 2005) or "China Rising" (*National Geographic*, September 2006).

25 A successful sort of this consumer subject is the flexible citizen, the elite class of multiple passport holders, who are able to efficiently exploit both political and economical systems transnationally (Ong 1999).

26 After the completion of this chapter, Li Yang became a news sensation once more in 2011 not for his business success but for domestic violence (Morris). Under public pressure, Li admitted and apologized for battering Kim Lee, who consequently won her divorce case against him with a settlement of US$1.9 million (Liang).

88   Homo economicus

Works cited

Ahmad, Aijaz. *In Theory: Classes, Nations, Literatures*. Oxford: Oxford UP, 1992.

Anderson, Benedict. *Imagined Communities: Reflection on the Origin and Spread of Nationalism*. New York: Verso, 1991.

Appadurai, Arjun. *Modernity at Large: Cultural Dimensions of Globalization*. Minneapolis: U of Minnesota P, 1996.

Balibar, Etienne. "Subjection and Subjectivation." *Supposing the Subject*. Ed. Joan Copjec. New York: Verso, 1994. 1–15.

Berry, Chris. "Getting Real: Chinese Documentary, Chinese Postsocialism." *The Urban Generation: Chinese Cinema and Society at the Turn of the Twenty-first Century*. Ed. Zhen Zhang. Durham: Duke UP, 2007. 115–34.

Berry, Michael. *Speaking in Images: Interviews with Contemporary Chinese Filmmakers*. New York: Columbia UP, 2005.

Bhabha, Homi, ed. *Nation and Narration*. London and New York: Routledge, 1990.

Bové, Paul A. "Afterword: Can We Judge the Humanities by Their Future as a Course of Study." *Globalization and the Humanities*. Ed. David Leiwei Li. Hong Kong: Hong Kong UP, 2004. 274–84.

Brown, Wendy. "Neo-liberalism and the End of Liberal Democracy." *Theory and Event* 7.1 (2003): 1–43.

Burchell, Graham, Colin Gordon, and Peter Miller, eds. *The Foucault Effect: Studies in Governmentality*. Chicago: U of Chicago P, 1991.

Castells, Manuel. *The Rise of the Network Society (The Information Age: Economy, Society and Culture Volume 1)*. Malden: Blackwell, 1996.

Chakrabarty, Dipesh. *Provincializing Europe: Postcolonial Thought and Historical Difference*. Princeton: Princeton UP, 2000.

Ching, Leo. "Savage Construction and Civility Making: Japanese Colonial Discourse and Taiwanese Aborigines." *Japan and Cultural Imperialism*. Ed. Gennifer Weisenfeld. A special issue of *Positions: East Asia Cultures Critique*, 2000. 795–818.

Chow, Rey. *Primitive Passions: Visuality, Sexuality, Ethnography, and Contemporary Chinese Cinema*. New York: Columbia UP, 1995.

Davidson, Adam. "Ford's Jaguar-Land Rover Division May Go to India." *All Things Considered: National Public Radio*. http://www.npr.org/templates/story/story.php?storyId=17822418.

Deleuze, Gilles, and Felix Guattari. *Kafka: Toward a Minor Literature*. Trans. Dana Polan. Minneapolis: U of Minnesota P, 1986.

Dirlik, Arif. "Chinese History and the Question of Orientalism." *History and Theory* 35.4 (1996): 96–118.

Dirlik, Arif, and Xudong Zhang, eds. "Postmodernism and China." A Special Issue of *boundary 2: An International Journal of Literature and Culture* 24.3 (Fall, 1997): 1–275.

Elegant, Simon. "China's Me Generation." *TIME*. (November 5, 2007): 46–51.

Foucault, Michel. "Technologies of the Self." *Technologies of the Self: A Seminar with Michel Foucault*. Eds. Luther H. Martin, Huck Gutman, and Patrick H. Hutton. Amherst: U of Massachusetts P, 1988. 16–49.

Giddens, Anthony. *The Consequences of Modernity*. Stanford: Stanford UP, 1990.

Gifford, Rob. *China Road: A Journey into the Future of a Rising Power*. New York: Random House, 2007.

Gordon, Colin. "Governmental Rationality: An Introduction." *The Foucault Effect: Studies in Governmentality*. Eds. Graham Burchell, Colin Gordon, and Peter Miller. Chicago: U of Chicago P, 1991. 1–51.

Harvey, David. *A Brief History of Neoliberalism.* New York: Oxford UP, 2005.

———. *A Companion to Marx's Capital.* London and New York: Verso, 2010.

Izod, John, and Richard Kilborn. "The Documentary." *The Oxford Guide to Film Studies.* Eds. John Hill and Pamela Church Gibson. New York: Oxford UP, 1998. 426–33.

Jameson, Fredric. "Preface," *The Cultures of Globalization.* Eds. Fredric Jameson and Masao Miyoshi. Durham: Duke UP, 1998. xi–xvii.

———. "Third-World Literature in the Era of Multinational Capitalism." *Social Text* 15 (1986): 66–88.

Kotkin, Joel. *Tribes: How Race, Religion, and Identity Determine Success in the New Global Economy.* New York: Random House, 1993.

Kuan-Hsing, Chen. *Trajectories: Inter-Asia Cultural* Studies. London and New York: Routledge, 1998.

Latouché, Serge. *The Westernization of the World: The Significance, Scope and Limits of the Drive towards Global Uniformity.* Trans. Rosemary Morris. Oxford: Polity P, 1996.

Lee, Leo Ou-fan. *Voices from the Iron House: A Study of Lu Xun.* Bloomington: Indiana UP, 1987.

Liang, Yiwen. "'Crazy English' Founder Ordered to Pay US 1.9m." *People's Daily Online* (February 4, 2013).

Liu, Alan. *The Laws of Cool: Knowledge Work and the Culture of Information.* Chicago: U of Chicago P, 2004.

Liu, Kang. "The Internet in China: Emergent Cultural Formations and Contradictions." *Globalization and the Humanities.* Ed. David Leiwei Li. Hong Kong: Hong Kong UP, 2003. 187–212.

Lloyd, David. *Anomalous States: Irish Writing and the Post-Colonial Moment.* Durham: Duke UP, 1993.

Lott, Eric. *Love and Theft: Blackface Minstrelsy and the American Working Class.* New York: Oxford UP, 1995.

Lu Xun. "Preface to *Call to Arms.*" *Lu Xun: Selected Works (Volume One).* Trans. Yang Xianyi and Gladys Yang. Beijing: Foreign Languages P, 1956/1985. 33–38.

Lyotard, Jean-François. *The Postmodern Condition: A Report on Knowledge.* Trans. Geoff Bennington and Brian Massumi. Minneapolis: U of Minnesota P, 1984/1997.

Massey, Doreen. "A Global Sense of Place." *Marxism Today* (June, 1991): 24–29.

Miller, Peter, and Nicolas Rose. *Governing the Present: Administering Economic, Social, and Personal Life.* Cambridge: Polity P, 2008.

Mitchell, Lawrence. *Corporate Irresponsibility: America's Newest Export.* New Haven: Yale UP, 2001.

Miyoshi, Masao. "A Borderless World? From Colonialism to Transnationalism and the Decline of the Nation-State." *Global/Local: Cultural Production and the Transnational Imaginary.* Eds. Rob Wilson and Wimal Dissanayake. Durham: Duke UP, 1996. 70–106.

Morris, Kevin. "Li Yang-Kim Lee Divorce Case Sparks Debate about Domestic Violence." *The Daily Dot* (October 31, 2011). *http://www.dailydot.com/news/spousal-abuse-divorce-china-li-yang-kim-lee/.*

Mullen, Bill V., and Cathryn Watson. *W. E. B. Du Bois on Asia: Crossing the World Color Line.* Jackson: UP of Mississippi, 2005.

Murji, Karim. "Ethnicity." *New Keywords: A Revised Vocabulary of Culture and Society.* Eds. Tony Bennett, Lawrence Grossberg, and Meagan Morris. Malden: Blackwell, 2005. 112–14.

Nichols, Bill. *Representing Reality: Issues and Concepts in Documentary.* Bloomington: Indiana UP, 1991.

Ong, Aihwa. *Flexible Citizenship: The Cultural Logics of Transnationality*. Durham: Duke UP, 1999.

———. *Neoliberalism as Exception: Mutations in Citizenship and Sovereignty*. Durham: Duke UP, 2006.

Osnos, Evan. "Crazy English: The National Scramble to Learn a New Language before the Olympics." *The New Yorker* (April 28, 2008): 44–51.

Peters, Michael. "Neoliberalism." *Encyclopedia of Philosophy of Education*. London: Routledge, 1999. *www.vusst.hr/ENCYCLOPEDIA/neoliberalism.htm*.

Phillips, Jerry. "Cannibalism qua Capitalism: The Metaphorics of Accumulation in Marx, Conrad, Shakespeare and Marlowe." *Cannibalism and the Colonial World*. Eds. Francis Barker, Peter Hulme, and Margaret Iversen. Cambridge: Cambridge UP, 1998. 183–203.

Poggi, Gianfranco. *Money and the Modern Mind: Georg Simmel's Philosophy of Money*. Berkeley: U of California P, 1993.

Pratt, Mary Louise. *Imperial Eyes: Travel Writing and Transculturation*. London: Routledge, 1992.

Qu, Weiguo. "Identity Politics and Re-politicization of English Learning." *Chinese Culture, Identity, and Language Anxiety: An International Conference*. Hong Kong: City U of Hong Kong, June 22, 2007.

Robertson, Roland. *Globalization: Social Theory and Global Culture*. London: Sage, 1992/1998.

Rofel, Lisa. *Desiring China: Experiments in Neoliberalism, Sexuality, and Public Culture*. Durham: Duke UP, 2007.

Rogin, Michael. *Blackface, White Noise: Jewish Immigrants in the Hollywood Melting Pot*. Berkeley: U of California P, 1998.

Rose, Nikolas. *Powers of Freedom: Redefining Political Thought*. Cambridge: Cambridge UP, 1999.

Said, Edward W. *The World, the Text, and the Critic*. Cambridge: Harvard UP, 1983.

Shen, Lixia, and Yihong Gao. "What *Crazy English* Means to Chinese Students." *The Social Psychology of English Learning by Chinese College Students: Motivation and Learners' Self-identities* (in Chinese). Eds. Yihong Gao et al. Beijing: Foreign Language Teaching and Research Press, 2003. 190–201.

Shih, Shu-mei. *The Lure of the Modern: Writing Modernism in Semicolonial China, 1917–1937*. Berkeley: U of California P, 2001.

Slaughter, Joseph. *Human Rights, Inc.: The World Novel, Narrative From, and International Law*. New York: Fordham UP, 2007.

Szeman, Imre. "Who's Afraid of National Allegory? Jameson, Literary Criticism, Globalization." *South Atlantic Quarterly* 100.3 (Summer, 2001): 804–27.

Tomlinson, John. *Cultural Imperialism*. Baltimore: Johns Hopkins UP, 1991.

Tong, Qing Sheng. "The Bathos of Universalism: I.A. Richards and his Basic English." *Tokens of Exchange: The Problem of Translation in Global Circulations*. Ed. Lydia H. Liu. Durham: Duke UP, 1999. 331–54.

Tucker, Robert C. *The Marx-Engels Reader* (2nd ed.). New York: W.W. Norton, 1978.

Wang, Hui. *The End of the Revolution: China and the Limits of Modernity*. London/New York: Verso, 2009.

Zhang, Rui. "The Business of English." *China.org.cn.* January 10, 2006.

Zhang, Zhen, ed. *The Urban Generation: Chinese Cinema and Society at the Turn of the Twenty-First Century*. Durham: Duke UP, 2007.

Part II

Homo sentimentalis

The transformation of family and intimacy

3 Neoliberalism's family values

(Re)production and (re)creation in Ang Lee's trilogy and Zhang Yimou's *Happy Times*

If Part I, *Homo economicus*, is a cinematic sampling of capitalist economy's domination of preexisting forms of life and labor, Part II, *Homo sentimentalis*, scrutinizes how its grid of self-interests and entrepreneurial spirits alter the historical modes of sociality, affecting how people relate to one another and feel about themselves. Though once considered a privately experienced psychological phenomenon, emotions are now widely understood as materially and socially conditioned. Critical insights on the interpenetration of economic structures and individual subjectivities since Capital's First Coming are also gaining increasing acceptance. As early as the 1970s, Eli Zaretsky identifies in a manner reminiscent of Polanyi on capital's "splits" of economic production. The first is "the removal of labor from the private efforts of individual families or villages" that occurred in the primitive accumulation of Europe, like its recent reiteration in *Ermo*'s China. The second is the separation of work and life, the split of "the outer world of alienated labor from an inner world of personal feeling," that secured its estranged existence in postwar liberal welfare capitalism (29–30). Similar to Zaretsky but focusing more on its temporal dimension, Tamara Hareven's study of capitalist development in early New England highlights its division of *Family Time and Industrial Time*. Extending Zaretsky and Hareven with her groundbreaking empirical research of the 1990s, Arlie Hochschild illuminates a surprising reversal of the home and work alienation in Capital's Second Coming and its apparent resolution of "the time bind" (1997/2000). There need not be an estrangement of economy and emotion, according to Hochschild, if neoliberal capital is able to effectively absorb individual physical and psychic energies into its productive processes. By turning the time-space of work for the fortunate elite labor force into one of stimulation and fulfillment, home may not necessarily be a "haven in a heartless world" (Lasch), an ideal engendered in the older institutions of liberalism; it can be downgraded in the age of neoliberalism to a space of drudgery in need of individual transcendence.

While the industrializing or newly industrialized Chinese-speaking regions may not have yet experienced its full impact, the painful contradiction entailed by capitalist development between work and home, the individual and the family, production and reproduction are being felt in the nooks and crannies of everyday life. It has already become a subject of intense cinematic mediation and meditation.

In this chapter and the next, we shall analyze films that delve into the struggle of sentiments, caught in the opposing spatiotemporal logics of capitalism and pre-capitalism, as they manifest in both "family" and "intimacy." While romantic rela-tionships will be our investigative focus next, I start deploying "(re)production" and "(re)creation" in this chapter as an interpretive framework to elucidate the changes in, after Raymond Williams, the familial "structures of feeling." (Re)production denotes the cultural imperative governing precapitalist and early capitalist societ-ies and subjects, while (re)creation refers to the neonorm that inverts social pri-orities and incites individual liberties in Capital's Second Coming. The tension between (re)production and (re)creation articulates more specifically the kind of power governing the management of life and administration of the body that Michel Foucault calls "biopolitics" (1990, 2008). In naming and centering the con-tradiction of (re)production and (re)creation in the Second Coming of Capital, I shift from Foucault's critique of the state's disciplinary functions to an alternative critique, à la the Frankfurt School, of capital's more pervasive control of the bio-logical and social body.

The contestation of emotion and ethics in contemporary family and individual life foregrounds the trilogy by Ang Lee 李安 – *Pushing Hands* 推手 (1992), *The Wedding Banquet* 喜宴 (1993), and *Eat, Drink, Man, Woman* 饮食男女 (1994) – and Zhang Yimou's later film *Happy Times* 幸福时光 (2000).[1] From antiquity to not too long ago, the life span of a human being was conceived as an ineluctable passage from crawling on four legs in the morning, walking on two at noon, to hobbling along on three at dusk. The lesson of the Greek Sphinx riddle is embodied and enacted in the Confucian ideal of filial piety. The agrarian Greek and Chinese share a truly catholic conception of the natural reproductive cycle: they concur that an appropriate response to the immutable biospheric law of birth, growth, decline, and death must result in a social arrangement mindful of the individual subject at both ends of its vulnerability and respectful of the natural environment that sustains humanity. If precapitalist Chinese communities are rooted in a social order of (re)production that privileges a localized linear temporality, a genera-tive time for species perpetuity, the precipitation of Capital's Second Coming in East Asia disrupts this practice in the promotion of individual (re)creational time. (Re)creation is not simply an act of emancipation from the repressive regime of procreative sexuality, but a far more complex nexus of governmental reason and individual conduct in global capitalism.

For Ang Lee and Zhang Yimou, the transition from a societal and subjective preoccupation with (re)production to that of (re)creation ushers in an abstract loss of chronological order and "the blurring of life-cycle" (Castells 494). The loss signals a crisis of generation, a "systemic perturbation in the sequential order of phenomenon," as Castells puts it (Ibid.). In this sense of temporal disturbance and loss, (re)creation stands for "a sequestration of experience" wherein "the lifespan emerges as a separate segment of time, distanced from life cycle of the genera-tions" (Giddens 144–46). It is a unique spatiotemporal segregation that emerges with Capital's First Coming and one of the most important forms of splits in life and work we have intimated in the preceding précis. With the Second Coming of Capital, the sequestration of (re)creational experience has evolved into a new raison d'être, having acquired the biopolitical power of dictating both economic production and individual subject formation. In the sense of entertainment, or amusement through sensorial stimulation and satisfaction, (re)creation practically drives the engine of our playful consumer economy. It is precisely in this merry market of constant competition and commodity choice that the ideal subject of neoliberal capitalism is compelled to refashion himself or herself like Madonna or Lady Gaga. When (re)creation begins to embody the principles and practices of ephemeral pleasures, not only are we conditioned to throw away coffee cups, encouraged to constantly revamp our social relationships inherited and/or chosen, we are also pressured to detest the stability of our own selves in favor of newer models, yearn for possibilities and potentialities in the endless performative games of an eternal and euphoric now.

(Re)creation does not just drive the incessant production of objects, experiences, and its desiring subjects in global "economic centralization"; it does so by privileging distance over time so that the "lateral space" of planetary capitalism, in the words of Teresa Brennan, "increasingly substitutes for the (linear) time of local-generational production and consumption" (277). Furthering the contribution of Zaretsky, Hareven, and Hochschild by confirming capital's incremental removal of productive power from the familial and the local, Brennan correlates the waxing of profits directly with the waning of local-generational cares. While the ideal (re)creational subject may freely roam in the horizontal plane of the global market, the problems of (re)production persist at both societal and subjective levels. Can the (re)creational subject voluntarily remove himself/herself from the vertical chain of generation before s/he has time to grow into and assert himself/herself as an atomic unit of an autonomous enterprise? By the same token, while capital may wish for zero-drag growth without having to pay adequately for the labor it needs or replenish the nature it exploits, where will there be an ecology for a voracious consumer base to keep the market alive? Because of its recalcitrant natural time duration and estimable costs, human/labor reproduction seems incompatible with the rapacious desire of capital for instant surplus value. At the core of the (re)creation and (re)production contradiction thereby lies the conflicting time schemes that Ang Lee's and Zhang Yimou's films formalize and tease out: "the generational time of natural reproduction, and speed – the artificial time of short term profit" (Brennan 274–75).

1

Much of Ang Lee's earlier status as a world-class director rests on his cinematic mediation of familial reorganization and gender transformation under the duress of capitalist progress. While these concerns may be cryptic in *Sense and Sensibility* (1995) and *The Ice Storm* (1997), they are pronounced in the "father trilogy," starring the superb Taiwanese actor, Long Xiong. Beginning with *Pushing Hands* (1992), followed by *The Wedding Banquet* (1993), and concluding with *Eat, Drink, Man, Woman* (1994), the father figure in the trilogy illustrates the waning of filial piety, the respect and responsibility, and the economic and emotional reciprocity between the generations that ideally ensure the cultural continuity of biological lineage over individual mortality. Although seemingly arcane, the questions of reproductive anxiety Ang Lee poses with the father figure are no more extraneous in our time of Capital's Second Coming than before. They are Sphinx-like in universal aspiration, but specifically grounded in contemporary circumstances: what if there arises a global inclination toward the severance of infancy and dotage from the life span as an embodied and inescapable biological destiny, toward the privileging and the pillaging of a young adult when one is most able-bodied as the normative self-possessive individual, and thus most autonomous in the alienation of one's labor? What are we supposed to do with the most fragile ends of one's biological journey when neither the family nor the state, let alone carefree capital, cares for the beloved subject of presumptive liberty?

Ang Lee's answers may look contradictory. However, his provisional or revisionist responses in the evolution of the trilogy concentrate on the nucleation of the extended family. After all, it is through the Chinese extended family that the ethical and emotional authority of filial piety, the practice of mutual support, and attendant feelings of belonging have been historically sustained, surviving both Mao's revolution on the mainland and Chiang Kai-shek's nationalist reign of Taiwan. Lee's staging of filial piety's predicament in *Pushing Hands* is both succinct *and* stereotypic. The father of the story, Mr. Chu, is a widower and a retired martial artist from the People's Republic of China. He is visiting his only son Alex Chu in the US – a Chinese American married to a Caucasian American, Martha – and their son, Jeremy. Lee anticipates the challenge his film's diasporic location and mixed-race casting pose. To make it readily intelligible for his audience, both English- and Chinese-speaking, Lee has coded the generational differences in a shorthand of geographic and ethnic incompatibility. Hence, the father begins to stand for China/tradition, his daughter-in-law for America/modernity, and his son, the Chinese American, a cultural in-between, playing the role of an indefatigable yet hopelessly inept mediator between the father/tradition and the wife/modernity. Lee streamlines the patterning of characters with imaging of superficial differences between Mr. Chu and Martha Chu – calligraphy versus typing, tai chi versus jogging, braised pork and steamed rice versus fresh salads and graham crackers – that culminates in a head-on collision experienced by Alex Chu. Though the Chus' suburban house is quite roomy by average American standards, the father and daughter-in-law are unable to share the domestic space. In a fit of pent-up frustration at his own failure to facilitate a harmonious coexistence between his father and wife under the same roof, Alex bangs his head on the wall, dents the sheetrock, and makes a hole in it.

It should have by now become obvious what Ang Lee has resorted to is the conceptual convenience of "Orientalism" (Said). Given the tremendous difficulty of screening between cultures, it seems the rusty conceptual kit from the long history of colonialism will have to be deployed before it can be repurposed. By casting the conflict of multigenerational cohabitation through an Orientalist opposition, Ang Lee has both made his story accessible to a crossover audience and anticipated dramatic resolution of its tensions. Some qualifications are in order, however. Although Alex Chu's head-banging betrays a sentimental excess, the violence of his self-infliction does not obtain "the eternal mythical qualities" typical of melodrama's archetypal contestation between "Good and Evil" (Altman 287). Neither does his painful gesture of torment suggest "a persecution of the good" that shall result in the "final reward of virtue" in the classic plotting of melodrama (Brooks 4). In fact, the antagonism between the East and the West is hardly constructed in the extremes of virtue and villainy, despite Ang Lee's deliberate polarization. This absence of absolute value judgment is a point to which we shall shortly return.

Nevertheless, the films in the father trilogy are melodramatic, because they are sense-making efforts at centrally confronting the processes of industrialization, which, as Peter Brooks notes in the context of Capital's First Coming in Euro-America, not only created a society deprived of an organic and hierarchical order and consolidated the bourgeois nuclear family, but also gave rise to melodrama as a generic negotiation of these social changes (Ibid.). Ang Lee's is a melodrama of Capital's Second Coming, however. His is a form of "minor melodrama," as I would like to put it, for its pronounced ethnic cast and situations, for its tempered emotionalism, and for its eventual moral relativism. Lee tackles this last minor difference as a consequence of compressed capitalist developments and its correspondent ethical bewilderment. An invalidation of older norms of personal duty coupled with a yet incomplete assimilation of individual sovereignty has put Alex Chu in an inarticulate mental confusion. All the pent-up frustration and bewilderment finally leads to a violent outburst against the wall, when the junior returns home after a futile search in the city only to find the missing senior escorted back to suburbia by the police.

This head-banging is a minor melodramatic expression of contemporary Chinese American immigrant experience. Alex Chu has embodied two great historical transformations at once and is only now coping with their ambivalent effects. The first, as indicated by his transpacific migration, is reminiscent of Karl Polanyi's diagnosis of Capital's First Coming. When immigrating to make his life in America, Alex Chu embodied the practice of possessive individualism and economic independence: the original economic purpose of administering and sustaining life as though in a household, locally, morally, and on the ground was "substituted for that of gain" (Polanyi 41, 46). Succeeding this substitution of social cohesion for material acquisition is a practice particularly pronounced in the Second Coming of Capital that Alex Chu also embodies. This is when "lifespan as a separate segment of time, distanced from the life cycle of the generations," as Anthony Giddens puts it, has become compulsory for the autonomous subjects of advanced capitalist nations (146). In both psychosocial transformations, the abstract principal of possessive individualism has reigned supreme: it is apparent in the compartmentalization of the self and the social, evident in the thinning of a longitudinal familial destiny, and manifest in the becoming of natural and normal of individual sovereignty. If a "generation" was in the precapitalist China of the Chu's origin, "a distinct kinship order which sets the individual life within a sequence of collective transitions," the global expansion of the market, labor migration within and without the nation-state, and the "creative-destructive" tendencies of capitalist production have practically emptied the "strong connotations of renewal" the word "generation" originally carries (Ibid.).

Instead of being an essential anchor of collective transition, Mr. Chu has to be transferred elsewhere: this is because the old order of (re)production he represents effectively impedes familial nucleation and individual (re)creation. Capitalist growth requires both material restructuring of the family and the ethical and emotional rewiring of the individual psyche. The truth must be made self-evident that each individual is to lead his/her own independent life in the brave new world of the marketplace. The removal of the grandfather from home is a requisite object lesson for the grandson's subject formation as well. Jeremy Chu should learn what his grandpa seems clueless about, although it is most likely that he will be plotting his permanent leave-taking long before reaching the legal majority of eighteen. After all, the attenuation of generational affective ties is a precondition of capitalist economic expansion, since the discontinuity of generational rites of passage is presumed to accentuate individual mobility.

Socialized in a culture once suspicious of such laws of reason and rules of feeling, Alex Chu is understandably torn, especially in view of the film's revelation about a life-and-death situation in the traumatic frenzy of China's Cultural Revolution. Then, Mr. Chu had to face a fateful choice of either saving his wife or his son, and he opted for the latter. One could say that Alex owes his present success not only to his father's rearing but also to his critical rescue; in order to save him, Mr. Chu has sacrificed his wife, resulting in his solitary status as a widower and his unwanted residence in his extended American family. In the (re)productive chain of filial piety, the nurture of the younger generation is incomplete without the nursing of the old. Refusing to continue and complete the cycle is indeed intolerable, according to this generative governmentality of old. Like his father before him though without his fatal circumstances, Alex Chu has to choose between an allegiance to him, the symbolic past, and an allegiance to his wife Martha, the symbolic present and future. Alex may have scaled the Great Wall of China and made it in affluent Westchester County, New York, but in order to achieve full independence and (re)creation of the self, he has yet to remove the retention wall of his memory that has so far buttressed his ethical integrity.

Lee does this with yet another (melo)dramatic episode. Without announcement, Mr. Chu leaves Alex's Westchester home for Chinatown, working as a dishwasher and lodging in a cramped rental unit. Because he refuses to be fired by his boss and beats up the gang of youth hired to physically remove him from the kitchen, Mr. Chu is arrested by the police and thrown into jail. Martha catches it on local news, and Alex rushes to bail his father out. It is in the prison cell of black bars and dark shadows, typical of film noir's visual set-up, that the audience finds Alex beseeching his father's return home. Rather than the Hollywood shot–reverse shot format suturing a normative individual subjectivity, Lee puts the senior and junior Chu in a medium shot together, with the father's profile on the left of the screen staring at the cell wall and Alex facing him. They are framed within the dim light of the American Dream, in a box within which any thinking beyond it would be a challenge. To Alex's request of homecoming, Mr. Chu retorts, "whose home?" "My home is your home," Alex whispers. "Forget it," responds Mr. Chu. Having thought it through, he resumes, what matters is the happiness of Alex, Martha, and Jeremy. All he wants for himself is contemplative solitude. If Alex still has a "filial heart," he should rent him an apartment near Chinatown and bring Jeremy to visit the grandfather if the (nuclear) family is free. "That way," Mr. Chu concludes, "we'd still have 三分情 or 'three cents of feeling.'" "All I wanted during those years of hard study and work in the U.S.," Alex says choking with tears, "was to build a family, to bring you here to live years of good life." Weeping turns into wailing as the senior Chu holds the distraught junior, folding his son's head into his chest and muffling his cry. The camera cuts to a wider shot of the father and son huddling together, silhouetted against the iron bars of the holding cell.

Cut to the suburban sunshine of Alex and Martha's new white house, impeccable against the wide expanse of the manicured lawn. It could be the Great Gatsby's dream house had Lee located it on Long Island. Following Martha's voice for Alex's help, the camera enters the roomy interior of the guest room reserved for Grandpa, where she tries to hang his sword straight on the wall. There goes Ang Lee's not-so-subtle metaphor of the resolution of generational divisions and developmental oddities, when Martha asks Alex if her father-in-law would visit. Alex cites the ubiquity of Jeremy's presence as his father's inevitable house calls and the couple engage in a game of "pushing hands," "tai-chi for two," a balancing act not unlike the marriage. As Alex and Martha intertwine their hands in a hitherto unseen intimacy arisen in the absence of their father, the audience may heave a sigh of relief that the establishment of emotional equilibrium has been simplified to the conjugal dual, made possible though through Mr. Chu's choice to voluntarily extricate himself from his son's nuclear sanctuary. The father's self-removal has given his son an automatic moral alibi, for the core of their ethical conflict – the irreconcilability between the historical insistence on reproductive continuity and the modern necessity of recreational individuality – is effectively removed along with the patriarch's apparently self-willing displacement. As the senior Chu has told his son, he has always put his "happiness" first and shall continue to do so in his spiritual retreat. Precapitalist tradition and capitalist modernity are shown to be capable of coexisting without conflict after all, as long as mutual acceptance is achieved and liberal tolerance ritualistically observed.

The fact Mr. Chu's removal has to happen seems to be Ang Lee's unwitting admission that it is a necessary condition of nuclear familial restoration: the obsolescence of on-site filial care is as inevitable as the triumph of neoliberal self-care is indisputable. However, this sobering lesson of stark (re)productive defeat at the declining end of life's one-way traffic is not what the director hopes to impart, because it will be hard for the audience both to accept affectively and justify ethically. After all, it is an unspoken commandment of liberal democratic capitalism that there are only gains in compulsory cultural change without attendant costs, only winners and no losers. To that end of ideological mystification, Lee has led the audience to believe that Mr. Chu's departure is a positive development, and indeed an ideal solution to familial difference, thanks to a sudden and superfluous surge of love between the generations.

What is in effect the result of a normative cultural coercion is presented as volitional individual choice. Where the sanctity of the nuclear family and the evident economic dependency of the elder have compelled the father figure's face-saving exit is now seen as Mr. Chu's enlightened liberalization and his kin's devotion. The legendary power of the Chinese patriarch, the kind mythologized in Zhang Yimou's *Raise the Red Lantern*, is nowhere found in Ang Lee's father trilogy. Instead, Mr. Chu's impotence betrays a genuine decline of authoritarianism in the extended and hierarchical family form as well as the rising hegemony of the bourgeois nuclear family with its appropriately autonomous subjects and egalitarian ethos. Given this changed social condition in East Asian capitalist development, it is not surprising that the patriarch in a minor melodrama is no longer the feudal lawgiver obstructing his children's freedom, but the affectionate facilitator of their happiness. Changes in generational roles only bespeak the rise of a new biopolitical order as Ang Lee's Chinese diaspora finds its identical manifestation in liberalizing South Asia. As Sangita Gopal remarks in her discerning study of the new Bollywood cinema, the disappearance of the extended family's absolute power means "its coercion is [now] affective rather than legal or economic" (77).

But affective coercion implies such a strong-armed emotional blackmail that seems realistically unavailable to the elders in an already inverted structure of generational power. It also appears so unbecoming of dominant liberal persuasion, upon which the success of the film's reception has to rest. Mr. Chu has not resorted to guilt trips because he has by now become fully cognizant of the futility of their activation. The hierarchical order of a multigenerational family compound is literally in ruins, because the "household" – *Oikos*, the origin of both "economy" and "ecology" – has been nucleated, splitting into atoms by the radical compression of Capital's Second Coming. With the disintegration of day-to-day, face-to-face economic and emotional communion, and the intensive integration of the able-bodied atomic subject into the global market, the natural authority and organic appeal of the old patriarchal figure have obviously been thrown into the dustbin of history.

Mr. Chu's resignation to historical progress has precluded a classic melodramatic resolution of *Pushing Hands*, for the binary constitutive of the film's initial ethical opposition has evaporated in Lee's "sentimental fabulations" (Chow). The contrarian criteria of individual and social conduct do remain, but in a minor melodrama of Capital's Second Coming. The uncouth "moral polarization and schematization [and] inflated and extravagant expression," typical of classic melodrama of Capital's First Coming, has to be neutralized in filmic image as well as in audience pathos (Brooks 4). The "strong emotionalism," arising from "the loss of tragic vision" and also informative of melodrama's unique historical constitution, is expected to morph into a version of "emotivism," a doctrine that turns "all evaluative judgments," especially of the moral kind, into "*nothing but* expressions of preference, expressions of attitude or feeling" (MacIntyre 11–12). A crude clarification of what is right or wrong based on some consensual standard is certainly to be avoided at all costs so as to ensure that the film audience can feel good and buoyant as the screen goes dark and the lights go up, before they go back to their uncinematic lives undisturbed. A key moment toward the satisfaction of this aesthetic of positive affect and ethic of emotivism occurs at the tour of Alex and Martha Chu's newly acquired larger house. The camera pans to a room the son has especially set aside for his father, and Jeremy, the grandson, has come to check it out. In the prominent physical absence of Grandpa is the ostentatious display of his sword on the wall. The room reservation is a benevolent token for the grandson of his living ancestor and the hanging sword a reminder of Grandpa's future visits. The family appears practically intact and happier even, despite or rather because of Mr. Chu's actual removal.

Modernity's ruthless discontinuity is resuscitated as tradition's respectful recognition. The literal exclusion of the still breathing ancestor/martial artist is substituted by a symbolic inclusion of his inanimate instrument. Grandpa's sword is carefully preserved as though a treasured item of antiquity or a totem pole in a museum. It is as empty and as lifeless as the reserved room itself, as impotent as the historical practice of filial piety, yet vibrant as a liberal fetish of reproductive perpetuity. As can be expected, the last scene of *Pushing Hands* is set in a street flooded with sunshine, contrary to the claustrophobic interiors throughout much of the film. Ang Lee has decided not to lament the loss of vertical succession between the generations and seems blasé if not entirely euphoric about the second chance of horizontal solidarities. Here in the park, Mr. Chu meets and chats with Mrs. Chen, a widow similarly exiled from her daughter's home. In contrast to their adult children's previous attempts to marry them off, much to their objection, this concluding scene is one of apparent consent and conviviality between the window and widower. It is a scene of sweet sorrow: the mutual mourning of a bygone (re)productive ideal is brightened by the (re)creational possibility of the two seniors, casting a ray of hope for their coupling and care.

If *Pushing Hands* shows how the disengagement of individual life span from the collective life cycle has made substantive generational continuity and care unfeasible, *The Wedding Banquet* renegotiates the potential of kinship ties in a different kind of "family romance," not in the classic sense of Freud. The biological family in question, the Gaos, consists of Mr. Gao, a retired army general, and his wife, Mrs. Gao, from Taiwan, and their adult Chinese American son, Weitong, a successful slumlord in New York, who, unknown to his parents, has a loving gay partner. Because Mr. Gao is in poor health and Weitong seems to have surpassed his ideal marriage age, his parents are anxious to see him wedded and see a grandchild before the senior's passing. At the suggestion of Simon, Weitong's white boyfriend, a titular marital ceremony is set in motion. With this setup, a melodramatic tension – between the model of (re)creation, with its emphasis on subjective development and open-threshold self-fashioning, and the (re)productive model of generational procreation – naturally ensues.

For Chris Berry, the film actually combines two melodramatic traditions, the European and American one "based on psychology and its expression" and the Chinese one "based on ethically defined social and kinship roles," roughly akin

to the antinomy of (re)creation and (re)production we use to tease out generational contradiction (238). By demonstrating how Lee eschews the point-of-view
shot in order not to seek audience identification with a single character and how
he arranges "the characters in *mise en scène* so as to give the audience access
to the different reactions," Berry presents a quite convincing case that neither
code of ethics, implicit in the respectively distinct American and Asian melodramatic conventions, is able to dominate *The Wedding Banquet* (Ibid. 240). "At no
point is any serious criticism of either set of values voiced within the film itself,"
whether it is Mr. Gao's "obsession with the family line" or Weitong and Simon's
"self-expression" and "sexuality." As a result, "the film's ambivalence itself is an
ideological move appropriate for the sustenance of globalized liberal capitalism,"
Berry concludes, "for it enables that system by finding a way to maintain simultaneously two otherwise incompatible values systems that it brings into proximity"
(Ibid. 240–41).

Indeed, Ang Lee's melting of melodramatic conflict in comic relief has enabled
a reconciliation between the father and the son, between heterosexuality and
homosexuality, and even between the self and society conflict inherent in the
liberal conception of the self-possessive individual. However, this apparent harmonization of (re)productive and (re)creational difference, like the displacement
of the patriarch and the placement of his sword in *Pushing Hands*, appears as yet
another cinematic performance of liberal masquerade. Berry's "globalized liberal
capitalism," or what we call neoliberal capital, indeed welcomes a diversity of
values (with a lowercase "v") on the very condition that the Value of the bottom
line (with its capital "V") is not affected. In other words, the vitality of global
capitalism requires the difference of "cultures" as individual lifestyle choices.
Otherwise, the identical clock of ceaseless commodity production, constituted by
a heterogeneity of race, ethnicity, sexuality, class, and so forth, shall stop ticking.
The production of profits as the ultimate goal of capital has meant a necessary
outsourcing of (re)productive costs, though with immeasurable consequences on
social arrangements, subject formations, and individual sentiments.

In view of this, the "American" and "Chinese" signifiers of value prove quite
inadequate for a conscientious cultural analyses of *The Wedding Banquet*, because
as soon as we begin to participate in neoliberal capitalism, the local culture in
which we are embedded, as Slavoj Zizek puts it brilliantly, "is always already
de-naturalized," to which I should add, it is denationalized and degendered as well
(144). Simply said, we cannot think about culture without simultaneously thinking about it through material history. One only needs to recall that the Puritans of
"the Plymouth Plantation" were as obsessed with the family line as Mr. and Mrs.
Gao were, and keep in mind too that the need for self-expression is shared by not
only Weitong and Simon but also by Weiwei, Weitong's tenant turned bride, who
is an illegal Chinese immigrant and a struggling painter.

It could be said that Ang Lee's scheme of minor melodramatization depends
less on conflicting values than shared interests, because the harmonization of different interests can be easier to reach than the reconciliation of opposing moral
standards. To start, the marriage between Weitong and Weiwei is one of explicit

convenience, serving multiple parties' interests. First of all, Simon came up with this plan to appease Mr. and Mrs. Gao's wish for their son's matrimony so that he could continue his gay relationship with Weitong in peace and secret. Second, Weiwei played her role of the bride because of her desire to secure a green card through Weitong's US citizenship. By the end of the film, the older heterosexual couple saw both their son's marriage and their grandchild's birth, and the young homosexual couple came out to the elders and had their union both sanctified and strengthened. Weiwei, too, is expected to acquire her permanent residency in the US. After all the melodramatic turns and twists, everyone seems happy in the end, having got what s/he has always wanted. A harmonious coexistence of "two otherwise incompatible value systems" appears to have become reality, as the satisfaction of individual interests in the Ur-system of global capitalism dissipated their apparent former differences (Berry 241).

But actual difference of interests does not disappear; it is only disguised or displaced. The bride's immediate pregnancy – an unintended effect of her willful "liberation" of Weitong from the "confusion of [his] homosexuality" when they were both lecherously drunk – has literally trapped Weiwei with such (re)productive responsibilities that cannot be readily reconciled with her project of self (re)creation. The begetting of a child, in short, interferes with Weiwei's original objective of making it in democratic and upwardly mobile America as a self-reliant Chinese American painter. However, this is an unlikely concern for the majority of the film audience. This is because the relative infrequent use of point-of-view shots that Berry praises as disfavoring the subjectivity of the film's major characters also significantly sidelines the interiority of such a minor character as Weiwei. As a result, we may easily slip into the roles of the Gaos or of Simon and Weitong regardless of our sexual orientations or generational designations, while we are ill-prepared by the camera either to empathize with Weiwei or to step into her role as an impoverished illegal immigrant. Though submerged by the cinematic apparatus, the potential for Weiwei to rupture an otherwise progressively pleasant détente of cultural wars the director has so far engineered is still palpable. For this reason, just as *Pushing Hands* has to patch the crack of the extended family by smoothing the removal of Mr. Chu with a symbolic unity of separate but equally happy nuclear families, *The Wedding Banquet* has to overcome the contradictory modes of (re)production and (re)creation that Weiwei has come to embody. In short, the film's psychoethical equilibrium cannot be obtained, first, without covering up the actual gender, class, and nationality hierarchies constitutive of its cast of characters, and second, without dressing down the discriminatory distribution of different values for different subjects. Finally, the eventual melodramatic merriment of the film's major characters depends on the satisfactory repositioning of Weiwei, its minor character.

It is to Ang Lee's credit that his plotting of suspense and surprises are successful and his cinematic curve balls remain consistent with his characters' trajectories and traits, except for Weiwei, however. While Mr. and Mrs. Gao, Simon, and Weitong are presented throughout as determined and desiring subjects, the image of Weiwei swings from being a fiery independent woman in the beginning to a demure and domesticated one in the end. Lee does include Weiwei's strong reservations about carrying through her pregnancy, but a change of heart more abrupt than Mr. Chu's preference for the senior home soon takes place. The transformative moment occurs on her way to the abortion clinic. An irrepressible craving for a hamburger suddenly seizes Weiwei and Simon has to stop their car. Yes, it is a life-affirming American hamburger rather than a Chinese bowl of noodles that functions as a catalytic converter: for it is precisely there and then that Weiwei, the ambitious and articulate artist, begins to think and act out of her usual character. The hunger for the hamburger works like an oracle, reminding her of her would-be motherhood and urging her to eat for the sake of the would-be baby. It is as though Weiwei's natural voracity makes her a natural mother, her natural appetite an instinct to nurture, that the scheduled visit to the clinic is aborted and the car heads back home in affirmation of motherhood. With a quick succession of cuts, this switch of the minor female character from a career-minded painter to a modern-day Madonna is complete, served more rapidly than a fast-food burger.

Neoliberal capitalism indeed tolerates the incompatible value systems in the global marketplace. It does so not through the processes of democratization, an equitable distribution of (re)productive labor and (re)creational love, an optimal balance of social sustenance and self-expression among differently positioned subjects of the same society. Instead, it accomplishes the semblance of cohesion through structural division of social groups, designating a few subjects as appropriate for self-fashioning and fulfillment while consigning others to the necessary task of reproductive labor and capital generation. As a matter of fact, global capitalism depends on social differentiation to mobilize profit making, and in this light, *The Wedding Banquet* reveals itself to be a rather socially regressive piece of artwork, not ideologically "ambivalent" as Berry holds it (240–41).

To see how this works, we can evoke the spirit of parody and subject the melodramatic resolution of the film to a cost-benefit analysis, so dear to the neoliberal valuation of the world. The addition of the baby, for example, will not affect negatively Weitong and Simon's relationship: by all available indicators the sexual, self-determinant, and self-expressive nature of their romantic liaison shall persist. Theirs will remain a horizontal partnership of the same generation, defined by consensual affiliation and democratic self-sufficiency, at once productive and pleasurable. For them the arrival of the baby is an enrichment of life experience, a net gain without pain. Weiwei's life, on the other hand, will be irrecoverably altered against her individual interests: she will become a primary if not a sole caretaker of her and Weitong's child rather than continue her professional pursuit as an artist. She shall lead a life of vertical generational encumbrance, as a single mother tending the biological needs of her child without any reciprocal affective fulfillment from a partner. Aside from the normative expectation of a "psychic income" from child-rearing, Weiwei has everything else to lose (Foucault, 2008, 244). No matter how effective the simulation of warm sentiments the end of *The Wedding Banquet* appears to be, Weiwei's loss of independence and her obligation within an airtight mother–child bond are hard to ignore.

In a predictable "power geometry" of globalization (Massey), the third-world immigrant woman has again become the vessel and vehicle of patriarchal desires, both heterosexual and homosexual, enabling at once the Gao family's wish for a male heir and Weitong and his partner Simon's friction-free consummation. Although the trio promises an alternative formation of the family under the same roof, the question of sexuality and labor has turned out an inevitable wedge that divides the subjects into those who either deserve the (re)creational pleasure of romantic love or the (re)productive labor of breast-feeding and diaper changing. This particular division of labor between (re)creational impulses and (re)productive imperatives in the respective lots of Weitong, Simon, and Weiwei clearly naturalizes the class hierarchy in the Second Coming of Capital, where different codes of ethics indeed coexist without apparent conflict but the third-world woman is expected to at once sacrifice her (re)creational possibilities, service the desires of major characters/dominant classes, and shoulder the burden of (re)productive costs.

2

Pushing Hands fades out with Mr. Chu muttering, "没关系 it does not matter; 没关系 it does not matter," suggesting the father figure's resignation to the nucleation of the family and to the naturalness of individual life's sequestration and (re)creation. When literally translated into English, 没关系 means, however, "there is no more relations." *The Wedding Banquet* concludes with a point-of-view shot of the trio, Weitong, Simon, and Weiwei, seeing the Gaos off at the airport. Passing the security check, Mr. Gao raises his hands overhead as though in helpless surrender when the image finally freezes. Despite its climax of ritualistic harmony and happiness, this last frame seems to destabilize the film's own painstaking effort at being picture-perfect. If *Pushing Hands* fails to proffer an entirely satisfying solution to the needs of the senior on the waning end of the life span, and *The Wedding Banquet* perpetuates, beyond its progressive treatment of homosexuality, a gendered and classed division of (re)production and (re)creation, *Eat, Drink, Man, Woman* attempts a way out of its precursors' ambivalence. The solution, which comes as a true revelation toward the end of the film, is unexpectedly funny and indisputably fantastic.

The time-space of *Eat, Drink, Man, Woman* is Taipei at the height of its economic boom. The opening shot of an intersection packed with cars and scooters overwhelms the audience with the immensity of a commerce-driven commotion. Cut to an aerial long shot of a tranquil courtyard where Mr. Zhu, a legendary chef of retirement age and the widower of the house, is preparing his Sunday feast for his three living-in grown daughters. A series of close-ups reveals Zhu's delicate yet expeditious knife work, as the credits roll and sumptuous dishes take shape one after another. An unidentified woman calls and Zhu picks up, interrupting his cooking. The conversation, brief yet familiar in tone, meanders from inquiry about lunch, cooking tips for dinner, to their discussion on the most appropriate time for their disclosure. What to disclose is, however, concealed for now, as the sound of psalms ushers in Old Zhu's eldest daughter Jiazhen (家珍 "family treasure"), a high school chemistry teacher and devout Christian, on a bus to Mass. Next, with the clicking of the computer keyboard, and the screen of annual flight analysis from Athens to Zurich, ushers in Jiaqian (家倩 "family beauty"), the middle daughter and an executive at Central Airline, working overtime in her spacious high-rise office. The sizzling sound of fries precedes the appearance of Jianing (家宁 "family tranquility"), the youngest daughter and a college student working at Wendy's.

When this initial sketch of the family is complete, the camera intercuts quickly between the activities of the father at home and his daughters elsewhere: Jiazhen at church, Jiaqian making out at her boyfriend's, Jianing with her would-be husband outside the fast-food restaurant, and Old Zhu himself either in the kitchen or around the courtyard where he keeps his chicken coop and his jars of specialty sauce, roasts his duck, and airs the family laundry. In their respective turns, the daughters reluctantly rush home as though compelled by centripetal forces and assemble themselves at the round dining table in a semicircle until their father finally emerges from behind the round window that partitions the kitchen and the dining room, setting down the last dish before taking his seat with his daughters whose given names, not incidentally, all contain the character 家 ("family"). At present, the circle appears complete. However, despite the image of roundness symbolic in traditional Chinese culture of familial perfection, will the center hold? Is the nuclear family arising from Capital's First Coming a functional and fruitful social formation in Capital's Second Coming?

I wish to probe these implicit questions in Lee's trilogy through an alternative lens of "liberalism's family values." "Even as the familial subject naturalized by the classic liberals is patently in crisis today," writes Wendy Brown in an excursion from her focus on Western liberalism: "the possessive individualism of the liberal civil subject is being affirmed from Beijing to Budapest" (139). While liberalism's global spread is not her focus, Brown's cursory remark lends itself to our further examination of Ang Lee's Taiwanese family in economic liberalization. For Brown, who seems to have recapitulated Zaretsky and Hochshild in a nutshell, liberalism is characteristically dualistic, manifest both in the gendered division of the "civil and familial domains" and in the separation of the familial and the civil subjects (137). On the one hand, we have "the masculinism of the civil subject cut loose from the family that constructs and positions women and men in socially male terms in civil society and the state" (139). On the other hand, the same masculinism maintains "the domain of avowed and naturalized encumbrance" as "the private, familial, sexual, and reproductive domain(s), the domains through and within which women are marked and positioned as women" (156). The dualism of liberalism operates through a "dependence upon, and disavowal of the subordinate term" (Ibid. 152). Thus, "liberal liberty's opposite" is not "slavery," but "encumbrance, constraint by necessity" (154). The autonomous liberal subject, on the other hand, "disavows the relations, activities, and subjects that sustain him in civil society from their sequestered place in the family" (158). Because abstract "liberty" is always already conceived as male and "necessity" is

almost always encumbered and embodied by women, Brown states, "the autonomous woman – the childless, unmarried, or lesbian woman – is within liberalism a
sign of disordered society or nature gone awry" (157). Consequently, liberalism's
family values are buttressed by "a private/public division," contends Brown,
where "men do paid 'productive' work and keep women in exchange for women's
unpaid work of reproducing the male laborers (housework), the species (child
care), and caring for the elderly or infirm" (184).

Indeed, the recurrent conflicts in Lee's trilogy between the productive and self-
interested acts of (re)creation and the indispensable and other-interested labor of
(re)production are uncannily telling of liberalism's inherent gendered inequality and its neglect of life cycles. Lee's representation of the Chinese family in
rapid capitalist development both concurs with Brown's systemic analysis and
complicates it, however. With the compulsory conversion of the autonomous
female painter to a figure of naturally respectful motherhood, *The Wedding Banquet* agrees with Brown's argument that the emancipation of particular "biological [wo]men can be 'purchased' through subordination of substitutes" (164, my
brackets). It also demonstrates how a liberal version of a gay relationship could
seamlessly sustain itself without fundamentally altering the capitalist structure of
inequality. If transcendence of liberal dualism through categorical substitution,
be it race or class, is insufficient in *The Wedding Banquet*, and if the trouble with
"the elderly" and "the infirm" is unsatisfactorily dealt with in *Pushing Hands*,
Lee is grappling with new cinematic alternatives. Instead of displacing the tension
between (re)creation and (re)production, of work and home, onto an implicitly
racialized cultural conflict between modernity and tradition, figured respectively
by Caucasian and Chinese partners in the first two films, *Eat, Drink, Man, Woman*
deals with such tension as an indigenous issue within a Taiwanese society already
integrated in the global neoliberal economy. With this last film in the trilogy, the
director's approach is two-pronged and contradictory. First, Lee wants to radically revise the gender dualism in liberalism, exhorting a gender-neutral form of
(re)productive labor as positive and pleasurable. Second, however, he seems also
to affirm what liberalism and neoliberalism, along with their self-possessive and
entrepreneurial subjects, have constitutively disavowed (i.e., nature's reproductive cycles and life's biological clocks). Suffice it to say, it is Lee's most politically conservative denial of generation's temporal limits that contributes to the
explosive humor at *Eat, Drink, Man, Woman*'s end. A minor melodrama eases into
a romantic comedy only to engender the kind of laughter that provokes critical
thinking and action.

As we have observed, Brown's dissection of liberalism's gender differentiation has found its perfect spatial expression in the opening scenes of *Eat, Drink,
Man, Woman*, although with a notable difference. Lee's is an unconventional map
of gender partition, between Old Zhu's predominant space of domesticity and
his daughters' participation in civil society. Contrary to critics who label him a
"resuscitated patriarch," Old Zhu is a practically biological man cast in the role
of a cultural woman, both bound by the reproductive obligation of nourishing his
children and delighting in the task of feeding and caring for them (C. Liu 1).[2] Ang

Lee constructs his male protagonist as though through Wendy Brown's delineation of womanhood in (neo)liberal capitalism, at once defamiliarizing the private and the public domains, deconstructing the masculinist divide of liberty and necessity, and illuminating the mundane but indispensible (re)productive work. While Zhu is shown as a culinary master who has to be summoned in order to rescue a banquet going awry, the public and remunerating dimensions of his job receive far less attention than his cooking at home throughout the film.

Old Zhu is an exception to classic liberalism's schema that constructs the household as a place for its quintessential masculine subject "to retreat *to* and emerge *from* rather than a place to *be*" (Brown 149). For Zhu, home is indeed where he resides and reigns, not only preparing his elaborate but underappreciated meals but also washing, airing, and folding his daughters' clothing. His misplacement of feminine underwear is a frequent source of the daughters' grievance, much to the delight of the film audience. On top of it all, Old Zhu also takes as his extrafamilial duty to prepare the neighboring girl Shan Shan delicious lunches, because her mother Jinrong, an old friend of Jiazheng and now a single mother with a busy insurance agent job, hardly has time. By situating Old Zhu in the domestic domain, deeply embedded in the daily relations of encumbrance and actively involved in routines of bodily survival and sustenance (eat, drink), Lee has concocted a male character who not only acknowledges the existence but prioritizes the quintessence of reproductive space and time in his performance of the everyday. In him, we see a feminist vision of redistributed private and public labor, of paid and nonpaid work, and of liberty and necessity. Old Zhu seems a notable Chinese figure in transition to the total dissolution of liberalism's separation of the civil and familial subjects, and holds hope for a more timely and more egalitarian constitution of society and subjectivity.

But the film's revision does not simply stop here. If Ang Lee portrays Old Zhu as a super(wo)man in the body of a gerontic man, minding both home and work with efficiency and taking double shifts without grievance, he has also endowed him with a biological timelessness that is naturally incredible. For sure, *Eat, Drink, Man, Woman* does return to the familiar grounds of its precursors. The downward cycle of decline and disease – the martial artist's retreat to a retirement home in *Pushing Hands* and the ex-general's heart attack in *The Wedding Banquet* – find their variations in the character of Old Wen, Zhu's associate chef and lifelong friend as well as his middle daughter Jiaqian's favorite "uncle." Wen's emergency treatment reminds Jiaqian of her own father's senility. Unbeknownst to Old Zhu, Jiaqian's accidental discovery of her father in a hospital gown at the cardio diagnostic lab furthers her worry. Although the three daughters' discussion about who shall ultimately stay with and care for their father seems unending, their attempt of matching him with a widow, Mrs. Liang, the grandmother of Shan Shan and mother of Jinrong, is explicitly evocative of the adult children's solution to their widowed parents in *Pushing Hands*. The successive marriage and departure of Jianing, the youngest daughter, and Jiazhen, the eldest daughter, along with the middle daughter Jianqian's promotion and imminent posting in Amsterdam have made it patently clear that Old Zhu will be on his own.

While arranged marriage for adult children is irredeemably archaic, oppressively antimodern, and antiromantic, an arranged marriage for seniors with deceased spouses appears a very liberal and liberating alternative. Failing that, an aging parent's irredeemable dependency is truly a migraine – endemic to the still robust vast army of migrant labor disembedded by the needs of global capital – that no modern medicine promises any satisfactory cure. Nor does Ang Lee the film director seem to possess the magic potion to cure it, either, until this last of the father trilogy. Like the predecessor films, the director of *Eat, Drink, Man, Woman* again summons up the trick of dismissal. However, while the issue of human dependency and vulnerability was partially dismissed in previous films with relative success, its disappearance in this last film is total. By persistently portraying Old Zhao as a model of self-care as well as a caretaker of others, Lee has simply freed the elder from the probability of infirmity and the destiny of decline, effectively eschewing the emotional and ethical challenges the contradiction of (re)production and (re)creation entail.

This portrait of near omnipotence comes to a comic climax in what turns out to be the final family feast, when Old Zhu assembles his daughters, sons-in-law, and the neighboring family of Mrs. Liang, Jinrong, and Shan Shan at his round dining table packed with his usual scrumptious dishes. In slight agitation, Old Zhu raises his glass to all members of his extended family before proceeding to toast Mrs. Liang, the presumptive future Mrs. Zhu in the minds of nearly all present. He eventually lets out a secret that the audience was given a tantalizing hint at the film's opening credit sequence. The disclosure has an effect like the dining table had been turned upside down, as it literally does moments later. Presenting her a certificate of his health from the hospital, Old Zhu beseeches Mrs. Liang's permission to marry her daughter, Jinrong, with a genuine promise to cherish her and Shan Shan for the rest of his life. Jinrong volunteers her consent in public as well: referring to her lover as "Zhu Ba" 朱爸, literally "Father Zhu," which the English subtitle mistranslates as "Mr. Zhu," she seeks everyone's approval of her lifelong partnership with him.

After the ensuing scene of chaos and ruckus, the camera cuts to the spacious sun-soaked apartment of the newlyweds. Now shown fecund with his child, Jinrong gives her doting husband a peck on the cheek, before sending him on his way for his farewell dinner with Jiaqian. Riding a cab to his former home, Old Zhu is identified for the first and last time in the film with the hustle and bustle of Taipei traffic, becoming one with rather than standing apart from the contemporary flow of commerce and commotion. A point-of-view shot follows him disembarking the taxi at his old house with a huge "SOLD" sign on the gate, inserting his old keys before realizing that they no longer work. Once let in by Jiaqian, Old Zhu looks pensively but not nostalgically at the deserted courtyard. Like the martial artist's sword in *Pushing Hands*, the house has become a ceremonial token of historical and sentimental value, as though a signature sauce that Zhu has preserved in one of the jars that used to sit around the courtyard, only not to be unsealed and used for his future dishes anymore. *Eat, Drink, Man, Woman* concludes with Old Zhu's reconciliation with Jiaqian and his recovery of his sense of taste, once thought of as being gone for good but now evidently whetted by his renewed sexual appetite (man, woman).

With his recuperated masculine vitality, unaffected by gerontic frailties and unlimited in energy, Zhu proves to be a consummate figure of the self-possessive individual in his perpetual prime. Hyperbolic and hilarious, the figure seems to refute two prevailing perceptions, one specific to Euro-American contexts of reception of Asian male asexuality and the other shared by Eastern and Western audiences of househusbands' femininity. Both seem stereotypes of (neo)liberalism's gender split, one with racial overtones. What is of greater importance in the male figure's fantastic ageless vigor is Lee's eventual dissolution of the tension between (re)creational impulses and (re)productive imperatives that has troubled his trilogy from its inception – a tension that is inherent in the liberal capitalism of C.B. Macpherson's original critique as well as such feminist rejoinders by Joan Tronto, Wendy Brown, and Martha Fineman. There is something undeniably progressive in the dissolution of gendered division that the father in *Eat, Drink, Man, Woman* begins to represent: in this figure lies first the director's full acknowledgment of necessary domestic labor that sustains the cycles of life and thus ongoing economic productivity of capitalism, and second, his almost automatic affirmation of male participation in the ethic of nurture and practice of care. In this, Ang Lee gestures toward possibilities that revise the abstract autonomy of masculinity central not only to liberalism, but also to preliberal and neoliberal notions of the independent male subject, and he even demonstrates with concrete cinematic representation how such masculinism could be reformed in the minutiae of daily life.

However, contradictions also abound. Indifferent to the natural limits imposed by biological clocks, the father figure comes back to affirm the sovereign self central to (neo)liberalism and speaks for the film's implicit rejection of human dependency and decline. In this manner, the character of Old Zhu seems indicative both of Manuel Castells's description of the late capitalist "blurring of life cycles" and Foucault's correspondent proposal of "the technologies of the self" to deal with it (Castells 475; Foucault 1988). For Castells, the organizational, technological, and cultural development of capitalism has reached such a stage that it calls into serious question "the biological determination of roles in society," "undermining the orderly life-cycle" in "the principle of a sequential life" (475–76). If the Sphinx riddle used to convey a universal life span distributed through the democratic cycle of birth, growth, and death, the culture of capitalism is breaking down that rhythm. "Depend[ing] on their social, cultural, and relational capital accumulated throughout their lives," observes Castells, "the social attributes of [the aging] will differ considerably, thus breaking down the relationship between social condition and biological stage at the roots of the life cycle" (Ibid. 476).

What appears to bother Castells (i.e., capital's disturbance and differentiation of biological time and its integration of wealth, health, and longevity) is for Foucault perhaps the proper biopolitical sphere of liberal reason, which requires not only an "*ethos* of government . . . a recurrent critique of state reason," but also, as Barry, Osborne, and Rose argue, "its *techne*, its organization as a practical rationality directed towards certain ends" (10). Biological condition should be socially and subjectively modified, as Foucault encourages "individuals to effect by their own means a certain number of operations on their own bodies and souls . . . so as to transform themselves in order to attain a certain state of happiness, purity, wisdom, perfection, *or immortality*" (1988, 18, italics mine). It is unfortunate in Foucault's view that such transformative agency to "take care of yourself" is historically obscured by the motto of "know[ing] yourself," informed both by "Christian morality" that makes "self-renunciation the condition of salvation" and by a "secular tradition which respects external law as the basis for morality" (Ibid.: 22).

A way out of such external prohibitions and ascetic habits from our inherited conditions of history, be it Christian or Confucian, is to embrace self-examination as mere stock-taking. Using Seneca as his ideal subject, Foucault writes:

> Faults are simply good intentions left undone. The rule is a means of doing something correctly, not judging what has happened in the past . . . [Seneca] is a permanent administrator of himself . . . It is not real faults for which he reproaches himself but rather his lack of success. His errors are of strategy, not of moral character.
>
> (1988, 33–34)

Remarkably, it is the instrumentality of ends and effects that governs individual agency rather than historically and communally instituted ethical standards that motivate Foucault's account of "the technologies of the self." This particular "emphasis on *techne* gains further significance," as Barry et al. rightly point out, "when one comes to consider the way in which liberalism has been reconfigured in its neoliberal incarnation" (Barry, Osborne, and Rose 10). This neoliberal biopolitics is manifest in the arena of state policies as well as the domain of the individual subject.

We could productively engage the evolution of the father figure in the trilogy through the terms of Foucault's technology with which the self learns to continuously alter his conduct, not according to the determination of historical norms or life cycles but to operate on social and biological time self-reflexively to ensure success. From being the outcast of capitalist nucleation of the family, the elderly severed from generational continuity in *Pushing Hands*, to a "flexible citizen" managing new age procreation in *The Wedding Banquet* (Ong), to the senile and supposedly infirm in *Eat, Drink, Man, Woman* who turns out to be a super(wo)man, the father figure has undergone so many of Ang Lee's makeovers until he eventually embraces the idea that his life span has to be detached from the life cycle of the generations, thus almost attaining – let me evoke Foucault – "a certain state of immortality" (1988, 18). The transformation of the patriarch/ protagonist is a neoliberal triumph of governmental reason that overrides even the moral sentiments informative of classic liberalism. What Ang Lee has Old Zhu learn from his precursor characters is precisely Foucault's pedagogical wisdom of biopolitical self-management. First, it is futile to hang onto the historical yet presently weakened networks of social and generational support based on an intuitive understanding of biological finitude and species collectivity. Second, in the wake of this neo-understanding, it is necessary to have Old Zhu initiate measures to administer his own welfare individually and effectively. With its comic relief in *Eat, Drink, Man, Woman*, the father figure has finally relieved Ang Lee of his enduring ethical dilemmas and conclusively liberated himself from his previous "errors of strategy" (Foucault, 1988, 34).

In making him the paragon of self-sufficiency with surplus capacity for biological and social reproduction, Lee has created in Old Zhu a male familial subject who not only defies the Sphinx riddle but also marches confidently toward what Castells considers with ambivalence the direction of "social arrhythmia" (475). A cross-generational conjugal union indeed disturbs natural biological time and social conventions of similar age partnership, as well as romantic ideals forged through the First Coming of Capital. But in the constant individual invention characteristic of Capital's Second Coming, and with a clear certificate of health from his cardiologist, who can deny Old Zhou's jubilations of the heart, however irregular, as an entitled exercise of his (re)creational rights? Two counterpoints to any opposition to his matrimony of incompatible ages seem in order, however. First, the age discrepancy is as much a phenomenon of feudal societies as it is of contemporary neoliberal societies; although Old Zhu's case seems an exception to this, we are witnessing the extreme concentration of wealth with an increasing coupling of people of sharp age difference (Madonna and Demi Moore included). Second, in light of the dominant biopolitical logic that regards reflexive modification of individual conduct perennially essential, it seems unreasonable not to conceive of Old Zhu's marriage as a perfect expression of successful entrepreneurial self-management.

Granted, Old Zhu seems still unable to entirely shake off his habitual obsession with (re)production, as Jinrong's pregnancy reveals. However, Ang Lee has given his audience enough evidences to draw the conclusion that the sign of the future child is perhaps none other than a supplemental effect of Old Zhu's self (re)creation, an additional satisfaction that exceeds his original act of libidinal liberation. To put it in starker and simpler terms, the new Old Zhu in his second marriage is impossibly identical with the old Old Zhu in his first marriage and widowerhood. While the old one enacts a model of (re)production in which the fulfillment of self is sought both within *and* without the biological span of the individual self, in and through familial and generational continuity, the new one seems to have adopted the (re)creational practice that refuses fulfillment through substitution and seeks satisfaction within the singular self. The history and the idea of a life cycle – evident in the practice of filial piety and the Sphinx riddle – is epistemologically, emotionally, and ethically enervated if not entirely extinguished. Forsaking vicarious generational and historical realization, the mode of (re)creation also exacts incredible toll on the individual life span. For the agent of (re)creation is now expected to stretch the limit of his/her atomic life exponentially, if not indefinitely through spatial expansion and temporal compression, and pack within it the fulfillment of dreams that used to be accomplished collectively over both historical and generational time.

The new Old Zhu is an utterly benign and jovial symbol of a propensity toward the global affirmation of (re)creational subjectivity. A combined figure of apparent "perfection" and "immortality" (Foucault, 1998, 18), however, Old Zhu personifies the neoliberal life of excess, overcoming nature's limits in an unstoppable accumulation of surplus values and experiences, interests, and affects. He seems to summarize at least two aspects of neoliberalism's family values. The first is "the privatization of care" in which all reproductive encumbrances, if acknowledged at all, are to be dealt with individually or within the nuclear family (we are reminded once more of Thatcher's infamous claim that there is no such a thing as society; there're only individuals, and very much as her afterthought, families). The second is "the technology of self-care" that promotes the making and market modification of the individual in the spirit of endless growth. What appears glaringly absent from this triumphal biopolitical figuration of subjective sovereignty are two inescapable conditions, however: the uneven individual capability to cope with vulnerability and thereby the ubiquitous need for social welfare, on the one hand, and the natural limits to individual biological life and thus the necessity of collective survival on the other. *Eat, Drink, Man, Woman* seems to have exorcised the specters of dependency that haunted the father figure in *Pushing Hands*, written off the quintessential tasks of tending to the vulnerably old and young in *The Wedding Banquet*, and rather unwittingly turned itself into a neoliberal farce of biopolitical extravagance and excess. It turns out a filmic fantasy of neoliberalism's family values.

3

Having read passions in *Red Sorghum* as expressive of the emergent liberal subject and his self-possessive interests, it is hard to imagine Zhang Yimou would shortly turn away from his preoccupation with (re)creational exuberance to (re)productive encumbrance. The shift has actually occurred, however, beginning with *The Story of Qiu Ju* 秋菊大官司 (1992), a dramatic feature about a peasant woman seeking justice for her injured husband. The extravagant display of exotic colors and customs and the joyful celebration of the repressed spirit yearning its rightful release that characterize *Red Sorghum*, *Ju Dou*, and *Raise the Red Lantern* have remarkably vanished. Instead, *Qiu Ju*'s drab documentary look appears to be Zhang's deliberate withdrawal from the mythical Chinese past and his renewed focus on a contemporary China caught in the sharp relief of the rural and the urban. The waning of romantic overtone and the commitment to cinematic realism continue with *To Live* 活着 (1994), a family saga of suffering and endurance, and *Not One Less* 一个不能少 (1999), the tale of an adolescent girl fighting for public education.

If the racy story of forbidden love and its transgression in the pre–*Qiu Ju* period corresponds with China's unprecedented opening up in the 1980s, representative texts of the post–*Qiu Ju* period engage the 1990s when the Second Coming of Capitalism became entrenched, "the concept of the market" eclipsed "the concept of society," and privatization accelerated the devolution of the state's social responsibilities (H. Wang 121).[3] Similar to Ang Lee's self-revision in his trilogy, Zhang Yimou has undergone stylistic as well as thematic changes in his growing oeuvre. An aesthetic of self-possessive and affective individualism preoccupies his earlier period: a rebellion against the state's proletarian dictatorship is disguised as a peasant revolt against feudal landlords while the seizure of their original romantic objects are rationalized as the rightful engagement of liberal enterprise. In contrast, gloomy mise-en-scènes and gritty textures of social life dominate Zhang's later productions as the intimate cuts and individual close-ups give way to more long takes and the panoramic panning of the social eye/I. Zhang's camera no longer lavishes attention on the sovereign captains of capitalism, but turns instead with great fondness toward the ordinary and homely Chinese mass at the edge of the market society, who lack the normative sovereignty necessary for neoliberal survival, let alone successful self-administration, in the nation's unprecedented saturation of market governmentality.[4]

Symptomatic of his directorial shift is *Happy Times*. A romantic comedy, initially driven by an apparent marriage plot propelling its male protagonist in a passionate quest for a wife, the film narrative quickly meanders toward an entirely unanticipated direction. The self-interests of the bachelor become helplessly intertwined with the needs of a stranger that beseech his address. In deliberately sidetracking his story, Zhang is able to demonstrate the emerging laws of market exchange, first revealing the extent to which they have infiltrated every form of social arrangement and practice from intimacy to family, and second, revising their meaning and measure by exposing the hidden dimensions of their social delinquency. As neoliberal economics appear to have acquired the fundamental status of ethics and dictatorial power over personal emotion in China and elsewhere, Zhang Yimou is increasingly concerned both with the endangerment of communal ethos and the enabling role of cinema for more humane forms of sociality and society. *Happy Times* appears, to allude to Martha Fineman, an allegory of "the autonomy myth," an advocacy for the "theory of dependency," and finally an unabashed cinematic argument, to borrow Joan Tronto, for an "ethic of care."

The film starts with a steady establishing shot of a café interior with "the fat lady" and her suitor, Old Zhao, in the foreground and through a floor-to-ceiling glass a busy street in the back. Both in their fifties, they swap personal information over orange juice and peanuts, with an explicit aim of entering into a verbal marital agreement. Since the woman's obvious obesity and her children from prior marriages do not deter Zhao, who reinterprets such conventionally construed dual baggage respectively as a quality of "warmth" and merit of "life experience," she proposes her terms of consent that he come up with fifty thousand Chinese yuan to shore up their wedding ceremony. For his matrimony to materialize, Old Zhao, a welder living on a downsized wage from a state factory under economic restructuring, has no other choice than immediately embarking on his frantic fundraising. None of Zhao's contacts seems in such a position of financial security as to loan him any money. But his former protégé, Little Fu, mentions an abandoned bus in the park, and like a true entrepreneur bent on primitive accumulation they instantly claim the rundown bus as their own, take possession of it, and fix it up to accommodate for a fee young dating couples wandering by, anxious for a moment of privacy. The guerrilla-style privatization of a former public means of transportation at once satisfies a market demand and elevates Old Zhao into the enviable class of property owners of what he designates as "Happy Times Little Hut."

With swift and succinct montage, Zhang shows his audience both the network of causalities and the logics of calculation that govern the emotional and economic exchange of his characters. The liberalization of planned economy and the opening up of a real estate market bear witness not only in the figure of his "fiancée," with intimacy for sale, but also in Old Zhao's own informal exercise of property rights, both of which evidence the overall expansion of "the values and activities of exchange into all aspects of [contemporary Chinese] life" (H. Wang 72). In bringing love interest and economic interest into the same frame, Zhang seems to anticipate the French novelist Michel Houellebecq, who, in a novel published two years after *Happy Times*, regards "sex" and "money" as equivalent systems of social differentiation in Capital's Second Coming: "Just like unrestrained economic liberalism, and for similar reasons, sexual liberalism produces phenomena of *absolute pauperization*," a planetary polarization of the "haves" and the "have-nots" in both arenas of economy and emotion (99). More presciently perhaps, *Happy Times* at once ushers in Yu Hua's blockbuster historical farce that casts China's cutthroat capitalist competition through the romantic wheel of fortune of a pair of *Brothers* (2005/2010) and forecasts the "Bachelor Padding" syndrome when the privatization of residential housing entails homeownership as "lonely single men" are reportedly "creating China's dangerous real estate bubble" (Lake).

Given Zhang Yimou's incipient coupling of romantic passion and property acquisition, the audience may naturally expect the "fiancée" to raise her original stakes of fifty thousand Chinese yuan, thus further frustrating Old Zhao's fantasy of conjugal union. Little would they expect that the rotund woman would seize on his boast of his purported managerial status for the unfolding of another design. The presence of her children in her apartment is surely an "inconvenience" for their "intimacy," she complains, but it is an easily resolvable problem, she insists. Having trapped Old Zhao in her original plot of seduction, she begins to compound it with additional (self) interests: she demands that he find ways to relocate her stepdaughter from the family apartment and to place her in a remunerated job. The ostensible justification is Wu Ying's abandonment by her biological father, who has ditched both his teenage daughter and his second wife for the new venture capitalism in Shenzhen without leaving them any means of subsistence. To the original investment of fifty grand in his long-term marital bliss, Old Zhao is now given the additional task of practically executing the divestment of his "fiancée's" daughter, to evict her from her residence and to deprive her entitlement to her adopted family.

Though one might count this cinematic turn of the screw as an extra hurdle on the road necessary for the eventual reconciliation and consummation of the lovers, generic mandates of romantic comedy of which *Happy Times* seems both an intentional and indisputable parody and pastiche, I would consider Zhang's move in a different light. For me, the inauguration of Wu Ying as a main character of the film fundamentally disrupts the romantic dyad of the middle-aged singles that have so far set the scene and driven the story. As an atypical "third party" and an "asexual love interest" at that, the figure of the stepdaughter, while triangulating and thus complicating the film's web of relations, cannot be constitutively harmonized out of existence according to the conventions of romantic comedy. There, an intruder of the intended intimate dual can be ejected, and all forms of social divisions and communicative difficulties can be surmounted for the ultimate heteronormative matching of the predestined couple. But the happy ending of the couple's actual or implied consummation is not at all Zhang's intention. Although the character Old Zhao is yet insufficiently aware of the odds against his romantic fantasy, Zhang the director has cast the stepmother's request of her daughter's riddance in a decisive inquiry about liberal subjectivity and neoliberal personal management in matters of the heart. The "fat lady's" insistence on Wu Ying's removal is not merely compatible to the sacred privacy of the romantic dual, sequestered from generational considerations, it is more seamless with the normative subject of self-sufficiency in market competition, regardless of its circumstances of ascription. By making Zhao's realization of conjugal union contingent upon Wu Ying's successful alienation of her labor, Zhang is turning the stepdaughter's becoming the "sole proprietor of [her] own person" into a cinematic study of the neoliberal biopolitical imagination (Macpherson 263).

With her additional demands, the audience immediately intuits the impossibility of Zhao's marriage to the fat lady, for the sums of their exchange simply shall not compute. For one thing, the bus serving as "Happy Times Little Hut" is hauled away in the city's beautification campaign, wrecking Old Zhao's only chance of financing his wedding and finding the stepdaughter any potential employment. For another, Wu Ying is legally blind. The doom of the film's tantalizing marriage plot, however, triggers its new turn as Wu Ying is spotted frozen and fear-stricken in the middle of the street, helpless against the frenzy of night traffic. The scene seems Zhang's deliberate reiteration of De Sica's *Bicycle Thieves*, when the son of Ricci, while running after his father chased by the criminal-catching crowd in Roman streets, is terrified by the oncoming cars.[5] This gestural tribute to the Italian master reveals Zhang's resonance with post–World War II cinematic neorealism, known both for its exposé of social misery and emphasis for communal survival. Not only does this show a significant departure in his own oeuvre, as indicated earlier, but it also resonates in tone and theme with identifying features of "the Sixth Generation" of prominent younger Chinese directors that I shall explore in Chapter 5. The allusion to De Sica signals a crucial change of *Happy Times* from the marriage plot of romantic comedy to the mundane moments of domestic comedy. It practically transforms the story of a couple's romantic love in its normatively synchronic and horizontal flow of intimacy into a virtual father–daughter plot similar to *Eat, Drink, Man, Woman*, at once defined by a diachronic and vertical love of existential needs provision and satiation, and yet betraying a nonfilial form of generational association. With this, *Happy Times*'s inchoate (re)creational instinct has succumbed to its director's revisionist (re)productive drive. Similar to Ang Lee but from a different national and developmental context, Zhang has subjected both the agrarian Greek Sphinx riddle and the Confucian filial piety to their unavoidable contemporary challenges. If Lee has imagined a heterosexual–homosexual combination of a new family formation in *The Wedding Banquet*, however unsatisfactorily, Zhang seems to wonder if the much-refined and diversified nuclear family of Capital's First Coming will prove adequate for the Second Coming of Capital. How could biopolitics, in its impulse not at control but in ensuring species and human thriving, develop means beyond residual natural blood relations as well as stifling commodity relations in order to cultivate egalitarian and empathetic forms of affiliation? How could cinema contribute to the construction of enabling families?

Guiding the blind girl to safety on the sidewalk and condemning her mistreatment by her stepmother, Old Zhao gives Wu Ying shelter in his cramped studio apartment and goes out to find her a job. Though still harboring illusions of matrimony, the poor and sincere Old Zhao begins to embody a spontaneous economy of "other-care," as opposed to Foucault's better-known "technology of self-care." Unlike Ang Lee, whose use of melodrama is more muted because of his ethical ambiguity, Zhang Yimou's deployment of melodrama appears more pronounced or even strident. The *de jour* stepmother and the symbolic but *de facto* stepfather form such melodramatic contrast of malevolence and beneficence that the audience is encouraged to identify with Old Zhao, the director's chosen party of moral decency, and embrace his ethic of fairness, justice, and care. By placing narrative weight on the resolution of Wu Ying's proper placement in terms of her work and home, *Happy Times* has come to restore and center the concept of social contract at a time when the free market appears to be the miraculous solution to everything. It is through this cinematic correction of his previous passion for Capital's Second Coming in China that Zhang starts to suggest a possible recovery of precapitalist values and practices.[6] With a focus on the figure of disability and displacement, *Happy Times* reconsiders the laws of acquisitiveness and self-interest that underlie *Red Sorghum*'s legitimization of capitalistic enterprise. More importantly, it foregrounds a question of which neither classic liberalism nor neoliberalism can easily dispose: namely, what are we going to do with the individual among us who is not able and therefore cannot enter the relationship of market exchange proficiently and profitably?[7]

Turning from the intrigue of (re)creational romance to the problem of (re)productive dependency immediately challenges the audience to think through the irreducible interrelationship of individual, state, and capital in globalization. *Happy Times* actively participates in the progressive intellectual arguments against the neoliberal dogma of 1990s China. It resonates with the critique of excessive individual liberty at the expense of greater democracy and it joins the call for the state to mitigate the hardships of its citizens as the nation transitions to a market economy (Yang; S. Wang). The film also becomes a screening of "a nascent Chinese public sphere," "the vast discursive space" between "a thriving, omnipresent market and a retreating, decentralized state power" (Zhang 316). If Wu Ying's abandonment by her biological father and her stepmother represents the flight of capital, the withdrawal of the state, and the subsequent outsourcing of care, her adoption by Old Zhao precisely figures the difficulty of fulfilling the needs of both self-interested liberty of individual (re)creation and the society's interest in (re)production, as interests are significantly shortchanged by and subordinated to the exorbitant demands of capital growth.

Herein lies Zhang's comic creativity and dynamic social conscience. Learning about Wu Ying's prior training in massage therapy, Old Zhao recruits Little Fu and his old friends in retirement on a mission to build a massage parlor for her. Clueless as to what it looks like, this group of low-end consumers feigns patronage in a luxurious downtown establishment before building a version of it in their deserted factory.[8] Rusty sheet metal is welded to frame the parlor, and used hemp sacks are picked up and wrapped around to give the feel of softened wall panels. Leftover material from a dilapidated socialist economy and Soviet-style heavy industry is recycled just as its downsized labor, made unproductive and redundant by market efficiency, is able to devote its excess energy into creative care of another less fortunate person. When Old Zhao and friends find the silence of the place deafening, they tape the sound of city streets to play back in their parlor. When they realize the absence of actual clients, they assume their roles. When they can no longer afford to pay Wu Ying with real money, fake currency is put into circulation. Nowhere else but in this abandoned factory, both physically at the outskirts of global capital and metaphysically apart from its logic of commodity exchange, lies Zhang Yimou's vision of a utopian community of (re)productive care through conscientious charade.

Two scenes stand out in the film's persistent investigation of exchange, both as a form of value abstraction and a form of affection unaffected by the commodification processes. One is in Beida Street, the actual space of commerce as well as society, and the other in the massage parlor, the ideal space of an extemporaneously existing utopia. In the first, Wu Ying wants to treat Old Zhao to ice cream since she has income for the first time. He volunteers to treat her instead. Unable to afford even one scoop at the Häagen-Dazs chain, Old Zhao buys her a Popsicle at a stand, sits down with her on the sidewalk, and they strike up a conversation (the shot of the pair side by side on the pedestrian walk is again visually reminiscent of De Sica's Ricci and son). In the second scene, after no one is able to produce real cash for tips, Auntie Liu comes up with the idea of fake money. The retirees try it on Wu Ying, who, having detected the forgery, willingly accepts the currency and plays along authentically. In both scenes, money determinedly mediates human exchange.[9] However, by playing on its visibility and invisibility, detaching the sign from its supposed value in the second scene, Zhang Yimou is able to follow Georg Simmel in distinguishing between money's quantitative and qualitative dimensions, thus opening up a space for a different practice of exchange, both economic and emotional. Writing in "Metropolis and Mental Life," Simmel states,

In a complete money economy, money takes the place of all the manifoldness of things and expresses all qualitative distinctions between them in the distinction of "how much." To the extent that money, with all its colorlessness and its indifferent quality, can become a common denominator of all values it becomes the frightful leveler – it hollows out the core of things, their peculiarities, their specific values and their uniqueness and incomparability in a way which is beyond repair.

(330)

Simmel's judgment on the reductive effect of money on individuality and sociality is intriguing, for his is qualified by the condition of a capitalist totality in which the money economy is notably "complete." The Chinese economy of the *Happy Times* Zhang captures is peculiarly incomplete due both to the abrupt takeover by the Second Coming of Capital of China's socialism and to the communist party's ill success of totally dismantling, through its abortive industrialization and ideological campaigns, of the ancient agrarian structures of feeling. Because of the speed fundamental to the Chinese capitalist developmental experience, it has contained within itself a ragged "residual," á la Raymond Williams, which appears to hold promise to reverse money's equation of the qualitative with the quantitative (122).[10] Indeed, Zhang repeatedly represents the residual as a source of comedy and a resource of culture resistant to the cash nexus.[11]

To the frightful flattening effect of money, Zhang adds feeling, "the imponderable components of affect laden relations" (quoted in Poggi 65). Feeling is figured literally as touching, as Wu Ying moves her hands over Old Zhao's facial contours to round out in her mind's eye the abstract kindness that the stout man embodies. When she recognizes what in her hands is indeed not real money, feeling again guides Wu Ying's sensorial ascertainment of the authenticity of affect and accentuates her appreciation of the priceless immaterial value with which the brown paper bill is associated. Here in the series of shots gliding between her hands and her face and between her fingering of the paper and the expectant facial expressions of her "uncles" and "auntie," the audience finds Zhang Yimou's deliberate execution of an alternative affective association. They discern the possibility of (re)productive sustenance and (re)creational support beyond the nuclear family and the free market, a promising nonfilial and noncommodity affiliation. The scene reveals the relationship between people as people, not as private owners of alienable intellect, affect, and labor, engaged in self-interested exchange of things, free of any personal attachments. In laying it bare as a mere piece of paper, the scene strips the magic of money as the sole bearer of universal value and prepares for the rise of an imponderable feeling against the superficial valuation of a cup of Häagen-Dazs and a Popsicle. It resists quantitative substitution because the depth of its meaning resides in the particular quality of the human being and the reciprocity of empathy. The affecting affects recuperated through Zhang's camera are therefore not the same as those "recycl[ed] lost faculties, or lost bodies, or lost sociality" that the market manufactures through the culture of simulacra: "People no longer look at each other, but there are institutes for that. They no longer touch each other, but there is contactotherapy" (Baudrillard 13). Rather, they seem to stem from a residual recognition of the mutual dependency of human subjects that the sheer objectivity of monetary and market relation has not yet been able to totally eradicate.

Not paradoxically, physical disability and economic denial are the very circumstances under which an independent valuation of plenitude and penury and a cultivation of collective responsibility for (re)productive dependency come into viable play. Zhang Yimou appears to have seized on Wu Ying's visual impairment for its full dialectic significance. Blindness incapacitates Wu Ying's entry into the capitalist market, aborting her effort to competently alienate her labor in exchange for the normative freedom of the possessive individual that money confers upon it. Blindness also frees Wu Ying from the daily bombardment of simulacra, the colonization of a transnational visual culture that transforms libidinal images into commodities and prescribes possible life trajectories via mass mediation (Appadurai 53–54; Shohat and Stam). In this respect, Wu Ying's blindness, as accidental immunity to the precipitation of deterritorialized images, appears a sanctuary for a relatively autonomous space of subjectivity to survive in ways that Ermo cannot.[12] Similar to Wu Ying's visual disability, Old Zhao's inability to adequately participate in the new regime of consumption seems also to warrant his continual practice of the older structures of feeling, laden with imponderable affects.

An island of contentment, Wu Ying and Old Zhao chat heartily on the sidewalk of Beida Street, as though a local defense against the saturation of global capitalism. However, just as the Häagen-Dazs shop is a mere step away from the Popsicle stand, the local and the global are already coextensive. While blindness temporarily secures local difference, making possible the happy times of Wu Ying and Old Zhao, Zhang Yimou makes visible that the utopian sociality his characters embody is severely restricted in its sphere of influence, for precisely no other reason than being local, forced to become "the vagabonds" as opposed to "tourists" (Bauman 77–102). In the "manic logic of global capitalism" that enables some "people and nations to take sudden leaps into modernity" and promotes the "exploitation of the weak by the strong," Old Zhao and Wu Ying are unmistakable signs of privation and immobility, the true definition of the local and the weak as people who cannot move (Greider 12).

What *Happy Times* deals with consequently is the all too pressing presence of the disabled and the immobile among us to whom a predatory neoliberal global capitalism turns a blind eye. In this sense, the film dignifies the existential materiality of the displaced as it demands a civilized social collectivity so that people of divergent capabilities and circumstances are given equal opportunity to achieve, as Amartya Sen advocates, development as freedom. In their painstaking construction of the massage parlor and their caring contrivance of its continuity, Old Zhao and friends have at least two significant accomplishments. They have compelled a recognition of "dependency as both universal and inevitable," a human condition for which society is ultimately responsible (Fineman xvii). And they have put "a theory of justice" into the practice of increasing the advantage of the least favored groups in society (Rawls). A particular version of the cultural, as the practice of everyday life laden with care, is finally recuperated, for the construction of an alternative social collectivity that combats what Bourdieu terms 'the tyranny of the market.' A supreme irony remains, however, since Old Zhao and friends are themselves as disadvantaged and in need of succor as Wu Ying, for the forcibly downsized and the unfortunately disabled are the social outcasts of China as they are elsewhere in the contemporary world: they are neither competent consumers in the social sphere of commodity consumption nor empowered citizens capable of mobilizing the state for their political and economic rights. With all their conscience, care, and civility, Old Zhao and friends are hardly capable of either resuscitating the nuclear family or constituting from the cinders of a socialist state a liberal civil society, believed to be able to bear the brunt of global capital as the state retreats from its democratic commitments and provision of social security.[13] What, then, are the fate of their ideal society and the fortune of (re)productive care?

Zhang Yimou struggles between two narrative resolutions of *Happy Times* after Wu Ying's stepmother breaks up with Old Zhao openly and officially. In the version released by Sony Classics in the US, Old Zhao is hit by a truck and slips into a coma. Little Fu and friends find the bloodstained letter Old Zhao addressed to Wu Ying in the name of her delinquent biological father and they also find Wu Ying's taped message that discloses her awareness of the whole charade, expresses her deep gratitude to her uncles and auntie, and explains her decision of departure. She does not want to further burden them and reassures them of her survival. Replaying Wu Ying's message, Little Fu reads Old Zhao's letter, which renews the father's promise to find a cure for the daughter's blindness. As the reading drowns the sound of the tape recorder, the camera cuts to a teary Wu Ying walking alone in the street accompanied by the tick-tack of her probing stick and Zhao's words of comfort, "everything will be alright." The conclusion released by Beauty Culture Communications in China, however, does not contain the truck accident. Old Zhao walks Wu Ying to work one morning only to find the factory and the massage parlor bulldozed. Declining to confess the charade as Little Fu encourages him to, Old Zhao leads Wu Ying to the still standing massage bed and reads her the letter, reiterating a father's commitment to the daughter's welfare.

Both dénouements pronounce the apparent death of utopia and an end of happy times. In the American version, Old Zhao is seen on life support while Wu Ying strikes out on her own. There are at least three layers of meaning to this conclusion. First, the narrative turn of the individual protagonist traveling alone on the open road can be an unambiguous affirmation of the autonomy myth: not only is it desirable for Wu Ying to realize the significance of self-sufficiency, but such strong conviction also seems tantamount to its attainability. Second, this apparent nod to the ideology of possessive individualism and the efficiency of the market to provide, however, is simultaneously undercut by the introduction of the stick that aids Wu Ying's hesitant movement in the city. One cannot but be reminded of her frightened paralysis amid rush-hour traffic and Old Zhao's involuntary rescue earlier in the film. Now, in the absence of any specific social support, the stick is shown as the only material reliance Wu Ying has in the precarious street, the metaphoric avenues of capitalist traffic. However, this exposed limitation of liberty is complicated by a third dimension of the treatment, namely the film's deployment of voice-overs. It is here that the letter by Zhao and the message by Wu are super-imposed upon each other in an audio montage, achieving a kind of discursive dialogue without the material presence of the interlocutors. This symbolic substitution of the physical person, Old Zhao, with his partial embodiment, his voice, is reminiscent of Ang Lee's conclusion of *Pushing Hands*, where an object, the sword of the grandfather, begins to stand for grandfather, the individual subject. Zhang's juxtaposition of the voice-overs, instead of reminding the audience of the comatose state of a caring society and the urgency of its revival, functions more or less as aesthetic kitsch, and a powerful kitsch not unlike Lee's. In conjuring up a mental image of Old Zhao and Wu Ying's togetherness both offscreen and in time immemorial, the protagonists of the film have become at once figures of discursive disposability and objects of nostalgia. Old Zhao and Wu Ying are no longer active agents of the real social world: they are dematerialized except for being "simulacra" of some golden past in Baudrillard's sense, signs without value, cinematic images whose sole worth rests on an audience's feel-good resignation to the death of utopia (22).

The political passivity and aesthetic escapism in this American narrative closure of *Happy Times* betrays a condition of "cruel optimism" that Lauren Berlant derives from her analysis of the cultural contradiction in the post–Cold War neoliberal US, where for the working poor in particular fantasies of the good life do not seem to wane with real diminishing opportunities. In his deployment of cinema as none other than nebulous *communitas*, Zhang could be appealing to the American ideological obfuscation Berlant clarifies and condemns. Or, he could be anticipating a Chinese need for the similarly successful American biopolitical management via the very production of "cruel optimism." In the People's Republic of China's determined transition from the fictions of *1984* to that of *Brave New World*, a cinematic form of "soma" that induces the veneration of asocial sovereignty and individual material success against the overwhelming odds of downward mobility seems very much in order.[14] Otherwise, China's Americanization in Capital's Second Coming would indeed be woefully insufficient.

Much to his credit, however, Zhang's cut of the Chinese version is devoid of excessive artificial sweeteners and melodious mystifications. The death of the short-lived utopia that Old Zhao, Wu Ying, and company cultivated does not accompany the disappearance or elimination of the main characters. It is instead attributed explicitly to the objective economic force, that is, global capital's constant remaking of physical and social landscapes. Razing the massage parlor at the end reinforces both imagistically and symbolically similar scenes at the beginning of the film, namely the abandonment of the bus and then its demolition after Old Zhao and Little Fu turned it into "Happy Times Little Hut." With the deliberate double exposure of such violence of removal, Zhang Yimou insists on gauging the aftermath of capital's creative destruction and the means of coping with its consequences. If the debris of an ancient edifice can be readily hauled to the dump, what will happen to the humans of those dwellings? Contrary to the American version in which characters are dispatched to another place and another time, in the Chinese version Old Zhao and Wu Ying stay recalcitrantly on the screen as subjects of history, still bound by their physical proximity and psychosocial interdependency.

The closing shot is panoramic: sitting on the message bed amid the rubble and against the steel skeleton of the now gutted factory, Old Zhao reads his letter to Wu Ying in the name of her biological father. The eschewal of close-ups of the kind used in the last sequence of the American version and the steady focus of the long shot betray Zhang Yimou's intention to chart the individual plights of his protagonists against the palpable social plane. The image of Old Zhao and Wu Ying in the same frame at the same time in the open arena, with its almost painful duration and persistent denial of motion, compels the audience to come to terms with the characters' shared encumbrance as a matter of public concern. In coupling the destinies of two biologically unrelated characters together in asexual affective affiliation, Zhang Yimou declines to confine the question of care as an issue of the domestic nuclear family. In focusing on their struggle in securing the satisfaction of their basic needs, the director has also transcended the privatized understanding of care, when "care is devalued conceptually through a connection with privacy, with emotion, and with the needy" (Tronto 117). Unlike the "cruel optimism" of the American version where a form of irrational exuberance erases the lesson of the Sphinx riddle, this father–daughter scene relentlessly restores in stark realism as well as a Gramscian "optimism of the will" the displaced natural condition of biological dependency, disability, and decline. This willful register-ing of biological dependency of individuals within a universal *communitas* makes the project of its alleviation and emancipation a pressing social need as well as a public priority both in China and elsewhere.

Happy Times shows us that the biopolitics of neoliberal (re)creation has played havoc with precapitalist psychic habits and ethic codes, but the cultural as a mode of noncommodified difference and (re)productive social practice is not entirely drained of its agency of resistance. Zhang Yimou seems to invest equal faith as Terry Eagleton does in a concomitant construction of a common and caring public culture. "[W]hat has come about in our time," Eagleton observes, is "an increas-ingly close interweaving of all three of [Raymond] Williams's categories," the dominant, the residual, and the emergent:

> The dominant culture, itself an unequal composite of the "high" and the post-modern, of civility and commercialism, increasingly undermines traditional identities, thus pressurizing the residual to the point where it reappears as the emergent. The beleaguered family, region, community, moral code, religious tradition, ethnic group, nation-state or natural environment inspires a move-ment which in challenging the dominant culture of the present, lays claim to what might lie beyond it.
>
> (123)

Recycling industrial waste from a communist past, Old Zhao constructs a space of solidarity in late capitalism, both drawing from values and experiences of previous social formations and revitalizing them for the present. Although the recuperated material for the ideal society is again reduced to rubble at the film's end, Zhang Yimou seems dogged in deploying cinema as a vehicle of cultural critique and utopian contemplation. Old Zhao's is truly a cinematic model of cosmopolitan collectivity, a conscientious form of affiliation extending beyond the biological and the nuclear family. What this model reveals is not only the irreducibility of human dependency and the grassroots creativity that arises to meet the needs of care and sustenance that capital has refused to duly pay for, but also the insufficiency of the nuclear family unit to shoulder the sole responsibility of supplying and caring for the source of labor when capital is given free rides by the deregulating state. In eschewing the logic of commodity exchange as human exchange and in extending care beyond filiation, Old Zhao and friends have performed a laudable form of local cosmopolitanism, which is neither elitist nor bloodless, promising solidarity in a world of solitude, solipsism, and social neglect. The collapse of this community seems to indicate that small-scale communal invention cannot really sustain the burden of collective care where state intervention and capital investment are incumbent.[15]

The film's unflinching confrontation of the challenges and costs of care is an explicit philosophic critique of neoliberal notions of liberty couched both in the myth of individual autonomy and the mirage of the laissez-faire market. In fact, *Happy Times*'s yearning for a more equitable condition of (re)productive as well as (re)creational thriving expresses a return of the residual: it revises the radical individualism of *Red Sorghum*, which indicts the psychosocial frustration of self-realization under Mao's communism. A necessary and enabling instrument of opposition to the totalitarian suppression of personal initiatives, this possessive individualism of exclusive (re)creational self-interests has during the compression of Chinese capitalist development metamorphosed into a dominant force of oppression, whose rampant disregard of social welfare once more compels the search for alternatives. In this sense, Old Zhao is clearly a trope of the pressurized residual that reappears as the emergent. Not incidentally, Old Zhao as the altruistic and protective paternal figure marks the figurative return of Luohan, the brotherly overseer of Grandma's distillery in *Red Sorghum*. In approximation to Brown's definition, both Luohan and Old Zhao are feminized and failed figures of romantic masculinity (162). In the current commonsense criteria of scoring in both economic and emotional arenas of action, Old Zhao is a figure of totally failed masculinity compared to the partially failed masculinity of Old Zhu from *Eat, Drink, Man, Woman*. Old Zhu's selfless sustenance of domesticity is sexually compensated in the film's final revelation, whereas Old Zhao's comparable psychosocial needs, as he answers Wu Ying's query on their way to the dismembered massage parlor, are indefinitely deferred.

While Old Zhao does not have the competitive edge in the marriage market demarcated by surplus values and material resources, he has, however, a surplus of selfless devotion to a daughter not of his own in a house he does not own. What Old Zhao has failed in the fulfillment of his personal (re)creational needs he has succeeded in an excess provision of socially necessary (re)productive care. In this idealistic casting of Old Zhao, Zhang Yimou has heroically revised the gendered division of love and labor and proposed an alternative conception of emotional economy that integrates individual fulfillment with nurturing sites of social continuity.[16] Old Zhao's endeavors are exemplary practices not of a "bad utopia" in the "purely subjunctive mood" but of a "good utopia" which "finds a bridge between the present and future in those forces within the present which are potentially able to transform it" (Eagleton 22). The same could be asserted of Zhao's artistic progenitor Zhang: against the neoliberal end of history in Capital's Second Coming, his cinema comes to perform the potentials of an emergent egalitarian and emancipatory family values, in which "the [imaginary] past returns, this time as the future" (Ibid. 123).[17]

Notes

1 Like *Red Sorghum, Happy Times* also draws from the literary work of Mo Yan, the Chinese Nobel laureate, this time his novel, *Shifu, You'll Do Anything For a Laugh*, from which Zhang has taken much greater creative liberty.

2 A self-proclaimed "feminist" reading, Liu's essay suffers from essentialist assumptions of race and gender, a glaring omission of class, and a sorry methodological individualism that fails to recognize Lee's contradictory mediation of family and intimacy in late capitalism.

3 The formal fissure in Zhang Yimou's cinematic corpus roughly parallels a watershed event in Chinese history, the 1989 Tiananmen Square massacre, when popular demand for democracy was quelled in cold blood. The first film to appear three years after the crackdown, *Qiu Ju*'s quest of retribution for the wrongful wounding of her husband by the village party chief unmistakably functions as a somber political allegory of state governance and social justice. The confusion of justice that the film addresses mediates a series of value competitions in the wake of China's embrace of global capitalism. The film's repetitive and insistent shuttling between the agrarian and industrializing modes of life spatializes the rivalry between saving face in a face-to-face village and the faceless abstraction of property rights in the global village.

4 This general shift of style and ideology must be qualified by Zhang's later return to cinematic spectacles (see note 17 of this chapter). Of great intrigue here is the parallel shift in Yu Hua, author of the bestselling *Brothers* and Zhang's contemporary. In the 1980s Yu thrived on aesthetic experimentalism, while in the 1990s he switched to social realism to deal with the lives of rural migrants and the urban poor (K. Liu 102–26).

5 A more direct reworking of De Sica is Wang Xiaoshua's *Beijing Bicycles* 北京单车 (2001).

6 The forfeiture of original narrative objectives turns out to be a typical strategy of Zhang's post–*Qiu Ju* production. The damage of a laptop and the struggle for its compensation structure the story of *Keep Cool* 有话好好说 (1997), but the film concludes with an admirable formation of fraternity. *Not One Less* is initially driven by a peasant girl's quest for fifty Chinese yuan in exchange for her work as a substitute teacher. It ends, however, with her becoming the populist cause célèbre against the Chinese state's negligence of rural education.

7 Zhang has clearly joined other Chinese directors in their unflinching examination of disability and disposability in a quickly capitalizing Chinese society. The retarded brother in Zhang Yang's *Shower* 洗澡 (1999), the petty thief in Jia Zhangke's *Xiaowu* 小武 (1997), and the migrant miner in Li Yang's *Blind Shaft* 盲井 (2003) come immediately to mind.

8 The camera slides seamlessly between the bustling service economy of the city center and its peripheral industrial wasteland only to jolt the audience into an epiphany of what Old Zhao and company experienced at the hotel's revolving glass door: the world has been sharply divided and its desirable part denies majority access.

9 Contrary to Simmel and a body of writing that deplores money's devastating flattening of social ties, Zelizer argues that money can indeed be incorporated into "personalized webs of relationship, family relations, interaction with authorities, and forays through shops and businesses" (2). While the first scene may show the social meaning of money in Zelizer's sense, I'll read the second scene along Simmel's lines.

10 Williams defines the residual as "experiences, meanings, and values, which cannot be expressed or substantially verified in terms of the dominant culture," but "nevertheless lived and practiced" (121).

11 The scene of Old Zhao sitting at the doorstep of "Happy Times Little Hut" refusing to have the door shut for the dating couple is just another instance of the residual. The notion of a public ethical standard that he feels obligated to maintain contradicts directly with his wish to earn money by charging the couple for their paid privacy. This incomplete understanding of property, of possessive and affective individualism, may well explain Old Zhao's altruistic accommodation of Wu Ying.

12 Contrary to Wu Ying, the female protagonist in Zhang's *Not One Less*, Wei Minzhi, actually learns to manipulate the monetary value of the "mediatized sign," suggesting an appropriation of visual culture not for individual interest but for the collective good (Chow 148).

13 As Wang Hui notes, the civil society imagined in the context of contemporary China completely leaves out the working class and the peasants. Because of the conflation or collusion of the global political and economic elite in Capital's Second Coming, the liberal concept of civil society as a force of mediation between the state and the market is scarcely feasible in practice (87–88, 177–79). For the ambivalent role of civil society in Latin America, see Yudice (95 108, 184 86).

14 Soma is a drug of bliss and oblivion commonly used by fictive citizens of Huxley's dystopia, very much like speed in our actual world of globalization. The end of the Cold War and the triumph of the Reagan-Thatcher-Deng Xiaoping Revolution could, in my view, be metaphorically apprehended as the literal victory of the literary *Brave New World* over *1984* and *Animal Farm*.

15 See Fineman for an analysis of care concerns and policy proposals, and Nussbaum and Cohen, and Cheah and Robbins, for discussions of cosmopolitanism.

16 Not incidentally, *Together* 和你在一起 (2002) by Chen Kaige, also deals with a single father raising a child not of his own descent. This gendered revision of masculinity in relation to (re)productive care seems to resonate with an overall feminist demand to reorganize home and work in global capital (Hochschild 2003).

17 In appearance, Zhang's return to Orientalist spectacle in *Hero* 英雄 (2002) and *House of Flying Daggers* 四面埋伏 (2004) would invalidate the periodic shift and the corresponding formal and thematic changes that constitute my analyses. Contrary to Evans Chan's quite hyperbolic charge of the director as the "fascist myth-maker," I would argue that his pair of kung fu capers only reiterates Zhang's persistent yet contradictory desire for individual autonomy and social welfare. To continue allegorically, I take *Hero* to be a tale that betrays a nationalist longing for solidarity. While such longing articulates a wish for the strong state to rein in schizophrenic capital, its invitation of self-submission to the absolute sovereign, epitomized by the emperor Qin, is deeply disturbing. In essence, *Hero* seems a belated aesthetic justification of the 1989 military suppression of popular unrest that in reality removed the roadblocks for the Second Coming of Capital in China. Intriguingly, *House of Flying Daggers* revises *Hero*'s cult of the emperor and eulogy of the sacrificial subject in the name of an ideal state. It questions instead all forms of political loyalty and advocates a sole allegiance to personal preservation and happiness. Not only do these two films reenact the swing of pendulum characteristic of Zhang's periodic dyad, but their recurrence also insists on thinking through the condition in which individual liberty and social solidarity are to achieve optimal balance. His oeuvre appears to have shown how easily communitarian desires could slip into totalitarian fantasies, and asocial and atomic individualism into anarchies.

Works cited

Altman, Rick. "Casablanca." *The Oxford Guide to Film Studies*. New York: Oxford UP, 1992. 287–88.

Appadurai, Arjun. *Modernity at Large: Cultural Dimensions of Globalization*. Minneapolis: U of Minnesota P, 1996.

Barry, Andrew, Thomas Osborne, and Nicolas Rose, eds. *Foucault and Political Reason: Liberalism, Neoliberalism and Rationalities of Government*. Chicago: Cambridge UP, 1996.

Baudrillard, Jean. *Simulacra and Simulation*. Trans. Sheila Faria Glaser. London and New York: Verso, 1988.

Bauman, Zygmunt. *Globalization: The Human Consequences*. New York: Columbia UP, 1998.

Berlant, Lauren. *Cruel Optimism*. Durham: Duke UP, 2011.

Berry, Chris. "*Wedding Banquet*: A Family (Melodrama) Affair." *Chinese Films in Focus II*. Ed. Chris Berry. New York: Palgrave, 2008. 235–42.

Bourdieu, Pierre. *Acts of Resistance: Against the Tyranny of the Market*. Trans. Richard Rice. New York: The New Press, 1998.

Brennan, Teresa. "Why the Time Is Out of the Joint: Marx's Political Economy without the Subject." *South Atlantic Quarterly* 97.2 (Spring, 1998): 263–80.

Brooks, Peter. *The Melodramatic Imagination: Balzac, Henry James, Melodrama, and the Mode of Excess*. New Haven: Yale UP, 1976/1995.

Brown, Wendy. *States of Injury: Power and Freedom in Late Modernity* Princeton: Princeton UP, 1995.

Castells, Manuel. *The Rise of the Network Society (The Information Age: Economy, Society and Culture Volume I)*. Malden: Blackwell, 1996.

Chan, Evans. "Zhang Yimou's *Hero* – The Temptation of Fascism." *Film International* 8 (March, 2004). *http://www.filmint.nu/netonly/eng/heroevanschan.htm*.

Cheah, Pheng, and Bruce Robbins, eds. *Cosmopolitics: Thinking and Feeling Beyond the Nation*. Minneapolis: U of Minnesota P, 1998.

Chow, Rey. "*Not One Less*: The Fable of Migration." *Chinese Films in Focus: 25 New Takes*. Ed. Chris Berry. London: British Film Institute, 2003. 144–51.

Eagleton, Terry. *The Idea of Culture*. Oxford: Blackwell, 2000.

Fineman, Martha Albertson. *The Autonomy Myth: A Theory of Dependency*. New York: New P, 2004.

Foucault, Michel. *The Birth of Biopolitics: Lectures at the College de France, 1978–79*. Ed. Michel Senellart. Trans. Graham Burchell. New York: Palgrave Macmillan, 2008.

———. *The History of Sexuality: An Introduction*. Trans. Robert Hurley. New York: Vintage, 1990.

———. "Technologies of the Self." *Technologies of the Self: A Seminar with Michel Foucault*. Eds. Luther H. Martin, Huck Gutman, and Patrick H. Hutton. Amherst: U of Massachusetts P, 1988. 16–49.

Giddens, Anthony. *Modernity and Self-Identity: Self and Society in the Late Modern Age*. Stanford: Stanford UP, 1991.

Gopal, Sangita. *Conjugations: Marriage and Form in the New Bollywood Cinema*. Chicago: U of Chicago P, 2011.

Greider, William. *One World, Ready or Not: The Manic Logic of Global Capitalism*. New York: Touchstone, 1998.

Hareven, Tamara. *Family Time and Industrial Time: The Relationship between the Family and Work in a New England Industrial Community*. Cambridge: Cambridge UP, 1982.

Hochschild, Arlie Russell. *The Commercialization of Intimate Life: Notes from Home and Work*. Berkeley: U of California P, 2003.

────. *The Time Bind: When Work Becomes Home and Home Becomes Work.* New York: Henry Holt, 2000.

Lake, Roseann. "Bachelor Padding: How Lonely Single Men Created China's Dangerous Real Estate Bubble." *Foreign Policy Magazine* (September 28, 2012).

Lasch, Christopher. *Haven in a Heartless World: The Family Besieged.* New York: W. W. Norton, 1977/1995.

Liu, Cynthia. "'To Love, Honor, and Dismay': Subverting the Feminine in Ang Lee's Resuscitated Patriarchs." *Hitting Critical Mass: A Journal of Asian-American Cultural Criticism* 3.1 (1995): 1–60.

Liu, Kang. *Globalization and Cultural Trends in China.* Honolulu: U of Hawaii P, 2004.

MacIntyre, Alasdair. *After Virtue: A Study in Moral Theory.* Notre Dame: U of Notre Dame P, 1984.

Macpherson, Crawford Brough. *The Political Theory of Possessive Individualism: Hobbes to Locke.* Oxford: Oxford UP, 1962.

Massey, Doreen. "A Global Sense of Place." *Marxism Today.* (June, 1991): 24–29.

Nussbaum, Martha, and Joshua Cohen, eds. *For the Love of Country: Debating the Limits of Patriotism.* Boston: Beacon Press, 1996.

Ong, Aihwa. *Flexible Citizenship: The Cultural Logics of Transnationality.* Durham: Duke UP, 1999.

Poggi, Gianfranco. *Money and the Modern Mind: Georg Simmel's Philosophy of Money.* Berkeley: U of California P, 1993.

Polanyi, Karl. *The Great Transformation: The Political and Economic Origins of our Time.* Boston: Beacon, 1944/1957.

Rawls, John. *A Theory of Justice: Revised Edition.* Cambridge: Belknap P, 1999.

Said, Edward W. *Orientalism.* New York: Vintage Books, 1979.

Sen, Amartya. *Development as Freedom.* New York: Anchor Books, 1999.

Shohat, Ella, and Robert Stam. "From the Imperial Family to the Transnational Imaginary: Media Spectatorship in the Age of Globalization." *Global/Local: Cultural Production and the Transnational Imaginary.* Eds. Rob Wilson and Wimal Dissanayake. Durham: Duke UP, 1996. 145–72.

Simmel, Georg. *Georg Simmel on Individuality and Social Forms.* Ed. Donald Levine. Chicago: U of Chicago P, 1971.

Tronto, Joan C. *Moral Boundaries: A Political Argument for an Ethic of Care.* Routledge: New York/London, 1993.

Wang, Hui. *China's New Order: Society, Politics, and Economy in Transition.* Ed. Theodore Huters. Cambridge: Harvard UP, 2003.

Wang, Shaoguang. "The Changing Role of Government in China." *Whither China: Intellectual Politics in Contemporary China.* Ed. Xudong Zhang. Durham: Duke UP, 2001. 123–60.

Williams, Raymond. *Marxism and Literature.* Oxford: Oxford UP, 1977.

Yang, Gan. "Debating Liberalism and Democracy in China in the 1990s." *Whither China: Intellectual Politics in Contemporary China.* Ed. Xudong Zhang. Durham: Duke UP, 2001. 79–102.

Yudice, George. *The Expediency of Culture: Uses of Culture in the Global Era.* Durham: Duke UP, 2004.

Zaretsky, Eli. *Capitalism, Family, and Personal Life.* New York: Harper & Row, 1976.

Zelizer, Viviana A. *The Social Meaning of Money: Pin Money, Paychecks, Poor Relief and Other Currencies.* New York: Basic Books, 1994.

Zhang, Xudong, ed. *Whither China: Intellectual Politics in Contemporary China.* Durham: Duke UP, 2001.

Zizek, Slavoj, ed. *First as Tragedy, Then as Farce.* London/New York: Verso, 2009.

4 The deregulation of affect and reflexive individualization in Hou Hsiao-hsien and Yang De-chang

Although Hou Hsiao-hsien 侯孝贤 is best known for his penetrating historical observation and persistent recuperation of memory in his virtuoso trilogy, *City of Sadness* 悲情城市 (1989), *The Puppetmaster* 戏梦人生 (1993), and 好男好女 *Good Men, Good Women* (1995), his sensitivity to the striae of feeling that emerge in Taiwan's rush toward (post)modernity is also evident in *Dust in the Wind* 恋恋风尘 (1986) and *Millennium Mambo* 千喜曼波 (2000). Though less epic in tone, the diversity of emotional responses to the island state's capitalist industrialization again takes center stage in *Three Times* 最好的时光 (2005). Similar to contemporary Chinese women directors who embed intimacy and family in between generational and psychological temporalities, *20/30/40* (2004) by his compatriot Sylvia Chang (张艾嘉), *Summer Snow* 女人四十 (1994) and 男人四十 (2002) by Ann Hui of Hong Kong (许鞍华), Hou grounds his treatment of emotional life in the historicity of body and society. This explains the film's composition of a triptych, three vignettes in an odd antichronological order, featuring the same actors of Shu Qi and Zhang Zhen as the romantic duo, but situating them in the respective years of 1966, 1911, and 2005. With this eccentric narrative order, *Three Times* achieves simultaneous cinematic crystallization and compression. On the one hand, it periodizes the shifting norms of gendered subjectivity, throwing varieties of eroticism and emotion in sharp historical relief. On the other hand, it provides an overview of the assortment of affects approached in Hou's oeuvre as though in cinematic stenography, evoking such spirit of particular eras as in *The Boys from Fengkui* 風櫃來的人 (1983), *Flowers of Shanghai* 海上花 (1998), and *Millennium Mambo* (2000).

For all its epitomic and economic form and Hou's trademark "ascetic realism" (Yeh and Davis 134), *Three Times* introduces us to the "deregulation of affect" that centers not only Hou's titular film but also the last three films of Edward Yang De-chang 扬德昌, his comrade-in-arms of the Taiwanese New Wave.[1] Ventriloquizing the mantra of neoliberal economics, I argue that the act to deregulate, to remove the governmental check on erratic market mechanisms, is only secondary to incitation of emancipating subjects from the social constraints of their desire. More than we would readily recognize, unleashing the hitherto tempered forces of neoliberal economy requires a mobilization of "the inner energy that propels us toward an act":

> While emotion is not action per se . . . [it is] the "energy-laden" side of action . . . [that] implicate[s] cognition, affect, evaluation, motivation, and

the body. Far from being pre-social or pre-cultural, emotions are cultural meanings and social relationships that are inseparably compressed together and it is this compression which confers on them their capacity to energize action. . . . [T]he making of capitalism went hand in hand with the making of an intensely specialized emotional culture and that when we focus on this dimension of capitalism – on its emotions so to speak – we may be in a position to uncover another order in the social organization of capitalism.

(Illouz 2–4)

Calling it "emotional capitalism," this is for Eva Illouz a culture in which "emotional and economic discourses and practices mutually shape each other" (5). While Illouz unfortunately refers to its making in the past tense, as though a fait accompli, Hou, Yang, and other Chinese directors have captured emotional capitalism in its remaking over historical time. The nature of capital's incessant revolution of the relations of production entails a constant "revolution of the heart" (Lee). If industrial capitalism evolves from goods production to service production to the production of experiences (Pine and Gilmore), erotic attachment and emotional sustenance have undergone a parallel historical passage "from obedience to intimacy." By the nuanced account of Stephanie Coontz, contemporary love's conquest of marriage – in its historical role of property transmission and biosocial reproduction – is a mixed blessing, at once promising individual freedom and furthering fragility of social bonds (1–12). If the liberalization of economy in the Second Coming of Capital hinges on the trope of governmental deregulation, such loosening of normative control over economic production cannot be divorced from a parallel if not a prior change of emotional orders and ethical parameters.

In the previous chapter, Ang Lee and Zhang Yimou showed us the types of emotions, while struggling to disassociate themselves from the confines of the family in both its extended and nuclear formation, still palpitate with an observation of ethical restraints that the development and dissemination of neoliberal capital are not yet able to eradicate. Solidarity, whether filial or afilial in structure, actual or imagined in nature, retains its tentative hold on discourses and practices of the everyday in Chinese-speaking societies of speedy capitalization. In this chapter, we focus on Hou's and Yang's mediation of romantic feelings in late capitalism apparently already detached from the moorings of kinship and marriage. If the historical forms of marriage and family constitute the normative structures of feeling in preliberal and liberal societies, does an independence from their apparently regulative and repressive functions usher in more liberating affects of individual and social thriving? If marriage in the past did much of the work markets do in the Second Coming of Capital (Coontz 9), could romance for its own sake fulfill the subjects' longing and belonging while transcend their dependency on the global market? Moreover, if intimacy has by now constituted its own sovereignty of feeling and governmental reason in the exclusive terrain of market choice and reflexive individualization, would the deregulation of normative cultural logic and social affect result in "the democratizing of personal life" or simply lead to "the normal chaos of love" (Giddens 188–92; Beck and Beck-Gernsheim)? When love is the esteemed postfamilial, poststructural, and reflexive affect, becoming "liquid" while mimicking the conditions of "flexible capitalism" and "liquid modernity," would it make us more satisfactory lovers and consequently freer human beings (Bauman 2000, 2003; Harvey)?

1

Three Times serves as an inaugural inquiry of such affective metamorphosis in the social reorganization of capital. Instead of following its original order, the time of Taiwanese industrialization in 1966, the time of the Chinese Republican Revolution in 1911, and the time of global capitalism circa 2005, we will read the film's middle triptych first, adopting a chronological order of interpretation before proposing an answer to the director's eccentric narrative sequencing.[2] To begin, "Dreams of Liberty" (1911) is set at a parlor house in Da Dao Cheng, where the geisha/courtesan played by Shu Qi and her gentleman caller by Zhang Zhen rendezvous. The pair remains anonymous, as though conveying character types of the era rather than individuals. The exclusive interior space is dark, though not without the occasional warmth illuminated by oil lamps and coal stoves. Shot in a pre-talkie mode, the entire episode is silent except for the songs Shu sings to the accompaniment of her *pipa* (a Chinese lute) that at times alternate with the nondiegetic sound of a piano solo.

Zhang is a father with a wife and children, an heir of a wealthy family, and a nationalist devoted both to Taiwanese independence from Japanese rule and to the success of the Chinese Republican Revolution from the Manchu Dynasty. Apparently in favor of equality for women, he publishes op-ed pieces against the system of polygamy. When Shu's sister gets pregnant by a patron, however, he donates money to redeem her from the house of ill repute so that her consummation into concubinage becomes viable. While Hou's camera lingers tenderly on Shu and Zhang's intercourse of politics and poetry, betraying the couple's rare intimacy of minds beyond their sexual liaison, it keeps in plain sight the hierarchy of aristocratic gender relations as well as the exchange of women as commodity. When Shu finally poses the question of "her future," proposing implicitly a lawful marriage to Zhang in either monogamous or polygamous form, the fighter of political liberty eschews a direct personal answer. An epistolary response comes in the mail later. Citing Liang Qichao's poem to celebrate the Chinese overthrow of the Manchus and lament Japan's continual annexation of Taiwan, Zhang makes explicit his inability to act on Shu's wish and the inevitability of their separation. Tears streaming down her cheeks, Shu fingers his characters on the rice paper. With the faint monotone of the *pipa* droning on, she fades into the gloom, condemned forever to her indentured servitude.

"Dreams of Liberty" is a trenchant indictment of Zhang's hypocrisy as his political idealism fails miserably Shu's wish for personal freedom. With his long take of the gendered liberty in shorthand, Hou reiterates a contemporary Victorian contradiction in the Taiwanese context: while married women are considered asexual, their husbands are sanctioned to seek sexual gratification beyond the wedlock. It is through this split of the sexes, secured by the condition of men as possessive individuals of natural desire and women not only as properties of their fathers and husbands but also vessels of procreation and vehicles of sexual gratification, that the reproduction of the feudal and early capitalist family is perpetuated. In this political economy of emotional arrangement, Shu remains the caged bird that sings, her song plaintive, piercing through the room partitions and wooden window grids, but her body continues to be kept inside the haute bordello, unable to fly away.

The parlor remains the mise-en-scène in *Three Times*'s first triptych, the second in our chronological reading, "Dreams of Romance," but it is no longer an airtight space of explicit disciplinary enclosure or contractual sexual exchange. Instead, in this episode set first in 1966's Gao Xiong, the pool parlor stands for a space of postadolescent dating amid the quickened pace of industrial capitalism when Taiwan becomes an American protectorate in the Cold War. The story follows Zhang as A Zhen, a high school graduate about to enter compulsory military service, and Shu as Xiu Mei, a pool hall hostess. A shot of the protagonists in two ferries passing in opposite directions introduces us to the cranes and container ships dotting Gao Xiong harbor with robust economic activity and it leads us to the couple's acquaintance at the pool parlor in a quiet street. A game of billiards to "Smoke Gets in Your Eyes" kindles their romantic flame, and A Zhen gets permission from Xiu Mei to write her. Three months later, the reticent young man's love letter arrives, wishing for her eternal beauty and expressing his affection for her through the pop song of the time, "Rain and Tears."[3] True to the spirit of the sentimental lyrics, "something here cannot be denied . . . when your heart's on fire" by the Platters, and Aphrodite's Child's "give me an answer of love . . . when you feel the rainbow of waves," A Zhen and Xiu Mei click and connect, conquering the separation of space and time.

With this contextualization of American popular cultural colonialism, Hou documents a moment when historical Japanese colonialism as inflected in "Dreams of Liberty" has collapsed. Unlike expressions of love constrained by feudal hierarchies and enclosed compounds, A Zhen and Xiu Mei appear to move with their own will and volition, following the prompt of their hearts with all the "rain and tears." The Shu character has transmogrified her former figure of a geisha into a young woman in the emerging entertainment and service economy. Instead of transitioning between the patriarchal households of the father and the husband, Xiu Mei is a self-possessive subject for hire, moving from one pool parlor to another in search of an economic mobility that only the capitalist market encourages.

This first triptych is Hou's unapologetic and nostalgic endorsement of the post–World War II American-style consumer capitalism in Taiwan. It represents for him a liberalization of authoritarian governance and the rise of an alternative emotional economy, a sentimental soft core of gender relationships if you will, to the unequal economic access and oppressive social strictures that precede it. No more do madams or matchmakers matter in this new age of heterosexual companionate affiliation when individual economic self-sufficiency is achievable. Even

Xiu Mei's mother, who makes a brief appearance in "Dreams of Romance," is no more than a mere facilitator directing the hard-pursuing A Zhen to her wandering daughter. With images of his spinning bike wheels and the township names rolling by his bus windows, A Zhen eventually locates Xiu Mei in Hu Wei (The Tiger's Tail). No handshake or bear hug when the romantic duo reunites, face to face, after months of epistolary exchange. After Xiu Mei gets off from work at the pool parlor, the young couple in love at length gets to share bowls of steaming dumplings at a wayside shack. It is right before their parting, because A Zhen has to report to his barracks, and under a big umbrella that Xiu Mei and her intended come into physical contact. In a rare close-up, their hands are seen tentatively brushing against each other before the fingers at last lock, virginally. To "Rain and Tears" by the Platters, A Zhen and Xiu Mei stand side by side at the bus depot in the moist and mysterious night before slowly fading out.

"Dreams of Romance" is for Hou Hsiao-hsien "A Time for Love," the kind of "romantic love" whose presence was first felt in eighteenth-century Western Europe. It was then, according to Anthony Giddens, "the complex of ideas associated with romantic love for the first time associated love with freedom" (40). While Giddens only points out "the emergent ties between freedom and self-realization" (Ibid.), it seems incumbent on us to couple the rise of the romantic love complex to the rise of industrial capitalism, and to the rise of the novel that does the cultural work of supplying a narrative of the possessive individual, who ultimately owns his/her body as well as its feelings. Hou's film narrative shows romantic love as an individualized form of affect contingent upon relative economic independence and awareness of self-identity not dictated by stringent social mandates. Although the director does not portray the marital bond subsequent to A Zhen and Xiu Mei's courting, it is not difficult for the audience to imagine their union, given the episode's ample suggestions, as "a joint emotional enterprise," both "disentangled from wider kinship ties" and "having primacy even over their obligations towards their children" (Ibid. 26).

Such monogamous coupling based on reciprocity of autonomous selfhood seems to have vanished overnight in the last triptych, "Dreams of Youth," when A Zhen, now a photographer and owner of a photo-printing business, and Chen Qing (by Shu Qi), an epileptic and a pop singer with her own fan base, simply hook up. Both are "semi-detached-couples" with their respective partners yet both are also "relationship revolutionaries" in the deregulation and restructuring of capitalism "who have burst the suffocating couple bubble" (Bauman 2003: x). After all, the time is the 2005 of Taipei, and as though reflecting the fin de siècle, the couple is brought onto the screen in a motorbike, rumbling on elevated highways and zipping by rows and rows of high-rises. After a brief pause at an exit ramp for Chen to overcome her seizure, they end up in A Zhen's apartment making out in no time, revealing an efficiency of sexual transaction comparable only to electronic trades of Wall Street. When A Zhen emerges from his apartment afterwards, the camera positions him behind a commercial poster at the street corner. Ever so appropriately for the moment, the ad line reads: "Quick Maintenance: Speedy Oil Change."

When asked to compare his generation's idea and practice of romance with the millennials, Hou seems a bit coy. He professes his confusion about contemporary youth but does not shy away from observing that they are absolute realists: unlike us in their age, they don't idealize, neither do they project their life in the future through literature or cinema, he remarks. For them, nothing is impossible because they are immersed in the absolute real.[4] The denial of limits and the proclivity toward the unsentimental real are expertly rendered in *Three Times*. Finding yourself and knowing your lover now take place postcoitus. It is only after the exchange of bodily fluids that A Zhen discovers on Chen Qing's blog her autobiographical statement. The declaration at once reveals her worldview and her coping mechanism: "An epileptic of pre-mature birth, with fractured bones, a weakened heart, and a near blind right eye," writes Chen Qing, "I have a dollar sign on my chest. I want to sell my soul; so please name a price! There is no past nor future, only the hungry present." With this blasé embrace of both radical contingency and the immediacy of life, driven by an individual survival instinct, Chen Qing and A Zhen come to stand for the youth in the new millennium, personifications of exhaustion in the global "risk society." Gone is the romantic love ideal of 1966, "the one and only" and "the forever" mode of emotional liaison that a regulated postwar capitalist economy appears to have both initiated and steadied. It is arguable if "Dreams of Romance" represents a perfect ideal of heterosexual affiliation of both gender equality and social equilibrium, but the Second Coming of Capitalism shown in "Dreams of Youth" is surely a nightmare of exuberant business transactions as well as emotional desperation and desolation.

The audience will have by now grasped the directorial intention of *Three Times*'s narrative order. Against an automaticity of world history as a necessary teleology of progress, Hou Hsiao-hsien has put 1911 and 2005 after 1966 in descending order of his emotional and ethical valuation and preference. For him, "Dreams of Romance" is the most humane and liberating, and thus the best of times. Neither the feudal era nor the neoliberal one comes close in comparison to the golden age of Hou's own sentimental education, which, not coincidentally, is also the romantic era of welfare capitalism in Taiwan as well as in its palatine state, the US. Devoid of an inclination toward cinematic didacticism, to which his colleague Edward Yang seems prone, Hou refrains from any explicit political commentary on personal sentiments. However, his unrelenting portrayal of cold intimacies in "Dreams of Youth" marks the unmistakable coming into hegemony of flexible capitalism in Taiwan, whose volatile and voracious appetites now compel the flexible bonds of individuals for the fast accumulation of profits/pleasures (Illouz). His depiction of the affectless engagement of sex – a "speedy oil change," as it were – brings him closer in spirit to the island's younger directors, most notably Tsai Ming-Liang who, in such works of memorable misery as *Vive l'Amour* (1994), *The Hole* (1998), *What Time Is It There?* (2001), and *The Wayward Cloud* (2005), has presented with poignancy a pathological emotional wasteland of the Taiwanese economic miracle. But to fully appreciate the urban jungle of loneliness and loss amid the near-instant wealth of the island state in Capital's Second Coming, we need to turn to Edward Yang, who, more than his contemporary and compatriot Hou Hsiao-hsien, Tsai Ming-Liang, and Ang Lee, has engaged the risks of loving and living in Taipei with uttermost clairvoyance.

2

From his first full-length feature *That Day on the Beach* 海滩的一天 (1983) to his last magnum opus *Yi Yi* 一,一 (2000), Edward Yang has tracked Taiwan's economic boom and bust with eye-opening precision through his characters' emotional wheel of fortune. As early as 1992, he became a principal subject of Fredric Jameson's scholarly tome, *The Geopolitical Aesthetic*, and as late as 2000, he won the Best Director award at the Cannes Film Festival, showing a rare combination of both academic and popular critical acclaims. In Yang's *Terrorizer* 恐怖分子 (1986), Jameson identifies the compressed processes of Capital's Second Coming in East Asia. For a critic convinced that the text is essentially a political fantasy articulating the actual and imagined social relations constitutive of the individual within a political economy (Jameson 1982), Yang's cinema necessarily aestheticizes the coexistence of the West's "more homogeneously modernized condition" and the rest's "situation of incomplete modernization" (1991, 310). "Powerful expressions of the marginally uneven and the unevenly developed issuing from a recent experience of capitalism," Jameson writes on Yang, "are often more intense and powerful, more expressive, and above all more deeply symptomatic and meaningful than anything the enfeebled center still finds itself able to say" (1995, 155). Yet, he is also annoyed by Yang's "archaic" recuperation of such modernist narrative as the "synchronous monadic simultaneity" (SMS) and thematic trope as "art versus life," especially when such "prim and pietistic moralizing" is "irrelevant or at least inoperative . . . in the international urban society of late capitalism" (Ibid. 116, 121, 127, 128).

In what I call "the monadic trilogy," *A Confucian Confusion* 独立时代 (1994), *Majiang* 麻将 (1996), and *Yi Yi: A One and a Two* 一,一 (2000), the last three films before his premature passing in 2007, Yang continues to deploy ensemble characters in simultaneous and multifarious story lines and use binary opposition in character types. It is with such cinematic technologies and through a host of partial subjects amid the uneven force fields of economy, emotion, and ethics that Taiwan's recent experience of capitalism achieves faithful filmic representation.[5] Instead of a "waning of affect in postmodern culture" that Jameson identifies as the dominant sentiment of late capitalism of which the metropolis of Taipei is becoming a part, Yang regards such flattening of feeling and deregulation of affect a troubling symptom of social perturbation: Yang refuses to concede to the disappearance of the individual subject and "whole metaphysics of the inside and outside, of the wordless pain within the monad" (1991, 10–11). Not anachronistically but assertively, Yang captures Taiwan's convoluted economic rise with its people's increasing emotional bewilderment, only to try to puzzle out the "ethical and pedagogical-formative" in Capital's Second Coming necessary for the subject of "precarious freedoms" (Beck and Beck-Gernsheim 1; Jameson, 1995, 130).

The dialectic engagement of developmental unevenness betrays itself in the bilingual title of *Duli shidai/A Confucian Confusion. The Age of Independence*, as the Chinese title reads, is simultaneously an era of fuzzy feelings for the descendants of Confucius. Although the sudden liberation of the individual from the bondages of social hierarchy and material scarcity is attributed to the promise of Capital's Second Coming, the deregulation of historical practices of emotion and ethics has its own inescapable predicaments. Yang approaches this ambivalence of independence at present with an allusion to *The Analects* of antiquity. *A Confucian Confusion* is intriguingly prefaced with an excerpt from the chapter of "Zi Lu," in sharp white characters against a pitch-black screen:

> Confucius travels to the state of Wei, riding on the carriage driven by Ran You. "This is really a populous country," Confucius comments. "With such a large population," Ran You queries, "what needs to be done?" "Enrich the people," Confucius replies. "And after that?" the disciple asks further.
>
> (142–43)

Curtailing Confucius's answer, Yang cuts to the next frame with the following statement: "Two millenniums later, within the short span of two decades, Taipei has become one of the world's wealthiest metropolis."[6]

In juxtaposing statements from different times to frame the film, Yang identifies the wealth of nations as a shared problem between pre-Christian Wei and contemporary Taiwan, opening up the possibility of mapping Taipei in its complex historical sediments as well as present sentiments. In omitting the original Confucian response, Yang also seems to set up the monadic trilogy as his own Confucian approximation. From an irrepressible suspicion of "sincerity" in *A Confucian Confusion* to the radical uncertainty of "wants" in *Majiang* to the rumination in *Yi Yi* of the apparently autonomous yet highly administered self is Yang's cinematic quest of existential clarity in the muddles of deregulated or "disorganized capitalism" (Lash and Urry). But this line of inquiry raises immediate issues of interpretive relevance. Does a dynastic conception of society and subjectivity remain appropriate in a free market economy? If so, is Yang's cinematic Confucianism a version of the scholarly neo-Confucianism that rationalizes the rise of East Asian capitalism as culturally indigenous and distinctive?[7]

Yang's correlation of agrarian Wei and postmodern industrial Taiwan is not meant to conflate but to subject tradition, initially encoded as Confucian, to historical evaluation. Indeed, by seizing on the sage's treatise of the hypothetical wealth of a nation that has never acquired material actuality until its relatively recent realization in industrial capitalism, Yang makes it clear that the ambivalence of "independence" his bilingual title imparts is a general problem of late capitalist abundance. *A Confucian Confusion* is a long take of this ambivalence from the spur of Taiwanese economic growth, for what Confucius says and Yang has encrypted is simply "to educate." Education should succeed the enrichment of the population, a surprisingly progressive idea of biopolitical management from 500 B.C. feudal China that anticipates, in spite of itself, its own materialization in Western liberal democracy two millennia later (*The Analects* 143). Yang's challenge is to translate this pedagogical formative, Confucian or Enlightenment European, into a persuasive film practice. To better apprehend the director's structural design and educational mission, I venture an imaginary encounter between Adam Smith and Guy Debord in the spirit of *The Analects* that Yang has framed the inaugurating piece of his monadic trilogy:

> Smith and Debord travel to the island state of Taiwan. Observing the material prosperity in the city of Taipei, Smith cannot help but exclaim, "look at another success story for *The Wealth of Nations!*" to which Debord answers, "economic growth liberates societies from the natural pressures of survival, but they still need to be liberated from their liberators."
>
> (Debord 28)

Taking this hypothetical encounter as the overarching mise-en-scène, we are able to finally grasp *A Confucian Confusion, Majiang,* and *Yi Yi* as Edward Yang's conscientious cinematic reconsideration of the Confucian imperative in Debordian dialectic, his pedagogic formative against "the normal chaos of love."

"Life is theater; to live is to perform": the voice-over of Birdy precedes the unveiling of the film's title. Responding to journalists that he plagiarizes for commercial success, the hot-ticket playwright on roller skates shouts out, "The box office is the most democratic: tickets are the same as votes!" In quick cuts, Yang has set the stage for his ensemble characters between appearance and reality. The audience is introduced to Molly, a confidant of Birdy, an heir of a family fortune and a division head of a multimedia company, of which her sister is the television host of a popular show on relationships. It turns out Birdy is seeking copyright permission from her now estranged novelist husband. Because of her sister's rejection of Akeem, a young and witless businessman with a silver spoon in his mouth, Molly is in an arranged marriage with him. Larry, Akeem's financial adviser and life coach, a married man involved with Feng, a dancer/actress, is seducing Molly. Qi Qi and Xiao Ming, long time fiancés, are having a fight over Molly, the boss of the former and the school buddy of the latter. Meanwhile, Ming's officemate and bosom friend Liren is making out with Feng, who also tries to seduce Ming. Amid frantic business deals and heated affairs, an ensemble cast of characters from every conceivable social strata of Taipei materializes just as the urban landscape of the city comes to constitute a postmodern space of SMS in a quintessential modernist plot-formation (Jameson, 1995, 115).

As Jameson explains elsewhere, SMS first arises from the condition of "monopoly capitalism,"

> when the phenomenological experience of the individual becomes limited to a tiny corner of the social world . . . but the truth of that daily limited experience of London . . . is bound up with the whole colonial system of the British Empire that determines the individual's subjective life.
>
> (1988, 349)

Because the structural coordinates governing life are neither "accessible" nor "conceptualizable" for the subjects in question (Ibid. 350), the SMS plot emerges to "reunite these isolated monads . . . in the most fitful relationship with one another," "reassuring us [of] the Providence-effect" (1995, 115). The sealed modern subject may at best feel his/her relatedness to social totality only as a compensatory aesthetic effect. Jameson distinguishes this modernist SMS from both its precursor and successor forms. SMS is distinct from the narrative omniscience of Victorian realism where a providential worldview remained dominant and moral judgment and "matters of characterology" viable. SMS also departs from its postmodern incarnation in late capitalism where "the depth model" of "appearance-and-reality" is overwhelmed by mere "textuality," "a conception of the succession of various surfaces none of which [is] somehow metaphysically or ontologically privileged over the other" (1988, 349; 1995, 127, 148).

Like *Terrorizer* before and *Majiang* and *Yi Yi* after, Yang's dispersal of his characters and deployment of SMS in *A Confucian Confusion* at once observe the succession of surfaces and blatantly insist on the depth model. Indeed, the chance connection of his caricature-like characters in offices, cars and cafes, studios, sports bars, and streets, manifests the contingent nature of market exchange as well as its correspondent form of sociality. Haphazard and horizontal, this fluid mode of deregulated sociality is overtaking the older vertical form of sociality hinged on pre-given kinship relations and rooted in physical locations. Not surprisingly, we have a sentimental revision in a heart to heart between Molly and Larry in the episode captioned, "there are few Chinese who do not understand this." Akeem, the sole investor of Molly's company, sends Larry there to investigate its financial soundness. Trying his leverage as Akeem's adviser with an intent to rope Molly in romantically, Larry delivers a lecture on a supposedly ubiquitous Chinese cultural practice of "Qing" 情 (i.e., "sentiment, affect, or feeling"). Foreigners do not make the best businessmen, according to Larry, because they know nothing but laws and interests. The Chinese are much superior because of their command of sentiments. "Money is about investment; so is sentiment," Larry intones. Therefore, "You Qing" 友情, the feeling among friends, or friendship, is like "a long-term savings account," while "'Qing Qing' 亲情, the feeling among relatives, such as your family's or Akeem's," as he stares at Molly, "is just like ancestral property." "Whenever 'Qing' 情 is present, whether it is in fiction or film, your sister's TV show or your brother-in-law's romance novels, it is bound to sell," Larry says. "That's why the cultural business your sisters are engaged in is the easiest and the most lucrative."

With Larry's pontification on Qing, Yang evokes two parallel histories of emotion, the history of sentiment in China and the history of "the passions and the interests" in the West (Hirschman). "The Cult of Qing" – emerging in sixteenth-century imperial China through the May 4th Movement of 1919 – is a process of psychosocial transformation in which individual desire continuously negotiates with constraints of state and familial orders (Huang; Lee). In so far as this process signals the shift from an acceptance of socially ascribed norms to aspirations in favor of individual determination of authentic feeling, the history of Qing appears analogous to "the transformation of intimacy" in the post-Enlightenment and "post-traditional order" of "[Western] modernity" (Giddens 1992; 1991, 2). It resonates with the historical trajectory of marriage from "obedience to intimacy" as well, when individual feeling arises triumphant from its earlier submission to social demands (Coontz).

In his wishful redefinition of Qing, however, Larry seems to have conflated and combined the genealogies of the East and West affective evolution in a singular fulfillment of self-interest. For him, the ultimate value of Qing is not emotional but economic, not altruistic but lucrative, hence the natural circulation of sentiments as necessary currency from kinship webs to transactional networks. Larry has made a powerful use of the Adam Smith of *The Wealth of Nations* (1776) against the Adam Smith of *Theory of Moral Sentiments* (1759) – so much so that there is no more room for sympathies for others nor social commitments for self-satisfaction, only a full-blooded pursuit of gain. Qing has to be instrumentalized to serve this acquisitive instinct of capitalism: it must be manufactured, sold, and consumed.

With Larry's unsentimental and interest-driven account of affective change, Yang exposes the effects of the near-simultaneous arrival of industrial and informational capital in Taiwan and provides a telling instance of the intense mutual constitution of emotion and economy in "emotional capitalism" (Illouz). Pointing out that "sentiments" constitute the engine of Molly et al.'s "cultural business" is also Yang's knowing nod to the original indictment of postwar US consumer capitalism by the Frankfurt School. Molly Inc. functions as the narrative hub of SMS through which the director tracks his characters' psychosocial confusion against Taiwan's compressed and convoluted capitalist development. Molly Inc. is the informational or cultural wing of industrial capitalism, whose mission – after urbanization's erosion of emotion embedded in the thick relations of extended families and local communities – is to fill the affective vacuum with its manufactured substitutions. It is only when indigenous and primitive institutions and the natural relations attendant to them are creatively destructed that the efficiency of the market to provide, not just concrete goods, but also services and simulated experiences, can become self-evident. Small wonder that the relationship show run by Molly's sister should dominate the actual family dinner time, just as Qi Qi is called by hers to watch her own commercial on TV and Ming's family and neighbors are summoned to the sports bar when an NBA game is broadcast on its large-screen TV. Here, we are reminded of Ermo's China and the televisual invasion of her village, at once confounding all the peasant subjects and putting the machine of local meaning-making out of commission.

Yang's Taipei is in a more advanced stage of capitalism with a far more reaching market administration of personal life, but his grasp of the cultural industry's domination of individual feeling matches if not surpasses that of Zhou Xiaowen's. At stake for the director of *A Confucian Confusion* are not only the means of meaning generation in precapitalist and late capitalist societies but also the purposes they serve. As Horkheimer and Adorno point out in the case of "cultural industry," of which Molly Inc. is doubtless a newer realization, profit motive has now infiltrated the arena of art as well as its inherent logic of practice formerly impermeable to commerce:

> What might be called use value in the reception of cultural commodities is replaced by exchange value . . . no object has an inherent value; it is valuable only to the extent it can be exchanged . . . the commodity function of art disappears only to be wholly realized when art becomes a species of commodity instead, marketable and interchangeable like an industrial product.
>
> (158)

But this interchangeability of objects has its ineluctable subjective dimension, because the reduction of all value to monetary value is tantamount to Larry's reification of sentiments into interests. What Yang has enabled his audience to see is the subtle imbrication between the production of cultural commodities in late capitalism, whose value lies in its interchangeability, and late capital's simultaneous reconstitution of the individual, whose original subjectivity forged in early capitalism, however, privileges bourgeois interiority with "an inherent value."

The dilemma confronting Yang's medley monads is perhaps best captured by Horkheimer and Adorno: when cultural meanings are imposed on the subject, disseminated en masse rather than internally generated, the idea of "the individual is an illusion" (154). The real challenge to individuality of the fundamental "self-possessive" and "inner-directed" kind (Macpherson; Riesman), as Yang unveils with his camera, is the dissolution of interiority at its core. This is the threat of "the society of spectacle" in Guy Debord's terms, when spectacle does not suggest "a collection of images" but "a social relationship between people that is mediated by images": "the spectacle proclaims the predominance of appearances and asserts that all human life, which is to say all social life, is mere appearance" (12, 14).

For a character like Birdy, life is always already theater, and relationships between people are but a show and a spectacle. For Larry, the distinction between the appearance and essence of a person sounds definitively archaic, for what matters is for the product, inclusive of human beings and his rather unteachable boss Akeem, to assume the appealing appearance for a successful sale. Marketing is meaning-making in booming Taipei. With no irony intended, he touts Qi Qi as "the most profitable cultural product" – "she embodies the sentiment that is most lovable: her image is ideal, full of sunshine, exuding warmth, harmony, and happiness." When reality does come in the way of shiny appearance, however, "the predominance of appearances" must be maintained at all costs (Debord 14). Such is the case of Molly's sister, the popular host of a TV romance and relationship show, and her husband, the reclusive writer who has moved out. To quell the news of their separation so that the veneer of her happy family life can continue to shore up her show's success, the host beseeches her husband's cooperation to partake in a social dinner with the media. His adamant refusal, instead of causing her shame in image manipulation, fires up her outright charge of Qi Qi as a "phony." In the end, amid the sea of phonies in her life even Qi Qi herself is no longer assured of her own innocence and integrity. Neither is her fiancé Ming, the other character in the ensemble cast with an atypical upright moral standing, who ends up in bed with Molly in yet another inadvertent act of confusion.

The fluid exchange of commodities and the flexible interchangeability of love objects are consequences of a desired independence for the new citizens of Taipei from their formerly encumbered, embedded, and heavily regulated social relationships. It is when these ascribed relationships and rules are rendered inoperative and invisible in the Second Coming of Capital, however, all values have become exchange values, all objects/subjects have become equivalences, and all the characters, like objects they trade for a living, have become subjects of remarkable "one-dimensionality" (Marcuse). This one-dimensionality has a foundational meaning in Jameson's definition of postmodern "textuality" and "waning of affect," as we saw earlier. Edward Yang's flattening of his characters in *A Confucian Confusion*, including ones that first appear to embody social sympathy and philosophical depth, thus resonates well with Jameson's description of a postmodern culture as a succession of synchronic surfaces. Contrary to Jameson's resignation to the domination of textuality as "metaphysically or ontologically" neutral, however, Yang's working of SMS will not let go of aesthetic distinction and exercise of ethics. Although the genuinely good characters in his film cannot seem to escape psychosocial bewilderment in the sudden surge of affluence, the lapses in their judgment and the torment they experience afterwards distinguish them from the majority of their scheming peers, putting them in an entirely different aesthetic and affective order of empathy and worthiness. Not only is the binary opposition of the real and the fake and the right and the wrong deliberately executed, the maimed couple who stand for authenticity and decency in the film, Qi Qi and Xiao Ming, are seen at the film's closing in an unexpected and uplifting reunion, as though forgiven for their errant experiences and rewarded eventually by the inherent virtues of their character. In an ocean of open horizons and appearances without actualities, the young couple has eventually rediscovered each other, tangible in flesh and solid with meaning, ready to embrace an intertextuality of shared reference.

3

As Yang's unapologetic pedagogic formative, *A Confucian Confusion* demonstrates that it is not just material prosperity by precipitous capitalist development but also the proliferation of market media that confound the mental orientations of the newly independent Taiwanese subjects, who, with one foot still in the weakened state and family structures and the other inching toward spectacular speculative flows, have found themselves not quite knowing if the abrupt autonomy thrust upon them is real – and if it is indeed real, why it is not truly enjoyable. The problem of confusion is therefore treated as a problem of referentiality in capital's reorganization of social significance, a problem of wants in their constant conversion by capital into needs, and a problem of self-definition in the borderless geography of global capitalism. While tackled with moderate optimism, these interrelated problems of (re)cognition and emotion return in the second of Yang's monadic trilogy with another animating look. "*Mahjong* for me is a post-*Confucian Confusion*," Yang claims, "a post-Confucian outlook on the future" (Kraicer and Roosen-Runge). "Future" refers to the younger generations Hou Hsiao-hsien admits difficulty in understanding, but with whom Yang wishes to enter into productive dialogue. Instead of the thirtysomething professional managerial of his precursor film, this one features the characters in their late teens and early twenties in Taipei's informal economy, young and restless mobsters with their own brand of entrepreneurialism.[8] As such, they form the film's narrative nodal points for legitimate investors, architects, salon owners and hairdressers, car mechanics, and the semilegitimate escort services, fortune tellers and whatnot, making up the synchronic monadic simultaneity of cosmopolitan Taipei now named after a Chinese tile game, *Majiang* (1996).

There is no waning of auteurial pedagogical impulse, as Yang continues his scrutiny of affect, affectation, appearance, and authenticity. As explicitly expressed by the title, *Majiang* figures gambling and gaming as a normative lifestyle in Capital's Second Coming, as entrepreneurial risk-taking in a world that has been turned into a borderless market. The film's cast is understandably international, or racially diversified if you will, when European adventurers once again swarm East Asia, where, as one British character puts it, "lies the future of the western civilization." No wonder we have Marcus, the London welfare recipient turned hot Taipei architect; Ginger, the redheaded American, a one-time David Copperfield assistant turned escort madame rubbing elbows with locals like Jay, the gay owner of a trendy hair salon; and John, a businessman, while the young but not callow gang wait for their turn in the wings of the Hard Rock Cafe, knowing well that the trajectories of their transactions shall soon intersect.

Ethnic varieties aside, the name of the game has reduced humanity into two distinctive types, "the swindlers" and "the suckers." This is a lesson Hongyu Chen, the don of the youth gang, has learned from his delinquent father Winston Chen, now in hiding from his creditors in a multimillion-dollar scam of kindergarten chains. Once cheated out of his fortune by a Hong Kong woman, Angela, Winston has since Bernie Madoffed his way to the top, becoming a swindler supreme and sweeping in money of suckers ever since. The moral of his father's fall and rise forms the twofold lesson Hongyu relays to his new inductee, Lunlun, a daytime car mechanic. The first is about mind over body: "Don't ever get sentimental. When flooded with sentiments, you lose your mind." The second is about knowing your clientele: "People in today's world do not know what they want. Tell and sell them what they want, and they'd be grateful." As "Qing" 情, feeling or sentiment, persists in the ever-wider circulation of capital, so seems the need for interests to override the reign of affects. Not only is there the necessity for the subject not to relate to fellow humans with dewy eyes and a soft heart, but s/he must also learn to feel the pain of their yearning so as to supply the objects of their desire. The irony of this new age teaching is not lost on the Chinese viewing audience, however, since the character "lun" in the character "Lunlun" 纶纶 also rhymes homonymically with the other more commonly used character, "lun"

伦, as in 伦理 (ethics) or 伦常 (relations and immutable laws of the Confucian social world). Characteristic of what Jameson considers as the director's archaic method, Yang again maps Taipei and its citizens in binary terms, Hongyu as embodiment of interests and instrumental reason, and Lunlun as sentiments and sympathy, though as an initiation ritual Lunlun has already become Hongyu's instrument in a staged accident of Jay's pink Mercedes.

Hongyu's small syndicate operates like old musketeers turned modern marketers and his new product line involves a pair of women and their affective profitability. We have Marthe, Marcus's jilted Parisian girlfriend presently in Taipei to reclaim her "love," and Alison, Marcus's current local girlfriend, whose family connections have ensured her boyfriend's designing successes. As both women are to varying degrees suckers for romance, Hongyu attempts to swindle them into becoming his cash cows. With Marthe, his approach is You Qing 友情 (as we recall from Larry's discussion with Molly), or friendship. Friendship as generous offerings from Hongyu shall in his estimation entail obligation from Marthe. Using Lunlun as a translator, Hongyu thinks he is able to indenture Marthe into sexual servitude through her dependence on and indebtedness to him, thereby beating his competitor Ginger by sheer indigenous advantage. With Alison, his trumpet card is "Ai Qing" 爱情, or romantic love, and his secret weapon, the card player, is Hong Kong, the gangster gigolo played by Zhang Zhen of Hou's *Three Times*. Where Hongyu fails with Marthe, he succeeds with Alison. Hong Kong has so enamored Alison with his "love" for her that for fear of losing it she wills herself to sleep with the rest of the mob (except Lunlun's refusal).

The joke in this sexual gaming and exchange of women is that no kiss is permitted by the bordello rule of "Toothpaste," otherwise known as "Little Buddha," the syndicate's feng shui specialist responsible for its bottom line via actuarial forecasts. True to the original Cartesian mind and body split and its later capitalist development that passions could be moderated and governed by acquisitive interests, the gang's code of conduct determines that a kiss shall cause impotence as well as loss of company profits. It is only through Angela, the mistaken target of Hongyu's revenge for her alleged bankruptcy of his father, that Hong Kong later learns the errors of his ways. Not only does Angela laugh at his superstitious withholding of erotic expression – "every man I kissed in the past is now driving a Mercedes" – but she also turns the table of gender exploitation around by turning Hong Kong into a communal toy for her band of opulent sisters. Shocked, humiliated, and disgusted as the sexually playful and predatory women stuff takeout dumplings into his mouth, Hong Kong chokes, throws up, and then doubles up on the floor, his wailing piercing through the giggling of the women as the camera lifts away from the interior of Angela's condo in an aerial shot of Taipei streets, with its indifferent traffic down below and the impenetrable dark blue sky above.

Hong Kong's cry of despair is Yang's cinematic tribute to Edvard Munch's *The Scream* as well as a rejection of Fredric Jameson, who in including Taipei in his mapping of late capitalism has invalidated the historically laden affects of the place and people (1995, 114–57). Such characteristic expressions of high modernism mediating Capital's First Coming as "alienation, anomie, solitude, social fragmentation, and isolation," as Yang emphatically shows, have not vanished but remained significant emotional responses to Capital's Second Coming in the Sinophonic Asia Pacific (Jameson, 1991, 11). The escalating domination of interests over sentiments, in other words, has not succeeded in flattening feelings of all the subjects of global capitalism, reducing affects into pure surface effects. In channeling Hong Kong's cry, Yang's camera becomes an "outward dramatization of inward feeling" (Ibid. 12). This artistic gesture both reflects the residual affects that refuse to wane in postmodernity and affirms simultaneously the "metaphysics of the inside and outside," thus the cathartic potential in the monad's emotional release and eventual recuperation (Ibid. 11, 12).

Such aesthetic resolution of affective disturbance is achieved through the characters of Hongyu and Lunlun, both of whom as it turns out are suckers for sentiments, and therefore unsuccessful swindlers. As an efficient crime syndicate, the gang is supposed to mirror Hongyu's capacity for rational calculation. Although money and its accumulation are his explicit goals of life, it is the kind of emotional bond and filial loyalty Hongyu never experienced while growing up that motivated his formation of the gang. The gang becomes his substitute family without blood ties and he the figurative father/provider. Hongyu's fatal attraction to personal allegiance also explains his revenge fantasy against Angela, which is also but a fantasy of his biological family's recuperation. Had the fantasy been fulfilled, Hongyu would have not only won over his negligent father and the way-ward husband for her mother; he would also have redeemed himself as the filial son who pulls everything together. The misidentification of Angela and the mishap of his father's unexpected suicide reveal just how Hongyu's residual modes of sentiments, his affection and allegiance, are absolutely misplaced in an amoral universe of ruthless calculation, pure chance, and mere commerce. The chain of events that results in his murder of Mr. Chu, Winston's old friend and another delinquent father figure, eventually spells the doom of his wishful redemption. Indulgent in filial sentiments, Hongyu the swindler has become a sucker, exiting the screen bawling, doubled up in agony like Hong Kong did. The moral here appears to be the importance of maintaining a healthy emotional ecology, the Pierre Bourdieu sort of habitus in and through which an orderly generational reproduction of positive affects and ethics may still be practiced.

In contrast to Hongyu, the unwitting gangster of Lunlun appears the most ethically and emotionally mature of all *Majiang*'s male characters, more affirmative in deeds and demeanor even than Ming Ming of *A Confucian Confusion*. Lunlun falls for Marthe at first sight in the Hard Rock Cafe when she comes to claim Marcus. Since then, he has helped her survive both Hongyu's and Ginger's attempts at pimping. It is only natural in Yang's cinematic administration of affective justice that the lonely heart, who joins the crime syndicate for solidarity, should eventually end his monadic alienation by merging with his true love. Going beyond Qi Qi and Ming Ming's hinted coupledom by the end of *A Confucian Confusion*, when the elevator door's closing and then opening suggests a hopeful future union, Lunlun and Marthe find each other amid the dense traffic of Taipei and the din of its evening streets. After swift cuts of their mutual loss and miss, the young lovers are seen at length spotting one another in the director's characteristic long shot. Reversing the upward camera movement that leaves Hong Kong as the disaffected monad in Angela's pied-à-terre, his Munch-like scream swallowed by the gloom hovering and enveloping the city, we watch Lunlun and Marthe on the ground as part of Taipei's thick and vibrant humanity, picking their way through the crowd with quickening pace until they pause, and kiss, first tentatively and then passionately. Marthe's kiss shall not bring Lunlun a Mercedes, but this sentimental shot of the decent and deserving young in tight embrace certainly warms those spectators on the shooting location as well as the audience in the theater: affective allegiance in the age of casino capitalism is not absolutely unachievable, as the closing image appears to say.

4

To kiss or not to regardless, Yang's artistic grappling with the economic and emotional phenomena of Capital's Second Coming has become by the last of his trilogy the most incisive and insightful. Aptly named *Yi Yi*, a repetition of the identical Chinese character "Yi" 一, which refers to the number one, the smallest positive integer, *Yi Yi* means *One One* in literal English translation.[9] This Chinese usage sounds outlandish, for as an adverbial phrase, "Yi Yi" or "one by one" is always followed by a verb, as in "Yiyi jieshao" 一一介绍, to "introduce one by one," suggesting a linear order of succession. When used as an adjective to modify two separate but the same type of nouns, as in "Yishen yishi" 一生一世 or "[one's] whole life," it signifies the integrity of a complete unit. Divorced from the noun and the verb, subject and agency, Yang's neologism *Yi Yi* lacks the sense of both temporal sequence and spatial completeness within the Chinese linguistic convention. But convention *interruptus*, both socioeconomic and psychocultural, is precisely the director's point about the state of Taipei and its dwellers. As a pair of a detached minimal whole, *Yi Yi/One One* comes to stand for the monads in our time, betraying nominally the accelerated atomization and privatization of human beings in Capital's Second Coming. As can be expected from his previous play of "independence" and "confusion" in the title, Yang's choice of *Yi Yi*'s English heading also intrigues. Indeed, the Chinese register of disengaged individualism in *Yi Yi/One One* is balanced by the English *A One and a Two*. As though a jazzy incantation, *A One and a Two* bounces back to the monadic state of *One One* only to indicate the improvisational potential of intersubjective recognition and constitution. Yang's bilingual play seems to propose the following. *A One and a Two* shall rescue *One One* from its capitalist sequestration so that the "absolutely simple entity" ("monad" n. 2. a. *Philos. OED*) is consequently reincorporated into the "individual," in its original but currently obsolete sense as "one in substance or essence; forming an indivisible entity" (adj. 1. *Obs. OED*).

This titular movement from *One One* to *A One and a Two* betrays the film's cinematic unfolding as well as the director's implicit change of his philosophical interlocutors. Yang has neither shifted his focus away from Capital's Second Coming in East Asia nor has he wavered from his preoccupation with its reorganization of emotional life. He has, however, ceased his intuitive cinematic conversation with theorists of postmodernity. The deceased subject and displaced morality, the disintegration of the family, and the decentered yet befuddled self omniscient in *A Confucian Confusion* and *Majiang* are still everywhere evident in *Yi Yi*. But the polarization of character types and dichotomy of the inside and outside seem not as significant in his last film, nor does Yang seem as interested in whether the depth model belongs to a bygone modernity or affective intensity necessarily wanes as global capitalism waxes. In his more insistent interrogation of his characters' inarticulate emotional turmoil amid Taiwan's economic boom, Yang unwittingly engages with scholars who are as responsive as he is to the condition of Capital's Second Coming as the postmodernists yet are self-designated as "reflexive modernists."

Reflexive modernity originates in a discontent with the grand narratives of the Enlightenment, arises with the disappearance of a bounded liberal capitalist state, economy, and citizenry, and culminates in an attempt both to break the stranglehold of a "the protracted debate about modernity and postmodernity" and to mobilize individual agency (Beck, Giddens, and Lash v–viii). In effect, though, a "progressive freeing of agency from structure" at the core of the reflexive modern resonates with the hegemony of "flexible capital" at the heel of the Reagan-Thatcher-Deng Xiaoping Revolution. The flexibility of capital investment, production, and consumption, in the words of Lash, both deregulates and dismantles "the rule-bound 'Fordist' structures" and demands a "self-reflexivity in that heteronomous monitoring of workers by rules is displaced by self-monitoring" (Ibid. 119).

Admittedly generated from the academic left, the privileging of the individual in the theory of "reflexive modernization" has an uncanny resemblance to the neoliberal cult of the same by Friedrich von Hayek and Gary Becker. Reflexive individualization is not about releasing the individual from feudal, religious, and precapitalist certainties and incorporating him/her into the rationalities of industrial capitalist democracy. Rather, it is a concerted call to liberate individuals from the postwar welfare capitalism of democratic nation-states in a march toward a "global risk society" of "manufactured uncertainty" (Beck 7; Beck, Giddens, and Lash 184). As Scott Lash recapitulates it, the program of post-Fordist reflexive individualization is best "rendered by Beck's 'I am I' in which the 'I' is increasingly free from communal ties and is able to construct his or her own biographical narratives (Giddens)" (Ibid. 163). Recognizing this late capitalist deregulation and reconstitution of the individual subject in the form of Beck's "I am I," *Yi Yi/ One One* engages, on the one hand, what Anthony Giddens calls the "reflexive project of the self . . . devoid of ethical content," while asking on the other hand if such a proposal of flexible self-management answers satisfactorily to the exacerbated condition of global risk society (176).

The film opens with a wedding and ends with a funeral with a birth placed in the middle. It centers on a multigenerational middle-class family in Taipei headed by NJ, a father, husband, and company head in his mid-forties, as though representative of the sandwich generation. Through him, his kinship relations, and social interactions with their neighbors, friends, schools, businesses, the local city space, and the global commerce, the audience pieces together the synchronic monadic simultaneity typical of Yang's cinema, a temporal and spatial coordinate that is not comfortingly harmonious but provocatively disjunctive. With its ensemble cast, the film tells a cradle-to-grave story, reiterating the biological destiny of human beings regardless of the specificity of, say, precapitalist or postcapitalist time. The fact that NJ is middle-aged and that the birth of the baby occurs in the middle of the film seems to manifest the in-between-ness of species subjects, always born and dying amid the course of humanity and the nexus of ascribed social relations. Like Yangyang, the son of NJ and Minmin, who tries with his camera to show people what is obscured from their perception, Edward Yang wishes to foreground a linear temporality with the recognition of an overlooked subjective in-between-ness. In doing so, *Yi Yi* acknowledges the narrative of (re)production in both individual and social senses of the term as we understand it in Chapter 3. The film also tries to link an individual's life and its limited purchase on biological time with a historical time, presumed to be continuous and transcendent of the monadic trajectory.

Yang's attempt to illuminate the much obscured if not obliterated conception and practice of (re)productive time is coupled with his acknowledgment of the individual's new spatial dispersion. The subjects of Taipei inhabit what Arjun Appadurai defines as a series of "ethnoscapes, mediascapes, technoscapes, fiancescapes, and ideoscapes" that stands for the disjunctive cultural flows of global capitalism (33). In this "modernity at large" or "reflexive modernity" of spatial and social convolution, what is synchronic and simultaneous is also disjunctive: the former insular integrity of time-space that (re)produced the historical subject prior to Capital's Second Coming has been opened up, the limited span of biological time that conditioned the crafting of individual biography has also been overtaken by the possibility of living on multiple planes in an apparent temporal infinity (Appadurai; Beck, Giddens, and Lash). (Re)creational individual agency no longer heeds the need of social perpetuity in its reflexive self-fashioning. Because Taiwanese citizens are no longer interpellated either in the biological family or in the state (Althusser), and because the family no longer serves as an elemental site for relatively stable subjectivities to evolve, Edward Yang has conceived *Yi Yi* as a cinematic contradiction between a delimited narrative temporal trajectory with a beginning and an end, and a recent runaway psychosocial space without boundaries. The film's representation of this time-space contradiction teases out the tension between those in favor of and in disagreement with reflexive modernity.

Writing like a true reflexive modernist, Aihwa Ong argues that in the post–Cold War world the cultural logics of flexibility have begun to inform the new "regimes of the family, the state, and capital" (3). Instead of being "coerced or resisted," "flexibility, migration, and relocations have become practices to strive for rather than stability," and the select "Chinese cosmopolitans" of her study come to "illuminate the practices of an elite transnationalism" and exemplify "the late modern subject" par excellence (Ibid. 19, 24, 3). Ong's optimistic embrace of disjunctive flows and affirmation of reflexive agency in the elite mode, however, stands opposed to neo-Confucian and neo-Stoic models of cosmopolitanism in the wake of capital's worldwide restructuring. For Tu Weiming, a contemporary Confucian self-development is still "based upon the dignity of the person, in terms of a series of concentric circles: self, family, community, society, nation, world, and cosmos" (1998, 302). In Martha Nussbaum's reworking of Hierocles, a local and global association is similarly "surrounded by a series of concentric circles." "The first one encircles the self, the next takes in the immediate family," she explains, "then follows the extended family, then, in order, neighbors or local groups, fellow city dwellers, and fellow countrymen – and we can easily add to this list groupings based on ethnic, linguistic, historical, gender or sexual identities" (9). Both Tu and Nussbaum posit the global subject in an ideal of social affinity through an image of spatial extension from the individual and the local to the national and global, in order to promulgate a transnational citizenship against jingoist fever and nihilist abandon.[10] Where such communitarian ideation and idealization of concentricity presumes the actuality of a shared center, the center is either forgotten or lost in the late capitalist society of "high reflexivity," where what matters for someone like Giddens is "the 'open' character of self-identity and the reflexive nature of the body" (Giddens 30).[11]

While sympathetic to cosmopolitan concentricity, Yang does not underestimate his cinematic challenge, for the centripetal forces of capital, its multiplication of spaces, and its siren call of reflexive mobility have already shaken the foundations of a solid modernity. He wants to make manifest that it is the radical forces of dispersion and pluralization that have muddied up the perception of the center upon which the multiple circles are supposed to radiate.

Yang frames the difficulty of clear vision as well as ontological and affective certainty earlier on with the wedding pictures. First is the ideal composition of the big family photo: families and friends saunter over and gather under the lush canopy for a group picture that symbolizes the vitality of the living tree and its ever-expanding roots and branches (Tu 1991). The serenity of nature's green, however, is followed by the crimson red of the banquet hall that suggests less festivity than the intense heat of contention. The groom's old flame, Yunyun, literally bursts into the wedding party, vociferously accusing the bride of hijacking her man while frantically apologizing to the groom's mother for failing to become her daughter-in-law. Amid the commotion, the gigantic photo blowup of the newlyweds, Adi and Xiaoyan, is misplaced. Heads down toward the floor, smiles turned into grimaces, it reverses optical logic just as the obvious pregnancy of the bride disrupts the old social sequence of marriage and child bearing. No wonder Popo, the mother of the groom and grandmother of the family, feels sick and goes home. "This kind of thing is everywhere nowadays," remarks her daughter Minmin in defense of her sister-in-law's unseasonable gestation. "We are no longer that rigid," she adds, betraying an acceptability of affective deregulation. But Minmin's reflexive tolerance or ethical flexibility sits uneasily with her daughter Tingting's moral innocence. "If Auntie Yunyun [the ex-girlfriend of Adi] is not a bad person," Tingting confronts her father NJ, "Auntie Xiaoyan [the bride] has got to have a problem." While the daughter's reaction appears a weaker version of moral Manichaeism than what is in *Confucian Confusion* and *Majiang*, the father's diplomatic equivocation, "we hardly know her," sounds similarly acquiescent as his wife's. Both father and mother, the sandwich generation living the radical shifts of moral sentiment, appear relatively accommodating. Their daughter's disapproval of affective deregulation, on the other hand, betrays a desire for ethical certitude befitting her Popo's age. NJ asks if grandma reproves the bride. "Not really," replies Tingting. "She just says she is old and I don't understand what she means."

Popo never gets to tell what she means since a stroke after the wedding sends her into a coma from which she hardly awakens, except for a magical moment before her death when she communicates with Tingting in the speechless art of origami.[12] A sagacious matriarch of a bygone age and a retired teacher who cannot talk, let alone instruct, Popo is Edward Yang's object-correlative for the newly built-in obsolescence of the old filial authority and normative morality. Contrary to the grandma figures in *Autumn Moon* (1992) and *Floating World* (1996) by Clara Law 罗卓瑶, Popo no longer has the residual capacity to either command or cajole her offspring, however impotently, through guilt trips or shaming tactics. To be able to whip her descendants into line would imply that the center of tradition and society still holds, the closure of the clan and the generational line remain essentially intact so much so that the mutual generation of filial meaning shall follow to make the shared destinies and goals of family life possible. When none appears readily tangible in a Taipei of mobile freeways and tenuous cell phone lines, the solidity of the biological family and the stability of national society are virtually rent asunder, the welfare of the collective, however conceived, now overtaken by the motive of economic profit.

Yang pictures the breakdown of generational interlocution in a cluster of carefully crafted scenes at Popo's bed. The doctor prescribes that the family "talk with" grandma to stimulate her brain and enhance her chances of revival. What is meant as therapy for the ancestor on life support turns out to be torture for the progeny. Son and groom Adi, the self-proclaimed champion talker, assures his mother that he is out of his perennial money trouble, but soon runs out of other words to say. Daughter Minmin gets so depressed by the poverty of her daily routine and the perfunctory minutes by Popo's side she cannot help but weep. Only Tingting has the real urge and content to communicate. Sneaking out of her bedroom in the quiet of the night, she beseeches Popo's forgiveness like a penitent, blaming herself for the tragedy of her grandma's accident. "If you do not wake up," she whispers, "I can never fall soundly asleep." But the metaphoric priest of filial order remains reticent, refusing the comfort of moral certainty and affective assurance that the burgeoning adolescent desperately seeks.

Popo's comatose state and Tingting's bewilderment about her uncle's marriage represent not just the collapse of a premodern Chinese tradition on a late modern stage. The fragmentation of filial or vertical and hierarchical authority also speaks of an attractive ascent of individual liberty that makes its earliest appearance with the European Enlightenment and Capital's First Coming. But the uneven, sped up, and convoluted development of capitalist modernity in Sinophonic Asia means that Yang has to consider an individualizing process that properly belongs to Capital's Second Coming. If the monadic subjectivity of the possessive individual entails the detachment from an economy of the natural family and the attachment to a state regulated capitalist economy, the reflexive subject of neoliberal individualization is expected to marshal the forces of the erratic market with few strings attached. A series of character portrayals by Yang – Popo and Tingting's traditional morality of the right and wrong, NJ and Minmin's permissiveness of their relatives' romantic choice and conduct, and the instantaneous instrumental rationality of Adi and Dada – reveal both the diversity of values in competition in Taipei's "ideoscapes, ethnoscapes, and mediascapes" and the director's anxiety about the viability of the reflexive project of the self. It is not anachronistic that his search beyond the reflexive modernist's alleged way out of the (post)modern should land him in a position similar to Alasdair MacIntyre's critique of the Enlightenment and the monadic subject of the Euro-American modern:

> the key question for men [sic] is not about their own authorship; I can only answer the question "What am I to do?" if I can answer the prior question "Of what story or stories do I find myself a part?" We enter human society, that is, with one or more imputed characters – roles into which we have been drafted – and we have to learn what we are in order to be able to understand how others respond to us and how our responses to them are apt to be construed.
>
> (216)

Sympathetic with him on the ascriptive condition of the self and the social conception of the good, Yang is hardly as prepared as MacIntyre to evoke a revival of Aristotelian traditions and "local forms of community" that are precapitalist and socially enclosed (Ibid. 263).[13] Yang is not "after virtue" either in abstraction or in nostalgia. For him, the "imputed characters" have necessarily become more complex after capitalist modernity and the local forms of community are no longer bounded with their own centripetal energy in globality. For Yang, both the optimism of MacIntyre, Nussbaum, and Tu in holding onto an immutable center with effective heteronomous regulation and the optimism of reflexive modernists about adjustable self-authorship are verging on the fantastic. As though figuring Zygmunt Bauman's analytical thoughts in sight and sound, Yang shows us the workings of both the panopticon and the synopticon on his characters' emotional lives in order to ask whether the release from explicit regulatory watch and the reflexive embrace of countless choices has meant the arrival of a new affective freedom (1998, 51).

If panopticon is Foucault's rendition of the disciplinary state, asylum, and school where "the few are watching the many" in terms of surveillance, Bauman writes, synopticon represents the state of the global village in which "the many are watching the few" through billboards, TV boxes, computer or cell phone screens (Ibid.). For Yang, these two different "scopic regime[s]" constitute the particular processes not only of viewing but also of subjective interpellation and emotional organization in Capital's Second Coming (Foster ix). The surveillance camera at the family's luxury high-rise apartment home frames Popo's return as it does capturing Yangyang at his school, sneaking out to fetch his developed photos during official napping time; still later it records a murderer's premeditation before his actual act. The mechanisms of heteronomous monitoring for societies of industrial capitalism have not been abandoned in the age of informational capitalism to allow independent self-regulation and free development of subjectivity. Rather, more psychologically invasive and more invisible means of panoptical power are now interlaced with the incitation of synopticon, as "the act of watching unites the watchers from their locality," transporting them "spiritually" into the "exterritorial web," points out Zygmunt Bauman, in which "distance no longer matters even if bodily they remain in place" (1998, 52).

Bauman seems to have extended Baudrillard's insight on an earlier synoptic power of soft discipline: "With the television image – the television being the ultimate and perfect object for this new era – our own body and the whole surrounding universe become a control screen" (quoted by Williams 236). In other words, synopticon not only obliterates geographical differences but also subjects the arrested spectators to forces of psychosocial identification over which they have little control. Borderless flow of images only exacerbates the bondage of human beings who cannot measure up, while the control screen of Baudrillard's reference has since exponentially multiplied. The coming into being of Adi and Xiaoyan's unborn baby is heralded on the ultrasound screen and its birth later witnessed via a camcorder viewfinder. The murder of the English teacher is broadcast on TV. After his mug shot accompanies the reportage, the television screen also displays a video capture of the electronic games to which the alleged teenage murderer is addicted. A tad trite perhaps, this linkage of gratuitous game violence to its deliberate execution in the real world ushers in Yang's cinematic dialectic of the interior and the exterior: the virtual decriminalization of homicide normalizes practical behavior of the same in the actual social universe. The technology-facilitated penetration of capital into residential, reproductive, and recreational spaces thus comes to stand for its colonization of the private and the biological, while the enactment of media-prompted slaughter, the transgression of boundary between the existential and the imaginary. Panopticon and synopticon act in sync in Capital's Second Coming to ensure the maximization of profits.

Not only does the infiltration of the invisible biological mystery preoccupy the director, but Yang also shows scientific domination of the human in a refreshing juxtaposition of voice-over and image. In a subsequent sequence, the audience is surprised into recognition that what they took to be a nurse's narration about the baby on the ultrasound screen is in fact a translator's explanation about the artificial intelligence of the computer. Ota, a Japanese computer wizard invited by NJ to rescue his company from its impending demise, is giving his presentation. "It has begun to acquire signs of human life," as the image of Adi and Xiaoyan's growing fetus with its thumping heart fades to the monotone and the poker face of the translator. "The reason we are unable at present to go beyond the games of fighting and killing has little to do with our limited grasp of the 'electronic brain' [computers]; it has everything to do with our failure to understand us humans." With this defamiliarization of the human–machine interface, both cinematically and thematically, Yang demonstrates the complex condition that N. Katherine Hayles calls "the posthuman" – where cognition and action increasingly take place in "information-rich and computationally embedded environments" (121). This environment of cybernetic capitalism, as Yang reveals it, precisely makes the exuberant "reflexive project of the self" dubious: the presumed weakening of heteronomous monitoring has not strengthened the capacity for autonomous regulation and self-fashioning (Giddens 176). Instead, it creates a psychosocial codependence in which human rationality and affectivity are prone to reflexively subordinate themselves to artificial intelligence. The cinematic conflation of the voice-over and image thus dramatizes the convergence of formerly separate realms of the sciences and the humanities, of "ethnoscapes, mediascapes, tech-noscapes, fiancescapes, and ideoscapes" that now hail both independently and in concert the subjects of global modernity (Appadurai 33). Not only may scientific knowledge of the natural world not necessarily enhance human control of the social world, but it also engenders other modes of discipline and other confusion of reason and conscience.

For Edward Yang, the challenge for the reflexive subject to constitute itself comes from the optical glare of the heterogeneous social landscapes typical of late capitalism. To supplement the motif of blurring spheres, Yang now makes ingenious use of abundant glass in metropolitan architecture, which, whether in Tokyo or in Taipei, is the transnational space his characters traverse. Unlike masonry walls of solid modernity, glass panes mark postmodern space without total delimitation, suggesting permeability, liquidity, and flexibility – qualities especially valorized in Capital's Second Coming. Yang foregrounds the visual prominence of the glass immediately before Ota's presentation when NJ and his colleagues ride in Dada's car, debating company salvaging plans and exit strate-gies. One suggests searching for a copycat of Ota in Taipei while another banters about Dada's destined retirement to San Francisco if their company falls prey to capital's revitalized engine of "disruptive innovation" (Lepore). The characters appear one moment through the windshield and disappear the next in the curve of the auto glass, as the reflection of office buildings in the uniform international box style rolls over, engulfing their visage. The medium of glass evidences an intertwined connectivity and intricate fluidity between global capital flow and the motion of local business and people. But this double play of transparency and reflexivity also becomes a larger metaphor for the apparent collapse of such older binaries constitutive of "the depth model" as the "latent and the manifest," "authenticity and inauthenticity" that Jameson finds prominent in Yang's earlier films (1991, 12).

No wonder the close-up of the windshield, mirroring the sheer opacity of the office buildings in motion as driven by both capital expansion and individual ambi-tion, is succeeded by a medium shot in a long take. This time, we vaguely see Adi and Yunyun, ex-partners, two of the most superficial characters in the film, having their rendezvous in Eslite Café. Barely visible through the café floor to ceiling glass as the shifting reflection of street traffic, passing cars, motorcycles, and pedestrians obscures and obstructs audience perception of their contours, Adi and Yunyun appear to embody nothing save for the imprints of their environments – a glass-sutured subjectivity, if you will, in reflexive modernity. The only thing standing out from this glass-retracted scene is their loud talk of stock holdings in AOL and Yahoo, the buzz of business revealing the bores they are.

Although privileging the depth of character favored in the earlier capitalist modernity of "inner direction," the director shows that the "other direction" turned reflexive subjectivity is not exclusive to Adi and Yunyun. Yang shares with David Riesman's post–World War II analysis that the telos-driven self-discipline of inner direction appropriate to industrial capitalism is yielding to a peer prompted and mass communication mediated other direction of consumer capitalism (Riesman 14–25). He seems specially sensitive to the sway of socialized other direction on his characters when Taiwanese society swings far more suddenly than American society did from a culture of relative scarcity to that of material abundance. In showing the speed and scale with which Taiwan is turned into a silicon island, Yang also illuminates the collective and crushing impact that the radical condensation of economic development has on individuals' increasing helplessness in responding to external stimuli.

Not at all a superficial person like her brother Adi, Minmin is also spotted repeatedly before mirrors and windowpanes, as though her identity is overwhelmingly determined by glass reflection or optical glare, extraterritorial forces and mirages. In the film's most heart-wrenching scene – reminiscent of Tsai Mingliang's unbearable closing shot for *Vive l'Amour* and Hong Kong's wailing in *Majiang* – Minmin can no longer conceal her anguish about life's monotony and her inability to have a meaningful existence. Yang frames the shot from inside the Jian's bedroom with a view of the hallway in their high-rise condo, revealing the depth of domesticity with many interior doors and equal number of bedrooms. Switching on the light, NJ enters after a long day at the office only to be greeted by Minmin's choked cry. Cut to Minmin in an extraordinarily long take, in which she agonizes over the fact that she has nothing of interest to report to Popo. "Life is such a blank and I've got mine wasted," she says to NJ, with tears streaming down her face. The back of her head is visible from her dressing table's mirror on which are also posted a small photo of Tingting at a younger age and Yangyang's more up-to-date shot. This visual rendition is to anticipate her son's photographic exercise of taking pictures of people's backs – to reveal "the other half of the truth," as he puts it. Sitting with her face toward NJ and their wedding photo on the wall to the left of him, however, Minmin cannot possibly see her children's photos, neither does she seem to truly see her husband in her present picture of life. Though his characters seem blind and unaware, Yang the director has framed the domestic and personal life of the Taiwanese professional managerial class as one emptied of its own significance in Capital's Second Coming. The familial frame of reference, though available, has failed to register coherence as well as its centripetal pull. While the semi-open venetian blinds to Minmin's left filter in the intermittent light of car traffic below, the audiences are reminded that the doors of the Jian's condo are shut in general, with such instances as Yangyang locking himself in the bathroom, Popo incapacitated in her bedroom, and Tingting praying in a room of her own. The spaces of the generational family in reflexive modernity do not connect despite flexible capital flow. Having shut their bedroom door to spare their children unnecessary sorrow, NJ stands sidelined by their wedding photo on the wall and suggests to Minmin, "Let's have the nurse read Popo newspapers." But his soft voice is being drowned by the bicker of their next-door neighbors. The camera cuts outside the condo in a long shot, with street lamps in the distance, headlights rushing toward us, and the reflection of the house lights mixed together in the same composition. The apartment next door is then illuminated at the upper right corner of the screen, showing the silhouettes of lovers in a bitter squabble against the indifference of nocturnal city motion down below. Continuing this exterior shot, the camera pans further left, back toward the Jian's unit, looking into the domestic sphere of the suffering couple. Minmin is still crying, as NJ paces toward the window, slowly closing the venetian blinds as though to contain the troubles. The audience can no longer see what is inside and behind, but we are overwhelmed by the outside in the glass: the windowpane-reflected urban panorama of pitch darkness is broken by dotted white lights, of street lamps and automobile headlights, the neighbors' wrangling now commingling with Minmin's whimpering.

Glass as a visual trope of dimensions that one can see through or dimensions that are overlaid with reflection and refraction thereby comes to denote horizontal "other direction" in reflexive modernity, a deregulated formation of subjectivity that displaces the centrality of teleological "inner direction" of an earlier regulated capitalism. Glass also figures the growing indistinguishability of the inside and outside that Michael Hardt and Antonio Negri characterize the generation of "imperial subjectivity." "The enclosures that used to define the limited space of the institutions have broken down," they argue, "so that the logic that once functioned primarily within the institutional walls now spreads across the entire social terrain" (196). This is the logic of Capital's Second Coming and the correspondent logic of absolute reflexive individualization, of "*Yi Yi*/One One," "I am I," apparently free from surveillance but actually subject to the siren calls of endless (re)creational fulfillment. The sequence on Minmin we have followed amply illustrates the invasion of the outside, or the internalization of the logic of flexible capital and limitless growth that has engendered much psychological and social instability in our time. What the director shows is that husband and wife are scarcely the principal agents of their own ennui but subjects in reaction to social forces in a much larger nexus of economic and emotional exchange. The transparency and reflexivity of the glass enables Yang to establish visual simultaneity and spatial complementarity not only between the two apartments in a luxury condo but also their relation to the global city as an engine of capital's constant revolutions and innovative deregulations. Although the residents may entertain an illusion of their sovereign existence in separate units, Yang convinces us that they actually inhabit the same condominium of "the lonely crowd" without optimal escape routes (Riesman).

To drive this point home, the director frames Minmin once again before a mammoth window, this time at her company. We see her at the beginning of the shot almost completely immersed in the gloom, standing motionless and staring blankly at the void, which as we recognize all too quickly is the reflection of the city below. In the distance is the reflection of the steady flash of a stop signal positioned precisely where Minmin's heart would be if we had X-ray vision. The audience is absorbed in the rhythmic beat of the red light at the intersection of a far away surface street, the perpetual swishing of the tires on the nearby freeway the only sound audible. The heart is where the light is, their separate pulses governed by a parallel surge of synergy and a parallel arrest of stagnation. One is reminded here of *Nighthawks*, the well-known painting by Edward Hopper of company men drinking alone in a tavern. But Yang goes much further in replacing the pub, a designated commercial space of supposed sociality with the office, the space of omnipresent capital as well as personal life, with the bar and the bottle overtaken by cubicles and computer screens. Similar to the previous juxtaposition of the baby's ultrasound image and the translator's soundtrack, the human–machine interface is reconfigured here in this cinematic overlayering, a breathtaking image of the total interpenetration and interpellation of society and subjectivity, and of exteriority and interiority of capital as culture. "Haven't you gone home already?" inquires Nancy the officemate and friend after she steps in and switches on the fluorescent lights. After what feels a long-drawn-out moment, Minmin replies, "I have nowhere to go."

5

The sense everywhere of having nowhere to go is symptomatic of reflexive modernity, a global risk society, whose predicament is defined by Ulrich Beck as "unintentional self-dissolution or self-endangerment" (Beck, Giddens, and Lash 176). As NJ puts it to the comatose Popo after Minmin has left home for her Buddhist meditation with the monks, "I am not sure about anything these days. Every morning, I wake up feeling uncertain." "If you were me," he asks Popo, "would you like to wake up?" The vanishing certainty about old social structures entails the use of a new decentralized expert system, according to Anthony Giddens, wherein the reflexivity and circularity of social know-how can help the subject change her condition of action (Ibid. 187). As though literate in Chinese and aware of the phrase 危机, Giddens takes Beck's sense of risk 危 as an opportunity 机. What is for Beck self-endangerment is for Giddens a chance to exercise individual agency by appropriating the expert system of nonjudgmental advice with nonnegotiable fees. Here the private and intimate are taken to new heights when the intercourse between husband and wife is expertly decommissioned to make way for the cottage industry of family counseling. Consistent with themes in *Confucian Confusion* and *Majiang*, Yang links in *Yi Yi* the crisis of wants and ennui to the capitalistic process of deskilling. Although never explicit in its indictment of the systemic production of risk, the film's suspicion of Giddens's proposal of an individual reflexive management is unmistakable.

While indicating the codependence of the traditional folk or new age spirituality with other burgeoning expert systems in reflexive modernity, Minmin's
retreat to the Buddhist temple, a Chinese equivalent of the therapist's couch in the
West, is the subject of Yang's scathing satire. The master monk is later shown as
a minstrel minister, for instance, coming down the mountains in order to recruit
NJ for "couple therapy" but returning happily with his fat check. The monk is
also a legitimate version of "Little Buddha," the pretender in *Majiang*. Besides
exposing material contamination in institutionalized religion when spirituality is
turned marketable expertise, Yang also uses this instance to raise doubts about
Giddens's affirmation of reflexivity on two other accounts. Yang is discontent
with Giddens's view that reflexive agency is purely a matter of personal management and adaptation, as market efficiency automatically overrides the concern
of moral legitimacy. He is equally dubious of the expert system as Foucaultian
"technologies of the self," and regards it instead as yet another form of discipline
in disguise, despite its objective appearance in the concealed power of panopticon and synopticon.[14] With this hermeneutic suspicion, Yang deliberately misses
"the central distinction between reflection (knowledge) and reflexivity (unintentional self-dissolution)," the basis of Beck's argument (Beck, Giddens, and
Lash 176). For him, if self-reflexivity is to have true meaning it will have to
involve self-reflection, not reflection as the bouncing back and forth of images or
the superficial suturing of subjectivity in optical glare, but as an individual ethical
engagement through apprehension of social totality.

This reflective search for knowledge makes Yang a proper early modernist
rather than late or reflexive modernist, and this quest is figured in the film narrative as dialectic of vision. Refusing the status quo of individualization and dissolution, *Yi Yi*'s principal pedagogical-formative seems a recovery of the monadic
self amid the bygone communal, the endangered collective, and the vanishing
social in global capitalism. As the boy protagonist puts it to his father NJ, "I can
only see what it is in front of me and not what's behind. Does it mean that we
can only see half of the world?" Yangyang is evidently a junior alter ego of director Yang. With all his intellectual precocity, the boy is concerned about vision and
cognition in at least two different senses. One is the urge to transcend partial and
peripheral for holistic vision, an attempt at grasping social and spatial interdependency and integrity beyond "*Yi Yi*" or "I am I." The other is the desire to recognize
a temporality of sight, to couple the forward-looking eye/I with the history of its
own immanence and the origin of its imminent becoming. If Yangyang pictures
the rear of people's heads to enable their self-perception, the director of *Yi Yi*
wants to locate the failure of constructing totality in the postmodern fracturing of
space and time.

It is not ironic that the loss of holistic vision results from a contemporary suf-
fusion of vision, a vision of life burdened with sensorial overload and its absolute satisfaction. "The relentless saturation of any remaining voids," as Jameson
notes, "[exposes the postmodern body] to a perpetual barrage of immediacy from
which all sheltering layers have been removed" (1988, 351). As "Fatty" sums
it up for Tingting after their trip to the movies that the invention of cinema has

considerably extended human life: "The experience we get through the movies at least doubles what we experience in real life." To illustrate, he cites the movie as a manual for murder. Only when Fatty is arrested for that crime does the audience realize the importance of this foreshadowing. The boundary between fantasy and reality has been abolished while the pursuit of intensified virtual experience in actuality becomes Yang's apt allegory of moral collapse. The attempt at extending one's own experience endlessly has resulted in the curtailing of another's life, as Fatty comes to embody "the aesthetic way of life" in his "attempt to lose the self in the immediacy of present experience." "The paradigm of aesthetic expression is the romantic lover who is immersed in his own passion," writes MacIntyre in his reading of Kierkegaard; "by contrast the paradigm of the ethical is marriage, a state of commitment and obligation through time, in which the present is bound by the past and to the future" (40).

If the audience has so far been frustrated by the random dispersal of families and friends, they are enlightened by the sequence of frames that intercut NJ and "Sherry" with Tingting and Fatty. It is Yang's design that centrifugal spatial movements are eventually recognized not as runaway paths but courses helplessly intertwined with temporal trajectories of a definitive beginning and an end. On learning his business visit to Ota, his now married first love Sherry flies from Chicago to Tokyo to meet him. The camera captures both waiting at a Japanese commuter train station, catching up on old times and new stories. "I get jealous as my daughter is growing into a woman," NJ says, "knowing that she'll eventually be with someone else." Before his voice tails off, a passing train obscures the sight of NJ and Sherry and the camera cuts to Tingting, who stands waiting at the corner of a Taipei theater. As Fatty slowly walks into view, the clucking of the Japanese train fades into the din of Taipei traffic. Tingting asks, "What's the time?" "Nine," replies Fatty. "It's almost ten now. Eight a.m. Chicago time," Sherry's voice jumps in, just before the camera cuts back to her. "Nine p.m. in Taipei," murmurs NJ, as they saunter toward a railroad crossing. Time and space of transnational proportions are radically compressed into living immediacy on the screen to exemplify the arrival for some of the condition of a global village, but for Yang global spaces remain identified both by local times and the primary locations of subjective dwelling.[15] Sherry remarks on the crossing's resemblance to the one near their school, harking back in late modern Japan to a modernizing Taiwan three decades ago.[16] "That's long gone," NJ updates her, "but I remember the first time I held your hand there, before our going to the movies." We hear this as the camera shifts again from the quiet night of the Japanese town to the hustle and bustle of the Taipei street crossing, where Tingting and Fatty are waiting for the pedestrian light to change, silently holding hands. "I'm holding your hand once again," continues NJ's voice, speaking to Sherry offscreen, "only at a different place, at a different time, at a different age." The lens closes in on Tingting and Fatty, hands clasped together, crossing the street, as Sherry's voice finishes NJ's sentence, "but the same sweaty palm." (The hand-holding in Yang's capture is almost identical to Hou's in the "1966" section in *Three Times*.)

In his correlation of amour in separate international time zones, different generations, and varied speeds of motion, Yang rejects the dominant temporality of late
capital that Manuel Castells labels "timeless time," the time of a "compress[ed]"
"instantaneity" or "a random discontinuity" (494). While the series of intercutting compresses the immediacy of concurrent intimate events, it crystallizes the
obscured order of succession in both generational distinction and identity. One
may say that Yang has put Castells's time schemes into filmic perspective when
the dominant frame of "timeless time" – with its "virtual" temporality, "instant
wars," and "split-second capital transactions" – is forced to confront "time discipline" with its "biological" boundaries and "socially determined sequencing"
(Ibid. 494, 495). The director of *Yi Yi* enables a virtual sight of timeless time
when NJ and Tingting are seen simultaneously in different geographic spaces.
Showing in comparison and contrast both the father and daughter in romance
also demonstrates their subjection to the time discipline of biological growth and
decline. Timeless time is thus set against the unchanging cycle of the generations,
of human procreation, of economic production, and of the origination of subjectivity in history and geography.

Yang has coupled the space of flow inextricably with place-bound time. While
global capital's perpetual manufacturing of difference and engineering of sensation threatens to compact our sense of time into ephemeral pleasures, Yang
wants us to see such simple beauty as the generational repetition and duration
of locked hands and hearts. Against the contemporary dispersion of subjectivity in the multiple spheres of work and leisure, Yang tries to cultivate a new
agency in globality that reckons with the limited human temporal purchase and
thereby a willful teleological necessity of historic continuity. *Yi Yi* is not content
with merely stating the finitude of human life; it wants the recognition of this
finitude to effectively counter timeless time's erosion of communal purpose and
promotion of instantaneous individual gratification. Individual biography cannot
be meaningfully crafted, however reflexively so, unless and until it is anchored
within historical time.

In this context, Fatty's formula of experiential expansionism in the episodic
mode – recall his quest to double his experience within the finite span of life,
migrating from one girlfriend to another – provides the backdrop against which
NJ's deliberation resolutely rails. Indeed, NJ's nostalgic interlude with Sherry in
Japan is not fundamentally different from the flights of fancy that plague Fatty
or his in-laws, neighbors, and friends, who all seek the thrill of novel experience in lieu of possible transcendence. The ensemble characters of Yang's cast are
susceptible to the quickened passage from industrial to informational capitalism.
They are all caught in the inevitable contradiction of the cultural logics respective
of two different historical eras, the "delay of gratification" of early modernity
and the "delay of payment" of late modernity (Bauman, 1995, 5). However, if
Yangyang's dialectical tale of hindsight and foresight is indicative, some are less
vulnerable and more capable than others to weigh the excitement of the moment
with the progression of teleology. It is in the consideration of time's unfolding
and its commitment beyond the moment that Yang's reflective project of the ethic

self departs from Giddens's "reflexive project of the self . . . devoid of ethical content" (176).

After considerable reflection – one in a silhouette behind a Japanese screen and another on an embankment stretching out to the ocean, both postures eminently evocative of Auguste Rodin's *The Thinker*, the artist and the figure of a bygone model of aesthetic and ethical depth – NJ meets with Sherry again. She proposes to start their life anew, presumably in America where she currently resides. Sherry has money and lots of it, and she offers to divorce her husband Rodney to reunite with NJ. In the beckoning of "this spectral form of civilization which the Americans have invented, an ephemeral form so close to vanishing point," in the enigmatic words of Jean Baudrillard, NJ must have suddenly seen "the best adapted to the probability – the probability only – of the life that lies in store" for him (10). He turns down Sherry's invitation, says "No" to the point of no return, and decides to go back to his Taipei family and software company. Historical reflection seems to have overcome the reflexive project of endless self-invention, as encoded in the postmodern promissory note: "Tomorrow is the first day of the rest of your life" (Baudrillard: Ibid. 11).

With Popo's passing, Yang brings Minmin back from her Buddhist retreat and puts her with NJ in the same frame on the film screen for the first time:

NJ: How was it up in the mountains?
MINMIN: It was as if they [the monks] were talking to Mom . . . and I was like my mother . . . I've come to realize that so much is in fact not complicated. But why did they ever appear so?
NJ: Right. Could I say this? While you were away I had a chance to relive part of my youth. I thought . . . things would have turned out differently. They turned out pretty much the same . . . [E]ven given a second chance, I would not really need it. It is quite unnecessary.

It is as though Minmin has emerged from the confusing complexity of reflexive modernity by having grasped the kernel of simplicity underneath, while NJ has refrained from choosing the apparent alternative to his perceived rut, a tantalizing prospect of the vanishing point. Having wandered lonely as a cloud in the lonely crowd, husband and wife have literally landed on their bed, an image of reembedding after their disembedding ventures.[17]

The reconciliation of the couple hinges on a shared refusal of endless experiential and emotional experiments, a rejection of reflexive adaptations, as well as a restoration of binaries, boundaries, and brakes that reregulate personal life: traffic lights and slow or stop signs abound in the film as cautions against reckless movements and unbridled mobility in the Second Coming of Capital. For Minmin, the realization that appearance can be deceiving leads to her conviction of an inarticulate essence. For NJ, that essence is defined by his reconceived needs and obligations as opposed to his equally reticent and ultimately repressed wants. Both husband and wife have embraced, through their individual routes of reflective discovery, a sameness, an identity, an elemental simplicity that is tied to a prior commitment and projected onto a certain future. The scene of the couple on their bed seems a moment of recovery, when a secular form of teleological time at once embodied in people and bound to place reemerges. Refuting the aesthete's indulgence in the infinite capaciousness of the moment for oneself alone, Minmin and NJ have come to reaffirm a generational cycle of perpetuity that entails a consensual curtailing of absolute individual gratification and a recognition of fundamentals. The centrifugal forces of reflexive modernity that engender much "Confucian" confusion in the incitation of *Yi Yi*, the monadic "I am I," have finally occasioned the much-needed critical reflections.

This affective regulation post-deregulation resonates with "the search of fundamentals," a common discourse emerging at the heel of the world risk society's time-space compression and disruption, and therefore must, argues Roland Robertson, be understood as a constitutive aspect of contemporary globalization (166). While this quest for fundamentals often appears as localized meaning-making, it is nonetheless a diffused worldwide phenomenon. As a reflexive structuring of preferences against "alienation, homelessness, [and] anomie," it is liable to fall into "the nostalgic paradigm" at best and the trappings of Christian and Islamic fundamentalisms at worst (Ibid. 169). With this in mind, differentiation seems in order in our approach to Yang's fundamental ideology and *Yi Yi*'s pedagogical formative. Although the site of the biological family remains the cinematic center of Yang's reflective recuperation from and within radiating reflexive modernity, the film is not endorsing either religious strictures or patrilineal governance. An earlier shot of Popo and Tingting holding hands, the symbolic gesture of affection between maternal grandmother and granddaughter, receives its visual encore in Tingting and NJ toward the movie's closing, suggesting at once an interruption of paternal heritage as well as a preservation of kindred sentiments. A similar visual matching is at work in the film's successive frontal pairing of Tingting and NJ, Yangyang and NJ, and Ota and NJ together behind the windshield, intimating a transgender, transgenerational, transracial, and transnational solidarity of the spirit of decency. By contrast, Adi's ride with his brother-in-law NJ is shot from behind just as NJ is put in the passenger seat when Dada drives: neither seems NJ's true fellow traveler nor shares with him his ideal universe. One cannot fail to observe that Yang has significantly revised the genealogical core of community in Tu Weiming and Martha Nussbaum's outline of concentric circles. Rather than bowing to the ascribed condition of filiation as the center of cosmopolitan sociality, Yang has made affiliation of ideals and ethical consensus central in his mapping of global interrelatedness. His concentric vision of an egalitarian planetary community thus defies a blind submission to both the fundamentalism of blood and the fundamentalism of the market.

It is small wonder that those who seek short-term interests, either in the arenas of emotional or economic exchange, fare much worse through Yang's lens than those who are committed to the durability of reciprocal benefits and larger social goods. If Adi's crass materialism is condemned in the rapid boom and bust of his fortune, Dada's chase of Ato, the copycat of Ota that cannot deliver, is also a lesson against instant profits. The kind of instrumental reason that matches means to ends in exclusive economic terms turns out neither ethical nor efficient. Such melodramatic Manichaeism is reminiscent of James's and Balzac's unveiling of the "moral occult," a "domain of spiritual forces and imperatives that is not clearly visible" but "believe[d] to be operative" in a "desacralized" post-Enlightenment West (Brooks 15, 20–21). An exemplary film at the turn of a new millennium, *Yi Yi* provides a similar yet more radical dramatization of Taiwan's passage into risk-ridden modernity in Capital's Second Coming. Here, the providential is no longer viable, the filial and the local no longer stable, yet rediscovery of ethical imperatives remains fundamental for the affective and social commonweal. Possessing an identical urge as the masters of early modernity, Yang wishes to register into consciousness the power of the residual, a weakened sense of historicity, a narrative conception of the self, and a teleology of the human species. Cultural capital properly belonging to a previous era yet not entirely eradicated in the mixed and compressed modernity of today seems to hold promise. Tingting, Yangyang, NJ, and Ota are emblems not of the past but of the potential of our future, for they have made evident the sham of a reigning cultural logic that the likes of Adi and Dada personify: maximum growth, instant profits, and flexible accumulation. That these are not the sole objective or the fundamentals of human actions constitutes *Yi Yi*'s primary pedagogical-formative.

"I'm sorry, Popo, It wasn't that I didn't want to talk to you. I thought whatever I told you, you would have already known," Yangyang says in tribute to Popo at her funeral. "I know so little, Popo. But you know what I'll do when I grow up? I will tell people what they do not know and show them what they cannot see." *Yi Yi* has shown us a world of jet travel, bullet trains, and instant electronic transfer of money, images, and information. But these signs of ever-expanding human conquest of space have not erased the incontrovertible limits of nature on human life, Popo's death being the most necessary of time's reminder. Just as it is self-deluding to have faith in the cybernetic salvation of humanity, the projected life's work of the boy Yangyang appears to lift the cloud of confusion for subjects of global capitalism so that they can see what they have been precluded from seeing, and they can act with nature's limits and the preservation of the living planet in mind.

"Throughout human history," argues Zygmunt Bauman, "the work of culture consisted in sifting and sedimenting hard kernels of perpetuity out of transient human lives [and] actions, in conjuring up duration out of transience," and in "transcending thereby the limits imposed by human mortality by deploying mortal men and women in the service of the immortal human species." It is not incidental that Bauman deploys the past tense in his summary of that history, for "demand for this kind of work is," as he puts it, "shrinking" (2000, 126). Bauman's concern with the waning of such demand and the devaluation of immortality is Edward Yang's as well, for both are preoccupied with the decisive turning point in human history, when the sovereign, solipsistic, and reflexive individual – the figure of "Yi," "the One," and "I am I" – is becoming the figure of hegemony in global modernity. No one can fully anticipate the consequences of radical reflexive individualization and its attendant deregulation of affect, but it is not premature to recall a cultural outlook that has sustained the divergent tribes of humanity thus far. "I miss you, Popo, especially when I see my still nameless newborn cousin. I remember that you always say that you feel old. I'd like to tell my cousin," Yang-yang declares, "I feel old too." Childhood and age, and innocence and experience, finally converge in this articulation of a continuous life narrative, and with it, a reiteration of an ethical imperative so often submerged in the fragments of Capital's Second Coming. Unlike the premodern resignation to biological fate and/or a postmodern deferral of death in the waning of affect and instant consumption, Yangyang's signification on Popo's silence suggests a potential collective triumph over monadic mortality, a cultural transcendence of individual earthly sojourn. A consummate work of cinematic art, *Yi Yi* has come to harness the errant energy of affective deregulation, to evoke both spatial and temporal limits so that an affect of care and conservation could effect a life-affirming planet.

Notes

1 For Taiwanese cinema in general, see Yeh and Davis, and Berry and Lu.
2 I prefer a literal translation of the section titles to the film's English DVD version (Hong Kong: First Distributions/Sinomovie Co. Ltd. 2005). Thus, I substitute the original "A Time for Love," "A Time for Freedom," and "A Time for Youth" with "Dreams of Romance," "Dreams of Liberty," and "Dreams of Youth."
3 "Rain and Tears," the 1968 global hit by Aphrodite's Child, is misattributed by Hou to the Beatles and placed two years ahead of its actual release. This does not invalidate the biographical fact, however, that when Hou was a young man about A Zhen's age, the Greek band reigned in the pool parlors of Taiwan ("In Dialogue with Hou Hsiao Hsien: Hong Kong Asian Film Festival" from *Three Times* DVD, 2005).
4 "In Dialogue" (*Three Times* DVD, 2005).
5 References to the films in text are based on the following editions and translated into English by myself: *A Confucian Confusion* (Video CD, distributed by Unlimited Film Sensation Ltd, 1994), *Majiang* (Video CD, distributed by Shu Kei's Creative Workshop Ltd, 1996), and *Yi Yi: A One and a Two* (DVD, Fox Lorber Films, distributed by Windstar TV & Video 2001). For an informative reading of *A Confucian Confusion* and *Mahjong*, see Tonglin Lu (116–54).
6 My translation of Confucius is based on chapter 13, "Zi Lu" 子路, of *The Analects*, from which Yang quotes.
7 See Chapter 2 for a reading of neo-Confucianism. An earlier Sinophonic appropriation of Confucius from Taiwan, Singapore, and Chinese North America to justify a Chinese right to capitalism is reiterated by the Chinese Communist Party amid China's own unprecedented economic growth. The sage is sanctified, after the Mao era's ruthless political criticism of him, as the classical source of cultural authority and social harmony (Osnos).
8 See Marchetti on "Gangland Taiwan" (94–123). Hong Kong director Fruit Chan's *Made in Hong Kong* (1997) also tackles problems of delinquent youths.
9 I am using the DVD version of *Yi Yi* (2001). All English citations in the text are based on this edition's subtitle and my own translation.
10 To read the Nussbaum and Cohen volume on cosmopolitanism and patriotism with de Barry's edition on Confucianism and human rights shall yield unexpected insights on the question of rights and responsibilities in globalization.
11 It behooves us to recall Pierre Bourdieu:

> It is perhaps no accident that so many people of my generation have moved from a Marxist fatalism to a neoliberal fatalism: in both cases, economism forbids

responsibility and mobilization by canceling out politics . . . [T]his fatalistic doctrine gives itself the air of a message of liberation, through a whole series of lexical
tricks round the idea of freedom, liberation, deregulation, etc.

(1998, 50)

12 The figure she made is a butterfly, which, in the context of "Zhuang Zhou Meng Die"
庄周梦蝶, when the Taoist master becomes the butterfly in his dream, has at least two
dimensions of significance: (1) as a self-referential commentary on fantasy and reality,
and (2) as a metaphor for the radical unpredictability of life, this time, in contemporary
Taipei or in global modernity.

13 See Horton and Mendus's collection on MacIntyre's corpus in general, and Haldane's
critique of his Roman Catholicism and Thomistic Aristotelianism in particular.

14 Scott Lash's lesson on "reflexive winners" and "reflexive losers" seems to bring back
an ethical critique of disorganized capitalism that Yang insists on in his film (Beck,
Giddens, and Lash 120).

15 Of related interest is Tsai Ming-liang's treatment of simultaneity of France and Taiwan
in *What Time Is It There?*

16 It is important to observe Yang's positioning of Japan as an idyllic country, a nostalgic
retreat from the metropolitan and cosmopolitan rush of Taipei, contrary to Wong Kar-
wai's more standard use of less developed nation-states (e.g., Argentina and Cambodia)
as escapes from Hong Kong.

17 It is worth noting that Edward Yang's resolution of tempting affairs in *Yi Yi* is identical
to Wong Kar-wai's in *In the Mood for Love* (2001). Both have favored an inhibition of
individual desire, an ascetic and ethic alternative very much against the aesthetic grain
of late modernity.

Works cited

Althusser, Louis. "Ideology and Ideological State Apparatuses (Notes Towards an Investigation)." *Mapping Ideology*. Ed. Slavoj Zizek. New York: Verso, 1994, 100–140.

Appadurai, Arjun. *Modernity at Large: Cultural Dimensions of Globalization*. Minneapolis: U of Minnesota P, 1996.

Baudrillard, Jean. *America*. Trans. Chris Turner. Ann Arbor: U of Michigan P, 1994.

Bauman, Zygmunt. *Globalization: The Human Consequences*. New York: Columbia UP,
1998.

———. *Life in Fragments: Essays in Postmodern Morality*. Oxford: Polity P, 1995.

———. *Liquid Love: On the Frailty of Human Bonds*. Cambridge: Polity P, 2003.

———. *Liquid Modernity*. Cambridge: Polity P, 2000.

Beck, Ulrich. *Risk Society: Towards a New Modernity*. Trans. Mark Ritter. London: Sage,
1992.

Beck, Ulrich, and Elizabeth Beck-Gernsheim. *The Normal Chaos of Love*. Cambridge:
Polity P, 1995.

Beck, Ulrich, Anthony Giddens, and Scott Lash. *Reflexive Modernization: Politics, Tradition, and Aesthetics in the Modern Social Order*. Stanford: Stanford UP, 1994.

Berry, Chris, and Fei Lu. *Island on the Edge: Taiwan New Cinema and After*. Hong Kong:
Hong Kong UP, 2005.

Bourdieu, Pierre. *Acts of Resistance: Against the Tyranny of the Market*. Trans. Richard
Rice. New York: The New Press, 1998.

Brooks, Peter. *The Melodramatic Imagination: Balzac, Henry James, Melodrama, and the
Mode of Excess*. New Haven: Yale UP, 1976/1995.

Castells, Manuel. *The Rise of the Network Society (The Information Age: Economy, Society and Culture Volume I)*. Malden, MA: Blackwell, 1996.

Confucius. *The Analects*. Taipei: Taiwan Xinshen News, 1984.

Coontz, Stephanie. *Marriage, A History: From Obedience to Intimacy or How Love Conquered Marriage*. New York: Viking Penguin, 2005.

Debord, Guy. *The Society of Spectacle*. Trans. Donald Nicholson-Smith. New York: Zone Books, 1967/1995.

Foster, Hal. *Vision and Visuality*. New York: New P, 1988.

Giddens, Anthony. *Modernity and Self-Identity: Self and Society in the Late Modern Age*. Stanford: Stanford UP, 1991.

———. *The Transformation of Intimacy: Sexual, Love, and Eroticism in Modern Societies*. Cambridge: Polity P, 1992.

Haldane, John. "MacIntyre's Thomist Revival: What Next?" *After MacIntyre: Critical Perspectives on the Work of Alasdair MacIntyre*. Eds. John Horton and Susan Mendus. Notre Dame: U of Notre Dame P, 1994. 91–107.

Hardt, Michael, and Antonio Negri. *Empire*. Cambridge: Harvard UP, 2000.

Harvey, David. *The Condition of Postmodernity: An Enquiry into the Origins of Social Change*. Cambridge: Blackwell Publishers, 1990.

Hayles, N. Katherine. "The Complexities of Seriation." *PMLA Special Topic: Mobile Citizens, Media States* 117.1 (2002): 117–21.

Hirschman, Albert O. *The Passions and the Interests: Political Arguments for Capitalism before Its Triumph*. Princeton: Princeton UP, 1977/1997.

Horkheimer, Max, and Theodore W. Adorno. *Dialectic of Enlightenment*. Trans. John Cumming. New York: Continuum, 1944/1989.

Horton, John, and Susan Mendus, eds. *After MacIntyre: Critical Perspectives on the Work of Alasdair MacIntyre*. U of Notre Dame P, 1994.

Huang, Martin W. "Sentiments of Desire: Thoughts on the Cult of Qing in Ming-Qing Literature." *Chinese Literature: Essays, Articles, Reviews* 20 (1998): 153–84.

Illouz, Eva. *Cold Intimacies: The Making of Emotional Capitalism*. Cambridge: Polity P, 2007.

Jameson, Fredric. "Cognitive Mapping." *Marxism and the Interpretation of Culture*. Eds. Cary Nelson and Lawrence Grossberg. Urbana and Chicago: U of Illinois P, 1988. 347–57.

———. *The Geopolitical Aesthetic: Cinema and Space in the World System*. Bloomington: Indiana UP, 1995.

———. *The Political Unconscious: Narrative as a Social Symbolic Act*. Ithaca, New York: Cornell UP, 1982.

———. *Postmodernism: Or the Cultural Logic of Late Capitalism*. Durham: Duke UP, 1991.

Kraicer, Shelly, and Lisa Roosen-Runge. "Edward Yang: A Taiwanese Independent Film Maker in Conversation" *Cineaction* 47 (1998): 48–55.

Lash, Scott, and John Urry. *The End of Organized Capitalism*. Madison WI: U of Wisconsin P, 1987.

Lee, Haiyan. *Revolution of the Heart: A Genealogy of Love in China 1900–1950*. Stanford: Stanford UP, 2006.

Lepore, Jill. "The Disruption Machine." *The New Yorker* (June 23, 2014): 30–36.

Lu, Tonglin. *Confronting Modernity in the Cinemas of Taiwan and Mainland China*. Cambridge: Cambridge UP, 2002.

MacIntyre, Alasdair. *After Virtue: A Study in Moral Theory*. Notre Dame: U of Notre Dame P, 1984.

Macpherson, Crawford Brough. *The Political Theory of Possessive Individualism: Hobbes to Locke.* Oxford: Oxford UP, 1962.

Marchetti, Gina. *From Tian'anmen to Times Square: Transnational China and the Chinese Diaspora on Global Screens 1989–1997.* Philadelphia: Temple UP, 2006.

Marcuse, Herbert. *One-Dimensional Man: Studies in the Ideology of Advanced Industrial Society.* Intro. by Douglas Kellner. Boston: Beacon P, 1964/1991.

Nussbaum, Martha C. "Patriotism and Cosmopolitanism." *For the Love of Country: Debating the Limits of Patriotism.* Eds. Martha Nussbaum and Joshua Cohen. Boston: Beacon P, 1996. 2–17.

Ong, Aihwa. *Flexible Citizenship: The Cultural Logics of Transnationality.* Durham: Duke UP, 1999.

Osnos, Evan. "Confucius Comes Home: Move Over, Mao." *The New Yorker* (January 13, 2014): 30–35.

Pine, II, B. Joseph, and James H. Gilmore. *The Experience Economy: Work Is Theater & Every Business a Stage.* Boston: Harvard Business School P, 1999.

Riesman, David. *The Lonely Crowd: A Study of the Changing American Character.* New Haven: Yale UP, 1961.

Robertson, Roland. *Globalization: Social Theory and Global Culture.* London: Sage, 1992/1998.

Tu, Weiming. "Human Rights as a Confucian Moral Discourse" in *Confucianism and Human Rights.* Eds. Wm. Theodore de Barry and Tu Weiming. New York: Columbia UP, 1998. 297–307.

——, ed. *"The Living Tree: The Changing Meaning of Being Chinese Today, A Special Issue." Daedalus* 120.2 (1991): 1–226.

Williams, David. *Imagined Nations: Reflections on Media in Canadian Fiction.* Montreal: McGill-Queen's UP, 2003.

Yeh, Emilie Yueh-yu, and Darrell William Davis. *Taiwan Film Directors: A Treasure Island.* New York: Columbia UP, 2005.

Part III

Homo ethicus

Toward ecological justice

5   The world of Jia Zhangke viewed

Neorealist aesthetics against neoliberal logics

Born and raised during China's radical shift from socialism to capitalism, the independent turned international art house favorite, Jia Zhangke 贾樟柯, is considered a consummate master of neorealist cinema and a clairvoyant chronicler of China's neoliberalization. As film aesthetics, neorealism not only concerns itself with norms of beauty but more crucially, in the original etymological meaning of the Greek *Aisthisis*, "the sensory experience of perception" (Buck-Morss 6). As a form of global capitalism, neoliberalism not only produces concrete goods and immaterial services but also fashions ways of thinking and feeling appropriate to practices of competition and circulations of commodities. Neoliberal logics is incomplete without its correspondent aesthetics. It entails a kindred form of perceiving the world and a structure of consumptive pleasure befitting an economy of the spectacle. Neoliberal capitalism in its characteristic "creative-destruction," as Joseph Schumpeter memorably calls it, is diametrically opposed to cinematic neorealism's insistence on observing and conserving a corporeal and material reality. Following Andre Bazin's famous formulation of the photographic image as that which "embalms [historical] time, rescuing it from its proper corruption," I consider neorealism as essentially a form of preservationist film aesthetics (1967, 14). Jia Zhangke's work, I argue, solicits a different sensorial response, cultivates a different social agency, and maintains a different ethics, functioning in its proper illumination as neorealist preservation against neoliberal creative destruction.

Millicent Marcus is instructive when she considers "Italian neorealism" as an aesthetic practice as well as an ideological position. The deployment of a specific set of visual technologies serves the neorealist directors' philosophical take of the world in their attempt to change it:

> location shooting, lengthy takes, unobtrusive editing, natural lighting, a predominance of medium and long shots, respect for the continuity of time and space, use of contemporary true-to-life subjects, an uncontrived, open-ended plot, working class protagonists, a non-professional cast, dialogue in the vernacular, [and] active viewer involvement.
>
> (Marcus 22)

Indeed, for Marcus and many critics on the subject, neorealism is first and foremost "'una nuova poesia morale' [a new moral poetry] whose purpose was to promote a true subjectivity" (Ibid. 23). Deeply immersed in China's postsocialist reality, Jia Zhangke's oeuvre is resonant of his Italian predecessors' ethical vision. Although devoid of their explicit didacticism, Jia's earlier films evidence an uncanny resemblance to their classic work. *Xiao Wu* 小武 (1997), the story of a small town pickpocket, conjures up in both theme and tone De Sica's *Bicycle Thieves*, while *Platform* 站台 (2000), a sort of road movie starring a song and dance troupe from a provincial town as China relinks with global capital, and *Unknown Pleasures* 任逍遥 (2002), a feature that dramatizes two delinquent teenagers feasting on popular cultural junk, hark back unmistakably to Fellini's *La Strada*.

While there seems no decline of his status as the preeminent storyteller both of the film medium and the contemporary Chinese condition, Jia's *The World* 世界 (2005) and *Still Life* 三峡好人 (2006) contain features that vociferously burst the seams of the neorealist form.[1] The animation sequences in *The World* and the surrealist flight of a UFO in *Still Life* are obvious stylistic departures. They seem to refute a standard neorealist insistence on the referentiality of reality and its ontological integrity with human experience. Since *The World* marked Jia's first ever aboveground entry into the Chinese film market after years of underground and overseas existence, and *Still Life* was distributed both at home and abroad, these formal ruptures raise suspicion as to whether the director bowed either to party censors or to commercial imperatives. The moments of jarring visuality in both films effectively preclude their reception as eye candy, however. They reject "enlightenment [of] mass deception" forecast by Horkheimer and Adorno about the "cultural industry," be it capitalist or communist.

Shot on location in the capital city of Beijing as well as at the theme park at its outskirts that bears the film's title, *The World* is both about the site, the World Park 世界公园, and its subjects, the stage performers entertaining the tourists and security guards maintaining the grounds. As a site, the World Park is a physical reproduction of cosmopolitan landmarks in the fashion of Disney's Epcot Center in Orlando, Tobu World Square in Japan, and the Luxor Hotel and Casino in Las Vegas as it anticipates other Chinese architectural appropriations, Shanghai's Thames Town and Shenzhen's own version of Interlaken, the Swiss alpine village in the snowless Chinese south.[2] As such, the World Park reconfigures the native contours of landscape and cityscape, revises the experience of the near and the far, and complicates irrevocably the perception of the real and the imagined. The amusement park is nothing short of being the materialization of a particular vision of a world, lifted from its multiple indigenous locations, presented in its shiny symbolic surface, conveniently compressed into 114 acres and readily consumed within 24 hours. As Jia's lingering shot of the park's neon slogan in the twilight impresses upon the audience: "You give me a day, and we'll give you the world!"

Still Life, a tour de force succeeding *The World*, leads us to yet one more actual site of extreme geographic makeover, roughly eight hundred miles away from the capital of Beijing, in the now submerged city of Fengjie on the mighty Yangtze River. *The Good Folks of the Three Gorges* 三峡好人, as the film is known in its original Chinese title, sets its characters on the largest construction site known to human history. The Three Gorges Dam, upon its completion in 2009, created a reservoir the size of Lake Superior. Its weight is so massive, according to a Discovery Channel documentary, that the mega-dam could "slightly alter the earth's axis and increase the length of every day by a microscopic amount."[3] Unlike the Discovery Channel narratives, which laud China's technological accomplishments while lamenting its inundation of tradition, *Still Life* directs the audience's gaze away from the feat of construction to the sight of demolition. Its subjects are the displaced locals as well as the migrants, invariably small people like the dancers in *The World*, whose participation in the grand scheme of progress and prosperity is punctuated with precariousness.

Combined, they are the director's global travel narrative in the Gulliver grain: *The World* is the land of Lilliput and *Still Life* the land of Brobdingnag. Together, the construction of the miniature and the gigantic and their cinematic mediation begin to manifest globalization as both "time-space compression" and "time-space distanciation" (Harvey 240; Giddens 64). The park, in bringing home the sights and sounds of faraway places, exemplifies an extraordinary speeding-up of social life and a concomitant shrinkage of physical and psychic space, precipitated by advancements in communication technologies. In abbreviating the time of freighting between the once landlocked Chinese interior and the port of San Francisco, the dam comes to demonstrate both new developments in transportation technologies and the increasing mutual dependency of distant institutions and local incidents. The frantic construction of the miniature and the gigantic articulates a unique Chinese capitalist modernity of developmental compression and mixed production. The massive scale of dam construction is reminiscent of the mode of Fordist capital, of a goods economy based on industrialization, manufacturing, and infrastructural building. The amusement park, on the other hand, represents the turn of post-Fordist capital toward service and experience economies, centered on informational technology and immaterial consumption (Harvey).

The World and *Still Life* seem cinematic tracking shots of Fredric Jameson's seminal thoughts. "In modernism," read the opening pages of *Postmodernism, or the Cultural Logic of Late Capital*,

> some residual zones of "nature" or "being," of the old, the older, the archaic, still subsist; culture can still do something to that nature and work at transforming that "referent." Postmodernism is what you have when the modernization process is complete and nature is gone for good. It is a more fully human world than the older one, but one in which "culture" has become veritable "second nature" . . . an immense dilation of its sphere (the sphere of commodities), an immense and historically original acculturation of the Real, a quantum leap in what Benjamin still called the "aestheticization" of reality.
>
> (ix–x)

Putting aside the descriptive felicity of postmodernity for our global condition today, Jameson's diagnosis of capitalism's remaking of nature has borne out in China's distinctive developmental compression. In this frame of reference, *Still*

Life visualizes an older technology of colonization, when the ground of human subsistence is conceived as a separate externality in need of artificial extraction and subjugation. *The World*, on the other hand, mediates the newer technology of colonization, when the very interiority of our mind and body, the site of our sensorium and the unconscious, is subject to capital's spectacular commodification. Tackling the amusement park as a simulated yet tangible form of social reality, the film conveys an overall sense of claustrophobia when its protagonists are overwhelmed by an outside world crushing in and crowding out the space of personal meaning-making. Moving from the global architecture of the city and virtuality to the physiognomy of the land in transformation and its residents' deracination, *Still Life* conveys the prevailing mood of agoraphobia, as the camera follows its protagonists wandering amid the open landscape, the gutted buildings, and demolished townships in search of signposts and memories.

Still Life stands out as Jia's exemplary cinematic contemplation on the interplay between sites and subjectivities, structures and sensoriums when capitalist creative destruction is changing irrecoverably their historical relations. Not only does it tilt the planet's axis, it has altered the climate, propelling the Holocene, the post–ice age warm period of the past 10–12 millennia, to the Anthropocene, the human-induced period of environmental change starting with fossil-fueled industrial capitalism.[4] In this chapter, we will examine exclusively the film's representation of still life made over on speed in an *Oikos* marred and maimed, as Jia correlates the disappearance of geographic markers with his protagonists' search for vanishing spouses. In conscientiously making visible the abstract political and economic forces that mobilize the transformation of physical as well as psychic nature, Jia is both revealing the altered relations of subjectivity and objectivity in the Second Coming of Capitalism and reframing a view of the world that may appear more hospitable to the conditions of our dwelling and the survival of the species. Because the artistic effects of *Still Life* derive from Jia's methodical application of neorealist aesthetics and his exceptional inclusion of surrealist techniques, because Italian neorealism is influential in the postwar and postcolonial constitution of world cinemas in opposition to Hollywood, and because the historical ascent and contemporary revival of neorealism seem cultural responses to particular moments of capitalist expansion, it is incumbent that our reading of *Still Life* be prefaced with a genealogy of neorealism's multiple historical and geopolitical manifestations from which Jia hails his artistic inheritance.[5]

1

As early as the making of his hometown trilogy of *Xiao Wu, Platform*, and *Unknown Pleasures*, Jia sets both his attention to the rapid social change and intention to "capture a transforming reality" against the "imaginary representations of traditional Chinese society common after the success of period pieces by directors like Chen Kaige and Zhang Yimou" (M. Berry 192). Jia's deliberate demarcation from Chen and Zhang reveals a definitional struggle between the Fifth and Sixth Generations of Chinese directors over significance of the real. We can better appreciate their difference by correlating the historical development of Chinese realism with Italian neorealism; Jia's antagonism to Chen and Zhang who once inspired his career and his own contrarian film practice shall gain clarity as a result.

In "The Concept of the Real in Chinese Cinema and the Impact of [Andre] Bazin," Ke Hu contends that the 1980s Chinese appropriation of Bazin is impossible without the native grounds of realism that predate his English translation to China in the 1960s.[6] According to Hu, an indigenous development of Chinese realist film aesthetics starts in the 1920s and reaches relative maturity with Fei Mu's *Spring in a Small Town* 小城之春 in 1948, a window of time coinciding with capitalism's first flourish in China. Corresponding roughly to the creative span of the Second Generation of Chinese filmmakers who favor "the aesthetic integrity of the true, the benevolent, and the beautiful," this formative period of "native social realism" is overtaken by the Third Generation active between the founding of the People's Republic of China in 1949 and the beginning of the Great Proletariat Cultural Revolution in 1966, when "social realism" of old is turned into "socialist realism" of the new (K. Hu 21). With the "Soviet model" in mind, Chinese socialist realism incorporates "cinematic production into the state's planned economy," demanding that it "reflect[s] the evolving revolutionary view of life" and conforms to the party's conception of reality (Ibid. 21–22). As a protocol of art, as Ann Anagnost remarks, "socialist realism dictates that art and literature must have a didactic function to represent ideal behavior for emulation" and what things are "supposed to be in a socialist society" rather than what they "really are" (54). The socialist reality becomes effectively a hegemonic fiction of the state in a teleological trajectory of realizing itself.

Despite the ideological stringencies of socialist realism, the release in mid-1950s China of such an Italian masterpiece as *Bicycle Thieves* – originally intended to expose the dark side of capitalism as a foil to the bright side of socialism – has inadvertently sparked the possibility of a contemporaneous comparative understanding between a "foreign" neorealism and the "native" realism of the Chinese Second Generation. While the introduction of Bazin in the early 1960s further confirms the aesthetic and ethical resonances between Italian and Chinese realisms of the late 1940s, a similar realist cinema also thrived, however briefly, with the Chinese Fourth Generation directors. Formally trained in the 1950s and 1960s and creatively suppressed until the early 1980s, the Fourth Generation at once "revive traditional [Chinese social] realism" and extend it with "a utilization of Bazin's concepts [of neorealism]" (Ni 26; K. Hu 22, 24).[7]

For Dai Jinhua, the Fourth Generation's appropriation of "Bazinian documentary aesthetics" is a "misreading" with which the directors could both evoke an earlier Chinese social realism and transcend the socialist realism of the Third Generation. Theirs is an outlook "from the leaning tower" that "casts its gaze at a disappearing reality": its "wish to tell the twisted fate of the individual can only result in the narration of a deformed history" (Dai, 1989, 3–7). The Fourth Generation's realistic reconciliation between self and society caught between a negative past and a changing present proves to be short-lived. Its creative heyday between 1979–82 is simultaneously the age of apprenticeship for the Fifth Generation from the Beijing Film Academy, who shall quickly eclipse the Fourth Generation with its unique negotiations of the real. The spectacular imaging of the barren yet majestic Chinese landscape in *Yellow Earth* and *Red Sorghum* performs a double turn, on the one hand toward a rethinking of the collective as it is figured in the timeless rural, while on the other hand toward an awakening of the individual as it is figured in sexual desire. Representation of observable contemporary reality is largely eschewed by the Fifth Generation, as their films assiduously and amorously mediate the Chinese reality of drastic political and economic change in an unmistakable mythical and allegorical mode. Such aesthetics, as is argued in my reading of *Red Sorghum*, both anticipates and prepares for the nation's transition from the socialist structure of public welfare to the capitalist mode of profit making, from the sentiment of proletarian solidarity to the feeling of possessive and affective individualism.

Although the Fifth Generation's subterfuge of referential reality is a purposive demolition of the "socialist-realist tradition," it reproduces the same idealizing tendencies endemic to the socialist realism it wants to replace (X. Zhang 204). Instead of abiding by a communist teleology as with the Third Generation, or confronting the reality of transition with ambivalence as with the Fourth, the Fifth Generation is obsessed with "aesthetic self-sufficiency"; this pursuit of cinematic idiosyncrasy has changed their implied audience "from a collective spectator [of the socialist state] to an international consumer," just as "[t]he marketplace [of global media]" has become "the predetermined destiny of the aesthetic style that hangs on in a changed social climate" (Ibid. 205, 207). Indeed, the short decade between Zhang's *Red Sorghum* and Jia's *Xiao Wu* witnesses the transition from a prior political predetermination to the present profit predetermination. Fifth Generation films that "squeeze through the narrow gateways [of socialist realism] to become self-conscious, marginal representations of an Other in Eurocentric culture," as Dai states wryly, "simply fell under the yoke of one discursive power in their attempt to escape from another" (2002, 50–51).

Whereas the Fifth Generation continues to ride on an Orientalist imagination both dependent on the global film market and in breach of the Chinese reality of massive capitalist industrialization, the classes of 1985 and 1987 at the Beijing Film Academy, the primary component of the Sixth Generation, face the disintegration of the studio system and "abandonment by the film industry" (Ibid. 80–81).[8] This unfavorable condition of cultural production prompts the Sixth Generation's close alliance with nomad singers and visual artists in their shared strategy of guerrilla fundraising and artistic survival, and fosters its intimate involvement with migrant laborers from the country and marginal groups in the city, uprooted by and alienated from the precipitous capitalist development. Zhang Yuan's *Mama* 妈妈 (1990) and *Beijing Bastards* 北京杂种 (1992), Wang Xiaoshuai's *Frozen* 极度寒冷 (1995), and Wu Wenguang's *Bumming in Beijing* 流浪北京 (1990) have all but confronted the immediate traumas and displacements of rapid industrializing China of which the Sixth Generation is an integral part.[9] As bookends of the Sixth, Zhang Yuan and Jia Zhangke come to exemplify

their generation's obsession with the postsocialist Chinese urban and its unflinching documentation of everyday change under capitalist reform, the manner of
which is superbly summarized in a Chinese critical biography devoted to them,
My Camera Does Not Lie 我的摄影机不撒谎 (Cheng and Huang).[10]

Such truth-telling impulse realizes itself in the "poetic melancholy of its
extreme documentary style," the necessity of "on location" shooting, and the
employment of "amateur actors and actresses," all of which coalesce into a generational aesthetics (Dai, 2002, 81, 82, 85). "The reality within the film (its content)
and the reality about the film (its processes and means of production), which [are]
distinctly separate in mainstream films, almost [merge] together in most Sixth
Generation films" (Ibid. 85, 94).[11] Reality as such is not about the ontology of the
cinematic image but an embedded relation of filmic representation; thus the subject matter and stylistic features particular to the Sixth Generation are grasped as
their dialectic engagement with contemporary Chinese circumstances. The operative word is "merge," an act that integrates cinematic production with creative
content to arrive at the perspective of "an ordinary person" and "the psychological world of the immediate sufferers" so that their reality achieves representation
(Ibid. 85).

In this manner, the Sixth Generation's documentary attentiveness to and empathetic identification with the margin and the mass conjure up practices of the
Second Generation active in China's earlier encounter with colonial capitalism
between the 1920s and 1940s. In face of the "suffering masses of laborers," writes
Leo Lee, the Second Generation manages to "tap into the anxieties of the Chinese audience not by injecting any blatant ideology" "but [by] employing a new
narrative mode" (100). Thematically, the "trope of city and country" serves "as
contrasting worlds of evil and good" (Ibid. 102). Cinematically, the preponderant
use of "long take, deep focus put[s] human beings in a larger environment and
create[s] a unity among them while manifesting their contradictions in the same
time and space" (Ibid. 103). The Second and Sixth Generations' shared practice
of realism also finds their affinity with the more established and better theorized
school of Italian neorealism, which, as Marcus shows, rallies documentary aesthetics as a directorial vehicle of "social criticism" and "moral statement[s]"
(22–23). The Second Generation's capture of "the social contradictions and alien-
ations that beset a modernizing society" and their deployment of a realist apparatus to tackle them, as Zhen Zhang describes it, should in my view be considered
as "a pre-neorealist neorealist cinematic practice": it is a de facto practice before
André Bazin et al. exclusively attribute a similar set of features to Italian directors of the late 1940s and endow them with the distinctive categorical existence
as neorealism.[12] In other words, the Second Generation of Chinese directors may
have independently pioneered in the 1930s the nascent philosophy and practice of
a (neo)realism that the Italian directors also developed indigenously in the 1940s,
to which the Chinese Sixth Generation of the 1990s could once again claim their
spiritual kinship.[13]

This genealogical affiliation of transnational and transhistorical practice of cinematic realism is not to identify unique origins and subsequent departures so as

to produce either national distinction or aesthetic hierarchy. Instead, the manifestation of contemporaneous neorealist orientations in China and Italy allow us to figure out their aesthetic and ethical commons despite their geopolitical discontinuity. As it should become evident by now, the singular thread woven through both societies at the time has been the economic instability and social polarity endemic to the First Coming of industrial capitalism. Shanghai of the 1930s, the principal site of cinematic production for the Second Generation, is a Manichean space riven by capitalism and semicolonialism, a "paradise for the rich, and hell for the poor," and a "paradise for the foreigner, and hell for the Chinese" (quoted in Shih 235). Late 1940s Italy, recovering from the horrendous world war symptomatic of the crisis in capitalism, is in the films of De Sica a space of massive unemployment and haphazard survival. And 1990s China, fervently relinking with the world system in capitalism's postcolonial Second Coming (Dai, 2002, 71), witnesses prodigious economic growth as well as human immiseration. The neorealist cinematic practice emerging out of these systemic conditions of everyday jeopardy in different phases of capitalism – with its on-the-ground perspective and documentary fidelity – betrays a shared artistic desire to render visible the precarious state of the vulnerable mass in order to forge collective social insurance. The self-inclusion of the neorealist as "part of the world [s]he records" eventually turns the "passive resignation" of observational impartiality into a potential for "neorealist activism" (Marcus 25).

Not paradoxically, this neorealist agency is derived from a commitment to a specific perspective relation, a subject and object correspondence, and a representational covenant. Thus, when André Bazin remarks that "the objective nature of photography confers on it a quality of credibility absent from other picture making [so that] we are forced to accept as real the existence of the object reproduced, actually *re*-presented," he does not simply show us "the virtue of [the photographic] transference of reality from the things to its reproduction" (13–14). He is insisting, moreover, on the pre-given-ness of a phenomenological reality of which photography merely provides an index. As Philip Rosen explains, Bazin's view of the cinematic image as an indexical sign is meant to maintain "some existential connection between a specific referent and the signifier," although "[i]ndexicality implies nothing necessary about the *form* of the signifier," "nothing for example about whether the signifier 'looks like' the referent" (13).

It is this desire to preserve the "existential connection" between the cinematic image and its referent that unite Zhang Yuan and Jia Zhangke in their mutual opposition to the Fifth Generation's pursuit of absolute aesthetic self-sufficiency. Although an understandable reaction to historical subordination of art to politics, the Fifth Generation's radical break with socialist realism has also inadvertently discredited the social relevance and referentiality of cinema, which Bazin's concept of indexicality critically entails. In the achievement of this aesthetic autonomy as production of the commodified sign, the referential relationship of art form to material reality and the association between artistic production and social responsibility are dissolved. Art, artists, and audience are now detached from society except when such complex social relations are reduced to the simple market relations of supply and demand, of goods production and consumption among self-willing, self-discriminating, and self-possessive individuals.

The pain people experience under neoliberal economic and social makeover "show[s] me how to capture the transformation of my surroundings with a kind of sensitivity," Jia remarks, "which should always be the responsibility of the director" (M. Berry 193). This unwavering "responsibility" for reality at once allies Jia with his Chinese and Italian neorealist predecessors and expresses a greater cultural unease than pure aesthetic differences from his Fifth Generation forerunners. His is a general apprehension of cinema's success to become mere image and spectacle, which, as Guy Debord and Jean Baudrillard cautioned us, would herald the absolute disappearance of the referent as such. The Sixth Generation's recuperation of neorealism must be properly seen as an active response to the imminent danger posed by "the society of spectacle," which threatens to evaporate the referential relationship at the heart of representation, both political and aesthetic. If "representation stems from the principle of the equivalence of the sign and the real," writes Baudrillard, "simulation" is the "death sentence of every reference" (6). In following Bazin's conviction in the pre-given-ness of phenomenological reality prior to cinematography, and Baudrillard's insistence on the inalienability of the representational dyad, the Sixth Generation resolutely retains the relationship between the cinematic sign and its material and historical referent. Theirs is a retention that preserves the semiotic as well the social and material in the face of global capitalism's dramatic dissolution of preexisting forms of human perception and communication, and its wholesale liquidation of all social relations into sole relations of exchange and extraction. The subjectivity that emerges out of this preservationist instinct is neither a sovereign domination of whatever stands without it nor is it "the blindness of insight" (De Man), a flicker of self-realization which excludes anything outside the very narrow personal apertures. Instead, it compels "viewers to abandon the limitations of a strictly personal perspective and to embrace the reality of 'others'" (Marcus 23). What issues forth is an inclusive reciprocal relation with others, "be they persons or things" that may initially appear peripheral to the camera eye/I but are in effect constitutive components of and constitutively prior to the representation of subjectivity as such (Ibid.). For the lack of a better term, we shall refer to this cinematic alternative to the neoliberal subjectivity "neorealist subjectivity."

2

Jia Zhangke's *Still Life* exemplifies the principal features of neorealist aesthetics in its deliberate deployment of location shooting, natural lighting, in-depth shot and lengthy take, uncontrived plot, and absence of narrative closure. The film begins with an establishing shot of a ferry on the Yangtze, followed by a series of contiguous lateral panning through the diversity of its passengers and cargos before dwelling on a middle-aged man with the muscular build of a manual laborer, who is later revealed to be Han Sanming, a protagonist of the film (the actor is an actual relative of Jia and a coal miner). The boat docks and Sanming embarks on Fengjie, a riverside city of two thousand years to be submerged within two, once the Three Gorges Dam is complete. Sanming is in town to look for his long-lost wife but the house is now at the bottom of a man-made lake. The precious address recorded on a cigarette wrap, which he kept for the past sixteen years as the only physical trace of his spouse, has become truly a referent without a corresponding object. Capitalistic development entails creative destruction of existing reality. Even the new computer at the county office is unable to retrieve the whereabouts of the addressee; the machine, as the female clerk explains to Sanming, is temporarily dead.

Thus inaugurates Sanming's dead-end journey in the hometown of his former wife and the camera's unfolding of its gutted landscapes, the occasional shots of the newly erected township on the hilltop and the persistent capture of mostly rubbles as well as remaining structures marked by 拆, the Chinese character for demolition. It is amid the course of Sanming's search that the audience is later introduced to Shen Hong, a thirtysomething woman with the appearance and attire of a city resident, who lands in Fengjie to locate her estranged husband. A story of quest for past affiliations, *Still Life* intertwines the narratives of Sanming and Shen Hong on a parallel hunt for their respective partners. Although coming from the same Shanxi Province as their life trajectories crisscross the city of Fengjie, 150 miles upstream from China's hydroelectric mega-dam in construction, the two protagonists of *Still Life* in fact never meet or appear in the same frame in the film. Contrary to the familiar convention of Hollywood romance, where the pre-destined union of the heterosexual couple always drives the film to its anticipated consummation, Jia refuses to contrive a togetherness for his characters. While the two stories proceed with an intelligible chronological order, achieving resolution with Shen Hong's request of divorce from her husband, Guo Bing, and Sanming's hinted reunion with his once abducted wife, Yaomei, to describe *Still Life* in strict plot layout, as Shelly Kraicer notes with savvy in *Cinema Scope*, seems not only "misleading" but also "beside the point." This is because in the film "information is presented piecemeal" and "narrative expectations are constantly thwarted."

Small wonder, then, that the seemingly random movements of Sanming and Shen Hong should have one frustrated critic of the *New York Times* complain about the film's lack of "obvious connective tissue": "things happen, though not necessarily as a consequence of what took place in the previous scene" (Dargis). What this critic has missed is precisely Jia's inclination to simply let the events, in the manner André Bazin characterizes Giovanni Pastrone's *Cabiria* (1914), "befall its inhabitants" (1971, 84). In *Still Life* as in *Cabiria*, a unique neorealist logic realizes itself in the befallen nature of narrative events: there, as Bazin explains, events "occur as an effect of 'vertical' gravity, not in conformity to the laws of 'horizontal' causality" (Ibid.). If we take Bazin's vertical gravity to mean the force of nature, the volcanic eruption of Mt. Etna in *Cabiria*, for example, and horizontal causality to mean free will and individual desire, *Still Life* seems indeed a film very much saturated with the spirit of vertical determinism. But the gravitational pull may not be necessarily or exclusively natural; it could assume, as we shall soon see in detail, the abstract force of the social (industrialization and globalization), or the phantom form of the supernatural (UFO), over which the characters have little control. At the core of Jia Zhangke's observance of verti-cal gravity in the unfolding of minor events and incidental bits is his obdurate rejection of the very horizontal causality – the artificial condensation of image sequence to execute a presupposed meaning and reaction – with which the *New York Times* reviewer judges him.

Still Life suffers from no lack of causality; it is infused instead with an alterna-tive causality, soliciting a different spectatorial response and audience affect. Its apparently fragmented stories are in fact faithful citations of Roberto Rossellini's *Paisan* (1946), the gritty neorealist classic about the liberation of Italy in World War II. As we recall, *Paisan* is composed of six seemingly disconnected visual vignettes with the personal adventures of the two protagonists that, in Bazin's analyses, "blend into the mass of other adventures":

> In the course of making one's way one sees in the eyes of those who stand aside the reflections of other concerns, other passions, other dangers along side which one's own may well be merely laughable. Ultimately by chance, the woman learns, from a wounded partisan, that the man she is looking for is dead. But the statement from which she learned the news was not aimed at her . . . The impeccable line followed by this recital owes nothing to classical forms that are standard for a story of this kind. Attention is never artificially focused on the heroine. The camera makes no pretense at being psychologi-cally subjective . . . the pathetic aspect of the episode does not derive from the fact that a woman has lost the man she loves but from the special place this drama holds among a thousand others, apart from yet also part of the complete drama of the Liberation of Florence.
>
> (1971, 36)

As typical of Bazin's espousal of film form, the previously quoted analyses blend the aesthetic perspective with the ethic one, hinting toward an understanding of the aesthetic as inevitably ethical. The camera's revelation of other concerns, passions, and dangers enables, for Bazin, an objective and thus more admirable vision of social totality beyond individual romance or matrimony, transcending the limits of "classic forms" at "being psychologically subjective" (Ibid.).

Still Life's alleged absence of obvious connective tissue betrays Jia's eschewal of the classic montage that Bazin decries in Griffith (1971, 28) and his appro-priation of Rossellini's use of mise-en-scène. In lieu of montage's imposition of subjective meaning by juxtaposing images and dramatizing durations, Jia exploits the epistemological promise of referential images mise-en-scènes provide. For Jia as for Bazin, the inclusion of incidental, contingent, and marginal images drawn from the immediate environment proves instrumental in the audience's access to the "real," and consequently their comprehension of the complexity and ambigu-ity of reality. Not incidentally, the kind of depth of shot pioneered by Welles and endorsed by Bazin – to retain the temporal and spatial "*continuum* of reality" and to "reveal the hidden meaning in people and things without disturbing the unity natural to them" – becomes a signature Jia Zhangke style (Bazin, 1967, 35, 37, 38). In *Still Life*, in-depth shot and long take often combine and dominate storytelling; doing away with classic montage, Jia frequently relies on neorealist mise-en-scène both to unfold the actors' movements within a fixed framework and to provide crucial information for the audience to gather the connective tissue.

Sanming's entry into the county administrative office and his inquiry about his missing wife, for example, are framed by a scene of ruckus where we overhear relocated residents aggrieving about unequal treatments. A similar commotion greets Shen Hong's entry into the manager's office of a now bankrupt state factory, where her husband used to be a salesman. A medium-shot long take of the office introduces the center of the controversy: a man with a missing arm sits in silence at the background while his relatives are demanding his living assistance. Arguing that the accident occurs off-site and after the factory's closure, the manager denies responsibility. As the brother-in-law of the disabled man accuses the manager of secretly selling state property to a woman from Shamen (who is later revealed to be the real estate developer that Shen Hong's husband Guo Bing works for and is involved with), thus causing the dismissed workers to seek employment elsewhere, the injured man stands up to get water. The camera tracks his movement to the water tank at the door and in walks Shen Hong. A close-up follows: as Shen Hong elbows her way to refill her water bottle, she is blocked by the face of another woman, the wife of the man with an amputated arm who, as it suddenly dawns on the audience, is the same woman who once offers to turn a trick for Sanming. From this and other uses of mise-en-scènes, Jia's neorealism appears almost as a cinematic practice of "consilience," "the interlocking of causal explanation across disciplines" that Edward Wilson advocates for the unity of knowledge (325, 8–13). A web of previously invisible relations and causalities emerges in *Still Life* not only revealing without didacticism the nexus of official corruption and property theft in the name of devolution and development, but also the displacement of disposable labor and the dissolution of families in its wake.

It is amid these "minor" mise-en-scènes to foreground presumably the two "major" stories of Sanming and Shen Hong that Jia makes visible a third story in the background of no lesser power and poignancy. While the handicapped man and his wife forced into prostitution remain anonymous in *Still Life*, their copresence with the protagonists in the film's frame shows Jia's heuristic method to "establish the image of history even in its most inconspicuous fixtures of its existence, its rejects."[14] Not only is the couple's life story shown to be linked through mere degrees of separation with the lover of Shen Hong's husband, the female tycoon at the heart of Fengjie's creative destruction (who appears only once in a framed photograph at the "entrepreneur's club"), but their indignities are revealed as the collateral damage of neoliberal development. History's rejects achieve dignity through his lens as Jia follows up the damaged couple with two additional scenes, one in which Sanming walks to their apartment as an unknowing messenger of its destined demolition, learning about the wife's decision to head south looking for work, and the other in which Sanming chances upon her at the dock ready for departure. Brief as it is, this second parting shot is at once elegiac and enigmatic.

Consistent with the film's overall documentary look, the dock scene is marked by "the crispness of the line, in the almost brutal sense of contrast between hot whites and dim blacks" (Kraicer 4). The silhouetted dark crowd, enhanced by HD technology, gives the scene an acute "video-ness," suggesting "an immediate, direct transcription of reality" in its stark matter-of-factness (Ibid.). The fast falloff between the human mass, the sky, and the water obscures the fact that Yaomei, Sanming's missing wife of sixteen years, comes out of the throng right under his nose, walks by him, and steps out of the frame without his recognition. While the harsh rendition of the dock makes it hard on the audience to make out the rich details embedded in the setting, Jia has blurred the distinction between major and minor plot lines with just such a mise-en-scène, entrusting his audience in their ability to edit the film with their own eyes, connecting the dots of the characters' lives in a way that we attempt to decode our confounding reality. One cannot but imagine the separation and union of partners – in this case, Yaomei's possible return to Sanming, and the departure of the disabled worker's wife – as involuntary effects of the tumultuous motion of capital in its constant perturbation of human attachment. The act of viewing is turned into an aesthetic and affective process through which the underlying and intertwined causalities of life on- and offscreen are discerned, and the hope of collective redemption revived.

Jia Zhangke's cinematic practice recalls Hannah Arendt's critical conception of aesthetics as the building of a *sensus communis* or common sense. As Arendt has it, aesthetics is inalienable from politics: "[t]he common element connecting art and politics is that they both are phenomenon of the public world" (1982, 218). Because they share the necessity of "public appearance," the "love of beauty" is always already encompassed within "political judgment" (Ibid. 214). Crucial to Arendt's reading of Kant's "critique of aesthetic judgment" is her introduction of the "judging spectator" who apprehends cultural and political appearances and her emphasis on the insufficiency of "rational thought to agree with itself" (Ibid. 219–20). The individuality of the judging spectator, according to Arendt, has to be reconciled with the plurality inherent in judgment itself. Just as Bazin insists on the neorealist vision with which "one sees in the eyes of those who stand aside the reflections of other concerns" (1971, 36), Arendt believes aesthetic judgment "must liberate itself from the 'subjective private conditions'" and rely on "the presence of others" "without whom it never has the opportunity to operate at all" (1982, 220–21):

> Taste, in so far as it . . . appeals to common sense, is the very opposite of "private feelings." In aesthetics no less than in political judgments, a decision is made, and although this decision is always determined by a certain subjectivity, by the simple fact that each person occupies a place of his own from which he looks upon and judges the world, it also derives from the fact that the world itself is an objective datum, something common to all its inhabitants. The activity of taste decides how this world, independent of its utility and our vital interest in it, is to look and sound, what men will see and what they will hear in it.
>
> (Ibid. 222)

In releasing taste from the conceptual stranglehold of individual senses and sentiments, Arendt is not disavowing that judgment entails "a certain subjectivity." Rather, she locates subjectivity in "an objective datum" of the world "common to all its inhabitants [subjects]" so that instrumental reason and self-interest at the heart of the capitalist enterprise may be overcome (Ibid.).

Still Life's mise-en-scène aesthetics realizes Arendt's humanistic view of culture as the public forum and facilitates the construction of a *sensus communis*. Given the particular treatment of his settings and characters, Jia's self-proclaimed responsibility has to be construed as an aesthetic "responsiveness" both accounting for the referential reality of filmic representation and answering the needs of the viewing public. When Jia insists that his "aesthetic taste and goals don't allow" him to "neglect reality" as "some [Fifth Generation] directors [do] in their work" (M. Berry 193), he resonates with Arendt's conclusion on taste as that of a *cultura animi*:

> Taste as the activity of a truly cultivated mind comes into play only where quality-consciousness is widely disseminated . . . As such, taste and its ever alert judgment of things of the world sets its own limits to an indiscriminate, immoderate love of the merely beautiful . . . Taste debarbarizes the world of the beautiful by not being overwhelmed by it; it takes care of the beautiful in its own "personal" way and thus produces a "culture."
>
> (1968, 224)

While Arendt's endorsement of *cultura animi* might be misread as elitist, the very condition necessary for its efficacy, the wide dissemination of quality-consciousness, has anchored the cultivated mind firmly in the body politic/public, endowing it with a remarkable democratic quality. The world of Arendt as is that of Jia is therefore fundamentally social and relational rather than autonomously individual. Its beauty is not the spectacular beauty of some Fifth Generation films, so "immoderate" in its sensuousness and "barbarous" in its nonreferential sovereignty that it is meant only for speedy visual consumption. For the director of *Still Life* "the merely beautiful" is never sufficient in and by itself because "taste decides not only how the world is to look, but also who belongs together in it" (Ibid. 225, 223). Evocative of Arendt and Bazin's humanism, Jia Zhangke considers it the irrefutable task of the filmmaker to "take care and preserve and admire the things of the world," reconstituting with his candid camera not only the world we see and our ways of seeing but also our means of relating and belonging to it (Ibid. 225).

3

The neorealist mise-en-scènes and the slow panning shots of *Still Life* enact Walter Benjamin's panoramic conception of history, as "history merges into the setting" and "chronological movement is grasped and analyzed in a spatial image."[15] Jia wields his lens as a double-edged sword. On the one hand, the camera is his recording device to "embalm time, rescuing it simply from its proper corruption" so that the landscapes, townscapes, and "ethnoscapes" of Fengjie are preserved in enduring cinematic form before their imminent inundation and irrecoverable disappearance – "change mummified as it were," in Bazin's most memorable phrase (1967, 14–15).[16] On the other hand, it is his cinematic apparatus of revelation to unearth the hitherto hidden causes that propel the creative destruction of the phenomenological world. On-site at the Three Gorges Dam, the setting of China's most spectacular Promethean project to harness nature, Jia is representing a reality in a spatial image rooted in the radical historical transformation of the representational relationships.

As soon as Sanming lands on the shores of Fengjie, he is hustled against his will into a warehouse on the dock, where a magician performs a card trick of currency exchange while his gang extorts money from the intercepted and bewildered audience, tellingly called "intellectual property charge." Jia uses the scene to set the dam construction in the context of China's sudden shift to a market exchange and money economy, on the one hand foreshadowing the big-time robber-baronism and small time gangsterism at the film's background while on the other hand revealing the shadow of capital as the engine of labor migration and creative destruction of nature. With the magician's sleight of hand, the Chinese yuan is turned into US dollars and then euros in the bat of an eye, suggesting both the infiltration of the Chinese hinterland by border-transcending capital and its drastic generalization of value through the domination of the monetary sign. This scene of currency exchange as a magic trick anticipates the subsequent panning of Sanming picking his way amid Fengjie's rubbles, concrete structures of Chinese socialist history already succumbing to the abstract power of money in its reshaping of human habitation and natural environment. The shots of repetitive sledgehammering of the buildings and the recording of its insistent echo reinforce audiovisually just this impression: the scenes of detritus are not the effect of natural erosion and decay but the disconsolate chronicle of incessant and artificial capitalistic growth.

Not only does Jia Zhangke bear cinematic witness to the debris of development, preserving a slice of material reality in its historical indexicality, but he also uses his camera as a vehicle of imagistic inquiry on the nature of aesthetic representation in relation to other forms of representation. If the magic show of international currency exchange at the dock sets the primal scene of capital flow and nature's conquest, the tracking of Sanming's sojourn in Fenjie probes deeper into the representational meanings of money in its complexity. By now Sanming has joined the demolition crew, and he was asked over cigarettes at his makeshift dorm if he had seen Kuimen on his way to Fengjie. On receiving his negative answer, one migrant laborer produced a ten-yuan RMB (*renminbi*, "people's money" in literal translation), revealing the engraving of the Kuimen gorge on the Chinese currency. "My home province is also on the money," Sanming replied, pulling out of his wallet a fifty-yuan bill with a picture of a landmark waterfall from Shanxi. Displaced from actual home and removed from any tangible relationship to ancestral land, Jia's characters have held onto the ultimate commodity fetish, which uproots them from the land of their birth, provides them with an abstract frame of reference in exchange value, and symbolically satisfies a sense of belonging. With this lead-in, the camera cuts to a medium shot of Sanming against the backdrop of the actual Kuimen: his eyes slowly take in the sight of the gorge as he measures it against the RMB in his hand. A close-up of the ten-yuan bill follows, one of the few of such shots ever used in *Still Life* emphatically aimed at an object, as the audience looks through Sanming's point of view at the portrait of Mao crowding the scene of nature off the screen. As though evoking the earlier magic show, the bill is then reversed, with a flip of Sanming's fingers, to the side of the engraved scenery, the picture of Kuimen on the money now completely overtaking the physicality of the real Kuimen itself.

With this sequence, Jia seems to have brought André Bazin and Martin Heidegger into the same frame of philosophical reference, opening up critical vistas of apprehending the "ontology of the photographic image" and "the age of the world picture" in China's massive capitalist makeover. This sequence both affirms and negates Bazin's neorealist reverence for the pre-given-ness of the phenomenological world:

> The stones of which a bridge is constructed – their reality as rocks is not affected when, leaping from one to another, I use them to cross the river. If the service which they have rendered is the same as that of a bridge, it is because I have brought my share of ingenuity to bear on their chance arrangement; I have added the motion which, though it alters neither their nature nor their appearance, gives them provisional meaning and utility. In the same way, the neorealist film has a meaning, but it is *a posteriori* to the extent that it permits our awareness to move from on fact to another, from one fragment of reality to the next, whereas in the classic artistic composition the meaning is established *a priori*.
>
> (1971, 87)

In first showing the physical Kuimen on the screen, Jia has reproduced it affirmatively as an a posteriori image, at once following Bazin's analogy that cinematography is merely an aftereffect, an artificial use of the stones in the river in the form of a bridge that does not fundamentally disturb the reality represented and preserving Kuimen with a neorealist respect for nature's a priori. In shooting Kuimen's takeover by the ten-yuan RMB, however, Jia has foreshadowed its imminent disappearance upon the dam's completion and has drawn our attention to the clear and present danger of neoliberal capitalism that for the sake of surplus value will never leave the chance arrangement of the phenomenological world alone.

Incidentally, Jia has bridged the philosophical insights of André Bazin and Martin Heidegger on the idea of representation and its reordering of nature. Bazin's bridge made of rocks in the river is essentially indistinguishable from Heidegger's "old wooden bridge [on the Rhine] that joined bank with bank for hundreds of years" – both of which, however, are in contradistinction to the new "hydroelectric plant set into the current of the Rhine" (Heidegger 16). While the wooden bridge just as the bridge made of river rocks does not affect the essence of the river, a power plant built on it will forever alter the river's nature. "In the inter-locking processes pertaining to the orderly disposition of electrical energy," writes Heidegger, "even the Rhine itself appears something at our command . . . What the river is now, namely, a water power supplier, derives out of the essence of the power station" (16). The wooden bridge is to neorealist cinema just as the hydro-electric plant is to classic montage. However, in the latter form of representation, as Bazin and Heidegger would concur, the essence of the represented no longer corresponds to that of the original object of representation. Similar to Bazin's grievance against an implicit anthropocentrism in classic cinematic composition ("meaning is established *a priori*" when human intention takes precedence over the world [1971, 38]), Heidegger rages against the artificial reduction of nature into mankind's "standing reserve [*Bestand*]" (Ibid. 17). Bazin and Heidegger cau-tion against the instrumental conquest of the world in mankind's discovery of its own power to "re-present" it has found its cinematic expression in Jia's capture of the two Kuimen in succession.

In addition to preserving the gorge in its pristine state, the first shot of Kuimen in its "natural" condition may be one already influenced by and inflected with an a priori meaning. While the cinematography of *Still Life* has been compared to clas-sic Chinese landscape painting, and by association to the Fifth Generation's suc-cessful translation of scroll aesthetics into a unique modernist film language, Jia's treatment of the natural setting in relation to its human subject does not replicate his predecessors'. Take the establishing shots of Chen Kaige's *Yellow Earth* and *King of Children* 孩子王 (1987), for example. Both situate the protagonists in the open mountainous terrain, and true to the spirit of the artistic convention, humans appear as tiny blobs against the magnitude of the landscape. Though the char-acters in Chen have already become the focus of cinematic vision – as opposed to the kind of human placement in classic painting that makes the figures diffi-cult to detect among the trees and rocks of nature – their presence on the screen remains dwarfed by the primordial power of the arid plateau and the moist moun-tain ranges, respectively. In these painterly panorama, the symbiotic relationship between humans and their environment is compositionally balanced, each in their own measure as it were, to betray Chen's own ambivalent reflection on Chinese culture in transition to capitalism. The epic landscape he has memorialized on the screen is for him the source and soul of "folk songs, drum dance, paper cuts, embroidery, and numerous legends," while it is also the cause of "ethnic cultural sterility, its incessant and eternal repetition of unchanging axioms."[17] No wonder the designated figure of enlightenment – be it Gu Qing of *Yellow Earth*, the army officer to bring Mao's antifeudalist ideas to the village during the war against Japanese invasion, or Lao Gan of *King of Children*, the "sent-down youth" to the country turned school teacher during Mao's Cultural Revolution – cannot pos-sibly succeed in their pedagogical conversions, personal salvations, or in nature's transformation. Gu Qing fades into the same yellow earth at the film's end as he first emerges from it, with the only difference of a farewell crowd dancing and chanting for rain, while Lao Gan leaves the thatch-roofed schoolhouse he is initially inducted into as the teacher and vanishes from amid the tree stumps. As with Chen's own commentary, these mise-en-scènes suggest that the nature of the villagers and village children, like the parched earth and dense forests in both films, remains largely untouched by communist enlightenment, despite Mao's claims of revolutionary mastery on the contrary.

Although Jia avails himself of the same elements of earth and sky as panorami- cally as Chen, his presentation of Sanming on the site of Kuimen is akin to Zhang Yimou's treatment of Grandpa's thrashing of red sorghum. The resemblance is not a matter of composition but perspective and proportion. The ratio of humans to nature on Jia's screen is dramatically different just as the irreverent stance Zhang's protagonist assumes toward the sorghum field is. With one third of the screen space occupied by his body in the foreground, heavy in hues of brown, and with Kuimen shrouded in a light blue mist at the background, Sanming evidences a human presence that no longer immerses itself in its environment but stands over and against it. This is hardly to contend that Sanming is a figure of enlight- enment, a stand-in of the director-intellectual Jia as in the case of Chen, nor is he the possessive individual turned romantic hero as Zhang's "Grandpa." What Jia shows instead is that a migrant worker like Sanming is now encompassed in a "civilizing" stance and participating as essential labor in Capital's Second Com- ing bent on the scopic and subjective command of the natural environment. Even without the ten-yuan bill of engraved nature in his hand, Sanming would have already betrayed a look that takes in Kuimen as a picture.

As Heidegger has famously said, "world picture" does not mean "some imita- tion," a copy of something, or "a picture of the world, but the world conceived and grasped as picture" (129). As a perspective shift heralded by Descartes's interpre- tation of man as *subiectum*, the emergence of the world picture has meant that "man becomes the relational center of that which is as such" (Ibid. 128). This modern representation of man as the subject of the world repudiates the medieval conception of human as "belong[ing] within a specific rank of the order of what has been created – and as thus caused, to correspond to the cause of creation" (Ibid. 130). It also rejects the ancient Greek definition of the human as one "who is looked upon by that which is . . . to be included and maintained within its openness and in that way to be borne along by it" (Ibid. 131). Both the medieval European notion of man and nature in "a ranked order of correspondence" and the classic Greek conception of man as being beholden incorporate a stance of mankind in the midst of all that is, a stance that is almost identical to the ancient Chinese ideal of harmony between the heavens and humankind (Ibid. 141). By Heidegger's account, the subject is present in these three understandings as that- which-lies-before-a-mountain, as reality confronts mankind in the power of its presence. Descartes, however, has fixed his attention on a reality that is present only as within his own consciousness. When this Cartesian perspective becomes hegemonic, the world is turned into a picture and man has decisively become a self-conscious representing subject of modernity (Ibid. 129–30).

This self-conscious representing subject of modernity is decisively the subject of Mao's revolution, epitomized by his well-known slogan, "Man is destined to conquer nature 人定胜天." But Mao's inheritance of the enlightenment legacy via his localized praxis of Karl Marx is hampered by the contradiction between his grandiose vision and its poor execution through state socialism. While abrogating the ideal harmony between the heavens and humankind, "Mao's war against nature," as Judith Shapiro describes China's socialist era, is fundamentally ill-equipped to alter China's ancient agrarianism; the vast Chinese hinterland seems scarcely subject to human imprint as Chen Kaige's shots have shown. While in concert with Heidegger's account of the world picture, Jia shows that a pure subjective stance is insufficient in nature's morphing. Though Chinese socialist modernity partakes a post-enlightenment "subjective" domination over the "objective" world through the "rational" deployment of science, technology, and bureaucracy, Mao has miserably failed to grasp Marx's insight on the revolutionary dynamics of capitalism to turn all "that is solid into air." Consequently, the Three Gorges Dam, though envisioned, is never built in Mao's lifetime.

Herein lies Jia's ingenious placement of Sanming's standing over and above Kuimen: the close-up of the ten-yuan bill in his hand hints at the missing element in Mao's modernity. The shot of the money not only explains Mao's historical misidentification of the engine of revolution but also identifies the Second Coming of Capitalism as the motor source of China's present geographic and demographic sea changes. The full power of man to bend the physical world to human will is not unleashed only until it is wedded to the political economy of unbridled capitalism. Kuimen's becoming of picture from its origin as phenomenological nature to its representation congealed in money form appears Jia's cinematic "objective correlative" of two major world historical processes since the European Enlightenment.[18] On the one hand, it is a telling of mankind's subjection and the subjugation of its perceived other(s). On the other hand, it pinpoints capitalism, just as the camera directs the audience's gaze at the money, as the political economy that aids, abets, and accelerates man's conquest of its existential space. The flipping of the bill functions more than Jia's simple illustration of how the relationship of origin and copy has been inverted when nature is to submit itself to human harness. It also illuminates China's sudden about-face, after the socialist decades of deliberate delinking to relink with a capitalist world system oriented toward the absolute extraction of all resources and abstraction of all values.

4

From the hydroelectric plant on the Rhine to the Three Gorges Dam on the Yangtze is the globalization of a "re-presenting relationship" of man who "'get[s] into the picture' in precedence over whatever is" (Heidegger 131). For Heidegger this mode of representation constitutes the heart of "humanism," which is "nothing but a moral aesthetic anthropology" "in a more strict historiographical sense" (Ibid. 131, 133). This anthropological core of humanism is for Dipesh Chakrabarty the dominant sociological code of historicism that subordinates "the story of human evolution/civilization – a single human history, that is" – to "a natural, homogenous, secular, calendrical time" (1997, 51, 37). Acknowledging a Marxist critique of capital as "indispensable," Chakrabarty nonetheless finds it "inadequate" because of its helpless complicity with the "metanarrative of progress" and its ubiquitous "obligation to be secular" (Ibid. 50, 52). Appropriating Heidegger's concept of contemporaneity, "the idea that things from different historical periods can exist at the same time but belong to different worlds," Chakrabarty believes we can rework Marx to account for actual temporal experiences within "the same horizon of capital and yet . . . disrupt the unity of that time" (Ibid. 49, 57). "The best medium . . . to make visible all the problems of translating diverse and enchanted worlds into the universal and disenchanted language of sociology," Chakrabarty concludes, is "fiction and film" (Ibid. 52).

What makes *Still Life* one of the best filmic examples of this historiographic translation, as we have already discussed, rests on Jia's adherence to a neorealist inclusion of incidental and marginal images, so much so that his cinematic "document of civilization" also unfolds at "the same time," in the words of Walter Benjamin, as "a document of barbarism" (1969, 256). What makes *Still Life*'s temporality even more intriguing is Jia's juxtaposition of Sanming and Shen Hong's life stories with such scenes as men in moon-suits spraying disinfectant over the torn-down buildings or Beijing opera singers in full traditional costumes playing with their cell phones. These incongruous images puncture the flow of Jia's neorealist film narrative and engender serious cognitive dissonance in the audience. Not only do they reveal the unruly archaic or the truly supernatural unfiltered by the lens of technological modernity, but they also serve as the director's visual puzzles on the Second Coming of Capital and its myriad manifestations.

The first striking instance of such imaging occurs in the mise-en-scène wherein the stories of Sanming and Shen Hong intersect with the appearance of a UFO. As Sanming takes a break at the riverbank, the camera cuts away from his figure by following his gaze toward Kuimen in the distance. Accompanied by an eerie boom, a disc emerges from the clouds atop the gorge as though an apparition, speeding to the right of the frame to Shen Hong on a higher elevation, who, momentarily mesmerized by the object, tracks its movement until its disappearance over the factory, the sound of sledgehammers tearing down the rusty pipes now drowning the mysterious drone. Besides its readily comprehensible function as a transitional device – connecting *Still Life*'s protagonists in the same time-space of the Three Gorges Dam – the appearance of the luminous saucer also disturbs the rational worldview behind the dam construction's assured conquest of nature. Jia conjures up the flight of the UFO as a phenomenological sign that troubles the anthropological centrality of humanism that Heidegger writes about and the homogenous filling of empty secular time that Chakrabarty characterizes historicism, for the disc is precisely an object that can neither be apprehended by the disenchanted discourses of scientific reason nor the teleology of capitalistic progress. The UFO is like a Heideggerian shadow, "not light's complete denial" in its commonsense understanding, but "a manifest, though impenetrable, testimony to the concealed emitting of light" (154). It demonstrates "the incalculable, that which, withdrawn from representation, is nevertheless manifest in whatever is, pointing to Being," as Heidegger would have it (Ibid.). As a concealed emitting of light and the incalculable, the UFO has effectively eluded the representing impulse, be that of anthropocentric humanism, historicism, or scientism, to conceive and grasp the world as a picture and to subject it to human calculation and control. As a cinematic sign of "radical untranslatability," the UFO betrays the possibility of other meaningful agents than human subjects in (an)other determination of the world (Chakrabarty, 1997, 39, 48).

While the UFO image deliberately bewilders the contemporary audience, in the very moment of their wonder Jia endeavors to recuperate a cosmic experience with which post-Enlightenment humanity has been by and large deprived. In this representation of the UFO, Jia avails himself of photography's power "to lay bare the realities" in the way André Bazin expects neorealist cinema to actually contribute "to the order of natural creation instead of providing a substitute for it" (1967, 15). The UFO must in this instance have ranked high "in the order of surrealist creativity because it produces an image that is a reality of nature, namely, a hallucination that is also a fact" (Ibid. 16). Jia's imaging of the UFO is only as confounding as Bazin's apparently contradictory equation of neorealist aesthetics with surrealist practices. For if we recall Philip Rosen's exact exposition that Bazin's take of the photographic image as an indexical sign is not about the particular form of the signifier but the "existential connection between a specific referent and the signifier" (13), it only makes perfect sense to see why Jia would want to digitally evoke a UFO. When the dominant mode of representation is trapped in the conception of the world as a picture and the singularity of secular and linear time, Jia is imbued with a Bazinian spirit of the neorealist filmmaker, who must dream and hallucinate in order to "unconceal" the diversity of phenomenological time and unpack surrealistic possibilities to blast open the homogenous course of history (Heidegger 10).

As Walter Benjamin notes, "the surrealists were the first to perceive the revolutionary energies that appear in the 'outmoded,'" just when "the objects [had] begun to ebb from them" (quoted in Wolin 131). In Hansen's persuasive reading, Benjamin has discovered in the surrealists the possibility of "a redemptive turn," a "radical crossing of the artificial flowering of images of second nature with a mode of experience traditionally reserved for those of an ostensibly more primary nature" (193). Jia's conjuring of the UFO seems very much an exercise of this Benjaminian "dialectical optics" that opens up "the whole field of surprising correspondences between animate and inanimate nature" and enables a perception of "the everyday as impenetrable and the impenetrable as everyday" (Ibid.).

Take another example of Shen Hong's visit to Dongming, her husband's friend and an archeologist scrambling to save the remnants of a burial site before its scheduled submersion. The sequence foregrounds an unusual looking concrete tower, presumably a partial structure for the dam construction, toward which a group of children run and behind it emerges a taxi carrying Shen Hong and Dongming. Cut to the interior of Dongming's apartment as Shen Hong is framed in a medium shot, craning her neck to look at a chain of timepieces dangling on the wall. Dongming is cooking lunch, surprised that Shen Hong is departing the next day. "Why are you leaving in such a hurry?" "It has been two years after all," she answers, referring to her separation from her husband while averting her eyes. The camera follows her pacing, panning slowly from right to left the wall behind her, revealing first a terrestrial globe on the desk, and then a thin wire above it strung with alarm clocks and watches, pocket, wrist, analogue, and digital, none ticking and all dead. On the balcony with the tower dominating the valley at the background, Shen Hong shows the last cell phone number Guo Bing left her: it remains seven digits while the area of Fengjie, as Dongming exclaims, has long ago advanced to eight. We return next to the tower at the center of the mise-en-scène before the break of dawn. After Shen Hong walks into the frame to hang her washing on the clothesline and exits, it sputters fire and lifts off as though a space shuttle.

Admittedly challenging in intelligibility, Jia has objects familiar and unfamiliar meet us with their impenetrable mystery. Recognizable timepieces are not moving whether mechanically or electronically, while a firmly planted and poured concrete tower shall jet into air. Not at all a whimsical juxtaposition, Jia seems to say with this sequence that while a neorealist fidelity to reality may be achieved through the rendition of accumulated objects, it must be supplemented with sur-realist dream images in order to make sense of the velocity of historical change otherwise impossible to convey. Dongming is not merely a professional arche-ologist but also a dedicated archivist like Jia, whose assemblage of time-telling instruments are spatialized ideas of a world being rendered obsolete in the devel-opmental clock of industrial capitalism. Unlike Salvador Dali's watch, which appears to have been melted by technological progress, the launch of the solidly grounded tower seems Jia's consummate image of lifting, when the vast Chinese peasantry is uprooted to become the industrial reserve army in Marx's original sense and nature itself is tapped as nothing but the "standing reserve" of energy (Heidegger 17).

But these defamiliarized objects, be they dysfunctional clocks, the flying tower, or the UFO, are not only emblems of temporal diversity in the global now, as the image of the planetary globe on Doming's desk preceding the panning of time pieces would urge us to puzzle out; they consequently correspond to the subjective experiences of time as split simultaneity. The time of Capital's Sec-ond Coming segregates people into radically different classes of travelers. Shen Hong is trapped in seven digits while Guo Bing travels in the realm of the eight: while the husband seems to ride headlong in rocket speed to the future, the wife appears frozen like the stopped watches against the wall, lagging behind if not fading into the past. Though sharing the same time, the biographical narratives of the husband and wife no longer synchronize. When Shen Hong and Guo Bing eventually meet face to face on the site of the Three Gorges Dam, they engage at the husband's insistence in an awkward and affectless social dance, looking ridiculously out of step with each other. Shen Hong proposes divorce and Guo Bing acquiesces. The closing long shot of the couple shows them walking apart in opposite directions against the background of the dam's completion: where the two sides of the gorges appear to have been connected with a bang, the conjugal union of Shen Hong and Guo Bing has dissolved with a whimper. So seems Jia's cinematic meditation on the creative-destruction of the neoliberal developmental narrative and its impact on the vicissitudes of personal life. His film aesthetics is one of correspondences, where macroscopic economic forces manifest in microscopic emotional turbulences and where objects and subjects encounter each other as well as the film audience "in the structures of frail intersubjectivity" (Benjamin quoted in Hansen 193).

But Shen Hong is not precisely the outmoded or the disposable in capital's headlong march in China. Her fissure with Guo Bing is succeeded with a promised fusion with a new partner as she sails from Fenjie down the Yangtze to Shanghai, a world metropolis and financial hub of Capital's Second Coming in China. The passage of the boat through the Three Gorges is accompanied by a voice-over narration of historical reconstruction, beginning with Tang Dynasty poet Li Ba's memorialization of howling monkeys in morning mist and concluding with a celebration of its imminent inundation. Jia interrupts his unfolding of the majestic and no more pristine looking gorges with a quick cut below the deck, centering a TV set that occupies much of the film screen in a manner reminiscent of the earlier shot of the money. Flashing through the TV is a fast relay of prominent figures from Sun Yat-sen, the founding father of the Republic of China, through Mao of the People's Republic, to Deng the reformer, when the voice-over touts the scheduled completion of the dam as a multigenerational collective national triumph over nature. Cut to Shen Hong in her cabin, an exhausted passenger on this boat of progress, and fade in Sanming atop the gorges, looking down expressionless at the Shen Hong's boat moving toward the ocean. In this sequence, Jia has combined montage and mise-en-scène to interweave subtly the official account of capitalist conquest led by mythologized great leaders with the broken biographies of the film's protagonists. The neorealist mise-en-scènes framing the average yet not insignificant agents of history not only stitch together Shen Hong's and Sanming's apparently unrelated life trajectories in an inclusive tapestry of globalization gone viral, but they also come to halt and haunt the sleek montage on the TV screen that simulates a smooth teleological progress of capital and its promised upwardly mobile prosperity.

While Sanming and Shen Hong inhabit the same time of neoliberal capitalism, they have never shared the same frame on the film screen, betraying Jia Zhangke's astute apprehension of globalization as spatially divisive and socially discrepant. With signs of her education and possession of cultural capital, Shen Hong is shown to be more dynamic in the reconstruction of her personal life, more adaptive to late modernity's temporal discontinuity and its normative expectation of reflexive renewal, and eventually more contemporaneous with capitalism's constant creative destruction. Sanming, in comparison, appears not quite unlike the ostensibly outmoded timepieces on Dongming's wall that have survived the revolution after the communist revolution but scarcely revolving according to the new rhythm of capital. He refuses Yaomei's offer to match him with a younger new partner and insists on getting his wife back by paying off her debt.

Their reunion takes place amid the man-made ruins in a gutted building that may have been worn down by Sanming's own sledgehammer. In a mise-en-scène that places the couple to the right half of the frame against a shaded wall with burn marks on the left half, showing a gaping hole through which is seen a cluster of high-rises in the distance, Yaomei and Sanming spend a quiet moment together, the husband squatting with his cigarette while his long-estranged wife stands. (The composition bears an unmistakable resemblance to a frame in Rossellini's *Germany Year Zero*, when the schoolboy is situated in a bombed-out building with rubble all around him.) Yaomei hands a White Rabbit toffee to Sanming, who, having peeled off the wrapping, bites it in half and hands the other half back to her. Putting it into her mouth, Yaomei squats, too, facing Sanming as they gaze at each other, sharing the candy in their inarticulate intimacy. Their dress and their body language are distinctively country and their modes of earthy communication expressive of the Chinese peasantry, not quite reformed or turned bourgeois. Unlike the collection of timepieces Dongming the archeologist is preserving, however, Sanming and Yaomei are not relics of a past but lively beings of a persistent present. Though endangered, they embody a historical sociality that remains stubbornly indifferent to the rhythm of waltz that Guo Bing and Shen Hong have apparently acquired. Appropriately, there are no point-of-view shots dramatizing what would conventionally be a scene of romantic rendezvous of amorous and autonomous individuals, except for the shocking implosion of the shiny glass office tower at the background, breaking their reverie. The couple stand up and turn to look, bewilderment etched on both of their faces.

Unlike the surrealist launch of the concrete tower earlier, the fall of the glass tower conforms to realistic expectations. Is the latter Jia's supplemental emblem to the former, hinting at an inevitable collapse of shaky structures after their shoddy construction, an ominous sign of harried unsustainable development hinged on a rapacious extraction of earth's limited standing reserve? Or is it another of Jia's digital revelations that the cycle of creative destruction has sped up right before our eyes, so that even new buildings are making way for newer ones? The couple's slightly confused and overall nonchalant reaction to the tower's collapse seems to yield yet another hermeneutic possibility. "The world has made another leap," in the words of Zygmunt Bauman, "and yet more of its residents, unable to bear the speed, have fallen off the accelerating vehicle": Yaomei and Sanming are part of this world of rapidly industrializing and capitalizing China but they have failed to catch up with the spinning hands of the developmental clock in a manner Guo Bing or Shen Hong seem to have managed (14). Placed on the open scroll of the Three Gorges in a social totality made over by capital, the two couples have represented Jia's incisive grasp of the dynamic and the residual that constitute the split in the Chinese now, revealing "the co-existence of realities from radically different moments of history" (Jameson 307).

Jia is not such a didactic film director that he would explicitly favor one type of character over another, but his fondness for the unadorned and his sympathy for the laboring people who have not assimilated the suave social dance and continue to socialize in their uncouth squat are also unmistakable. Similar to neorealist masters of a bygone generation, Jia feels obligated to represent the underclass in a mediated reality dominated by bourgeois subjects and their pleasures so that the existential actuality of the mass achieves cinematic recognition and our reference of the world becomes less partial, less self-possessive, and less wealth-growth obsessed. This aesthetic commitment to the inclusion of working people's struggles in spectacular capitalist development is also an ethical commitment to solidarity and equality as well as an artistic revision of the neoliberal teleology of history. Jia Zhangke recognizes the Second Coming of global capitalism as an earth-moving force that sweeps over landscapes and mindscapes of old, splitting humanity's shared space and time and propelling the world toward progressive extinction. He also registers his hope in his figuration of the not quite vanquished elements as both living and lived practices and resource of resistance to the forward motion of creative destruction.

Over liquor and cigarettes in the makeshift dorm, Sanming tells his demolition crew his decision of returning to the coal mine; though the work is more life threatening, the better pay would fulfill his dream of reclaiming Yaomei by clearing off her debts sooner. Weighing the odds stacked against them, the band of brawny laborers chooses to join their brother in arms. Daybreak sees them filing out of their dilapidated dwelling with their beddings and belongings, led by Sanming, into the heaps of rubble that initially greets his arrival in Fengjie and now bids him farewell. At the premonitory signs of progress's debris, Sanming pauses and looks back, as his brotherly battalion of industrial reserve army marches on. Here in *Still Life*'s closing shots we find a striking correspondence with Benjamin's delineation of Paul Klee's *Angelus Novus*:

> This is how one pictures the angel of history. His face is turned toward the past. Where we perceive a chain of events, he sees one single catastrophe which keeps on piling wreckage upon wreckage and hurls in front of his feet. The angel would like to stay, awaken the dead, and make whole what has been smashed. But the storm is blowing from the Paradise; it has got caught in his wings with such violence that the angel can no longer close them. This storm irresistibly propels him into the future to which his back is turned, while the pile of debris before him grows skyward. This storm is what we call progress.
>
> (1969, 257–58)

Sanming appears to be Jia Zhangke's angel of history: his confrontation of the present is simultaneously a staunch retention of the past under erasure and his determination to salvage his marriage a personal enactment of Benjamin's notion of a redemptive history, for "every image of the past that is not recognized by the present as one of its own threatens to disappear irretrievably" (Ibid. 255). In Sanming's unwavering affective allegiance to his wife, Jia seems to have found in the historical present affirmative structures of feeling that the logic of commodity production and consumption has not yet fully outdated, for Sanming believes in repair instead of replacement, in the renewable relationship instead of the disposable one. The appreciative recognition of Sanming's obstinate attempts at the resurrection of the apparently dead expresses Jia's own preservationist aesthetics/ethics at its best.

But there is no absolute reassurance of redemption in the angel's backward look, only cautionary signs essential for its materialization. As the audience follows in the direction of Sanming's gaze they observe together with him the remote silhouette of a stick figure suspended on a high wire between two partially demolished buildings against the mountains further back. The characters on-screen and the audience offscreen are all integrated at this moment of sighting in a continuum of the world that exists beyond the projected image, a world wherein "man himself is just one fact among others" (Bazin, 1971, 38). This long-take-long-shot neorealist image is not "the world as picture" that implies and imposes humankind's domination over the planetary environment, but the picture of "the world viewed," wherein "human beings are not ontologically favored over the rest of nature" (Heidegger 134; Cavell 37). The image effectively revises the earlier shot of the money laden with anthropocentric arrogance of man's subjective rule over the earth and restores the proportionate propriety of man's place in its objective universe. The shadowy figure on a thin line striving for balance also illuminates the precarious liberty and attendant anxiety that neoliberalism has subjected the global citizenry since the Reagan-Thatcher-Deng Xiaoping Revolution. One wonders if this image could be a philosophical update of Nietzsche's man as a tightrope walker and Jia himself a twenty-first-century Chinese Zarathustra coming down the mountains to readdress "the inner disorientation" of humankind as a result of its "conquest of nature" and "the associated rise of the industrial bourgeois society" now gone global (S. Rosen 37). One thing is certain in Jia's cinematic capture of the global existential and ecological crisis as well as its correspondent "normal chaos of love," however: the neoliberal course of capitalistic development is seen as a rickety rope hung on unsustainable foundations and it has put humanity and ecology in dire jeopardy (Beck and Beck-Gernsheim). For the citizens of the world to avoid their fall over the man-made abyss hollowed by the hunger of constant creative destruction and to secure the continuous survival and thriving of the earth and its species, as Jia indicates with his closing image, a political and planetary common must be imagined, and limits to endless capitalist growth evoked and enforced in perpetuity.

Notes

1 *Still Life* won the Golden Lion for best director at the Venice Film Festival in 2006.
2 See Kingsbury, "Postcard: Shenzhen" and Parr, *Small World*.
3 *China's Mega Dam* (Discovery DVCD Classics): Canada: Discovery Channel Communications, 2007. A longer and different version of the story is found in *Three Gorges: The World's Biggest Dam* (Discovery DVCD Classics): Canada: Discovery Channel Communications, 2006.
4 The term Anthropocene as a geological epoch was coined by Nobel Prize–winning chemist Paul J. Crutzen in 2000, and is now overwhelmingly accepted by scientific communities worldwide (Chakrabarty, 2009, 209–10).
5 On Italian neorealism and its global dissemination, see Laura E. Roberto and Kristi M. Wilson.
6 Ke Hu's historical mapping was shared by Chinese film scholars at "Rethinking Film Criticism and Theory: Commemorating the 90th Anniversary of Andre Bazin" (Shanghai: School of Film and Television Arts and Technology, Shanghai University, June 13–14). For a history of Bazin in China, see Cui, the Chinese translator of Bazin.

 7 Nuanxin Zhang's *Sha Ou/Drive to Win* (1981), Dongtian Zheng's *Linju/Neighbors* (1981), and Yigong Wu's *Chengnan jiushi/My Memory of Old Beijing* (1982) are exemplary films of the Fourth Generation (Ni 26).
 8 My reading in Chapter 1 of Zhang Yimou's stylistic and ideological change, with which Chen Kaige resonates, paints a more complex picture of both Fifth Generation directors than Dai's classification of their oeuvre as Orientalist. While her writing of generational distinction is insightful, it is critically incumbent that we attend to the Fifth Generation's own revisions over time.
 9 For an extended discussion of the Sixth Generation, see Y. Zhang (2007, 49–80) and C. Berry (115–34).
10 While Zhang Yuan as the inaugural voice of the Sixth Generation, the appearance of Jia Zhangke's *Xiao Wu* in 1997, in the opinion of Zhen Zhang, "effectively end[s] the era of the Sixth Generation" and heralds what she calls "the Urban Generation" (2007, 15).
11 When Dai speaks of "mainstream films," she could refer to either the Fifth Generation films or the state-sponsored "main melody" or propaganda films, or both. "The Sixth Generation" is also an umbrella term, which overlaps with other terms of classification. For Cheng and Huang, they are the "avant-garde film-makers born between 1961–1970"; for Zhen Zhang, they are "the Urban Generation" (2007, 1–45); and for Paul Pickowicz and Yingjin Zhang, they represent an "alternative film culture in contemporary China" that includes both "underground and independent" filmmaking. For Dai, it is the "low-budget features" and "new documentaries" made "outside the usual operations of the system" that distinguish the Sixth Generation (2002, 75).
12 The first phrase in quotation is from Z. Zhang (2007, 367, 385), while the last one is of my coinage.
13 Casual comparison of the Chinese Second Generation to Italian neorealists has been made, but not in a causal reasoning I have shaped to establish neorealist aesthetics as an alternative to the sensorial experiences and perceptive regimes appropriate for neoliberal capitalism (X. Zhang 219). For the connection between the Chinese and Italian directors of the 1940s, see Ma, Pickowitz, Y. Zhang (1999), Pang, J. Hu, and Z. Zhang (2005).
14 This self-description of Benjamin's critical methodology is quoted in the "Publisher's Note" of his *One-Way Street* (35).
15 Quoted in Sontag's introduction to Benjamin's *One-Way Street* (12).
16 Ethnoscape is a coinage of Appadurai, who defines it as "the landscape of persons who constitute the shifting world we live: tourists, immigrants, refugees, exiles, guest workers and other moving groups," "the woof of human motion" that is shot through with the warp of "relatively stable communities" (1996, 33–34).
17 The phrases in quotation are director Chen Kaige's, taken from Daoxing Li, *The History of Chinese Film Culture (1905–2004)*, and translated by myself (435–36).
18 "Objective correlative" is T.S. Eliot's term that describes the "exquisite balance between, and coalescence of, form and matter." J.A. Cuddon, *A Dictionary of Literary Terms: Revised Edition* (London: Andre Deutsch 1979): 457–58.

Works cited

Anagnost, Ann. *National Past-Times: Narrative, Representation, and Power in Modern China*. Durham: Duke UP, 1997.

Appadurai, Arjun. *Modernity at Large: Cultural Dimensions of Globalization*. Minneapolis: U of Minnesota P, 1996.

Arendt, Hannah. *Between Past and Future*. New York: Penguin, 1968.

———. *Lectures on Kant's Political Philosophy*. Ed. Ronald Beiner. Chicago: Chicago UP, 1982.

Baudrillard, Jean. *Simulacra and Simulation*. Trans. Sheila Faria Glaser. London and New York: Verso, 1988.

Bauman, Zygmunt. *Wasted Lives: Modernity and Its Outcasts*. Cambridge: Polity P, 2004.

Bazin, André. *What Is Cinema?* Trans. Hugh Gray. Berkeley: U of California P, 1967.

———. *What Is Cinema? (Vol. II)*. Trans. Hugh Gray. Berkeley: U of California P, 1971.

Beck, Ulrich, and Elizabeth Beck-Gernsheim. *The Normal Chaos of Love*. Cambridge: Polity P, 1995.

Benjamin, Walter, ed. *Illuminations*. Trans. Harry Zohn. Introduction by Hannah Arendt. New York: Schocken Books, 1969.

———. *One-Way Street and Other Writings*. Trans. Edmund Jephcott and Kingsley Shorter. London: NLB, 1979.

Berry, Chris. "Getting Real: Chinese Documentary, Chinese Postsocialism." *The Urban Generation: Chinese Cinema and Society at the Turn of the Twenty-first Century*. Ed. Zhen Zhang. Durham: Duke UP, 2007. 115–34.

Berry, Michael. *Speaking in Images: Interviews with Contemporary Chinese Filmmakers*. New York: Columbia UP, 2005.

Buck-Morss, Susan. "Aesthetics and Anaesthetics: Walter Benjamin's Artwork Essay Reconsidered," *October* 62 (Fall, 1992): 3–41.

Cavell, Stanley. *The World Viewed: Reflections on the Ontology of Film, Enlarged Edition*. Cambridge: Harvard UP, 1979.

Chakrabarty, Dipesh. "The Climate of History: Four Theses. *Critical Inquiry* 35.2 (Winter, 2009): 197–222.

———. "The Time of History and the Times of Gods." *The Politics of Culture in the Shadow of Capital*. Eds. Lisa Lowe and David Lloyd. Durham: Duke UP, 1997. 35–60.

Cheng, Qingshong, and Ou Huang, eds. 《我的摄影机不说谎》 *My Camera Does Not Lie: Archives of Avant-garde Filmmakers – Born Between 1961–1970*. Beijing: China Friendship Publishing, 2002.

Cui, Junyan. "Me and What Is Cinema?" *Rethinking Film Criticism and Theory: Commemorating the 90th Anniversary of Andre Bazin, a Conference Proceeding*. Shanghai: School of Film and Television Arts and Technology, Shanghai U, June, 2008. 9–18.

Dai, Jinhua. *Cinema and Desire: Feminist Marxism and Cultural Politics in the Work of Dai Jinhua*. Eds. Jing Wang and Tani Barlow. London: Verso, 2002.

———."Xiata: Chongdu dishidai/Leaning Tower: Re-reading the Fourth Generation." 《电影艺术》 *Film Arts* 4 (1989): 3–8.

Dargis, Manohla. "Those Days of Doom on the Yangtze." *New York Times* (January 18, 2008).

Debord, Guy. *The Society of Spectacle*. Trans. Donald Nicholson-Smith. New York: Zone Books, 1967/1995.

De Man, Paul. *Blindness and Insight: Essays in the Rhetoric of Contemporary Criticism*. Minneapolis, U of Minnesota P, 1971.

Giddens, Anthony. *The Consequences of Modernity*. Stanford: Stanford UP, 1990.

Hansen, Miriam. "Benjamin and Cinema: Not a One Way Street." *Critical Inquiry*. 25 (Winter, 1999): 306–43.

Harvey, David. *The Condition of Postmodernity: An Enquiry into the Origins of Social Change*. Cambridge: Blackwell Publishers, 1990.

Heidegger, Martin. *The Question Concerning Technology and Other Essays*. Trans. William Lovitt. New York: Harper and Row, 1977.

Horkheimer, Max, and Theodore W. Adorno. *Dialectic of Enlightenment*. Trans. John Cumming. New York: Continuum, 1944/1989.

Hu, Jubin. *Projecting a Nation: Chinese Cinema before 1949*. Hong Kong: Hong Kong UP, 2003.

Hu, Ke. "The Concept of the Real in Chinese Cinema and the Impact of [Andre] Bazin." *Rethinking Film Criticism and Theory: Commemorating the 90th Anniversary of Andre Bazin, A Conference Proceeding*. Shanghai: School of Film and Television Arts and Technology, Shanghai U, June 2008. 21–31.

Jameson, Fredric. *Postmodernism, or the Cultural Logic of Late Capitalism*. Durham: Duke UP, 1991.

Kingsbury, Kathleen. "Postcard: Shenzhen." *TIME* (December 10, 2007): 8.

Kraicer, Shelly. "China's Wasteland: Jia Zhangke's *Still Life*." *Cinema Scope* 29 (2006): *http://cinema-scope.com/cs29/feat_kraicer_still.html*.

Lee, Leo Ou-fan. *Shanghai Modern: The Flowering of a New Urban Culture in China 1930–45*. Cambridge: Harvard UP, 1999.

Li, Daoxing. *History of Chinese Film Culture (1905–2004)*. Beijing: Beijing UP, 2005.

Ma, Ning. "The Textual and Critical Difference of Being Radical: Reconstructing Chinese Leftist Films of the 1930s." *Wide Angle* 11.2 (1989): 22–31.

Marcus, Millicent. *Italian Film in the Light of Neorealism*. Princeton: Princeton UP, 1985.

Ni, Zhen. "Dianying yu dangdai shenghuo"/"Cinema and Contemporary Life." 《当代电影》 *Contemporary Cinema* 2 (1985): 20–27.

Pang, Laikwan. *Building a New China in Cinema: The Cinematic Left-wing Cinema Movement 1932–1937*. Lanham, Maryland: Rowman and Littlefield, 2002.

Parr, Martin. *Small World* (Text by Simon Winchester). Stockport, United Kingdom: Dewi Lewis Publishing, 1995.

Pickowitz, Paul. "Melodramatic Representation and the 'May Fourth' Tradition of Chinese Cinema." *From May Fourth to June Fourth: Fiction and Film in Twentieth Century China*. Eds. Ellen Widmer and David Der-wei Wang. Cambridge: Harvard UP, 1993. 295–326.

Pickowicz, Paul, and Yingjin Zhang. *From Underground to Independent: Alternative Film Culture in Contemporary China*. Lanham, Maryland: Rowman and Littlefield, 2006.

Roberto, Laura E., and Kristi M. Wilson, eds. *Italian Neorealism and Global Cinema*. Detroit: Wayne State UP, 2007.

Rosen, Philip. "History of Image, Image of History: Subject and Ontology in Bazin." *Wide Angle* 9.4 (1987): 7–34.

Rosen, Stanley. *The Mask of Enlightenment: Nietzsche's Zarathustra*. New Haven: Yale UP, 2004.

Shih, Shu-mei. *The Lure of the Modern: Writing Modernism in Semicolonial China, 1917–1937*. Berkeley: U of California P, 2001.

Wilson, Edward. *Consilience: The Unity of Knowledge*. New York: Vintage, 1999.

Wolin, Richard. *Walter Benjamin: An Aesthetic of Redemption*. Berkeley: U of California P, 1994.

Zhang, Xudong. *Chinese Modernism in the Era of Reforms*. Durham: Duke UP, 1997.

Zhang, Yingjin, ed. *Cinema and Urban Culture in Shanghai, 1922–1943*. Stanford: Stanford UP, 1999.

———. "Comparative Film Studies, Transnational Film Studies: Interdisciplinarity, Crossmediality, and Transcultural Visuality in Chinese Cinema." *Journal of Chinese Cinemas* 1.1 (2007): 27–40.

Zhang, Zhen. *An Amorous History of the Silver Screen: Shanghai Cinema, 1896–1937*. Chicago: U of Chicago P, 2005.

———, ed. *The Urban Generation: Chinese Cinema and Society at the Turn of the Twenty-First Century*. Durham: Duke UP, 2007.

6   Abiding by nature's time
The caution of cannibal capitalism in Fruit Chan's *Dumplings*

Old Zhu's dinners in *Eat, Drink, Man, Woman* or *Babette's Feast* (1987) assume rather different forms in *Eat the Rich* (1987), *The Cook, the Thief, His Wife, and Her Lover* (1989), *Silence of the Lambs* (1991), *The Human Flesh BBQ Buns of the Eight Immortals Restaurant* (1993), and *Dumplings* 饺子 (2004).[1] Not incidentally, the cinematic expressions of insatiable appetites and their sinister satisfaction find their literary analogies in Ian Wedde's *Symmes Hole* (1987) from New Zealand, Margaret Atwood's *Wilderness Tips* (1991) from Canada, and *The Republic of Wine* (1992) from China by the 2012 Nobel laureate in literature, Mo Yan. Such figurative haunting of the omnipresent cannibal, not incidentally, also coincides with the Second Coming of Capital and the successful spread of the Reagan-Thatcher-Deng Xiaoping Revolution. The persistent artistic preoccupation with man-eating-man practice could betoken a number of overwhelming cultural disturbances. They range from the fear of national boundary transgression by capital's annihilation of geopolitical time-space formerly impenetrable to its desire to the anxiety of capital's transformation of older caution of the individual psyche into new pleasures of consumption. The worldwide apprehension of being stripped bare and swallowed whole registers a profound identitarian crisis of bodily security, continuity, and sustainability only befitting a global "risk society."

Fruit Chan's *Dumplings* is especially eye-popping and soul-shattering in this broader context. Chan is internationally famed for *Made in Hong Kong* (1997), *The Longest Summer* (1998), and *Little Cheung* (1999), variably named the "1997" or the "handover" trilogy, and for *Durian Durian* (2000) and *Hollywood in Hong Kong* (2001), two of his intended yet incomplete "prostitute" trilogy. He is an independent Hong Kong director with a relentless historical bent, a sympathetic eye for the downtrodden, and a predominant style of neorealist filmmaking. A far cry from his guerrilla mode of low-cost production with nonprofessional actors and docudrama camera work, *Dumplings* boasts a big budget, a stellar cast, and a creative crew that includes such luminaries as Peter Chan and Christopher Doyle. The adoption of mainstream horror, however, has neither compromised Chan's social conscience nor his cinema's tendency toward cultural critique. Apparent entertainment value aside, *Dumplings* only enhances his repertoire in mediating issues of identity and marginality more suggestively, allegorically, and even comically and farcically.

Like *Durian Durian* before it, *Dumplings* is set in the borderlands between a post-1997 Hong Kong and a postsocialist China with Deng Xiaoping's "one country, two systems" policy well inscribed in the political and economic landscape. Unlike *Durian Durian*'s symmetrically split geography in its two-part narrative, where a drastic discrepancy of wealth between the former crown colony and its historical motherland speaks of a systemic difference, the action and plot development of *Dumplings* is primarily situated in Hong Kong. Frequent traffic of one main character up north and down south shows a more systemic integration of China, the political sovereign, and Hong Kong, the economic sovereign, as well as the invisible intercourse of supply and demand between them in the circulation and consumption of laboring or delectable bodies. Such (in)formal flow of commodity and capital between the two geopolitically distinct places finds its object-correlative in Chan's juxtaposition of his two female protagonists, Meiyi (Aunty Mei or Mei for short), an internal immigrant from the mainland with a clandestine small business, and Ai Qingqing, once the local darling actress and TV celebrity of Hong Kong, now officially Mrs. Li in retirement.

In her desperate desire to preserve her fading beauty, her only asset to retain the attraction of her business tycoon husband, the late-thirtysomething Mrs. Li tracks down Mei, a woman of seemingly similar age with much younger appearance, whose secret of youth is rumored to reside in the magic ingredient of her specialty dumplings. A tale of eccentric exchanges ensues as the two women's lives intimately intertwine along with an inclusion of a wider cast of characters in a larger network of commerce. By drawing Mei's and Mrs. Li's divergent trajectories together, Fruit Chan revises Deng's policy to claim a reality not of "one country, two systems" but "one system, two destinies." For despite their different experiences with it, Mei and Mrs. Li are shown in the same system of the open free market, apparently governed by the same rules of self-interested exchange, rational calculation, and competition characteristic of classic liberal capitalism of the First Coming. In its unambiguous allegorical figuration, *Dumplings* is saying that neither the People's Republic of China (PRC) nor Hong Kong constitutes anymore an *outside* to global capitalism in its fateful Second Coming. When industrial capitalism has become the de facto hallmark of human civilization, the opposition between the barbaric or backward Oriental Other and the civilized or advanced Occidental Self seems to disappear.

This inclusion of Mei and Mrs. Li as the same subjects within global capitalism, however, is troubled by their association with cannibalism, triggering more questions of identity and identification between China and the world, capitalism and cannibalism. As we recall, the collectivization of Hong Kong, Taiwan, the PRC, and diasporic Chinese film production, known as Sinophone cinema, hinges on a coupling of linguistic and phenotypical identities (i.e., the characters on-screen are to speak and look Chinese). *Dumplings* is a superb realization of this new critical classification: it casts actors from both Hong Kong and the mainland and it intermingles the use of Chinese dialects in remarkable Cantonese and Mandarin accents. While the regional variations so conveyed in speech is hardly lost on the audience of the Chinese diaspora, in its subtitled consumption on the global media market, however, such dialectic difference is ineluctably lost in (non)trans-lation. The specific monologue by Mei on Chinese legends of man-eating, when interwoven with the suggestive images of Mei and Mrs. Li engaged in actual acts of anthropophagy, is prone to fan and fortify a rather literal cannibalistic identi-fication of the Chinese. Because of its race-specific casting and place-specific mise-en-scène, the film's universal allegorical significance can be automatically particularized either racially, nationally, or both. The audience response could be one of ethnic "metonymic collectivity," when the part stands for the whole and the Chinese figuration begins to substitute for a Chinese reality (Li 65, 174–83). The great wall of neo-Orientalism – if I may update Said's treatment of Euro-American imperialism in the First Coming of Capitalism – seems to retain its epistemologi-cal power of partition in capital's planetary Second Coming. No longer outside it, China/Hong Kong could signify both visually and viscerally the *other* within, the cannibalistic threat in the new world order of borderless capitalism.

Is capitalism civilized? Is cannibalism evil? Is capitalism cannibalistic or is cannibalism merely capitalism with Chinese characteristics in another name? The challenge of cultural intelligibility *Dumplings* immediately poses has to do with its critical preoccupation with boundary maintenance and disturbance central to both the horror genre and the histories of cannibalism and capitalism, for they all delimit the parameters between self and other, inside and outside, norm and deviance. What makes *Dumplings* an especially complex film of social allegory and the task of its interpretation equally thorny has to do with Chan's choice to track and tackle capitalism's evolution in and through his experimentation of *Dumplings*'s own generic form. To do full hermeneutic justice to the film requires that we first grasp the two different comings of capitalism and their respective relationships to cannibalism. Second, we note Chan's deliberate departure from the horror genre's stock figures and resolutions and correlate the film's alteration of aesthetic convention to mutations in the modes of capitalism. In his identifica-tion of late capitalism as cannibalistic and mediation of Mei, Mr. and Mrs. Li's anthropophagy as mere mundane monstrosities, Chan provides us with a cine-matic scenario in which the Other of capital has disappeared as a viable geopoliti-cal alterity and geo-economic alternative. This deterritorialization of capital and disappearance of its effective regulation, as *Dumplings* makes visible, are driven by an overwhelming delirium that biospheric limits to life can be overcome with both autopoiesis and the forfeiture of reproduction.

1

Let us begin with the reality/fantasy of human flesh consumption and its repre-sentation in colonial contacts and capitalist developments, from whose long his-tory Fruit Chan's *Dumplings* emerges and to which our readings are compelled to respond. From the Greek narrative of Herodotus to the Chinese mythology of *Shanhaijing* 山海经, from Homer's *Odyssey* to the sacrament of the Eucharist, anthropophagy appears as endemic to humanity in universal textual evidence.[2] Since Columbus's voyage to the Antilles in 1492–93, as Peter Hulme argues, the island Caribs have entered the European lexicon and achieved special recognition as *Canibales*; "cannibalism" has accordingly replaced "anthropophagy" as a principal noun to describe ingesting flesh of one's fellow creatures. If the original Greek formation of *anthropophagi* is made up of two preexisting words, "eaters/ of human beings," "cannibals" in its Columbian conception identifies the people of the Caribbean specifically with the man-eating practice (Hulme 15). The naming of the "cannibal" achieves a double distinction. On the one hand, it differentiates the common figure of *anthropos* through the specific category of *ethnos*: what used to be mere "human being" is now distinguished by "race." On the other hand, what was conceived in ancient texts as universal is presently particularized as a practice unique to one place and one people.

While it has become common to situate the figurative evolution of the cannibal in European colonialism and see it as Western metaphysics' historical need to reinforce the "boundaries between a civilized 'us' and a savage 'them'" (Guest 2; Kilgour, 1990, 4), the civilization and barbarity dichotomy is not exclusive to the West.[3] In fact, it has a longer history of contestation and wider geopolitical involvement. As Peter Hulme points out, the cannibal's inauguration in Columbus's journal transpires precisely when the articulating principle derived from Marco Polo's narrative of Oriental sumptuousness switches to the Herodotean discourse of savagery (1986, 33, 20–34). The birth of the cannibal is precipitated by the abortive attempt of Columbus to find Cathay, the intended destination of his expedition for gold. Had Columbus reached Cathay, the "few chests of baubles kept in the holds of [his] three ships" certainly would not facilitate the much-fantasized China trade (Ibid. 39). Neither would he convince the Middle Kingdom – whose conceptualization of people beyond its landmass as barbarians is notorious – of the material and technological superiority of fifteenth-century Europe. While the dream of trading with the Chinese founders on the coast of Cuba, the failure to literally arrive in China turns out to be a strategic success in discourse. The absence on the Caribbean shore of "intelligent soldiers," "large buildings," and "merchant ships" of the "Grand Khan" relieves Columbus of the potential civilizational anxiety a real encounter with the Celestials may engender (Ibid. 20–21). In effect, it helps put to rest the psychic disturbance at the threshold of a European ascent so that its more assured claim on the world could be staked. By omitting the Chinese and identifying the Caribs as cannibals, Columbus turned the Antilleans into a real people of apparent monstrosity and made dubious the actuality of a glorious Asian civilization and the validity of Oriental opulence (Ibid.). This emergence of European colonialism thus reveals itself as a complex triad formation of deliberate dual disavowal. It is only through an "invention of the [cannibalistic] Americas" *and* a repudiation of civilized Asia that a "flexible positional superiority" is procured in which Europe emerges as the self-proclaimed subject of a new world history.[4]

The Columbian placement of the cannibal and its displacement of China have crucially redrawn the boundaries of civilization and barbarity in geographic, historical, racial, and cultural terms. In eclipsing its historical predecessor of Sinocentrism and eluding its reference, the incipient European Self then defined its new subjectivity against both its temporal and spatial Other(s). Forging itself against its own ancient regime of feudalism historically and the New World of its colonization geopolitically, this subject of the West has come to center the First Coming of Capitalism through the figure of the cannibal. As a sign of savagery, the cannibal is a racialized *other* fit for expropriation and extermination. It at once displaces colonial violence and rationalizes the European conquest of the Americas, the Asia Pacific, and Africa in the historical amassing of primitive capital (Barker, Hulme, and Iversen 3; Todorov). In addition, "the cannibal appetite [also becomes] the self-consolidating other of capitalist appetite as well as European civility" (Bartolovich 214). Since barbarity is signified in the literal ingestion of human flesh, voracious consumption of human labor and ruthless exploitation of nature have become comparative markers of civilization.

This European colonial figuration of capitalism as an expression of civilization is resonated by a famous Chinese identification of feudalism as cannibalism. Called "China's first modern short story" (Lee 53), the "emblematic voice" of "the then burgeoning New Culture movement" (Tang 49), also known as "the Chinese Enlightenment" (Schwarcz), Lu Xun's "Diary of a Madman" starts with the first-person narrator's paranoia that he is going to be devoured:

> In ancient times, as I recollect, people often ate human beings, but I am rather hazy about it. I tried to look this up, but my history has no chronology and scrawled all over each page are the words: "Confucian Virtue and Morality." Since I could not sleep anyway, I read intently half the night until I began to see the words between the lines. The whole book was filled with the two words – "Eat People."
>
> (trans. Yang and Yang 42)

It is not trivial to highlight that *Polynesian Mythology*, George Grey's nineteenth-century account of the cannibalistic Maoris, was one of Lu Xun's informing pretexts (Yue 64–66, 389–90). Lu Xun's "translingual practice" (Liu) – this embedding of a European construct in the emerging Chinese discourse of enlightenment and this registration of the cannibalistic Chinese – shows that indigenous subjective enunciation can hardly escape the tattered course of colonial history, and its desire for modernity is liable to find outlet in the teleology of capitalist material progress.

For Lu Xun, the cannibal is the ultimate figure of Chinese feudalistic stagnancy and self-consumption. Only by an anthropophagic self-identification and a rejection of the binary Sinocentrism could China achieve a radical break from its indigenous cannibalistic fate and become incorporated into modern capitalist civility at large. "Perhaps there are still children who haven't eaten men? Save the children . . ." (trans. Yang and Yang 51). While I shall not dwell on his Orientalist lapse, two brief points seem in order. First, like his European counterparts, Lu Xun's sense of national salvation seems to hinge on a necessary temporal displacement; the rejection of Chinese feudalism is a perquisite of civility and modernity. Second, his condemnation of an all-consuming Confucianism is predicated on his rosy reading of capitalism as a conservative force of universal civilization. The children of China could be "saved" because the nature of early capitalism and Western colonialism is hypothesized to be self-sustaining and worldly inclusive.

This hypothetical understanding is at the heart of Crystal Bartolovich's apparent Marxian interpretation of why the cannibal is logically incompatible with the spirit of capitalism. "The cannibal/capital binary in the early modern period," the period we call Capitalism's First Coming, provides "both an example of – and a limit text for – European proto-capitalist 'appetite,'" which, as Bartolovich has it, is contradictorily manifest in "the simultaneous drive to endless consumption of labor power by the capitalist, and the necessity of observing the limits to preserve production" (211). While capital's attempt to overcome its temporal obstacles is frustrated by the possible hours an agent of labor can be put to work in a given day, its absolute appetite to maximize accumulation is curtailed by a rational recognition that its own survival depends on both prolonging the use value of labor "without killing its agent" and maintaining "a minimal existence in which labor-power could reproduce" (Ibid. 212–13). Because labor and production were locally and nationally embedded in Capital's First Coming, let me historicize where Bartolovich generalizes: perpetuation of accumulation entails the reproduction of a local or national labor force and its correspondent citizenry, constitutive of the then still emergent body politic in the form of the nation-state. It is this spatial embeddedness and boundedness of economic production that determine the particular practice of capital in its First Coming: a continual production of surplus value demands a delay of total consumption and the durable supply of labor within a delimited national geopolitical economy. A virtue is thus "produced out of a capitalist necessity," as a higher if not consummate form of civility, Bartolovich argues, that capitalism "must be parasitic rather than cannibalistic" (Ibid. 214).

Contrary to Bartolovich's claim that capitalism cannot be analogically or allegorically equated with cannibalism because it depends on a transhistorically restrained consumption for the sake of its own reproduction, Jerry Phillips contends capitalism in fact "cannibalizes" its labor forces even in its First Coming, and this tendency "should be regarded as the permanent destination of capitalism" (186–87). Drawing from Marx's remark that "the veiled slavery of the wage-laborers in Europe needed the unqualified slavery of the New World as its pedestal," Phillips maintains quite convincingly that the colonial capitalist is "the vampire who gave life to the cannibal elite that ruled at home" (Ibid. 186). By illuminating the important Europe/New World and metropolis/periphery distinction in the cannibalistic exhaustion of natural and human resources, Phillips is able to indict capitalism as the cannibalistic ghoul in the colonies, citing again Marx's vivid rendition, "dripping from head to toe, from every pore, with blood and dirt" (Ibid.).

While both Bartolovich and Phillips draw their arguments from evidences in the First Coming of Capitalism – the period of Euro-American primitive accumulation, nation-state building, and colonization of the world – their different conclusions on capitalism's nature as either "parasitic" or "cannibalistic" have to be grasped on each scholar's definition of capitalism's proper subject and sovereignty. "Eating the other," to borrow bell hooks from a different context, is not cannibalistic because the *ethnos* is not integral to the subject of capital, constitutive of a civilized *anthropos*. Equally pivotal is the recognition that the practice of capitalism is also spatially differentiated in the parallel histories of Western capitalist and colonial expansion abroad and national consolidation at home. With her eyes exclusively on its metropolitan/domestic manifestation, Bartolovich mistakes capital's contingent preservationist impulse for its permanent parasitic nature. With a universal conception of the *anthropos* and assuming capital's absorption of labor is always already global and total, Phillips cannot but regard capitalism as cannibalism incarnate, its all-consuming nature fully realized in its First Coming.

While the projection of features particular to one time and place onto a transhistorical permanence of capitalism tends to mitigate their original critical purchase, Bartolovich and Phillips can yield new insights if we are sufficiently diligent in noting the historical difference in the evolution of capitalism. I will simply mention a point yet to develop fully that the parasitic propagation of labor is telling of a national conception of the laboring body and a self-possessive subjectivity distinctive of the First Coming of Capitalism, while the widespread cannibalistic practice and realization are more indicative of its Second Coming, of neoliberal capitalism's subordination of state and societal interests, its incitation of excessive appetites, and its speculation of growth beyond limits. Because of the geopolitical circumscription of capitalism in its First Coming, "the interest of proto-capitalist accumulation" predetermines that both natural and artificial resources previously squandered in a manner of aristocratic surplus consumption must, in the words of Bartolovich again, "be redirected into investment if capital were ever to emerge and reproduce itself" (215).

For Robin Wood, this "proto-capitalist" imperative of "reproduction" in its First Coming is in a nutshell "repression" of what she calls "patriarchal capitalism" (197), which, by turning "all human relations into relationships of a property principle," maintains "the monogamous heterosexual union necessary for the reproduction of future ideal inhabitants" (199, 198). Because the driving force behind Capitalism's First Coming remains reproductive of society as such, Wood argues, "the true subject of the horror genre is the struggle for recognition of all that our civilization represses or oppresses," while the monster in horror becomes nothing but a figuration of "the repressed/the Other" that exceeds the boundaries of civilization (201, 198). An artistic mediation of Capital's First Coming, the horror film is consequently torn between its own antithetical aesthetic and ideological impulses. While the genre's "progressiveness" lies in the figurative capacity of "the monster to arouse sympathy" in negation of "patriarchal capitalism," its "reactionary tradition" tends to insist on "the monster as *simply* evil" with a "'happy ending' typically signifying the restoration of repression" (Ibid. 216, 215, 201).

Although neither critic mentions Max Weber by name or extensively addresses Freud, the spirit of Protestantism and the discontents of civilization haunt the analyses of both Wood and Bartolovich. Their respective pairing of "patriar-chal capitalism" and "repression," and "proto-capitalism" and "reproduction," is reminiscent of the Weberian trope of "the iron cage" and the Freudian concept of "sublimation," from which Foucault shall later form his theory of disciplin-ary societies. Although conventionally understood as a visual vehicle for a con-straining instrumental rationality, the iron cage is also a metaphor of Christian asceticism with which Weber justifies the European origin of Capitalism's First Coming. What Weber characterizes as the iron cage of *The Protestant Ethic* – the secularization of calling, the conversion of Christian mission into capitalist accu-mulation, and the bureaucratic organization of social life under capital – is akin to the sacrificial narrative of Freud's *Civilization and Its Discontents*, wherein individual instinct is supposed to sublimate and egotistic happiness is offered on the altar of culture. The iron cage thus signifies the instinctual repression produc-tive and/or reproductive of an early capitalist civilization and spells out with its imagistic suggestiveness that the steely borders of the nation-state also delimit such civilization. Normative repression of individual libido and the reproduction of the body politic are constitutive of a capitalism still geopolitically rooted and bounded as well as socially contracted between capital, state, and labor.

This capitalism expresses itself as Fordism, a form of Keynesian economics, or welfare capitalism that dominated the waning decades of Capital's First Coming in the post–World War II West. In this mode of regulated and equilibrated eco-nomic growth the state puts brakes on the cannibalistic inclinations of capitalism to which Phillips refers, tames it into a parasitic form Bartolovich describes, and becomes the basis of Wood's analysis of the horror genre's ambivalence.[5] Broker-ing the competing appetites of capital, state, and labor by keeping them from can-nibalistic fulfillment, Fordism, or "embedded liberalism," represents a repressive yet not entirely unrewarding equilibrium of political and personal economy that socializes its subject into the mass production and consumption as well as capital-ism's indefinite reproduction (Harvey, 2005, 11–12). A similar kind of postwar Fordism, far less persuasive and far more totalitarian, is the Maoism of China, in which the state's monopolistic management of economy and society boasts a tra-jectory from today's equal opportunity poverty to tomorrow's communist cornu-copia. Both Fordism and Maoism are strangely bound by their respective faiths in social welfare, in the propagation of the patriarchal family and the protectionism of the state in order to facilitate biological and social reproduction. Regardless of the great ideological polarity and considerable material disparity in their respec-tive realization, the welfare state, be it Chinese or American, is "the first political form to understand obligations in immediately social, collective terms," accord-ing to Melinda Cooper, "to inscribe its relations of debt at the level of the biologi-cal. It undertakes to protect life by redistributing the fruits of national wealth to all its citizens" while asking for citizens' lives in national crisis as "a reciprocal obligation" (7). Having rendered the filial family obsolete, the modern welfare state seems to have assumed its inevitable historical caretaking roles.

This liberal ideal of reciprocal reproduction between the productive life of the laborer-citizen and the protective perpetuation of the nation-state seems relatively

short-lived, given the emergence of a neoliberal model of growth by all necessary means. The Reagan-Thatcher-Deng Xiaoping Revolution has terminated the
transnational reproductive consensus, East, West, North, and South. It ushered in
a post-Fordist neoliberal biopolitics indifferent to natural and social limits. Published three years after the 1989 Tiananmen massacre, which paved the way for
the unstoppable march of Capitalism's Second Coming in the world, Mo Yan's
The Republic of Wine constructs a chilling postsocialist China in which Lu Xun's
historical call to "save the children" is turned into to "sell the children."[6] In this
fictional world, the law of natural competition compels Mr. and Mrs. Jin Yuanbao
(which literally means "Gold Nugget") to get up at the crack of dawn so they can
beat their rival suppliers to fetch the best price for their biological son, Xiao Bao
("Little Treasure"):

SALESPERSON: Has the baby been specifically produced for this procuring depart-
        ment so that he is not human?
FATHER: No, he is not human.
SALESPERSON: What you sell is therefore not a baby but a special commodity,
        correct?
FATHER: Correct.
SALESPERSON: You deliver us your goods while we pay you your money, you're
        willing to sell while we're willing to buy, thus, this transaction is fair and the
        sale is final, right?
FATHER: Right. (88)

A transactional right has overcome human rights to have become the common
sense of political correctness. As though deliberately differentiating himself from
the modest proposal of Jonathan Swift, where Irish famine offers the satirical
pretext for survival cannibalism in Capital's First Coming, Mo Yan places his
fantasia amid the surfeit of China's economic boom and the gluttony of global
capitalism, when for a privileged and powerful few "eating is no longer to fill up
the stomach" but to "relish in variety and quality, like a philanderer perpetually
lusting for new playmates" (266). The novelist's sarcastic advice to all subjects in
a now enveloping Second Coming of Capitalism is to be "diligent and inventive to
fulfill such market needs" (Ibid.). Lu Xun's humanist utopia – where the children
of China will transcend their lot of being ingested in their native villages – seems
aborted in Mo Yan's enlightened capitalist civility of the global village, where
poor peasant parents have to be entrepreneurial producers of their own blood and
flesh for consumption. It is in this return of the repressed appetites without limits
that Fruit Chan joins Mo Yan with his cinematic allegorization of capitalism qua
cannibalism.

2

Dumplings comes in a short and a regular feature, with an additional plot twist and
an alternative ending in the full-length version.[7] The opening sequence intercuts

between movements of its two female protagonists, following pretty Mei through the customs at Shenzhen, China, with her lunch box of precious cargo, all the way to her dingy apartment in a dilapidated Hong Kong tenement complex, where Mrs. Li, a tastefully attired woman with fine features, finds herself after disembarking from her taxi. Mrs. Li is in Mei's domicile turned enterprise zone for her special treat(ment). Chan uses point-of-view shots to reveal the mysterious fillings of Mei's perfectly shaped artisanal dumpling, the reddish prawn-like substance from her lunch pail now minced and rolled into fresh dough skin. Although instinctual aversion may have accounted for Mrs. Li's initial grimace at the sight of her serving, involuntarily dropping her first serving, she regains her composure in no time and swallows the bowl's contents whole. This triumph over gastronomical inhibition is succeeded with an introductory cut to Mr. Li, a mogul in his fifties, on a recliner by the rooftop pool of a luxury hotel, enjoying his massage and flirting with a cute twentysomething masseuse, Miss Zhao, before he wolfs down the egg of a half-hatched chick. Cut to Mei back in a Shenzhen hospital with her emptied lunch box, and the embryonic connection of the film's principal characters becomes evident. To retain her husband's affection, Mrs. Li is determined to recover her premarital beauty, and Aunt Mei's fetus dumplings open the gate to her prelapsarian bliss.

As Mr. Li's adulterous adventure with the masseuse accelerates, Mrs. Li's demands for quicker and more potent remedies become increasingly desperate. Enter the anonymous schoolgirl and her mother into the picture, or more precisely, Mei's apartment in the projects. It turns out that chef Mei had a previous professional life in China as an obstetrician, and the mother pleads that she help terminate her daughter's five-month pregnancy, the fruit of an incestuous rape. While the schoolgirl dies in excessive bleeding, Mrs. Li devours her more mature rarity and soon begins to exude erotic charm, prompting Mr. Li to resume intercourse with her. As a dietary side effect, however, Mrs. Li also develops a rash.

The plots diverge between the film's short and feature versions from Mrs. Li's visit to the doctor for her skin discomfort. Mrs. Li is informed of her own pregnancy in the short version, which concludes with a scene of her curtailing her own gestation. In the full-length feature version, it is Mrs. Li who discovers the pregnancy of the masseuse, while her husband discovers her secret exchanges with Mei. Not only does Mr. Li take in Mei's dumplings but he also takes her ravenously on the dining table. Meantime, Mrs. Li pays off the masseuse to obtain her five-month-old fetus. In a purposeful nod to the slash-and-splatter genre, the feature ends with Mrs. Li raising the cleaver over her procured fetus, followed by a resolute chop.

Except for the closing shots where gory details are explicitly displayed for effects of a final shock, *Dumplings* looks visually subdued in its representation of violence and does not appear as a typical horror film in its mise-en-scène. There are no dark dungeons, eerie forests, haunted castles, or hideous-looking creatures. The characters traverse in ordinary places and built environments of a global city, riding taxis or walking in the streets both day and night. Even the primary *anthropophagi* of the film, Mr. and Mrs. Li and Mei, are charismatic in appearance; their visual normality if not star-image desirability hardly solicits the sort of involuntary fear and loathing to which horror spectacles resort. Complicating the absence of the visibly devilish in the film is the presence of its amorphous victims. Here, the aborted fetal matter of indeterminant form can never properly constitute "the Final Girl," which Carol Clover cannily identifies as the genre's unique stock figure. While the film's double victim, the uniformed schoolgirl of both incest violation and fetus harvest, could be developed into "the Final Girl," she remains sidelined in Fruit Chan's treatment, both anonymous and voiceless throughout. The vindictive murder of the schoolgirl's rapist father by her mother is also rendered offscreen, thus aborting another possible materialization of the mother as "the Final Girl." Without the female protagonist's initial terror at and her final victory over the monster, and without the figuration of the monster as "the repressed/the Other," visibly alien and/or abject, exceeding the boundaries of civilization and threatening the integrity of its imagined community, *Dumplings*'s claim on the horror genre seems tenuous indeed (Clover 82; Wood 198). *Dumplings* may be horrifying to watch, but is it horror cinema?

Tracing the origin of contemporary horror to the historical Gothic novel, Judith Halberstam makes a helpful distinction between the monsters of the nineteenth century that "metaphorized modern subjectivity as a balancing act between inside/outside, male/female, body/mind, native/foreign, proletarian/aristocratic," and "monstrosity in postmodern horror films that find its place," and she here evokes Baudrillard, in the "immediate visibility" that is "all body and no soul" (1). For her, the Victorian "monster itself is an economic form that it condenses various racial and sexual threats to nation, capitalism, and the bourgeoisie in one body," whereas "monsters within postmodernism are already inside – the house, the body, the head, the skin, the nation – and they know their way out" (3, 162).

While Halberstam does not correlate the conditions of modernity and postmodernity specifically to the unique features of capitalism in its respective First and Second Comings, her contrast of modern liberal subjectivity that (in)forms the classic horror genre with a postmodern neoliberal subjectivity concurs with our critical attempt to ascertain *Dumplings*'s special significance. *Dumplings* does not fit the convention of horror because the binary mechanisms of the norm and its deviance upon which the monstrosity of the horror hinges appear to be vanishing from the world of Capitalism's First Coming. After all, the mechanisms of distinction and discipline inherent in the original horror genre – as such critics of postcolonial proclivity as Hulme, Bartolovich, Phillips, Wood, and Halberstam have led us to conclude – are formal expressions of a historical antagonism between a Western colonial and capitalist civilization and that of the rest as yet unvanquished by capitalism and colonialism. Such opposition is geopolitically, economically, and ideologically maintained through the nation-state form, whose own raison d'être, be it capitalist, communist, or socialist, is to secure the boundaries of a normative national identity, suppress the efferent energies that subvert its imaginary solidarity, and consequently sustain the will of its own biological and social reproduction. Regardless of on which side one locates the subject, "the power of horror," to evoke Kristeva, regulates the operation of such social identity and makes possible the projection of a monstrosity that achieves its height of intensity in the heat of the Cold War. Anything falling outside of the homogenous and progressive time of Fordist or Maoist reproductive order is the Other.[8] The monsters of American horror are manifest refugees from the Fordist internment of sexual desire and manifest refuse from the welfare capitalist state's repression, sublimation, and commodity satisfaction of the individual body. What hide within but exposed through political struggle in the Maoist regime, however, are literally known as "Niugui sheshen 牛鬼蛇神," bull devils and snake demons, wayward elements of the communist revolution to be condemned and eliminated. In both cases, the integrity and longevity of the body politic demands a regulatory sovereignty of well-defined boundaries in the monster's repression and removal.

Dumplings signifies a new form of horror because the social and historical circumstances that give rise and continue to stabilize the original genre have undergone radical alterations. As we see, the main characters of Mei and Mr. and Mrs. Li resemble Halberstam's portrayal of "the postmodern monster," no longer "the hideous other storming the gates of the human citadel," because s/he has "already disrupted the careful geography of human self and demon other" and made "the peripheral and the marginal part of the center" (162). The *anthropophagi* of Fruit Chan's construction resonate with Halberstam's elaboration of Hannah Arendt's "banality of evil," because they are "both on us and in us," "replaced with a banality that fractures resistance" (162–63). While keen in her delineation of evil's dispersal in the everyday and its infiltration of everyone, Halberstam is paradoxically both content with mundane monstrosity as a postmodern surface effect and adamant in her rejection of "the humanistic urge to uncover the cause of violence and the way to end it" (187). Motivated by a foregone poststructural thesis that both disavows "an easy morality of monstrosity versus humanity" and privileges "indeterminable productions" of a "posthuman monstrosity that is partial [and] compromised," Halberstam refuses to clearly identify and historically account for why the monstrous has become mundane, the marginal has become part of the center, and resistance has been fractured (187–88).

Contrary to Halberstam's apparent liberal tolerance, Fruit Chan lends his lens deliberately to apprehend causal relations of horror's transformation in order to provide an unambiguous ethical indictment of evil's systemic saturation of the normal. Unrepentant in his humanistic urge, the director of *Dumplings* wants to show how the historical geography and temporality of the human subject has been transformed by the invasion of the invisible hand and how defamiliarizing the sinister turned banal may help recuperate resistance and restore human sanity. To begin, Chan constructs Hong Kong/China and its borderlands as a space of economic integration and collaboration, where the internecine ideological battles between the opposing blocks of the Cold War no longer figure. It is in the dissipation of tension between capitalism and communism, in the neoliberal consensus of expediting the flow of capital for endless growth in its historical Second Coming, that Chan locates the disappearance of the demon as well as the dramatic opposition in classic horror that finds cathartic resolution in the demon's expulsion.

As creatures of self-interested exchange and cutthroat competition, Mei and Mr. and Mrs. Li inhabit bodies of decent, respectable, and even pleasant appearance in Chan's casting because the director wishes to show how individual "greed," as he may well intentionally echo Oliver Stone's treatment of corporate body snatchers in *Wall Street* (1987), is now "for the lack of a better word" a global "good" that exceeds institutional regulation of the historical varieties. The ease with which Mei transports herself and her fetal commodity between the borders of Hong Kong and China, or the lack of interdiction of incest and rape, evidence a notable transformation of the state from a monopolistic apparatus of physical violence and moral authority of a national society to an instrument of global enterprise. The task of consolidating ideal citizens against others of different political, psychological, social, and ethical makeup, and the responsibility of securing its people from frailties of nature and ravages of the unrestrained market, hardly constitute anymore the state's own reason for being.

Although the police do make a brief and very much belated appearance toward the film's end, forcing Mei to relocate her business across the border, the ineffectualness of law enforcement is telling of Gary Becker's neoliberal model of "crime and punishment" that subjects "criminality to the economic rationality of cost-benefit analysis" (Foucault, 2008, 256). In the deregulated free enterprise zone, *anthropophagi* could just be the other side of autopoiesis. While Chan does not go so far as Mo Yan's fictionalization of the state's sanction of marketing babies for culinary pleasure, his treatment of state noninterference reveals an exhaustion of its will to discipline and accordingly the evaporation of ethics in favor of economic efficiency.[9]

3

In sidelining the disciplinary prohibition and reproductive function of the state, Chan is able to better illustrate the rise of the enterprise society and the entrepreneurial subject at the heel of the Reagan-Thatcher-Deng Xiaoping Revolution and identifies this rise as the source of horror's anonymity, banality, and ubiquity. In effect, *Dumplings* materializes Margaret Thatcher's infamous vision of a global market monopoly, where "there is no such a thing as society. There are individual men and women" (quoted in Harvey, 2005, 23). It is not that such individuals are free from social domination, but that they are readily subject to a neoliberal governmental reason that both obviates the state's traditional role intervening "between society and economic processes" and compels the state, as Foucault incisively points out, "to intervene on society so that competitive mechanisms can play a regulatory role at every moment and every point in society, a general regulation of society by the market" (2008, 145). Essential to this intensified and internalized regulation is turning the *Homo economicus* of classic liberalism from an individual "partner of exchange," "the object of supply and demand in the form of labor" into "an active economic subject," a neoliberal "entrepreneur of himself, being for himself his own capital, being for himself his own producer, being for himself the source of [his] earnings" (Ibid. 223, 225–26). Even consumption is reinscribed as "an enterprise activity by which the individual, precisely on the basis of the capital he has at his disposal, will produce something that will be his own satisfaction" (Ibid. 226).

Mei, Mrs. and Mr. Li, and even the young masseuse Miss Zhao exemplify the sort of entrepreneurial and speculative subject that Capitalism's Second Coming is intent on producing. Unlike the schoolgirl, the silent victim of sexual violence, the masseuse has an intuitive grasp of her own youthful beauty as capital and the optimal moment of fetching its best yield. When confronted by Mrs. Li about her pregnancy with her husband's baby, Miss Zhao flatly responds with the calculative reason befitting an ideal entrepreneur. She explains that with four more months of gestation she is going to "complete the job," delivering the baby in exchange for the promised material comfort later in life. "I'm young," she says, "I can afford time." With the clock ticking away painfully in her own body, Mrs. Li nevertheless believes in Mei's exclamation to Mr. Li after his shocking discovery postcoitus that she is sixty-four years old: "Age is an illusion; it is my body that counts." Convinced that her ingestion of other human bodies would arrest the natural advance of biological time and even reverse it, Mrs. Li proposes to "double" her husband's promised payment to Miss Zhao. Having considered her relative poverty and low-skilled labor capacity, and having weighed her comparative advantages in competing markets, the masseuse eventually decides to source her baby to a higher bidder, despite the buyer's insistence that her fetus be procured without anesthesia to ensure its uncontaminated natural potency.

With this matter-of-fact panning of his main characters' uniform conduct of calculation and competition, Chan demonstrates how the "enterprise form" has infected "the social body" by "extending the economic model of supply and demand and of investment-costs-profit so as to make it a model of social relations and of existence itself, a form of relationship of the individual to himself, time, and those around him, the group, and the family" (Foucault, 2008, 242). There appears also an integral process of degendering in the neoliberal deregulation of economy and emotion. The stereotypical demarcation of female sentimentality and male reason in liberal capitalism no longer holds while masculine predatory instincts are being normalized as gender-neutral requisites. At once biological women and individualized natural born entrepreneurs, Miss Zhao, Mrs. Li, and Mei have ceased to be the succorless victims of monstrous men, whose rescue signals classic horror's symbolic restoration of society. Chan is not overlooking the class discrepancy the Second Coming of Capitalism has sharpened, however. By putting the three women in the roles of the elite consumer, the illicit trafficker, and the serviceperson in the official, as well as "occult economies" of his filmic landscape, he highlights the role of transnational reproductive work in unequal labor relations as well as uneven emotional and economic exchanges.

As Comaroff and Comaroff explain, "occult economies" of "millennial capitalism" have two salient features. There is "a material aspect founded on the effort to conjure wealth by appeal to techniques that defy explanation in conventional terms of practical reason," and there is "an ethical aspect grounded in the moral discourses and (re)actions sparked by the (real or imagined) production of value through such 'magical' means" (310). Mr. Li's involvement in the "formal" aspect of "finance capitalism" for endless growth and Mrs. Li's participation in the "informal" aspect of "cannibalism" for perpetual youth turn out variant articulations of the same: both operations are based on "less than rational connections between means and ends" and on "a faith in probability," "a chimera knowable, tautologically, only by its effects" (310). "Does it [cannibalism] work?" asks Mr. Li as soon as he barges into Mei's apartment, her makeshift enterprise zone. Before an answer is even attempted, however, the audience sees him already wolfing down the dumplings, in a rush to action typical of Wall Street speculators, not guided by statistical reason but governed by a belief in magic.

What *Dumplings* has conjured up is thus neither Max Weber's disenchantment in institutional rationalization nor Sigmund Freud's sublimation through symbolic incorporation, but a far more troubling picture of an iron cage melted and capital unbound. If repression of direct and immediate individual desire for the reproductive continuity of the social body constitutes the logic of a "patriarchal" and "parasitic" capitalism in its First Coming and the very "form of civility" and rationality reserved for the metropolitan center (Wood 197; Bartolovich 214), this repression must itself be repressed to make way for reenchantment. For the Second Coming of Capitalism demands the kind of "repressive desublimation" that Marcuse forewarned, which, in the process of dissolving the boundaries of the self and the other, the literal and the figurative, is simultaneously removing the multiple historical constraints on unimaginable hungers and reconstituting a new subject on the fantastic satisfaction of these ferocious appetites (56).

For Fruit Chan, then, "desublimation" of the preliberal or the liberal subject is a reenchanting form of discipline that could turn the occult practices of man-eating in our neoliberal time thinkable, actionable, or perhaps even reasonable. Desublimation ushers in what Foucault calls the new "grid of intelligibility" that begins to subject formerly noneconomic relations and behaviors to the interpretation and generalization of market principles (2008, 243, 225). Thus, turning to the question of familial and social reproduction, Foucault illustrates how the provision of nourishment, affection, and education for the child is now understood as "an investment which can be measured in time," constituting a future "human capital" in the forms of both the child's "salary" when s/he becomes an adult and the mother's "psychical income," a "satisfaction" measurable by "both economic and psychological profit on the capital invested" (Ibid. 244). Despite demonstrating the novel ways of subjective interest calculation, Foucault's description of neoliberal human investment appears identical to the ideal liberal socioeconomic arrangement in Capitalism's First Coming. The primacy of biological and social reproduction remains an irreducible and nontranscendent political, personal, and physical reality, indefinitely sustained by the patriarchal division of reproductive labor and its exclusive psychic income for women.

For Fruit Chan, the neoliberal generalization of both economic rationality and the enterprising spirit has insinuated an anthropophagic and autopoietic orientation into the soul of society and the psyche of the self. Whether it is in the feature or the short version, the fetus of the masseuse or that of herself, Mrs. Li's resolute termination of pregnancy and the unambiguous suggestion of her subsequent ingestion in the two conclusions of the film betray the same delirium of immortality and definitive forfeiture of reproductive necessity. What Foucault calls "an investment which can be measured in time" is in Chan's treatment swallowed up in no time. In this casting of his characters, the director refuses to attribute "the destructive return of our ferocious buried hungers" in Capitalism's Second Coming to such enforced "ideals of transcendence" as "*sublimation*" or "mere *repression* of desire" in the First Coming (Kilgour, 1998, 259). He also rejects the optimistic regard of cannibalism as a possible "liberation from a discrete individual identity" and "a ritual of reunion" capable of "restoring social wholeness that has been violated by death" (Ibid., 246). No symbolic resurrection of social wholeness shall ever emerge from Mrs. Li's swinging cleaver, as the camera work makes it emphatic at the end of the feature, because her chopping represents the absolute severance of the individual self from the social body, and her consumption of fetal matter a literal subsumption of society by the neoliberal subject. Neither shall Mrs. Li ever obtain the satisfaction of eternal youth except for her wish's contrary realization in premature death, as shown at the end of the short, because temporal limits to individual biological life cannot be literally overcome.

While the neoliberal maternal subject in Foucault still finds fulfillment in the psychic income of reproductive labor, Mrs. Li, the degendered entrepreneurial subject of Chan's construction has totally lost faith in (an)other investment which shall require a durable measure of time. Why should the satisfaction from both economic and psychic profit be acquired indirectly through biological and generational substitution when it can be gained directly in and through the individual? Why should the ceaseless (re)creation of the self within its own lifespan be sublimated for the (re)production of society and the perpetuity of historical time? What should one choose when the repression of the social can be replaced by the practice of autopoiesis with apparently greater benefits to the self? Why would "I" wait for gratification when waiting could be reasonably taken out of wanting? These are the motivating questions behind Chan's uncompromising investigation of cannibalism's spatial/social, temporal/historical implications. The director also seems pushing envelopes of Foucault's rumination on "Technologies of the Self," especially the French philosopher's conviction in the capability of individuals to "effect a certain number of operations on their own bodies and souls" in order to "attain a certain state of happiness, purity, wisdom, perfection, or immortality" (1988, 22).

In the last scene of *Dumplings*'s short version, we find Mrs. Li pregnant, thanks to the alleged rejuvenating power of Mei's magic dishes, as she deliberates on what to do about it. The camera frames her soaking in the tub, glowing with a newly recovered beauty and energy. She toys with a hook-like medical instrument made of stainless steel before plunging it, ever so willfully, between her legs. The bathwater turns crimson as the camera closes up on Mrs. Li's face: a thin line of blood drips from her mouth, and in a shot deliberately resonant of the vampire genre, we see her serpentine tongue roll out to lick off the blood near her chin with a smirk.

In deploying a visual distortion characteristic of classic horror, Chan has blurred the actress's Chinese phenotype so that she appears as a (wo)man without ethnic distinction in a world of capitalist globalization. This deracialization of the protagonist's image reflects the deterritorialization and transnational incorporation of capital: having effectively extended the sphere of influence from its Euro-American origins to Asia, Africa, and beyond, the Second Coming of Capitalism appears near universal. Such deracialization and globalization of a restless consuming agency deconstructs the semantic basis "cannibalism" has historically accrued within the European lexicon since Capitalism's First Coming. It signals a collapse of two mechanisms that Bartolovich considers crucial for the "civility" of incipient capitalism. First, it is the capital and cannibal dichotomy enforced through a consolidation of the civilizing Self against the barbarous Other, and second, by the logical extension of the first, is capital's reluctant but continual reproduction of its domestic labor at minimal cost (214). The deracialization of the image thus restores the original meaning of anthropophagy as a human-eating-human practice rather than a region- or race-specific one. More importantly, this catholic identification of anthropophagic agent and general figuration of the act as a distinctive historical development of global capitalism indict the state's relinquishment of social reproduction and its protection of the citizenry against market incursions. For Fruit Chan, anthropophagy is symptomatic of a universal unreason in Capital's Second Coming, a life-extinguishing menace to humanity and ecology from within *anthropos* itself.

Whether in the feature or the short version of *Dumplings*, Mrs. Li personifies "the ultimate in possessiveness" (Wood 213). Her destructive appetite is an extreme expression of possessive individualism, exacerbated by the neoliberal revision of its proper subject as an autonomous "enterprise unit," in the constant investment and production of his/her own satisfaction (Foucault, 2008, 243, 225). It is in this predatory and privatized production of the self-satisfying subject, at once discrete and sovereign, both the parameter of the social and the older practice of individual satiation through sublimation and substitution are being eviscerated. If sublimation recognizes boundaries of the literal and the figurative, substitution registers the span of individual biological time and the continuity of generational time. While such classic, civil, and civic practice of time respects the wisdom of the Sphinx's lesson of the natural cycles, the biological and social boundaries it represents will have to be deregulated in Mrs. Li's "logic of singularity." In her compulsory "addiction to self-making or self transformation" lay the "maladies of agency and pathologies of will" (Seltzer 97).

With the delirious Mrs. Li performing self-extraction, Fruit Chan shows that capitalism qua cannibalism is not just the transgression of self/other boundaries or denial of spatial/social limits; it is also the conquest of one time scheme over another. Mrs. Li's unnatural death is Chan's cinematic illustration of "Why the Time is Out of Joint" in Capital's Second Coming, where Teresa Brennan's titular essay argues theoretically. Reworking Marx's labor theory of value, Brennan locates the impediment to capitalist accumulation in the "essential contradiction between natural energy and the time or speed of exchange" (264). For her, the distinction – between human labor as "variable capital" adding more to the finished product than it costs, and natural substances such as fossil fuels or technology as "constant capital" giving no more than they cost – is no longer a meaningful one. To get more products to the market in the shortest possible time, the profit maker will spend less on variable capital and more on constant capital because "profit depends on the difference that a living subject makes to a dead object" (265).

But Marx's subject/object distinction overlooks, in view of Brennan, the important interchangeability between "animate and inanimate natural substances" (267). Thus, she posits an affinity between labor power and power inherent in natural sources. By regarding them as equivalent commodities "capable of releasing and adding energy" on the one hand, and exchangeable energy entailing "certain time of natural reproduction" on the other, Brennan is able to establish the power of both human labor and natural substances as the common source of capitalist profit. "Labor-power and other natural substances are alike in that they are living, as opposed to technology, which is really dead," she argues, and as such, both human and natural resources are "sources of surplus value" and "should be treated as variable capital" capable of adding greater value in production than the cost of their reproduction (267–68).

In Brennan's formulation, both "Marx's [industrial] 'reserve army' and Heidegger's 'standing reserve' of nature" represent "living energy," both of which are subject to capitalist extraction and exploitation (269–70). Since the less it pays for the reproduction time of living energy the more surplus value production time generates, "capital will always, all other things being equal, take the cheapest option" for maximum profit (Ibid.). Capital accomplishes this by either discounting the "socially necessary" time of natural reproduction or speeding up reproduction by artificial means, or by engaging in both processes at once. Two temporal schemes are thus at fundamental odds here: "the generational time of natural reproduction, and speed – the artificial time of short term profit" (274–75). Living energy – be it humans or trees – has to observe the natural cycles of regeneration to ensure its continuous viability and vitality. Capital, on the other hand, "garners its energy by violent conversions" (278).

From Mrs. Li's initial disgust at Mei's dumplings to her insatiable desire for them is a cinematic capsule of how cannibalistic capital is "redirecting nature at its own speed," "literally altering the *physis* of the world, adjusting nature's inbuilt logic and spatiotemporal continuum to suit itself" (Brennan 278). When company CEOs rarely look beyond quarterly profits and the politicians the next election cycle, and when "each generation makes good capitalist decisions, the effect is collective suicide" (quoted in Foster, Clark, and York 45). While accelerating the commodification of animals and plants can enhance profit, contends Brennan, "the long-term effect" of this speeding is "an impoverishment of surplus value based on use value" as well as "an increasing debt to nature . . . even at the price of survival" (Brennan 272, 274).

"Surplus value is first and foremost the outcome of the exploitation of nature [and labor as part of nature, I shall add]," Barbara Adam agrees (64, 14). Because "the time of ecological give-and-take becomes subsumed under the time logic of economic exchange" in global capitalism, "the time-scale of [resource] reproduction stands in inverse relation to the time-scale of [its] use, degradation, depletion, and destruction," Adam resumes in an uncanny resonance with Brennan, "the result is out of the sync time frames" (14–15). By making visible capital's perturbation of nature's process and rhythms, Chan appears to both share Adam's insights and reinvigorate Brennan's thesis that "the absence of any natural check on speed" is "why time is out of joint": "We smell this around us and know it in our bodies . . . because it is the necessary economic consequence of the present course of capital" (Brennan 268, 278).

Whether the "present course of capital" is a fait accompli receives further artistic elaboration in *Dumplings*'s alternative endings. Notable in the concluding shots of both versions is the director's fleeting yet explicit rendition of gruesome violence. With the chopping of the masseuse's five-month fetus and the poking of Mrs. Li's own, *Dumplings* reverses its predominant portrayal of anthropophagy as normal, thereby recuperating "the power of horror" and the visceral shock inherent in the horror genre. In the last instance of her ghoulish appearance, Mrs. Li has indeed become the visible menace of a generic monster. This visualization of predatory threat makes the "partial, compromised," and "indeterminable production" of Halberstam's "posthuman monstrosity" impossible and her unwillingness to "uncover the cause of violence" questionable (187–88). While Chan's identification of evil is unambiguous and his urge to eradicate it irresistible, the two cuts of *Dumplings* nevertheless provide different foods for thought.

Contrary to the convention wherein the final shock is typically succeeded by the triumph of "the Final Girl" over the demonic, the *anthropophagi* in the feature version faces no rival and remains unremovable. Mrs. Li lives to laugh at the world, with neither symbolic retribution nor legal discipline. This treatment appears Fruit Chan's nod to Brennan's less than rosy estimate that there may be hardly any "natural check on speed" or any viable social deterrence to the voracity and velocity of cannibalistic appetite (268). Cannibalism is but a rescission of reproduction in another name, the victory of a warped rationality, and "the necessary economic consequence of the present course of capital" (Ibid. 278). By contrast, the conclusion of the short version shows Mrs. Li inflict violence both on herself and her invisible fetus. Here, in the competition between the natural rhythm of sustainable reproduction and the time-space compression of neoliberal capitalism, speed wins but self-destructs. This conclusion negates the feature version's implicit resignation to cannibalistic doom and calls instead for a halt of the current course of consumptive and cancerous growth.

At this point, we would be well rewarded to attend to Melinda Cooper's scintillating sketch of the parallel ascents of "biotech revolution" and "neoliberal revolution" (the "Reagan-Thatcher-Deng Xiaoping Revolution" in our reference). What both revolutions share is "a common ambition to overcome the ecological and economic limits to growth associated with the end of industrial production," as Cooper points out, "through a speculative reinvention of the future" (11). The exhaustion of geochemical growth that has sustained the life of Capital's First

Coming will have to be replaced with the extraction of hitherto noncommodified biological resources, or the life of Capital's Second Coming cannot really be resuscitated. Surplus value depends on surplus life (both produced through stem cells in immaculate laboratories and laid waste through welfare reforms), and survives on a speculative promise "in excess of the earth's actual limits" (31). Where Comaroff and Comaroff have delineated as the "chimerical" or the "occult" logic of neoliberal capitalism is for Cooper an unreferenced promise verging on "delirium." It ranges from the irrational exuberance of the finance market to the imperialism of US debt regime that "reproduces itself in a realm of pure promise" (Ibid.). When we come to Mrs. Li's gloating facial expression before her imminent metallic extraction of her life's potentiality, we encounter an every(wo)man caught in "the most insane form of capitalist delirium" (Ibid. 20). In this delirium, Mrs. Li begins to move from her figuration as a definitive cannibal in the feature version of *Dumplings*.

There, as an *anthropophagi*, Mrs. Li destroys the embryonic lives of others and disrupts both the universal lore of the Sphinx riddle and the scientific law of "cell growth, aging, and death" (Cooper 136). For all her gnawing at the somatic propagation of *Homo sapiens*, however, she seems unable to deny the generation of bodies in "vertical transmission," that is, the passing of hereditary information "from generation to generation through the germ line, reproducing itself in mortal bodies of living beings" (Cooper 136–37). Her dependence on Mei's supply of fetal matter and her consumption of the unborn in order to be born again remain implicit recognitions of "the intrinsic limits to the division and differentiation of somatic cells," and by extension death as the inevitable boundary of biological life (Ibid. 137).

Here in *Dumplings* the short, Mrs. Li suddenly imagines herself "as self-valorizing value: a life force possessed of its own powers of self-regeneration" (Ibid. 30). Instead of a parasitic and predatory dependence on the fetal matter of others, which reproduce germinally, sexually, and vertically, she deludes herself into believing in the infinite propagation of herself that negates mortality. Like the cancerous cell that avoids "aging and death by refusing to differentiate" in the pursuit of its own relentless growth, Mrs. Li is convinced of her chimerical capacity to self-accumulate, self-generate, and self-perpetuate (Ibid. 137). However, it is precisely at the instant when she starts to violate nature's spatial and temporal limits with absolute self-abandon, its inherent constraints exact their toll: a rampant desire to reverse aging has resulted in her untimely demise. While you may embrace the occult conviction in the indefinite deferral of debt to nature, the more you will your deferral the sooner it catches up with you, if not in the spectral shape of a scythe, then a stainless steel hook.

The image of the bloodied bath revives the shock effect of classic horror and stirs up the hitherto dormant moral sentiment in the audience. Most intriguing of all in his aesthetic mobilization of ethical judgment is Fruit Chan's integration of ingestion and immolation as identical acts of violence. Mrs. Li is not just helplessly devouring the other constitutive of the self but also destroying at the same time what the self is made of, for in the film director's artistic resurrection, nature is no more the other of culture than culture is exclusively generative and transformative; there cannot be any culture without nature. The *anthropos* and the *physis* of the world are finally identified as one and the same, visibly indivisible but mutually dependent and (re)generative. Chan has thus conjured up a material connection and a natural circulation of living energy that the Cartesian frame of dualism precludes and the capitalist logic of limitless conquest has hidden from view. The total subjective domination of the objective world, the hallmark of the post-Enlightenment industrial capitalist modernity over and against the physical barriers as well as psychical boundaries of original nature, is revealed to be untenable, at best delirious and at worst suicidal. Capitalism qua cannibalism in Fruit Chan's specialty *Dumplings* has come to illuminate twin truths: short-term growth is tantamount to preternatural and/or eternal death, while neither labor nor nature is inexhaustibly alienable. In giving us a picture of cannibal capitalism's creative destruction at its own peril, Fruit Chan has compelled us to abide by nature's (re)productive time, encouraging a world democracy of effective regulation and equitable distribution for the collective thriving of our planet and its living beings.

Notes

1 *The Human Flesh BBQ Buns of the Eight Immortals Restaurant* is a literal translation of the original Chinese title whose English rendition is *The Untold Story*. *Dumplings* is released in a Lion's Gate anthology of Asian horror, entitled *Three Extremes* (2004). The DVD includes three shorts: *Box* by Miike Takashi of Japan, *Cut* by Park Chan-Wook of South Korea, and *Dumplings* by Fruit Chan of Hong Kong, with an additional full feature. This is a follow-up of an earlier anthology, *Sangeng* 三更, meaning "midnight" or "small hours," rendered as *Three Extremes* and appearing as *Saam gang* (Applause Pictures 2002). I thank Chuck Kleinhans for introducing me to *Dumplings* and for his insightful essay, "Serving the People: *Dumplings*."
2 See Shirley Lindenbaum for a historical survey on "thinking about cannibalism." The reference to Herodotus is from Lindenbaum (476). The reference to *Shanhaijing* is from Yue, who translates it as *Book of Hills and Seas* (26). While Herodotus's record of cannibalism dates to 500 B.C., the anonymous Chinese legend is believed to have become a written record circa 270–230 B.C. I am indebted to Stephen Durrant for this dating.
3 William Arens's controversial classic, *The Man-Eating Myth*, marks the beginning of a postcolonial delineation of how the dominant discourse of cannibalism is constructed, while Maggie Kilgour's *From Communion to Cannibalism* signals the figurative turn. Both conceive of cannibalism as a binary category of inclusion and exclusion. See the introduction of Barker, Hulme, and Iversen for a synopsis of the scholarly debates, and Guest as a tribute to the literary and rhetorical foci that Kilgour pioneers.
4 The first phrase refers to Enrique Dussel's title book (1995), while the second is taken from Said (7). In regarding Eurocentrism as the triumphant outcome of a subjectivizing process through which Europe defines itself simultaneously and successively against its historical rivals, we are at once "provincializing Europe," to borrow Dipesh Chakrabarty, and "planetarizing" world modernity, to paraphrase Dussel (1998, 4). Such a move recuperates a prior history of cultural origins and "contact zones," while it renders absurd the miraculous conception of Hegel and Weber that the West's development is sovereign and its teleological embrace of the rest is inevitable (Pratt 6; Dussel, 1998, 3).
5 Though Fordism owes its formulation to Antonio Gramsci's *The Prison Notebooks*, which sees Henry Ford's system of automobile production as an advanced form of

capitalist productive organization, its suggestion of mass production as part and parcel of political regimes of full employment, welfare state, and mass consumption refers largely to Western capitalist societies after World War II. My use of Fordism intends both to analogize it with state socialism of the East and to frame its subsequent evolution into post-Fordism, when the capitalistic mode of production has become global and flexible (see Harvey, 1990, 125–97).

6 Though available in English as *The Republic of Wine*, my reference to Yan Mo's novel, *Jiuguo* 酒国, is based on the original Chinese edition in my own translation.

7 Unless otherwise noted, my interpretation is based on the feature version in the Lion's Gate DVD set of *Three Extremes* (2004).

8 I am alluding to Benedict Anderson's well-known thesis of the nation as "an imagined community" whose spatial boundary unfolds through the simultaneity of "homogenous, empty time" (26).

9 Though not dealing with cannibalism per se nor a reworking of the horror genre, Li Yang's *Blind Shaft* 盲井 (2003) and *Blind Mountain* 盲山 (2007), and Peng Tao's *Little Moth* 血蝉 (2007) are neorealistic treatments of predatory criminal practices that seem to thrive underground with the Chinese state's implicit tolerance, as long as they do not hinder the formal flows of capital.

Works cited

Adam, Barbara. *Timescapes of Modernity: The Environment and Invisible Hazards.* London: Routledge, 1998.

Anderson, Benedict. *Imagined Communities: Reflection on the Origin and Spread of Nationalism.* New York: Verso, 1991.

Arens, William. *The Man-Eating Myth: Anthropology and Anthropophagy.* New York: Oxford UP, 1979.

Barker, Francis, Peter Hulme, and Margaret Iversen, eds. *Cannibalism and the Colonial World.* Cambridge: Cambridge UP, 1998.

Bartolovich, Crystal. "Consumerism, or the Cultural Logic of Late Cannibalism." *Cannibalism and the Colonial World.* Eds. Francis Barker, Peter Hulme, and Margaret Iversen. Cambridge: Cambridge UP, 1998. 204–37.

Brennan, Teresa. "Why the Time Is Out of Joint: Marx's Political Economy without the Subject." *South Atlantic Quarterly* 97.2 (Spring, 1998): 263–80.

Chakrabarty, Dipesh. *Provincializing Europe: Postcolonial Thought and Historical Difference.* Princeton: Princeton UP, 2000.

Clover, Carol J. "Her Body, Himself: Gender in the Slasher Film." *Horror: The Film Reader.* Ed. Mark Jancovich. London and New York: Routledge, 2002. 77–89.

Comaroff, Jean, and John L. Comaroff. "Millennial Capitalism: First Thoughts on a Second Coming." *Public Culture* 12.2 (2000): 291–343.

Cooper, Melinda. *Life as Surplus: Biotechnology and Capitalism in the Neoliberal Era.* Seattle: U of Washington P, 2008.

Dussel, Enrique. "Beyond Eurocentrism: The World-System and the Limits of Modernity." *The Cultures of Globalization.* Eds. Fredric Jameson and Masao Miyoshi. Durham: Duke University P, 1998: 3–31.

———. *The Invention of the Americas: Eclipse of the Other and the Myth of Modernity.* New York: Continuum International, 1995.

Foster, John Bellamy, Brett Clark, and Richard York. *Ecological Rift: Capitalism's War on the Earth.* New York: Monthly Review P, 2010.

Foucault, Michel. *The Birth of Biopolitics: Lectures at the College de France, 1978–79.* Ed. Michel Senellart. Trans. Graham Burchell. New York: Palgrave Macmillan, 2008.

———. "Technologies of the Self." *Technologies of the Self: A Seminar with Michel Foucault.* Eds. Luther H. Martin, Huck Gutman, and Patrick H. Hutton. Amherst: U of Massachusetts P, 1988. 16–49.

Guest, Kristen, ed. *Eating Their Words: Cannibalism and the Boundaries of Identity.* Albany: State U of New York, 2001.

Halberstam, Judith. *Skin Shows: Gothic Horror and the Technology of Monsters.* Durham: Duke UP, 1995.

Harvey, David. *A Brief History of Neoliberalism.* New York: Oxford UP, 2005.

———. *The Condition of Postmodernity: An Enquiry into the Origins of Social Change.* Cambridge: Blackwell, 1990.

hooks, bell. *Black Looks: Race and Representation.* Boston: South End P, 1992.

Hulme, Peter. *Colonial Encounters: Europe and the Caribbean, 1492–1797.* London: Methuen, 1986.

Kilgour, Maggie. *From Communion to Cannibalism: An Anatomy of Metaphors of Incorporation.* Princeton: Princeton UP, 1990.

———. "The Function of Cannibalism in the Present Time." *Cannibalism and the Colonial World.* Eds. Barker, Francis, Peter Hulme, and Margaret Iversen. Cambridge: Cambridge UP, 1998. 238–59.

Kleinhans, Chuck. "Serving the People: *Dumplings.*" *Jump Cut: A Review of Contemporary Media* 49 (Spring) 2007. *http://www.ejumpcut.org/archive/jc49.2007/Dumplings/text.html*

Lee, Leo Ou-fan. *Voices from the Iron House: A Study of Lu Xun.* Bloomington: Indiana UP, 1987.

Li, David Leiwei. *Imagining the Nation: Asian American Literature and Cultural Consent.* Stanford: Stanford UP, 1998.

Lindenbaum, Shirley. "Thinking about Cannibalism." *Annual Review of Anthropology* 33 (2004): 475–98.

Liu, Lydia H. *Translingual Practice: Literature, National Culture, and Translated Modernity – China, 1900–1937.* Stanford: Stanford UP, 1995.

Lu, Xun. "A Madman's Diary." *Lu Xun: Selected Works (Volume One).* Trans. Yang Xianyi and Gladys Yang. Beijing: Foreign Languages P, 1956/1985. 39–51.

Marcuse, Herbert. *One-Dimensional Man: Studies in the Ideology of Advanced Industrial Society.* Introduction by Douglas Kellner. Boston: Beacon Press, 1964/1991.

Mo, Yan. *Jiuguo* 《酒国》. Taipei: Hongfan Books, 1992.

———. *The Republic of Wine: A Novel.* Trans. Howard Goldblatt. New York: Arcade, 2000.

Phillips, Jerry. "Cannibalism qua Capitalism: The Metaphorics of Accumulation in Marx, Conrad, Shakespeare and Marlowe." *Cannibalism and the Colonial World.* Eds. Francis Barker, Peter Hulme, and Margaret Iversen. Cambridge: Cambridge UP, 1998. 183–203.

Pratt, Mary Louise. *Imperial Eyes: Travel Writing and Transculturation.* London: Routledge, 1992.

Said, Edward W. *Orientalism.* New York: Vintage Books, 1979.

Schwarcz, Vera. *The Chinese Enlightenment: Intellectuals and the Legacy of the May Fourth Movement of 1919.* Berkeley: U of California P, 1986.

Seltzer, Mark. "Serial Killers (1)." *Differences: A Journal of Feminist Cultural Studies.* 5.1 (Spring, 1993): 92+. *Academic OneFile.* Web. Jan 30, 2015.

Tang, Xiaobing. *Chinese Modern: The Heroic and the Quotidian.* Durham: Duke UP, 2000.

Todorov, Tzvetan. *The Conquest of America.* New York: Harper Collins, 1984.

Wood, Robin. "An Introduction to the American Horror Film." *Movies and Methods (Volume II).* Ed. Bill Nichols. Berkeley: U of California P, 1985. 195–220.

Yue, Gang. *The Mouth That Begs: Hunger, Cannibalism, and the Politics of Eating in Modern China.* Durham: Duke UP, 1999.

Index

immigration 97
imperialism 13n9, 67–8, 82
in-between-ness 147
India 11
individualism 22, 38–40, 43, 48–9, 84, 97–8, 106–7, 129–65
industrial capitalism 21–2, 29–31, 38, 51, 130, 139, 172
industrialization 11, 27–8, 93, 97, 129
International Monetary Fund (IMF) 13n5
interpellation 35
interurban geography 52, 54n23
In the Mood for Love 163n17
intimacy 94, 130–1
Iraqi War 86n14
iron cage trope 205, 212
Italian neorealism 169–70, 173–6, 179, 195n13

James, Henry 161
Jameson, Fredric 28, 37, 54n20, 61–5, 85n4–5, 137–8, 141–3, 152, 156–7; *The Geopolitical Aesthetic* 135; *Postmodernism, or the Cultural Logic of Late Capital* 171–2; "Third World Literature in the Era of Multinational Capitalism" 62–3
Jameson, R.D. 76
Japan 28, 72, 79–82
Jefferson, Thomas 26
Jia Zhangke 12, 14n12, 85n2, 125n7, 169–97
Jiuguo (Mo) 219n6
Johnson, Lyndon 9
Ju Dou 23, 27, 113

Kant, Immanuel 181
Keep Cool 125n6
Keynesian economics 205
Kierkegaard, Søren 157
King of Children 185–6
kitsch 122
Klee, Paul: *Angelus Novus* 193
Kleinhans, Chuck: "Serving the People: Dumplings" 218n1
Kotkin, Joel 77–8
Kraicer, Shelly 178
Kristeva, Julia 208–9
Kuimen gorge 183–8

labor theory of value 214–15
Lanzhou University 59
Lash, Scott 146, 163n14
La Strada 170

Latouché, Serge 68–9, 72, 78, 86n16
Law, Clara 149
Lee, Ang 12, 93–128, 135
Lee, Kim 87n26
Lee, Leo 175
Liang Qichao 131
Liang Shuming 32
Li Ba 191
liberal capitalism 199
liberalism 9, 27, 40, 49–50, 53n4, 59–61, 64–70, 93, 102, 106–10, 210–11
Li, Daoxing: *The History of Chinese Film Culture* 195n17
Li, David Leiwei 14n11
lifting out 8, 33–5
Lindenbaum, Shirley 218n2
Linju/Neighbors 195n7
Lion's Gate 218n1, 219n7
Little Cheung 198
Little Moth 219n9
Liu, Alan 77
Liu, Cynthia 125n2
Liu Kang 85n3
Li Yang 59–61, 66–79, 85n2, 86–7n18, 87n26, 125n7, 219n9
Li Yang Cliz English Promotion Studio 59–60
Lloyd, David 70
Locke, John 38
logos 11
Longest Summer, The 198
Long Xiong 95
love 130–1
Lu Xun 54n19, 79–81, 85n5, 206; *Call to Arms* 81, 87n21; "Diary of a Madman" 202–3

Macaulay, Lord: "Minute on Indian Education" 67–8
MacIntyre, Alasdair 150, 157
Macpherson, C.B. 22, 38, 48–51, 110
Made in Hong Kong 198
Mahjong/Majiang 12, 135, 137–8, 142–6, 149, 155–6
Mama 174
Manchu Dynasty 1, 67, 87n21, 131
man eating. *see* cannibalism
Man-Eating Myth, The (Arens) 218n3
Manichaeism 149, 161, 176
Mao era 86n13
Maoism 205, 209
Maoris 202
Mao Zedong 3, 11, 22, 25–9, 33, 71–4, 96, 124, 185–7, 191

For Product Safety Concerns and Information please contact our
EU representative GPSR@taylorandfrancis.com
Taylor & Francis Verlag GmbH, Kaufingerstraße 24, 80331 München, Germany